MW01001967

# Closer to the Sun

ALSO BY GARTH DRABINSKY

*Motion Pictures and the Arts in Canada:*
*The Business and the Law,*
1976

# Closer to the Sun

*An Autobiography*

Garth Drabinsky

with Marq de Villiers

**M&S**

**Canadian Cataloguing in Publication Data**

Drabinsky, Garth, 1949-
Closer to the sun: an autobiography

Includes index.
ISBN 0-7710-5650-8

1. Drabinsky, Garth, 1949- . 2. Cineplex Odeon Corporation. 3. Live Entertainment of Canada Inc. 4. Businessmen – Canada – Biography. 5. Theatrical producers and directors – Canada – Biography. 6. Motion picture producers and directors – Canada – Biography. I. de Villiers, Marq, 1940- II. Title.

PN1998.3.D7A3 1995    338.7'6179143092    C94-932698-4

The publishers acknowledge the support of the Canada Council and the Ontario Arts Council for their publishing program.

**All dollar amounts in this book are in Canadian dollars, unless stated otherwise.**

Text design by Stephen Kenny
Typesetting by M&S, Toronto
Printed and bound in Canada on acid-free paper

McClelland & Stewart Inc.
*The Canadian Publishers*
481 University Avenue
Toronto, Ontario
M5G 2E9

1 2 3 4 5   99 98 97 96 95

For my mentors, Dick Roberts, whose erudition and love of life taught me so much, and Nat Taylor, doyen of Canadian motion-picture exhibition, who grounded me in the first principles of entertainment.

# Contents

# *Foreword*

"I was ever a fighter, so one fight more the best and the last. I would hate that death bandaged my eyes and forbore, And bade me creep past."

*– Robert Browning*

I am inclined to think that the moment Garth, without consulting his shareholders, made the astute decision to take leave of his mother's womb, he blinked in the searing light of the unsuspecting new world about him and cried out, "Who's got the concession?" When no response was forthcoming, and a deadly silence fell upon the universe, he began to negotiate, and he's been negotiating ever since.

Though he was born in that city of one-way streets – Toronto – (one way could also mean up), the pioneering spirit of this feisty young city pup resembled far more that of the prairie dog from the Saskatchewan plains, where some time ago his not too well-off Polish-Russian forebears decided to settle. From his first faltering step, he knew that to capture that special bone he craved he would have to forage for it, and forage alone. It is not too far-fetched to assume that, while immersed in the fight against early paralysis and the racking pain of polio, he was already forming nefarious plans to do battle with the future demons and dragons that would attempt to bar the gateway to his treasures. Somehow, he was able to build his blocks and, on his own, find himself. Impatient with his family's caution and little zest for life, the life he longed to relish, Garth was more than ever determined to hurl himself deep into its very core and, at whatever price, to make a reality of his sleepless dreams. Perhaps it was the rock 'n' roll revolution pounding away in his young ears, willing him to move as he lay in hospital beds and recharging his pulse with its heady beat, that first hooked him on "showbiz." But what clearly clinched matters was when, in Grade 9, he wandered into a rehearsal of a school play, ironically titled *The Imaginary Invalid*, that the magic really got to him, and he knew then that for the rest of his days he was to remain hopelessly and unabashedly stagestruck.

Realizing that his handicap could make acting as a career a mite difficult, he sought out the law, and armed with an LLB from the University of Toronto, he developed, for a spell, a successful entertainment law practice and wrote a textbook – *Motion Pictures and the Arts in Canada* – that remains a standard reference work. But the roar of the greasepaint eventually won in the end, and he began to set about building his empires in the sun. The rest, of course, is history or geography, as Stephen Leacock would say.

As complex a creature as Garth would have you believe him to be, I venture to imagine that his views on life, fate, and destiny have always been fairly straightforward, "upfront," if a trifle cinematic. There are the good guys – the gifted ones, the poets, the artists, the creative talent he is convinced he was destined to champion. Then there are the bad guys – the philistines, the preachers of convention, the high priests of compromise, and the rival entrepreneurial forces who sit smugly in their offices. "I've stared the dogs of adversity in the muzzle before," writes Garth, "and they hold no terror for me." This book is all about that: a suspenseful saga of corporate intrigue at once gigantic and sensational in its proportions; the tale of a young hustler who leaps across the chapters of his life with boundless and uncanny energy; the irresistible rise of a young upstart mogul in a land not particularly used to moguls, especially in the arts – a land notorious for its reticence and timid conservatism which quite predictably reacts with shock, disbelief, and seething envy at the phenomenal ascendancy of one of its native sons.

"Enfant terrible," "Monstre Sacré," "Darth Grabinsky," a megalomaniac who "has no spur to prick the sides of his intent but only vaulting ambition" – these are some of the nicknames and phrases that have christened him over the years. And though these may hurt for a second, he shrugs them off and presses on. For the professional side of Garth has taught him that the precarious voyage he has chosen collects strange passengers – enemies as numerous as barnacles. And as he gets to know them, he challenges and taunts them, almost welcomes them; he could even alter the Scriptures to include them – "and though I have all faith so I could remove mountains and have no enemies, I am nothing."

Something about Garth puzzles me however. It must be that face of his – that baby face – a face illuminated by a beatific expression of innocence, youth, humour, and permanent good nature; not a line nor a crease to suggest the passage of time or the pain of that passage, the angry struggle, the fearsome deals, or the ruthless guts it must have taken to force himself up the dark path and reach whatever Shangri-La he fancied. Once you get to know Garth, however, the enigma vanishes. He comes clean, he'll tell you the whole story, he'll spill the beans, no holds barred. I count myself fortunate to have been on that end of the line, that our paths have been crossing over some twenty years, and even more fortunate that, upon occasion, he has fallen into the quite comfortable but incredible habit of employing me. I have done some of my best work for Garth and some of my worst, yet still he persists in offering me the world and the moon together. His faith and loyalty are extraordinary.

I've seen him devote that same faith to hundreds of Canadian, American, and British artists, young and old, whom he has employed over the years. I have known him as an eager young producer who, frustrated with film exhibition and distribution in his country, would build his conglomerate to remedy the situation, turning it into a billion-dollar business – one of the largest of its kind in North America. I've watched him burst across the borders to align himself and hold his own with the biggest sharks in the ocean, who would kill for a piece of him. "I want an army I can shriek defiance at! Take off your dwarfs! Bring on your giants!" I've seen him become the master of marketing geniuses in Canada's film and theatre history – an entrepreneur extraordinaire of the grand old school. I've seen him fall like

Lucifer and rise like Lazarus. I've marvelled at his obsession for restoring theatrical landmarks otherwise doomed, giving them back their glory and, what's more, filling their seats with live audiences. I shall never forget when he returned my sos call to back a limping production of *Macbeth*, which he did without hesitation, transforming it into one of the highest-grossing Shakespearean productions ever. (In Toronto, it grossed over $1.5 million in two weeks.) Even I, as the unfortunate Thane, saw some of that gelt! This Joseph in his technicolour dreamcoat dares to risk failure and never thinks small – a modern-day Barnum, rare indeed, who helps fill his country's coffers and does it proud. Perhaps his proud country will one day come to him and, for his labours, recognize him as it should. There is no unsolved mystery that lies behind this life – no Rosebud motivates this driven citizen – he wears his secret on his sleeve and on every leaf of this engrossing and riveting confession.

A hundred years from now when we are all gone and history wonders in which direction Garth was assigned to go, the ghosts of Marcus Loew, Thomas Lamb, Nat Taylor, and a few of the shades from Roxy – everyone who haunted and inspired him while he lived – will be sitting together in the front row of some celestial grand theatre. And as the great chandeliers dim and the orchestra begins to play the overture, they look up and high above the gold curtain just below the ceiling in the centre of a frieze is a carved cherub staring down at them. There is something awfully familiar about that benign expression and the somewhat irritating self-contented grin stretched wider than any Cheshire cat's. It seems to be saying, "OK, boys! This time it's my turn! It's my show! It's my theatre! It's my popcorn! And guess who's got the concession?"

Christopher Plummer
Weston, Connecticut
November 1994

# *Preface*

The story speaks for itself, as stories should – but why tell the story at all? Why the story of my life so far, when we're only in episode three or four of what I profoundly hope will be a long-running series?

Why? Because my work is immersed in the magical worlds of theatre and music, and because my life has had its share of drama, comedy, passion, adventure, romance, conflict, resolution, and triumph. It is a story filled with fascinating characters: villains and heroes, traitors and loyalists, liars and cheats, adversaries and enemies, mentors, partners, and great, good friends.

Because I have created two major corporations in my time; and though I was stripped of one of them (as you will read), the other one has become the joy of my professional life.

Because I want to set the record straight about certain dramatic events that have made the headlines and filled both the entertainment and business pages of North American newspapers.

Because I care not so much about succeeding, but succeeding in work that is creative, emotionally satisfying, culturally significant, and pushes the boundaries of the art form.

Because I care about my country and want to contribute to it, and because I want to show others that Canada can serve as a wellspring of creativity, if only more Canadians could escape their cultural insecurity.

Because I am certain there are others who will follow me who are equally capable, equally determined, care equally about excellence, and who may learn a lesson or two along the way.

Because I love life and want others to see that. Because I have overcome adversity and want others to understand it can be done. Because I refused to yield and believe there is inspiration in that.

Because I am the impresario of my own destiny and want to share with others how much of a *rush* it has been.

December 19, 1994
Toronto

# Acknowledgements

Since I started writing this book almost seven years ago, I have benefited from the kindness and talent of many people who have helped,
encouraged, and, at times, provoked me. I began this project with
experienced arts writer Gina Mallet, but two developments in my
career interrupted the work: the attempt, in 1989, to purchase all the
shares of Cineplex Odeon Corporation and, subsequently, the fierce
demands placed on me during the difficult start-up phase of my new
company, Live Entertainment of Canada Inc.

In 1994, accomplished author and veteran journalist Marq de
Villiers joined me in completing the book. His finesse and style
brought a new dimension and perspective to the project. In all, I
believe the wait has been worthwhile, as the inclusion of my burgeoning career as a producer of commercial musical theatre has made the
book a more complete story.

My deepest gratitude goes to the late Dick Roberts, who assiduously revised the manuscript in its early drafts and who I will always
miss for his sage counsel; my steadfast partner and confrère, Myron
Gottlieb, whose infinite capacity for detailed recollection was indis-
pensable; my loyal colleagues at Livent, Lynda Friendly, Margaret
Livingston, and Lorraine Valentine, who stayed with me right
through the years at Cineplex Odeon; my wonderful assistant, Sharon

Turville, who painstakingly typed and retyped the manuscript; the invaluable Dennis Kucherawy, who helped research and edit the manuscript; Marty Bell, who contributed much wit and valuable advice; my lawyers, Ron Rolls and Mark Hayes, especially for their persistence in overseeing the book through to its publication; David and Marilyn Burnett, for their cogent insight; my dear friend and film collaborator, Joel Michaels, for his reminiscences; my editors, Jocelyn Laurence, and Pat Kennedy and Heather Sangster of McClelland & Stewart, for their rigorous scrutiny of the text; Avie Bennett and Doug Gibson of McClelland & Stewart for their good-natured patience and enduring faith; Scott Thornley, for his exquisite cover design; Toronto *Globe and Mail* editor William Thorsell for leading me to Marq de Villiers; and everyone who generously shared their thoughts and memories.

I would also like to express my love and thanks to my family, especially my wife, Pearl, my daughter, Alicia, and my son, Marc, whose devotion has remained constant in spite of my many preoccupations.

And finally I want to thank the great impresarios of the past: Zukor, "Roxy" Rothafel, Loew, Ziegfeld, and the countless others whose flamboyant, entrepreneurial spirits taught a young boy how to dream and aspire to greatness.

# Prologue

## Escape to Something Greater

I remember one day, in the torrid summer of 1953 when I was only three, running through the sprinklers my father had set up on the lawn, joyous in that innocent way children are joyous, shrieking in childish glee, and then . . . sometime later, I remember . . . falling down.

*And waking into a nightmare.*

How powerful that first memory, though, how clearly imprinted. The water cold as diamonds, glittering in the summer sun, the heat of the afternoon, the green of the lawn, the smell of wet earth; I remember most of all the wonderful freedom to run and run and run.

*And then the virus came, and the doctors, and my life disappeared for a while into a fog of pain and misery. The glittering water from the sprinklers metamorphosed into the glitter of surgical instruments in the unforgiving light of the operating theatre. After that my crippled leg dragged behind me like a useless club, and I ran no more.*

Well, I came back from that. I reached deep down and seized back my life, not only from the well-meaning surgeons who kept me in a hospital bed for so many summers during my first twelve years, but from the doubters and naysayers and sceptics and sneerers. I seized control of my life, and after that I refused to let it go.

It was a terrible ordeal.

But it has helped me often, in other dark moments.

Thirty-six years later, Friday, November 27, 1989. Black Friday.

The Cineplex Odeon Corporation boardroom. Noon.

The lowest point of my adult life, the nadir, the black cave under the rock.

*They are in the last bitter stages of trying to take my company away!*

The Minute Book of the corporation recorded blandly that "as Chairman of the Board, Mr. Garth H. Drabinsky acted as Chairman of the meeting." And so I did, for the final time, having one remaining card to play, though knowing that this was the crucial meeting, the one that would decide my fate, the last toss of the dice. The atmosphere in the room was one of acrimony, with anger simmering below the surface, as lawyers manoeuvred and directors traded alliances. The air was rank, everyone was sweating, bald domes and foreheads shining in the lights. There was victory, defeat, and a shifty kind of betrayal in the air.

For months I'd been fighting off a vote to fire me from my own company. I may have owned only 3.5 per cent of Cineplex Odeon Corporation, but over the previous ten years I'd built it from nothing into a billion-dollar company, a major presence in the theatre-exhibition industry and a force in Hollywood. As recently as April, I was sure I'd won this battle. At last I was going to get my major shareholder, the entertainment behemoth MCA, off my back by buying out the Charles Bronfman interests. MCA owned 49 per cent of Cineplex Odeon's shares, but under Investment Canada rules, it was allowed to vote only a third of them. Bronfman and others, through his company Claridge, owned 30 per cent of the non-MCA shares, which, combined with my 3.5 per cent and the 3.5 per cent owned by Myron Gottlieb, Cineplex Odeon's chief administrative officer and my long-time friend and comrade-in-arms, would give me *de facto* control of the company.

But the Bronfman interests had breached the deal. And so we got into this rancorous fight.

*Now – here they are, come to take my company away!*

I looked around the table to find a friendly face among the board members. Of course I looked first at Nat Taylor. *Mister* Taylor, a legend in the Canadian movie business. Nat was eighty-two, and there was nothing he didn't know about the business or those who ran it; in his time he had easily outfoxed both Famous Players and Canadian Odeon. Nat was my teacher and my mentor; the reason I was sitting in the hot seat was because I had bought into Nat's dream of creating a modest little multiplex cinema in downtown Toronto. Well, I'd come a long way from those first screening-room-sized theatres in Toronto's Eaton Centre. In just a few years I had turned Cineplex Odeon into the second-largest exhibition chain in North America and arguably the most powerful. When I glanced at him, his face was enigmatic, as usual. He had seen too much in his long life to waste pity on me.

But in the course of the fight that long afternoon, Nat would make one last impassioned plea on my behalf, one last, useless, generous, futile, marvellous speech. Bless him.

I knew Ted Pedas was sympathetic. Ted was one of the few gentlemen in the exhibition business. By that I mean you can shake hands on a deal with him and know it will be honoured. I shook hands with him and his brother Jim in 1987 when I bought the Circle movie theatre chain in Washington, D.C., from them. The Pedases drove a hard bargain, and some members of the board had complained that I had paid too high a price, but when you go after a key market, you have to pay the premium. What's more, I had locked up Washington, D.C., with Circle, having bought the Neighborhood chain there the year before. The Pedases weren't just exhibitors however; they were producers, eclectic producers, who backed moviemakers like the Coen brothers, Ethan and Joel, the creators of *Blood Simple, Raising Arizona*, and *Miller's Crossing.* Ted was upset at the way things were going. I knew he had been lobbying on my behalf, trying to convince the waverers. But when I looked at him, he was expressionless.

Jerry Banks. He was head of business affairs for Cineplex Odeon and an old friend. I was fond of Jerry. He used to cover for me at the

University of Toronto law school, taking copious notes while I cut classes to run my first business, putting out *Impact*, my little movie magazine. Jerry was about fifteen years older than me. I knew he was on my side, but he couldn't afford to show it. He was, after all, an employee of Cineplex Odeon, not my personal employee. He was in a vise, his loyalties in conflict. I didn't resent his anxious look.

I felt differently about Allen Karp, whom I had elevated to the presidency of Cineplex Odeon only a year before. Why did I do that if I didn't altogether trust the fellow? MCA had been pushing me to beef up the management of Cineplex Odeon. It was all part of their futile attempt to make Cineplex Odeon, and me, into something we weren't: foot soldiers in the sprawling MCA empire. I hired Allen from Goodman and Carr, Cineplex Odeon's Toronto corporate law-yers, after he'd been one of the counsel involved in pushing through the original deal with MCA back in the ancient history of 1986. But after all this time, Allen still didn't know much about the exhibition business; he was pushed by his wife, and he was badly starstruck, a hazard for the weak in our business. He always wanted to be the big shot, to impress people with the fact that he had arrived. He loved holding special screenings for friends in Cineplex Odeon's private screening room. Earlier in the year I had become uneasy about Allen. My hunch was that he had gone over to the enemy. I didn't know why I thought so; there was nothing I could put my finger on. It was just a suspicion in the back of my mind. But my instincts are pretty good on things like that.

I was also uncertain about Jack Daniels and Rudy Bratty. I didn't question their integrity, but they were ambivalent. Jack and I went way back. It was Jack who had helped fend off a bid to take over the presidency of Cineplex in 1982. Jack had brought in Rudy as a Cineplex Odeon investor in 1980. In the mid-eighties, they had become partners in Erin Mills, the billion-dollar development pro-ject, and they were among the first I called when I set out to secure financing to buy out the Bronfmans. Rudy, a big Daddy Warbucks look-alike, was enthusiastic right away, and Jack signed on from the South Pacific where he was vacationing. But MCA had recently been leaning on them, I could tell. And Erin Mills wasn't the power-house money-machine it used to be. As the real-estate boom began to expire, Jack and Rudy had to look to their own interests. I thought they would side with me if they could, but under the circumstances, they might go either way.

Jimmy Raymond, the president of Claridge, was present only in spirit, and not very much spirit at that – he was hooked into a confer-ence phone from his Toronto sickbed as though it were another intravenous tube. I couldn't help liking Jimmy. He was small and dapper, with a large, white, waxed mustache. I remember at an earlier meeting one lawyer laughing behind his hand, "Say, does anybody over five foot seven work for Charles Bronfman?" Jimmy thinks, sweetly but entirely erroneously, that he's a dynamite dealmaker, but he's really a nickel-and-dimer, which is what lost him so many deals. I think he really got a bang out of Myron and me, admiring what he took to be our buccaneering spirit. He came on the board when the Bronfman group bought into Cineplex Odeon in 1984. It's true that Jimmy's friendliness and ebulliness were often just a surface show that masked a coldness underneath, but in May 1989 he had gone further than he had to in warning Myron and me that MCA was going to move to fire us. I had wanted Jimmy to be here at this final showdown, but he had just groaned, "I'm sick, Garth, I can't help you." I muttered something back like, "You're sick, Jimmy, but I'm near death."

Sandra Kolber was next. How I disliked that woman! I always felt she was a phony. It irritated me the way she always said "Hi doll!" to the women in the office. But she was not really a factor. She was only on the board as a stand-in for her husband, Leo. Senator Leo Kolber, another little man, had been a bagman for Pierre Trudeau in Montreal; he was also Charles Bronfman's adviser, his *consiglière*. Leo was not a director of Cineplex Odeon and so was never invited to board meetings. He was in the room this day "by special invitation," a bad sign from my point of view. Six years earlier (though it seemed only a few months), Leo had made his falsely encouraging noises, "Garth, I want you to build me the biggest entertainment company in the world." What crap! I'd like to take those words and shove 'em down his throat. It was Leo's vacillations, his indecisiveness and lack of spine, that led directly to this terrible day.

Next to Kolber was Jack Richer, the third Claridge nominee. Someone once described him to me as "a sneering kind of accountant" and it's only too true. Negativity seemed basic to his character. He had been on my case for some time, determined to prove me wrong wherever he could, although he knew little about the business. It was Jack who kept harping on the need for Cineplex Odeon to produce profits from its core business – the theatres. I explained again and again that Cineplex Odeon was an entrepreneurial business of which exhibition was a part but not the whole, but he just never seemed to get it. I was sure Jack had been suborned by MCA, which was still angling to get another seat on the board. Skip Paul had certainly been cultivating him.

Charles S. "Skip" Paul looked like a Southern Californian Peter Pan, the kind of guy who spends a lot of time on the beach. He was close to MCA's president Sid Sheinberg. Sid and his wife, Lorraine Gary, used to take Skip on vacations with them, and Sid had made Skip the head of a new investment division of MCA, into which their Cineplex Odeon holdings had been shoehorned. In the last few years Skip had been calling Myron frequently, always in a bullying, hectoring, unpleasant tone. Myron was always perplexed by Skip. "He's awfully rude one day, and the next day he calls up and apologizes," he would say. Skip was manipulative. He was gunning for me. He had come to the meeting with a letter that accused Myron and me of everything but abusing small children. I had zero respect for him.

I passed by the two corporate MCA members, Eric Pertsch, one of its Canadian nominees, and Hal Haas, the MCA treasurer. I didn't need to guess where their loyalties lay. For the last three and a half years Hal had sat on our audit committee and okayed our accounts, and then wham: in the summer of 1989 one of our executives saw, peeking out from Hal's briefcase, an accountant's version of "the scarlet letter," a damning Kellogg report, with DRAFT stamped all over it. The report, an insiders' tip sheet, was published in the middle of our struggle with MCA and cast all kinds of unlikely aspersions on Cineplex Odeon's accounting practices. After that we had class-action lawsuits, and the shortsellers began closing in like jackals. But it was no use worrying about Hal. He was just a cog in the MCA machine.

Finally, I looked at Sid Sheinberg. I felt a mix of sadness, anger, and contempt. I had really liked Sid and I think he liked me. What had happened? There he was, sitting in his expensive threads, as he liked to call his suits. For nearly two decades Sid had considered himself the heir apparent at MCA. He thought he was in the catbird seat, his life all lined up; he was president and would succeed Lew Wasserman as chairman; it was as sure as God made little green apples, as predictable as a politician's tax grab, as certain as another earthquake. But supposing old Lew were to sell MCA from under him? I would never put anything past Lew. Sid was wearing one of his many pairs of granny glasses and was being sarcastic, as usual. I thought of what my old friend Norman Levy had once said. Norman had held numerous top jobs in Hollywood over the last decade, and when I told him in December 1985 that MCA was buying into Cineplex Odeon, he said, "This may be the way to build an empire, Garth, but the problem is you may wake up one morning and find you're not Caesar any more." Norman, Norman, how prescient you were! I knew Sid wouldn't waver now. There was no forgiveness whatsoever in Sid Sheinberg.

I made my pitch to all of them. I showed them how we could quickly and decisively eliminate a substantial portion of the company's debt by the realignment of key assets and by unloading non-essential assets – the value of which I had dramatically improved. I took them through the scheme patiently, but I knew I was losing them. It had been a brutal few months, and they were angry, weary, and, in the end, confused. They didn't want to listen any longer. They just wanted it to stop.

There was an adjournment. Leo and Sid huddled in my office, and the Bronfman–MCA treaty was sealed.

They came back into the room and I knew it was over. I had lost. I was out. I looked around at those faces again. The sound and the fury faded to a hum. I seemed to be existing in some kind of emotional limbo. I saw the light glinting off glasses, heard the snapping of brief-cases as loud as pistol shots, the scuffing of chairs, and noticed the evasive glances – *why don't they ever have the balls to look at you at times like these?*

As I got heavily to my feet, numb with fatigue, I thought, "They have come to take my life away from me again. Instead of the deadly virus and the surgeons' scalpels, they substituted the petty treach-eries, the furtive little compromises, the failed visions, the votes 'in the best interests of the corporation.'"

I went to my office and I locked the door. I put my head in my hands and sat very still, staring into the blackness within, but I didn't cry, not quite, not then.

After those long, long minutes, I went home and told my family.

They sat around the dinner table, staring at me, the children's faces shocked and scared. God, how I loved them! My wife, Pearl, who had gone through the endless, cliff-hanging months with me. Alicia, fourteen, and Marc, eleven, who had never seen their father defeated.

It was very painful. I had never had to confess defeat to them before, to make, in effect, a speech of explanation and apology to my own family. I think my children had always been proud that their father had built a sprawling empire in the movie world. They often went to screenings or to the theatres with me, and that's all they really knew about my corporate life and what I had created over the past ten years. Now it was gone, snuffed out, in a moment.

I tried to keep my voice calm, reasoned. "Tomorrow you'll read in the papers that your father is no longer in the motion-picture busi-ness. I'll no longer be at Cineplex Odeon. Don't be sad. There's plenty of opportunity and challenge in what I'm going to do next. Things aren't going to get boring."

I had hoped I was convincing. But I'm not sure that even I believed it then. I was still fighting my own demons.

I lay awake that night, depressed. My children's worried eyes haunted me.

Jerry Banks said to me the next day, "You know, Garth, it's only been a couple of hours. You have a right to feel sad."

In those dark days of corporate double-dealing, I would sneak down to the Pantages, the splendid theatre I was restoring. At first I would watch the workmen, taking pleasure in their unhurried competence. After the theatre's opening, I would sit in the magical place that I had built and listen to the haunting, exhilarating melodies of the wonderful music of *Phantom*, and I would feel inside the stirrings of optimism and energy that had always fuelled my life.

Now once again, from somewhere deep inside, I reached for this same reserve. I began to plan my new life. The day Myron and I bought Cineplex Odeon's live-entertainment division, which was to become our own Livent, I went to the Pantages Theatre and watched and listened to the rapt audience. After the show was over, I went up on the stage and, behind the closed curtain, made a speech to the assembled cast, musicians, and crew who for months had been troubled by the uncertainty and fearful for their own futures. "You're my corporate family now," I told them. And I believed it. We would build something grand, something beautiful; we'd construct new theatres, develop other plays, create magnificent music, delight entranced audiences, build another great corporation.

*When I was a child, I had run through the glittering water from the sprinklers, and then . . . that evil virus came and took away a part of my life.*

*But I seized it back and never let go.*

*So if I have anything to contribute, it is this: Never give up. Never yield. Always dig deeper. There is always another layer of the onion. There is always a way back. There is always opportunity to be mined from despair. Exhaustion is just another obstacle to be overcome, another knot to be unravelled. There is always a way to liberate creativity and then nurture it. Never be afraid to fly closer to the sun.*

*Not just escape. But escape into something greater.*

# PART

I

# CHAPTER

## I

### "THEM'S THE CONDITIONS THAT PREVAIL"

I wakened into the air-conditioned nightmare. It was September 1953, and I opened my eyes to find myself in a cavernous room lined with small, neat, white beds. I could hardly move. There was no one there I knew, no one to say comforting words, no one to hold my hand or hug me. Out of the corner of my eye, I saw there was someone in every bed, kids, some of them apparently whole but most just heads tacked onto giant metal cylinders, bodies, if there were any, wrapped in metal, imprisoned, entombed. It terrified me. *What had happened to take their bodies away?*

I suppose I was in a state of shock, too frightened to even whimper, so I just lay there, scrabbling for refuge in the far reaches of my mind.

I lay there for days, for nights, forever it seemed. At least once a night one of the cylinders disappeared, the kid in it wheeled out, never to reappear. What was happening to them? I tried to ask the nurse, but she only shushed me and wouldn't say a word. She, too, looked frightened. Every now and then I heard someone say the word "polio." I didn't know what polio meant, and no one explained it to me. I didn't understand why my parents, who were allowed to see me only occasionally, looked so white and scared. What I did know was that I couldn't move my leg. My left leg.

\*   \*   \*

About a month earlier I had developed a fever and begun to shiver and sweat. My mother called our family doctor, but he didn't come. For three days she called repeatedly, and for three days he put her off. And I just kept running around, although it was standard practice then (which my parents didn't know) to treat any possible symptom of the dreaded polio with immediate bed rest. Our doctor finally came on the fourth day, and then only after my mother called him and said, "You've got to come now because Garth fell over while he was walking."

Whenever I think of this now, anger floods my mind. Maybe, even if the doctor had come promptly, it would have made no difference. But maybe it would have made all the difference in the world. Maybe I would still have been able to run.

*Everything would have been different!*

After the doctor came and spread a belated alarm, my father picked me up in his arms. The next thing I remember, we were rushing downtown in a cab to the Hospital for Sick Children. When we got there, they did tests and then took my father aside. "Mr. Drabinsky, your son has polio," they told him. It must have been like being told a century earlier that your child had smallpox. Polio was a terrifying daily headline; children and young adults died within days of it being diagnosed. The disease was highly contagious, and I had a little brother, Sheldon, at home. My parents were torn between shock and horror for themselves, pity for me, and fear for Shelley, who had been born only the previous October.

Ironically, that summer the first anti-polio vaccine, the Salk, was being field-tested, and the virus for the vaccine was being grown in Toronto's Connaught Laboratories, no more than a few miles from our little Castlefield Avenue home. Too late, much too late for me. I was unlucky all round. Hundreds, thousands of others, Donald Sutherland and Francis Ford Coppola among them, had contracted polio in an earlier epidemic, but they came through without paralysis. Not so for me. Within a week my left leg was severely paralysed, all the way from the hip to the arch of my foot. Today I can bend my left foot only with great difficulty, and sitting down I can't raise my out-outstretched leg. Walking has always been an effort. A mile is, for me, a marathon. My hip aches; pain is a presence that fills my being.

*It wasn't supposed to be this way!*

After seven days in the trauma ward at Sick Kids, I was sent to Thistletown, the isolation hospital in suburban Toronto. There, in the vast room reserved for polio patients, I watched the muscles in my leg slowly waste away.

And that was just the beginning. Over the next eight years I would have seven major operations. The following year, when I was four, Dr. William Mustard, a public-spirited heart surgeon who had shifted to orthopaedics partly because of the terrible epidemic, operated on the muscles of my thigh to prevent my left leg from becoming deformed and shorter than my right. I remember vividly the first time I went under the knife. In those days they didn't use gas or a needle before they gave you the anaesthetic; they just slapped the chloroform mask over your face, pressing it down so you couldn't breathe without sucking the loathsome fumes into your lungs. When they did that to me, I thought I'd go crazy. I fought and tried to rip the mask off until, finally, I was put to sleep. For years afterwards, when-ever I had more surgery, I begged the doctors to give me a needle first. "Please," I said, "don't put the mask on me when I'm awake."

After that initial operation, I went home in a body cast that covered me from the waist down. My father had to carry me every-where, and I felt utterly helpless. Months later, after I got out of the cast, I was fitted with a leather-bound walking brace from the knee down, which had two steel posts that slotted into specially made Oxfords. The leather was hot, and when the shoes weren't painful, they were dreadfully uncomfortable. Worst of all they made me dif-ferent. I knew by the way the kids looked at the brace just how different I was as I lurched up the road to Allenby Public School.

My mother, however, was unbending on this matter; she refused to allow me self-pity and made me walk to school as though there were nothing wrong with me. Even later, when we moved two blocks further from the school to Briar Hill Avenue, I was expected to walk.

Those two blocks were like two miles, miles filled with obstacles and perverse traps. The only times my mother would pick me up in her car were in the slippery days of winter, because I kept falling over all the time. After a while I learned how to cushion myself by leaning into the fall, but even now I'm vulnerable on any slippery surface. Dick Roberts, for whom I articled as a law clerk and who subsequently became my second mentor, great friend, and cherished law partner, once remembered walking to a coffee shop with me soon after we met. The pavement was slippery and I fell down with a crash. But before he could say anything, I picked myself up and said, "Don't pay any attention. I do it all the time."

When I was nine, I was sent to Dr. Robert Salter, the surgeon who later became head of the orthopaedic department at Sick Kids. Salter operated on me six times – once it was twice in one week – during the next few years. These were not trivial operations, a few quick cuts, a slice here, a stitch there, and it's over. They were all major operations, down to the bone and the gristle, intended to straighten the leg, fuse the joints in my foot, and transfer the tendons and ligaments to different locations so that I'd have some mobility in my leg and foot. They hurt like hell. For a week after every operation, I'd scream to the nurses to give me another shot to deaden the awful, tearing pain; they had to wean me off the morphine. My left leg still looks like a battlefield. One of my scars is fourteen inches long.

To add to the pain, the operations always took place in the summer so I wouldn't miss school. I can understand this now, but at the time I believed they were doing it to torment me – *they were taking my summers away from me too!* For all of my childhood, the routine was to spend two to three weeks in the hospital followed by a month in a full-length cast, hobbling around on crutches, followed by six weeks in a "walking cast." Finally, I was given three to five months of physiotherapy.

Every year. From the age of seven until I was twelve. My entire childhood.

I used to dread my visits to Sick Kids. I hated walking into

Dr. Salter's office in the Medical Arts Building. Even then, I knew he was trying to help me, but every time I saw him he would tell me I needed another procedure, another operation, another summer in hell. I know he had a special attitude toward his patients; much later he told me that one of the most gratifying things about being a children's surgeon was that he could watch his patients grow and develop and see what became of them. I was – and am – grateful to him. He treated eight out of ten kids free, and for the rest it was essentially pay-what-you-can. So when I was given a Renaissance Man of Film Award at the Montreal World Film Festival in 1987, I asked Dr. Salter to sit at the head table as my guest; and when the hospital asked me for money during a fund-raising drive, I was delighted that I could make a significant contribution.

But at the time I hated the hospital, I feared Dr. Salter, and I dreaded the pain. The worst I remember was during the hour-long physiotherapy sessions that I was subjected to three times a week. Miss Brodie – I'll never forget her – was the head of physiotherapy. Ah, the prime of Miss Brodie! She was a disciplinarian in her soul and her sinew, and she was relentless; for her, pain was merely a necessary condition, a prelude to wholeness, a rite of passage, and she never let up. She made me try to straighten my leg so that I could walk, and she insisted I try to flex my toes and my foot muscles. I would sit on a bench and extend my left leg. Miss Brodie was determined to straighten the ligament in the knee; all I had to do, she said, was push. Huh! I thought I'd go through the roof. A hundred burning needles stabbed into my leg every time I pushed.

I wanted to strike out, to take control, but there was no one to hit, no one to hurt. They all wanted to do the best for me. But I thought they were killing me.

I still feel those wrenching emotions when I hear one of those old teen-idol songs, Paul Anka's "Lonely Boy," Bobby Darin's "Dream Lover." For other kids, those songs evoke love or romance, idle dreams and longings; for me, when I hear the Teddy Bears singing "To Know Him Is to Love Him," it reminds me of being driven down to

Sick Kids to see Dr. Salter to be told the dreaded news: more surgery. More knives. More Brodie. More pain. Another long summer gone.

On hot summer days I would look at the fields around Allenby, the endless fields made for childish running, and remember how it felt dashing through the sprinklers that last summer before polio struck. Then a sense of loss and sadness would overwhelm me, and I would feel suffocated by the unfairness of it. Sometimes all that emotion would break through and I'd strike out at whatever or whomever was near. Once, when I was six and my brother Shelley was three, it welled up and overcame me. I got so mad at him that I took my hated brace off and threw it at him as hard as I could. It cut him so badly above the eye that he had to be rushed to the hospital for stitches, and he still bears the scar. I missed his eye by a fraction of an inch.

This incident still troubles me – *I could have blinded my own brother!*

I mentioned it to my parents recently at a Passover seder. My wife and our kids were there too, listening intently.

"Do you remember," I asked, "when I almost knocked out Shelley's eye when I threw my brace at him?"

"No," my father said. "I forget."

I was astonished. I couldn't believe it – this memory that had been seared into my brain for so long. I abhor violence. I have never been a physical person, have never lifted a finger to my kids or anyone else. I'm confounded every time I hear the words "physical abuse." The idea of a man striking a woman appals me. I can't even begin to understand the attraction of hunting. I can't deal with killing of any sort. So I asked, "How could you forget? You were hysterical when I did it!"

My father's head sank lower and lower. Finally he said, "I guess I tried to blot it out of my mind, because it hurt me so much."

*The amateur shrinks have it easy. They can point to my polio and say, "See, it scarred you as a child, it shaped your life, it took your youth away, it stole years from your life, it's what drives you." They can easily see how different I am from my two brothers and my parents. They can point to my mother and father and say, "Oh yes, you were never able to see how they were wounded and scared and unable to cope with your illness, you saw only that they couldn't give you your life back. You felt abandoned."*

On the matter of the polio, they may be right, these amateur second-guessers. But whether it's a negative influence or a positive, in the end we'll leave it to others to judge. I do know that I learned how fragile life was, and how necessary it is to live it to the fullest, and how shabby compromise is. But on the matter of family, the amateurs cannot know. Family is always more complicated than outsiders think.

My parents were always there when I woke up after the operations, and I could see that it was torturing them inside to have me going through all this. They were there . . . but not there. We never managed to communicate with each other in a healing way. They never told me about their pain and I never told them about my fear. All I knew for sure was that I was a dreadful burden, a worry, and a constant expense. I knew that behind their bland and soothing faces they were wondering, like any parents with a disabled child, "Why us?"

I understand that, now.

My parents' outlook had been shaped by the Depression in Saskatchewan, where they both grew up. Both of them were second-generation Canadians; they were always worried about money. This worry consumed their every moment and action and in the end governed their lives. In 1947 they made their way to Toronto, and my father, Philip, eventually started his own commercial and industrial air-conditioning and refrigeration business. Later I could laugh when Nat Taylor, my mentor in the movie business, described with passion the first dime he had ever earned – to Nat, that dime was as exciting as a gold rush! But my father seldom had fun in his business. He got little satisfaction from his work.

My father's father, Isaac, arrived from Poland at the age of twelve and went to rural Saskatchewan, where the government was offering immigrants a square mile to farm. It sounded immense to migrants from Europe, but nobody troubled to tell Isaac that Saskatchewan was a notorious dustbowl. As well as contending with the weather, Isaac was impatient and had a terrible temper, and he soon lost his farm and eked out a living by running a small grocery store. My father likes to say he was born in a haystack, and until he was six, he spoke only Yiddish. As the eldest of three brothers, he became the *de facto* head of the family, as Isaac was always busy and his wife, Sophie, my grandmother, was often ill.

My mother's father, Chaim Gershon Waldman, came from Ukraine in 1912, missing the *Titanic* by thirty minutes. Harry, as he was called, was quite a guy. He was involved in all kinds of enterprises in Moose Jaw, Saskatchewan, ending up with a soft-drink bottling company. Among his ideas was a process for turning cornstarch into sweetener, and during the Second World War, he sold the process to the Army. After the war, he started the Jackson Bottling Company, using his partner's Anglo-Saxon name, which he thought would have greater local appeal. His brands were Suncrest and Nu-Grape. After his death in 1948, his son Harold took over the business and eventually locked up the Coca-Cola franchise for most of the province.

I'm named after Harry, my mother having ingeniously extracted Garth from Gershon. I don't know to this day how she came up with a name of Welsh origins. As a kid I wanted to be called John, a good Anglo-Saxon label. It was bad enough always having to spell Drabinsky. When I was asked my name, I'd say "Garth" and people would say, "No, I mean your first name." It wasn't a name of the fifties. But now I congratulate my mom: Garth is a name for the nineties.

What can I say about my family? I guess the best way to describe it is that, in my first eighteen years at home, my family hardly ever took a vacation together. Maybe we spent a week at a cottage in northern Ontario or went to Montreal for the occasional weekend, but those times were very rare. We never *hung out*. My mother, Ethel, would scrimp and save, even when she didn't have to. It's true that my mother's efforts allowed her and my dad to build up some kind of an asset base; they started, after all, with nothing. But the reality is that my parents never really savoured life.

My mother, sad to say, was often argumentative and from time to time managed to alienate one of her brothers or sisters. She was hard on family. It hurt me a lot, because I liked my uncles and aunts. I liked saying I had cousins. But we only saw them on Jewish holidays and family celebrations. It fell to me to attempt to be the family catalyst, to bring the family together. It was always me who called my mother's brother in Moose Jaw. I was like a young kid compared to him, but I was also like a younger brother.

My father should have been a doctor. He could have been a great doctor, I think, but he sacrificed his life for his father, mother, and brothers. His mother was a diabetic and was dying, so his father needed him in the store. He couldn't afford medical school. All he could manage was the engineering school at the University of Saskatchewan. His younger brother ended up becoming the doctor in the family.

My father was not an entrepreneur. He's a very caring man, and a man of great integrity, a perfectionist, but life intimidated him and so did risks. As a result, many of his decisions were tentative. Life could have been so much sweeter had he seen the future and how prices would multiply endlessly.

Our little two-storey house on Briar Hill was full of tension. The anxieties and pressures of operating his small business wore my father down.

*Am I saying this drove me into the life of an entrepreneur?*

*I don't know.*

*I love them, both of them, but I couldn't respond to their small view of life and I hated their caution.*

*Polio had grabbed me and tried to smash me down. I wouldn't let it. I wouldn't let anything smash me down.*

*Fighting back gave me a hunger for life that has never left me. I learned to do everything wholeheartedly, whether it was to love the arts, to work for charity, to build a company, to look after family. Do it well and do it totally. I became determined that I wouldn't repeat my father's*

*mistake and end up doing something I disliked and resented. Whatever I*
*decided to do – and I really had no idea at all what that might be when*
*I was young – I would do it because I enjoyed doing it.*

My own brothers are very different from me. My middle brother, Shelley, always laboured at school. My parents continually carped at him, telling him to work harder and to accomplish more, but Shelley loved to dream about going to faraway places and flying. . . . He loved reading maps. He lived in his own special world. I finally brought him into the company at Cineplex Odeon, giving him all the opportunities I could, while trying to discipline him in business. I was tough on him, I guess, and he may have resented it. Eventually he became very good at what he did, which was to be head of purchasing for all the concessions and supplies for the company. Then one day, without even giving me warning, he left the company for the travel industry – his first passion.

Shelley, who was three years younger than me, used to tag along after me when we were kids. He remembers one summer how we used to bike down Yonge Street from Lawrence to St. Clair – a distance of several miles – collecting Orange Crush bottle caps from the vending machines at variety stores. Under the cork of each cap there was a letter; if you could spell out the words "Orange Crush" in bottle caps you'd win a case of pop. My mother at one point had about forty cases of pop in the cold cellar – we just never stopped collecting and guzzling.

I was close to my kid brother, Cyril. He's eight years younger than I am, with a lot of spirit. He went into law school and came to work for me as an articling student. When I moved into Cineplex Odeon, he joined the company, and I found an appropriate niche for him in one of our operations, The Film House Group, which he ran with great efficiency and aplomb. When I finally sold Film House, he stayed on to run the company. He is now the president of Rank Organisation PLC's North American lab operations, including Deluxe Labs.

My family lived very simply. Most of my friends had money, but I never did. There were no trips to the theatre, no concerts, no museums. I was eleven by the time I had my first meal in a restaurant. The parents of my friend Marshall Devor took me out for a Chinese dinner. I thought I'd died and gone to heaven!

*A really sophisticated kid, no?*

*Well, it's easy to laugh now. But I was a kid with a hunger for life, who felt his life hadn't yet begun. I wasn't afraid. I was never afraid. I was always filled with a sense of possibility.*

Music came to fill the emotional gaps in my life. There was no phonograph in our house until I was twelve, and the single radio we owned was in my parents' bedroom. But, if they hadn't gone off to visit my Uncle Dave in Florida in the summer of 1958, the rock-and-roll revolution might have passed me by. I slept in their bed while they were away, and once I had turned on their curved, ivory-coloured table radio, I was hooked. Elvis Presley's "Hound Dog" and "Don't Be Cruel," Buddy Holly's "That'll Be the Day," and Fats Domino's "Blueberry Hill." Those wonderful songs poured out of the speakers, and soon I knew them all. The airwaves were crowded with the frustrations of young love . . . "they tried to tell us we're too young!" When I heard "Diana," I wanted it to go on forever. I was intensely romantic, and these songs were the first directly sensual expression I had ever experienced.

I needed music. I had to have it as a solace, to help me get through such a frustrating time. I was wildly competitive, yet I was either lying in bed or stumbling around in a cast when all I wanted was to be out with the other kids, playing games. I know my life would have been dramatically different if I hadn't had polio. Maybe I wouldn't have become an entrepreneur. I wanted so badly to be Jim Brown breaking a tackle or, later on, Jean-Claude Killy hurtling down the Alps.

Alas, reality interrupted my dreams. I could play baseball. But when the kids picked sides, I'd always be the last one they'd choose, and it always rankled. "Why did you pick me last?" I'd ask. "I can hit the ball as well as anyone. I can catch and throw. I can play first base." It was true – the crutches had developed my arm and shoulder muscles, and I could bat and throw the ball as far as anybody. But the truth didn't help. I couldn't tear up the bases. My running method, to my mortification, was an ungainly, awkward hop.

The kids would say, "You're no good to us." They would walk away from me.

I would never walk away. I would stay there and say, "I want to be part of this. It's important to me."

They paid no attention.

My sports ambitions frustrated, I took refuge in music and watched a lot of television. I didn't read very much, until I discovered Ian Fleming and James Bond. And board games . . . there wasn't a board game I couldn't win. I was unbelievably aggressive. Monopoly was my favourite game and I quickly became the local Monopoly champ. I would disconcert my opponents because I moved pieces so quickly. I knew the board like the back of my hand. Everything had to move quickly. That was the way I was. I also loved watching sports and became a sports fanatic. To this day I can recall the leading coaches in the NCAA. You want to know who coached Oklahoma in the sixties? I can tell you. My son can't believe it. I loved watching baseball, football, hockey, track and field, tennis, the Olympics; it didn't matter, I was a fanatic.

*I didn't spend my time in bed dreaming. But I did dream – about where I was going and what I would do. I dreamt of wonder and romance, the kind of dreams, I see now, that motion pictures and the theatre are made of.*

*Perhaps it's one reason why I am where I am.*

Later, card games took the place of board games. Poker and blackjack and this and that. I gambled a little bit. I'd take twenty dollars and . . . the adrenaline flowing, pushing to the edge. I loved the risk, that I could lose all the money I had by playing cards. I never feared losing. I suppose the reason was always pretty clear to me. I had already lost something in my life so I started living a little bit recklessly when I was young. But it's never so simple. I was also, on the other hand, doing things like learning the Torah.

Of course, even that was a gamble. I was seven when my mother sent me off to Hebrew school. It meant extra hours of study, but I didn't care. I loved it. That was the first place I felt accepted whole-heartedly. In return, I embraced Judaism. To this day I read Hebrew fluently and chant the prayers without a prayer book. Then my mother pushed me even further, saying, "I want you to go to the youth services at Beth Sholom Synagogue on Saturday mornings."

At first I enjoyed the services, mainly because I met other Jewish kids, and we were given free Coca-Cola and cookies from the Jew-ish bakery. But by the time I was twelve, I wanted to excel. Why shouldn't I read the Torah at the Saturday services the way the six-teen-year-olds did? My teacher, Rabbi Kirschenblatt, shook his head. "You can't. You haven't even been bar mitzvahed." Nonetheless, I insisted. I must have been insufferable. But Rabbi Kirschenblatt taught me well, and before I had my bar mitzvah, I was reading the Torah at Saturday services. My parents were proud of me, the con-gregation admired me, and, most of all, it did wonders for my self-confidence.

*I remember a conversation I had many years later with a friend:*

*"You were learning the Torah, the whole thing?" This in an incredu-lous tone.*

*"I wanted to see if I could."*

*"Why?"*

*"To see whether I could be good enough in front of hundreds of elders in a congregation, and master it, and do it, and be respected for it, chal-lenge myself in areas where I was able to, areas where my polio had no impact – that is, in the mind. It was enormously important to me, a way of overcoming my physical handicap, to see if I could do something better than others."*

*"So you were compensating for your disability?"*

*"No, not necessarily. Don't oversimplify. I made a conscious decision, to live life as fully as I could, because . . ."*

*"Because why?"*

*"Because it was mine."*

I learned to swim during those early years. Now it would be called therapy, but then it was just exercise. It was something I could be good at – I had strong arms and shoulders, after all – and later I would become a lifeguard for a while, something that helped boost my confidence. One of my instructors was Marilyn Bell, already famous for being the first woman to swim Lake Ontario. She was just a kid, still in her teens, but she helped out every Tuesday evening, either at the pool at Oakwood Collegiate in midtown Toronto or at the Lakeshore swimming club. It was a long time ago now, but Marilyn still remembers the emotional intensity of being able to help kids whose confidence had either been eroded or destroyed to regain some modicum of it. Many of the kids were much worse off than me – among her charges was a young girl, no more than three, who had been born without arms, and another kid who learned to swim though completely blind. Marilyn was a wonderful instructor, patient, strong, and warm, and she helped a lot of us more than she knew. For her part, she says she still gets a kick out of seeing my name in the papers and knowing that she knew me back then, when I was just a forlorn little boy.

The experience of attending Hebrew school and learning the Torah also grounded me in Judaism and for the first time gave me a moral and intellectual framework for my thinking. Jewish scholars have their own version of the Socratic method: they dissect, analyse, interpret, and argue over everything. Today, partly as a result of this training, I refuse to take anything at face value, which makes me hard to please. No wonder I've been called one of Canada's toughest bosses. What people don't realize is that I have a problem pleasing myself. It wasn't until I went to Jerusalem for the first time – and that wasn't until I was thirty-seven – that I really understood my own background. Jerusalem was a buzz-saw of argument. You can't survive in Israel unless you're willing to argue – about everything. I felt absolutely at home.

My school years were among the happiest of my life. I graduated near the top of my class at Allenby and then moved to North Toronto Collegiate, a school with one of the city's highest academic standards.

At first I was filled with dread. New faces, new teachers, the unexpected. The other kids' reactions to my limp. And I would be one of maybe a hundred Jews in a student body of twelve hundred.

I remember only the good things about North Toronto. I was a workaholic, but I didn't care. I was playing catch-up with a vengeance, and I would continue playing catch-up for a very long time. In fact, I don't think I've stopped yet. In Grade 10 I took nine courses instead of the mandatory seven. I even took a course in Russian! North Toronto was famous for its music department; I joined the choir and tried to learn the guitar. I won a Kiwanis award for public speaking, and I fell in love with my English teacher.

Oh, it was a heady time!

But it was in Grade 9, when I wandered into a Grade 13 drama group rehearsing Molière's *The Imaginary Invalid*, that I found myself. I knew right away I wanted to be part of this.

*And no, this is not just hindsight, the chairman of a major theatrical corporation talking. It was a moment of genuine epiphany. I loved it at once. To this day, it's the warmth that excites me. Making theatre is intimate and involving. The smell, the sights, the community of players, the egos, the magical pretense, the chameleon-like nature of theatre, the chance to lose oneself in character and story, everything.*

I'd never even seen a play, only movies. My first screen loves were biblical epics. They tied into my Jewish studies. Okay, so Charlton Heston now seems stiff and pretentious playing Moses, but when I was ten, the sight of him standing in front of the burning bush was tremendously stirring.

One particular movie stands out. Billy Wilder's *The Apartment* was the first movie my mother ever took me to. I at once fell hopelessly in love with Shirley MacLaine and had no difficulty at all in identifying with the poor schlemiel, Jack Lemmon. I, too, was unsure how women would relate to me.

But film musicals were best of all. I stood in line for an hour to see *West Side Story*, and when Richard Beymer's Tony and Natalie Wood's Maria sang "Somewhere there's a place for us," I bawled my eyes out.

That same year, Grade 9, I heard that auditions were being held at school for *Inherit the Wind*. I saw myself playing Clarence Darrow, destroying the forces of ignorance and intolerance as represented by William Jennings Bryan. But with my limp, I knew I'd be lucky even to get on the stage. And I was lucky – I managed to get on the jury. To me, it didn't matter how small, how inconsequential the part. I was hooked. Just putting on the makeup, listening to the audience, watching the people react to the actors was a wonderful experience. I continued my modest acting career at summer camp, Camp Rockwood, and many years later I briefly relived those days when my daughter, Alicia, auditioned for and won the role of Mary Magdalene in *Jesus Christ Superstar* at her summer camp. I was really impressed. I had never done as well as that.

The first years of the sixties felt filled with promise and the possibilities seemed endless. The shackles had come off – almost literally in my case, for I was finished with hospitals. I was into my teens. It was the time of Phil Spector. The music of the Beatles echoed in my head. It was a wonderful time.

The high point of my school career was when I was elected president of the student council. Remember, this was 1967, when the assassination of John Kennedy was still thought of as having happened only yesterday. Selma, Alabama, was becoming a code word for the struggle for civil rights; it was the time of Martin Luther King, Jr., folk music, protest; Vietnam was already a name of high emotion; and student unrest was starting to manifest itself across North America. Even North Toronto's *esprit de corps* was becoming tattered. Still, I was taken aback when Bob Wright, my history teacher, suggested I run for president. North Toronto was, after all, a bastion of the city's WASP establishment. It had never had a Jewish president of the student council, and I was far from being well-known, let alone popular.

As usual, though, I couldn't walk away from the challenge.

I'm not a cynical kind of guy at all. I really wanted to bring everyone together, so my platform included the idea for a house-league system that would give older and younger students a reason to cooperate on projects and so augment the school spirit. But I confess my winning ploy was pure hokum. I had a series of photos taken by a friend of mine, Gunther, a great photographer. Each photo we tried had a different look – Garth in black shades, Garth with the corporate image – but none of them was convincing. Then I had an inspiration. Gunther's three-year-old brother, who had long blond hair, was always hanging around us. I took this adorable kid in my arms, hugged him, and yelled at Gunther, "Shoot it!" And there it was: How Drabinsky Loves Kids! It worked, too. Posters of this disingenuous picture went up everywhere, and I won by the largest plurality in the history of the school! Ain't politics wonderful?

For me, this was an intoxicating time. The principal and the vice-principal were constantly asking my advice. I remember being in Grade 13 math class one day studying calculus when the phone rang. The teacher picked it up and said, "It's for you, Drabinsky." After speaking briefly on the phone, I said, "I have to deal with a problem here, sir," and off I went.

Could it get any better? Yes. In the spring of 1968, I produced at the school a musical variety show that I had begun for Canada's centennial year. It ran for four nights and every performance was sold out. What's more, it made a profit: $25,000.

I wanted to leave my mark on the school, so I spent the money on Canadian paintings for the newly refurbished senior administration wing. I didn't paint or sketch, and I knew nothing about either the principles or principals of art. But for one reason or another, I was always hypersensitive to my surroundings, and I responded immediately to painting, particularly abstract expressionism. It was wonderful to go shopping for art. I remember with particular fondness a landscape by Ray Cattell. In retrospect, most of them were good paintings but not great paintings; in my experience it's the difficult, intense paintings that really last, works in which the artist has taken an idea and infused the whole canvas with it, pushing that idea into every corner of the work. Nevertheless, these were the first paintings I had bought, and it was a deeply satisfying experience.

With the rest of the money, I had a new garden built with stone benches so students could sit and study. People still come up to me and say, "I was at North Toronto when you were president!" At the school's seventy-fifth anniversary a few years ago, I made a stirring speech about what the school had meant to me. It gave me a life, I said. It filled up all the empty corners, it made me see I could be an achiever, it gave me friendships and made me feel whole.

But was it all perfect? No.

Why not?

Girls!

I was an intensely romantic young man and, like all romantics, was an obsessive (and all obsessives are romantic, I think.) But for me, my leg, which made me *different*, was a problem.

*Sure, it screwed around with my head. Out of fear and insecurity, I developed a need to conquer in love very early, to overwhelm with attention and love and admiration and sheer presence and persistence, because I was always in fear of being viewed as different. To this day, I can't walk past a mirror and not notice it. I know it's more in my mind than in anybody else's, but it's there. When I was a young man, the idea of wearing short pants, and having one leg clearly thinner than the other leg, bothered me a lot. And one leg was very scarred from all the operations. I believed that had to be a turn-off for any woman.*

*I'm still very self-conscious when I walk up on a stage and four thousand eyes focus on me. I find it excruciating.*

*Later in my life, when I went up on a Broadway stage to receive the Tony for Best Musical, I remember thinking, "I hope the cameras are not on me as I go up the stairs."*

In the summer of my seventeenth year, I decided I wanted some real money. I wanted to buy decent clothes, I wanted to travel, I wanted to break out of my cocoon, to be a big man. My successes at the synagogue and at school boosted my confidence at home, so I asked my dad for a job. Without quibbling, he apprenticed me to his mechanics to learn the air-conditioning business from the roof down, so to speak; for that summer I heaved heavy tanks of Freon over the sweltering metallic roofs of shopping centres. It wasn't my idea of a good time, but I did what I had to do, and after eight weeks' work, I had

$2,000 in my pocket. I took myself off to Miami Beach and the Beau Rivage Hotel with my friend Fred Fruitman. It was my first airplane flight and I couldn't sleep the night before.

The hotel and the beach were filled with Americans, hip with their Levis and Bass Weejuns and cool attitude, and I longed to be a part of all that. This was the hottest summer of music, Neil Diamond, the Lovin' Spoonful. I wanted it all, to be immersed in it, to let the richness of life drift over me, like the spiced breezes of the tropical islands. I loved every moment of it.

After a couple of weeks on the beach, I flew to Los Angeles for the bar mitzvah of one of my Uncle Dave's kids. And on the way, my comfortable isolation from the war in Vietnam was pierced. A disruptive airline strike grounded me in Atlanta, which was one of the embarkation points for soldiers on their way to the war. I had never been much interested in soldiering, but I confess to a pang when I saw these kids, who looked no older than I was, on their way to war. They stood there helplessly in brand-new khakis, lugging their brand-new duffle bags, their faces untouched and defenceless. After that I became not only more conscious of the war but also of the difference that the pure chance of being born in one country rather than in another can make to your life.

Forty hours later, exhausted, I arrived in the L.A. of the Beach Boys, Malibu surf, and California girls. Every time I see the opening sequence of *The Graduate* with Dustin Hoffman riding the moving sidewalk of LAX and I hear "The Sounds of Silence," I feel a wave of nostalgia about my own anonymous and unheralded arrival.

*And no, I had no premonition of what L.A. would come to mean to me, no inkling that I would become something of a presence in this city, at least for a while, no suspicion at all that my life was to be bound up in any way with the weasels of Tinseltown and the mean and ugly world of Hollywood moviemaking.*

I came home to one of the most important jobs of my life: a carny barker at the Canadian National Exhibition (CNE). I'm not joking. Through that experience I learned more about the world and the people in it and myself. I got the job from my mother's cousin, Raymond Kives, who, along with his cousin Philip, owned K-Tel International, a Winnipeg-based industry that sold the world such gadgets as the Hair Magician, the Miracle Brush, and the Vegematic. Raymond and Philip would often visit us in Toronto. I was fascinated by Philip. He was my dad's age. He, too, had been "born in a haystack" and had had little formal education and less finesse. But he could sell anything. He was the P. T. Barnum of TV advertising. It was Philip who devised those insufferable ads that made K-Tel a household world.

Each year K-Tel pushed its products at the CNE, and I asked Raymond if I could run one of the tacky booths he kept at the fair (despite the fact that he didn't need them any more, for by then he was a wealthy man running a very large company). To me, you must understand, the CNE was glamorous, it had the whiff of show business. Megaphone in one hand, IBM card-sorter behind me, I ran K-Tel's handwriting-analysis operation. I'd bark into the megaphone, "Walk up, walk up! Learn about yourself! Are you truly a romantic? Are you destined for greatness?" Okay, so I knew I wasn't talking to PhDs. The crowds that flocked to my booth were blue-collar workers in jeans, their kids carrying dolls and stuffed toys and sucking candy apples. They paid a dollar and put their signature on a piece of paper, and then I'd take a stack of cards and run them through the IBM card-sorter, cry "Aha!" and pull out this bullshit analysis of the applicant's characteristics.

I could've pulled out any one of five cards – it didn't matter a damn. I was amazed at how credulous people were, how accepting of the most obvious con. I could hardly believe I was generating thousands of dollars a day, with virtually no overhead except the cost of renting the space.

The biggest lesson I learned was how to work a crowd. Barking got their attention, but the key to getting their cash, I discovered, was the manipulation of the line-up. I never ran the machine until I had a substantial line-up, and once it began to dwindle, I went back to barking and built it up again before starting the machine. Line-ups create more line-ups. Don't ask me why, but people get excited about other people standing in line. It works for more sophisticated audiences, too. I filed this piece of information away, and during those years when I was building my theatre circuit, I would instruct my managers in the early weeks of a tumultuous hit to line up people so they were visible to potential customers and passers-by. They in turn would be attracted to the line-up because it was a line-up. That's why I never moved crowds into the theatre lobby during the first weeks of a film's release. I wanted them outside, where they would attract attention. A line-up is always the best movie ad.

I learned so much about the psychology of people by doing that job. I also discovered that I loved being a salesman. Selling gave me the chance to be around people in an unselfconscious way. For the next couple of summers, I had a ball as a salesman for Town Shoes. I was a terrific salesman. I could have been the Prince of Shoes. See, I was just a kid. But I loved women, and I had good taste for a kid. I would lead them to a decision, turn them away from shoes they wanted that would make them look terrible. I would tell them, "No, you'll look lousy in those. Try these, this is what will work for you."

Oh yes, I learned how to deal with women through putting shoes on their feet. I've had to rely on my own taste, my own judgement, all through my career. Town Shoes helped me see how good I was at it. In one way, I was an arrogant little snot. On the other hand, I saw that they responded to it. They were so weary of having wishy-washy men serving them, men who never offered an opinion. So when a man, even a very young man, spoke with authority, saying, "You look good in that sling-back . . . that purse with that shoe is fabulous," they appreciated it, the thought that someone of the opposite sex was noticing them so closely, paying so much attention to them, judging them. It was a game. It was fun, it was sexy, it was instructive.

K-Tel and Town Shoes. A terrific education.

*I felt I was overflowing with life. My head was filled with the music of the times; I was the Graduate; I was filled with a sense of destiny, of possibility, of purpose.*

Remember, I was born, in the sense of being born into a consciousness of my own future purpose, with the wonderful music of the sixties filling the air. It affected me dramatically. I remember so clearly the first time I was exposed to the music of the Beatles. At the time I had never heard of the Beatles. I was clearly behind the rest of my generation in my musical tastes. One day I was coming back from a United Synagogue youth convention in the mountains of Ste-Agathe, Quebec, a cold winter weekend, but a wonderful, wonderful weekend for me, one of those rare, golden, escapist moments. All weekend I had been exposed to illuminating discourse and provoking thought, with the commentaries of intellectuals much older than I. On the train on our way back, about half past four on Sunday afternoon, everybody seemed to be really excited.

Someone said, "In just three hours I'm going to watch Ed Sullivan."

And I said, "Well, what the hell's going to be on Ed Sullivan?"

"The Beatles!"

"Who," I asked, "are the Beatles?" I felt like a complete fool. But that night I tuned in to Ed Sullivan and became as captivated as anybody.

*Of course, I didn't know at the time that I was witnessing the beginning of a musical revolution, the kind of revolution we'll never see again in our lifetimes. I did know that I was behind in my knowledge, that I didn't have all the inside information on what was going on, that I wasn't as hip as I wanted to be, but I also knew that the music appealed to an emotional part of my life that wasn't being expressed in any other way, that it filled me up in a way nothing else could.*

So many people were affected so profoundly by that music! Even now when I talk to my contemporaries, we remember the music with wonder and regret that nothing like it is being written any more. Of course, it came out of the deep social/political revolution taking place in the world at that time; the music reflected that revolution and helped foster it. Even today, when you put on a recording of Bob Dylan singing "Like a Rolling Stone," for example, and hear his poetry, or "Blowin' in the Wind," the lyrics seeming to penetrate to the heart of our existence. There was an emotional richness to our lives then that seems entirely lacking now. Contemporary music – music composed by the next wave of bands and songwriters – seems empty, devoid of meaning or any passion except anger and nihilism.

The life we led! When I was sixteen, my friends had their little cars, Peugeots and Volkswagens and Buick Wildcats, and we'd cruise Yorkville on warm summer nights and watch the people go by. We'd sit in the car and breathe in the fumes and watch the excitement of a neighbourhood coming to life. One day we finally parked the car and slipped into the folk music of Toronto, so similar to much that was happening in the Village in New York. We'd sit downstairs in smoke-filled nightclubs like the Riverboat and listen to Gordon Lightfoot or Sonny Terry and Brownie McGee, and Phil Ochs and Ian and Sylvia, Malka and Joso and Dylan and Simon and Garfunkel. We'd sip espresso and drag on cigarettes, watching the lights focus on the performers with a couple of hundred people around them, and the colours, the pinks and blues, would filter through the smoke. I knew that I was living in a special time, experiencing something quite remarkable.

*Almost thirty years later I presented Artie Garfunkel on one of my stages. It keeps happening – the people who affected me most in music have come back to touch me again. I've had the pleasure of presenting them: Art Garfunkel and Harry Belafonte, Burt Bacharach and Dionne Warwick, Barry Manilow and Nancy Wilson, so many others, even my first love, Shirley MacLaine. When I was up for a Grammy for the cast recording of* Kiss of the Spider Woman, *I was competing against the same people I had been in so much awe of earlier, people who had produced albums for the Beatles and who were now part of my working world.*

I still have an intimate knowledge and command of the music of the period, of the decade from 1958 to 1967. Play me the first four bars of any song and I can generally tell you who the singer is and what the song is, and with some thought I can even give you the lyrics. It's because it left such an indelible print on me. I don't think there's anything that makes me feel better than listening to the music of that era.

When I go to New York these days – and I'm there at least a day every week – I walk into my hotel room and turn on 101.1 FM, the CBS old-rock station, the best music station in America, bar none, for that music. And at once I'm reminded why I loved it so, the rich legacy of the lyrics and the haunting simplicity of the guitar, maybe a harmonica, perhaps even a drum somewhere in there, but it relied on emotion, not gimmick or technological stridency. The lyrics were not intricate at all, or complicated, but they spoke of love and relationships in the most beautiful way. They spoke to the young. They spoke to honesty and authenticity of feeling and. . . . After that, the world changed, for all time I think, and we blasted into the hard-drug era of the seventies, from which we have yet to emerge.

I miss it so much. I have never stopped missing it. It was innocent in a profound way. But it touched a nerve in our culture.

It wasn't just folk or rock. I loved all kinds of music. I'd visit Marshall Devor's house, and he'd be playing the music of Johnny Mathis, and I found it thrilling. I got equally stirred listening to the music of the jazz vocal group the HiLos or the Broadway shows *Gypsy* and *South Pacific*. At the same time, Marshall's older brother, David, was a fan of the music of Charles Aznavour, and I fell in love with that, too. I was only a teenager, and no one else in my age group knew who Charles Aznavour was. I went from there to Yves Montand and the other French *chanteurs*, Jacques Brel and Gilbert Bécaud, and so I continued my exploration of the world of music. I could never do homework without the radio in my room blaring or the record player on. I had to have Sinatra playing in the background or I couldn't study history. Streisand did the same thing for me. I can even remember putting on the 101 Strings playing the music of the movies from *Exodus* or *Lawrence of Arabia*. I had an incredible thirst for music.

Alas, I was never a performer. I studied guitar for a year and a half. Tried to perform, but couldn't. But I used to sing along with great zeal. I still do. When I feel good, I'll sing away. I may sing off pitch, but I still love singing.

Obviously that's one of the reasons I've been so passionate about musical theatre and why it's made the impact on me that it has. The emotional comfort of music is one of the staples of my life.

Once a week, I'd go down to Paradise Pizzeria at Avenue Road and Eglinton Avenue and have a pizza with double cheese, anchovies, and pepperoni and a Brio. From there I'd go down to Yorkville and have an espresso and listen to folk music, and I would say to myself, "What more can life be? It can't get any better than this!"

I had a handful of great friends in that period. It hurts me now to think that they were there and then they drifted away. One of them was Billy Novak, who became Lee Iacocca's biographer. He was a great guitarist and played with Sharon Salsberg, niece of J. B. Salsberg, the old labour communist. Sharon later married Herschel Ezrin, a key strategist in the Ontario government of David Peterson's Liberals.

After graduating brilliantly here, Marshall Devor went to Princeton and then to MIT, where he graduated in physiological psychology. He's now a professor at the University of Jerusalem and lectures and does research all over the world on the subject of pain. Marshall and I were very close. He used to go to the best summer camps because his father could afford their substantial fees. At one of them he learned about photography. On Saturday afternoons he and I would sit in his darkroom and process, develop, and print, and I would learn from him.

Across the street from me on Briar Hill was David Wolinsky. David's father, Leonard, had started a big hardware company, Acklands. David eventually founded Concert Productions International (CPI) with Michael Cohl and Bill Ballard. David's father, who had a lot of money, left his mother early on. His mother, Sylvia, was a sabra from Israel; she looked a bit like Lotte Lenya from the second James Bond movie, *From Russia with Love* – slightly sinister, as if the stiletto was about to come out of the shoe. But she was a great lady, so real, so honest, so full of life. David had his father's supercharged Buick Wildcat. He was into the playboy lifestyle, loved to have the best in button-down shirts and was probably the only guy who could tell you what GTO meant (Gran Turismo Omologata). The day I got my temporary driver's licence, David let me drive the Wildcat. We went to Niagara Falls, New York, to Peewee's Pizzeria, and I returned at midnight exhilarated – I had driven two hundred miles before I had passed my driver's test. My mother was ready to destroy me.

My close friends were quirky, I think now. They weren't into drugs or anything of that nature. They rejected all that. But they were intellectuals, sophisticated, quite unconventional, and they all ended up doing interesting things.

Still, as I said, they were all a little older than me. Most of them went away to college and some never came back.

Then it was time for me to go to college. I already knew I wanted to go into business – but what business? And how was I to get there? I enrolled in commerce and finance, a four-year honours-degree program at the University of Toronto, and dithered about whether or not I should aim at law school. More and more, I began to let go a little. It was the relatively unstructured environment that unnerved me, I think. I spent my time in the refectory at University College, smoking, drinking endless cups of coffee, and studying women. Or sitting on the grass in the quadrangle among the gracious architecture of the university, outside Hart House (where, again coming full circle, years later I would hold final auditions for *The Phantom of the Opera*). Or dreaming of an E-type Jaguar, an elegant two-seater to die for, and, after seeing *Goldfinger*, an Aston Martin DB5, like the one driven by Sean Connery. I couldn't have enough cigarettes and coffee. I became a bridge junkie. This wasn't the Garth Drabinsky of a year before – ambitious and motivated to succeed, student leader, speechmaker, producer of a successful musical.

For a while all I could think about was what fun I was going to have on my winter vacation.

David Cooper was a tall, good-looking friend of mine who knew something I didn't yet know – how to savour life to its fullest. He had the perfect car: a new blue Camaro Supersport that we were going to drive 3,200 miles to Acapulco over the Christmas vacation. The plan was to take Route 66 through the U.S. heartland, turn south at Laredo, Texas, south into Mexico, and on to the Pacific.

"You're out of your mind!" my mother said. Then she astonished me by adding, "I don't care what it costs. You're flying."

But I was adamant. I wouldn't have it. "No, no. I want to drive Route 66!" I wanted adventure; I was determined to see the guts of America. My parents reluctantly okayed the trip, and David and I drove off from Toronto in a sleet storm, the radio going all the time. The music this time was all Motown: Smokey Robinson and Diana Ross. We had dinner one night at the St. Louis Playboy Club, entirely unaware of how unsophisticated it was. The next night we were in Dallas, driving down past the Texas Schoolbook Depository and the infamous Grassy Knoll, the scene of Kennedy's assassination. Then Monterey, where we ate at the only Jewish deli in town. Then, on the fourth day, surviving the hairpin bends in the mountains after Mexico City, we reached Acapulco.

This was adventure! I was determined to make the most of it. I was tanned and feeling great. I went scuba diving for the first time, and we dove to the wreck of an Argentine ship sunk during the Second World War. Parasailing was the craze that winter, and without thinking twice, I strapped on the harness and zoomed over the Pacific.

We were feeling so good that neither of us paid attention to the fact that the special car insurance required for driving in Mexico was limited to twenty-one days. On Day 17, we arrived in Mexico City. It was me, who after all was the son of a very cautious father, who said casually some time during the twenty-first day, "Shouldn't we extend the insurance by at least a day?" But Dave didn't think it was worth it. By that evening we would be in Laredo, Texas, and out of the country.

I was driving as we left Mexico City. We were about seventy miles out of town, near Querétaro, when it began to rain and the roads became slick and greasy. It was a typical Mexican highway, with cows crowding along either side of the road and traffic meandering aim-lessly. About a mile ahead, a bus stopped and a crowd descended, fill-ing the highway. I applied the brakes. Nothing! My God! I saw the crowd of people and cows and just one car ahead of me. "Oh God," I thought, "if I don't veer, I'm going to kill twenty people at one shot." My only hope was to angle the car and veer away from the people. Which is what I did. Except that I miscalculated – I went over the side of the road, down a deep ditch, and wrecked the car. Fortunately, I only had a tooth knocked loose. Dave suffered bruised ribs.

In short order the cops arrived and promptly threw us in jail. There was no option left – I had to call my dad. This, as you can imagine, was not something I looked forward to. I hated asking him for money; I knew what it would do to him. And he lived up to all my expectations. But in the end, reluctantly, he asked, "How much do you need?"

My voice must have quavered as I said, "I need $6,000 wired to me, otherwise they're not going to let me out of Mexico."

It was a humiliating end. The totalled Camaro was hoisted on top of a trailer truck, and we were driven to the border. Then, tail between my legs, I flew home. My mother didn't have to say anything. I was the smart guy, and I suffered for it.

This was a major turning point in my young life. It was bad enough going into debt. Much worse was that I owed my father.

I vowed it wouldn't happen again. It became the motivation that pushed me to accomplish something, anything, and to acquire assets – fast.

# CHAPTER

## Beginnings

*She was wearing a yellow dress and yellow vinyl boots when I saw her. Her hair was dark and her expressive face was alive with intelligence and humour; she was laughing with a group of friends. She was utterly beautiful.*

When was this, exactly? I don't remember the date, but it was not long before my first college year ended. I was hanging out in the refectory when I saw her at the next table.

I went over and, in what I hoped was my best casual man-of-the-world manner, asked, "Where did you buy your boots? I bet they come from Town Shoes and that you're a seven-and-a-half."

*So suave! What a pathetic line! She, clearly, was not a bit impressed and brushed me off. I didn't care. Nothing could divert me now.*

The next time that I saw her in the cafeteria, Varsity Radio was playing "Les Comédiennes" by Charles Aznavour. Already I knew a great deal about her. I knew her name was Pearl Kaplan. I knew she was in honours French. I tipped my chair back, once again man-of-the-world style, and leaned over to ask her, "Do you know who's singing?" She shook her head. "How can you be majoring in French," I cried, "and not know the voice of Charles Aznavour?"

So all right, I lacked a little tact, didn't have much finesse, came on too strong. But I made up for it in enthusiasm. I wouldn't give up. I found out her home number and asked her out. She refused. I said, "What have you got to lose? An evening at the most." No dice. Then, a few weeks later, I went to see *Jacques Brel Is Alive and Well and Living in Paris* at the Bayview Playhouse and there was Pearl with her friend Valerie Weisman. My date that evening was a fabulously attractive second-year U. of T. Swedish blonde, and we had seats right up front, but I spent the intermission with my head turned to the back of the house, looking at Pearl. Of course, I persisted, and she finally agreed to go out with me.

Later she told me many of her friends thought I was ballsy. I think she was intrigued by my energy, my all-embracing pursuit of her; I was obsessed and it showed. How many young women attract that kind of attention? I was a romantic young man who would have done anything for her, who wanted to surround her, captivate her, possess her. She felt a little bewildered, a little intimidated, but considerably fascinated. And we did develop an intellectual bond, a connection.

*We walked down the street together. She was lithe, a young woman alive in her body, aware of her power; I limped beside her. What was going through her head? Was she . . . embarrassed? Did she think of the skiing we couldn't do together, the tennis we couldn't play? Did she think of the other men she was dating? Or did she think only of the conversations we were having? I don't know. I didn't care. I took joy in her presence and a fierce pride at having her with me.*

In the meantime I met her parents, Rachel and Harry Kaplan. They thought I was entirely wrong for their daughter; they were even more taken aback than she at my single-minded devotion. Her father thought I was a man of overly grand ideas who would one day end up cashing UI cheques. Yet to me, her parents were never less than warm and supportive. They were extraordinary people, European Jews who had fought in the Russian resistance during the Second World War. Harry had seen most of his family shot before his eyes. On their way to Kirkland Lake, Ontario, they had stopped off in Munich, where Pearl was born. Harry owned a fruit store in Toronto's Kensington Market, slogging it out from four o'clock in the morning to midnight, six days a week, for his first seventeen years in Canada. By sheer hard work, he'd made a very good living.

To them, they had this miracle daughter – like her sister Marilyn, a young woman of infinite promise. Why throw it all away on me?

But I never doubted myself. Not for a moment.

It was through Pearl that I met Marc Michaan, Valerie Weisman's fiancé. Marc was an Orthodox Jew whose family came from Iran, now living in New York, who had been captivated by the motion-picture industry. He wanted to make a movie from (future) Nobel Peace Prize winner Elie Wiesel's hundred-page story, *Night*. (In another example of life coming full circle, Wiesel years later gave the inaugural Drabinsky B'nai B'rith lecture in Washington, D.C.) I, too, had been enthralled by this gripping account of Wiesel's escape with his father from a Nazi concentration camp; to a Jew, the subject was inherently fascinating. Besides, nobody was then making movies about the Holocaust: it was all too close. But I was hot for the idea. I knew it could be a significant statement, a wonderful, powerful tale, a great story. Many years later, in 1993, Steven Spielberg proved I was right, proved there could be an audience for an emotionally wrench-ing story about the Holocaust, when he made the magnificent *Schindler's List*.

Marc said the movie would cost about $750,000. "And guess who's interested in directing it? Orson Welles!"

"You've got to be kidding!" I cried, as awestruck as only a young man can be. Welles, the maker of *Citizen Kane*, was a Hollywood giant. I was flushed with a sense of possibility. I was going to become a major-league player in the film business, I was going to finance the making of an Orson Welles movie – while I was still at college!

Financing was going to be easy, or so I figured. All I had to do was approach every prominent Zionist Jew in Toronto, all the big givers to the United Jewish Appeal, such as Murray Koffler, Leon Weinstein.... I had a long list. I couldn't miss.

Again, poor old Harry Kaplan. He thought I was a nut case. He kept saying to Pearl, "Don't even consider Garth. He's living in another world. He doesn't have his feet on the ground. He keeps thinking he can make movies or he's going to be in the entertainment business. He's got these delusions of grandeur. You don't need this. Marry someone who'll give you a respectable living, so you'll never have to worry."

For my part, I had learned two things about myself: I was receptive to any idea that was entrepreneurial in essence – that is, that would allow me to create something – and my interest was always piqued by anything connected to show business. Those two things were the sparks. Ignition was provided by the push inside me to *get things done.*

I hadn't fully understood it in high school, but showbiz had its hooks into me.

*Did this push derive from my childhood? Did it come from the fact that my childhood had been stolen from me? I don't know. Perhaps. I think it came from a deep need to escape and from the wellspring of romanticism that my need had created in my mind.*

In any case, I confidently set off to raise the money to allow Orson Welles to make our wonderful movie. And I was turned down forty-eight times. I was so naïve! I couldn't believe I could fail to sell an idea that had so much appeal for Jews.

The project fizzled. Welles cancelled the previously arranged meeting, and the film never got off the ground. I had wasted nine weeks of my summer vacation.

Somewhat disillusioned after this fiasco, I spent the rest of the summer doing menial work in a small downtown law office where my friend Fred Fruitman's father was a partner. One of the other partners was an eccentric by the name of Joel Sheldon Wagman. There was a character! Fast-moving, skating on the edge. I don't know if he's still a member of the bar. He used to walk into the office dressed to the nines, with immaculate French cuffs, groomed to the hilt, smoking a cigarette in an affected way, the whole shtick. But he was a guy who liked to make deals happen, and that's how I came to meet Malcolm Bennett, a breezy, smooth-talking Englishman who thought up deals in his sleep. One day when I was in the office, Bennett came in to see

Wagman. Bennett was an inventor of sorts, or represented inventors –
I was never quite sure which – and I became excited about what he
and Wagman were up to. "I'd like to help you find money for these
inventors," I told Wagman. I was nineteen years old, I didn't know
much, but many of my friends' parents were wealthy and my father
had some connections through business. How difficult could it be to
raise $10,000, $20,000? In spite of my disappointment, I wasn't dis-
couraged by my failure to raise the money for *Night*.

Soon after, Bennett brought in two brothers who had developed a
new type of door latch. Well, you ask, how can you get excited about a
door latch? But I did my research on door latches and found that most
people have no idea how they work. They're always pushing or pul-
ling or turning them the wrong way. Our inventors had come up with
a new mechanism that you couldn't screw up, no matter what you
did, and the whole thing was made of plastic. Money danced through
my head. You could mould the plastic into any shape the architects or
designers wanted, give it any colour you wanted – the world con-
sumes how many millions of door latches each year? The market was
gigantic. You had to be able to make a lot of money.

Pearl thought it was ludicrous to be spending part of a summer on
door latches. Her father's worst fears were being realized. And in a
way she was right: we never did get the money together and the latch
men went away. But Bennett and I continued our collaboration, without Wagman, and started talking about publishing ventures.

The first one he mentioned was *Employers' Digest*, which was to be
a biweekly tabloid listing job opportunities. Uhuh. I saw possibilities.
It was not the sexiest enterprise in the world, but it could make
money. Then he mentioned his idea for a film magazine, to be given
out free at motion-picture theatres, and . . . the spark hit the ignition.
I loved that idea.

But I had to store it in my memory bank for the moment. Pearl
was still my priority. The more I saw her, the more I had to be with
her. The idea of her consumed me. I simply couldn't stay away. I
told her I needed her. I told her I had to have her. She knew I meant
it. She still went out with other people, but I think she sensed the

inevitability of it. I was like an earthquake, an avalanche, nothing would get in my way. She was amused, irritated, awed, and finally overwhelmed by it all.

When I got back to University College, the adrenaline flowed. The bridge-playing wastrel was gone, history. I focused entirely on economics courses for my second year and shifted all my energy into studying. I got straight As. I had a few really impressive professors, men like Ed Neufeld, who went on to be deputy minister of finance and then chief economist of the Royal Bank. He taught me macro-economics. Mel Watkins, the economic nationalist, was there, and so were labour theoretician John Crispo, economic historian J. H. Munroe, and the great political scientist, Paul Fox. I loved all those guys.

Then Pearl asked me a pointed question.

"Where are you going with an honours degree in economics?" she asked, and I had to admit I hadn't worked it out, I had no idea. I had flirted briefly with the notion of doing postgraduate work at the London School of Economics, but had abandoned the idea. At Pearl's suggestion I decided to transfer to law school at the end of my second year. I wanted action. I wanted substance. I wanted to leave my house. I was contemplating marriage. I wanted money, a chance to make my dreams work. I was *ready*.

I was accepted by the law faculty at the University of Western Ontario in London, Ontario. But I would be in London, Pearl in Toronto. Intolerable! And I didn't have a car. Nor did I have money – I was still in debt to my father. I had heard from a friend about a resourceful banker at the Bank of Montreal branch at Spadina and Adelaide, and I went down to see him. His name was Wayne Squibb.

I asked for a car loan, and he wondered pointedly about security.

"I'm it," I said. "I'll give you my word and my signature. I'm going to pay the money back, and I will. I'm going to practise law."

So he gave me a character loan for my first car, a Mercury Cougar. Wayne subsequently became a good friend and a co-venturer in some business deals. He would go on to own a part of the Delta hotel chain.

At Western I lived with two guys in a small apartment, people I had known at school. They weren't as academically proficient as I was, so I struck a deal: I would tutor them if they cleaned the apartment. It was great. I would cook and they would clean the dishes. Perfect. I was a better cook than they were, anyway.

During the first half of the year, I worked so hard that I ended up with mononucleosis, such a bad bout that I contracted pleurisy as well. However, I was out of bed after six days and back into my life. It was typical of my body's ability to renew and refresh itself, *the triumph of metabolism!* This ability to recover rapidly from exhaustion has stood me in good stead many times in my life, especially later during my Cineplex Odeon days, when I set an insane travel and work schedule for myself.

After that first year, I made the Dean's List and transferred back to the faculty of law, University of Toronto. The U. of T. was a pretty good place to be in those days. But at the end of the day, there was something missing. And that was a sense of the institution as something to love and cherish, with a philosophy worth taking to heart. I was reminded of this again when I was analysing private institutions with my daughter, Alicia. Brown, Northwestern, Duke – they have a deep sense of camaraderie, a strong desire to perpetuate their institutional culture. In the screening process, they make it clear what they can do for a student, but in addition they always ask, "What are you going to do for us? What are you going to give us back, now and in the future? How are you going to make a difference?"

At the University of Toronto, now or in the future, a student is just a number. You get in on academic merit, you finish your four years, you move on, and, for the most part, you don't really care. It has no persona.

*In retrospect, I can see I rushed myself, I gave up a part of my life as a result of my insistence on doing things right away, at once. I deeply regret it now. I regret that I was never part of the intellectual and emotional community that a true campus life provides. Occasionally I would visit my friends at* MIT *or Harvard, and God, I was envious. Autumn in New*

*England. We would walk around Harvard Yard and down the Charles River to watch the oarsmen. The whole environment was so invigorating. Weekends there were special. Not just the parties between the men's and women's campuses, but the whole experience, the fraternities and sororities, the rich traditions, the wealth of memories, the gracious architecture. I visited Marshall at Princeton; he was now a part of an institution that was embedded in the literature and the history of our culture. I felt I had missed something significant.*

This is why I want my kids to go to school in the United States. I want them to get out, I want them to meet a whole different cross-section of society. I want them to be exposed to the optimism of America. I don't want them to be sucked down into the vortex of pessimism that permeates so many segments of Canada.

I've noticed American kids look back on their university experience as the absolute be-all and end-all, the high point of their young lives, far more than high school. For me, it was the other way around. It shouldn't have been that way. University was one of the great crashes of my life.

Pearl still hadn't made up her mind about me. She was a young woman, confident in the way only beautiful young women can be confident, secure in the knowledge that many men were attracted to her.

I felt more vulnerable than I had ever been in my life. I was devastated when she dated others; once I just sat on her family's porch and waited until she got back from a date. I waited and waited. Midnight came and went, one o'clock. She was out dancing somewhere, having a good time, and I sat on her porch and stared into the night. The image of her filled my head, there was no room for anything else. Two o'clock, two fifteen . . . and there they were. And there I was, making small talk to an astonished Pearl and her irritated date at two fifteen in the morning. The date, who had flown up from Washington just to see Pearl, finally wandered off disconsolately – I wasn't going anywhere! – and we went inside, arguing.

*"What are you doing?" she asked, furiously.*

"*I need you,*" I replied. "*I'm right for you. You know I am. We must get married. We must.*"

I couldn't lose her, I just couldn't. Everyone, she told me after-wards, was against the match. "He's different," her mother warned Pearl. "A man with an impediment like that is a man who has a lot to work out. It won't be easy." Her father was against it. "The boy's a dreamer, will never accomplish anything." Her friends were against it. "Who is this Drabinsky? Why him? He's too young for you! Why not one of the others? There are so many to choose from!" Even my own parents were against it. "What will you live on? Where will you get the money? How will you support her?"

Still, just before Christmas 1970, Pearl accepted my proposal.

Why did she do it? Now she says it was the connection we had somehow made, the bond that had grown up between us. After a while she found that, despite her reservations and the warnings she was getting, she was hooked, too. We could always talk about any-thing; she says she found me funny and smart. She was overwhelmed by my tidal wave of love and devotion; ultimately, she just couldn't ignore it. None of her other suitors had that. It was an emotion out of a great romance, not out of mundane life. How could she resist?

Awkwardly, I had to borrow half of the five hundred dollars I needed for an engagement ring from my future father-in-law. My own family were still against the whole thing. Nevertheless, we got married on June 22, 1971, at Beth Sholom Synagogue.

There was neither time nor money for a honeymoon, only time to settle into our new apartment in Don Mills on the outskirts of Toronto. Don Mills! Neither of us thought of ourselves as suburban-ites, but it was a compromise. Pearl was teaching French at Agincourt Collegiate while she completed her MA in French linguistics and French theatre. I had the car so I could drive each day to school. Pearl earned the money to keep us going for a while. But she admits she never needed to do that for very long. I was a young man in a very great hurry.

Before transferring to U. of T. law school, I wanted to work in still another lawyer's office in the summer, and I solicited my uncle's help.

Uncle Irv, who was married to my mother's eldest sister, Ann, put the squeeze on Willard "Bud" Estey, who later became a justice of the Supreme Court of Canada. A little nepotism goes a long way. Both men grew up in Saskatoon. I can imagine the conversation. "Bud," said Uncle Irv, "I've got this nephew doing great in law. We Westerners have got to stick together." Bud invited me to work in his office for the summer, writing speeches and doing research.

Bud Estey was a ball of fire, a salty, down-to-earth lawyer who worked at a staggering pace. Ironically, in light of later events, Bud was involved with Albert Gnat, one of his partners, in restructuring Canada's leading exhibition chain, Famous Players. His office had a lot of showbiz clients, including CBS, Warner Brothers, Twentieth Century-Fox, and Gulf + Western, which was then taking over Paramount Pictures, which in turn owned Famous Players. As for Al Gnat, later a senior partner at the law firm Laing Michener, he and I crossed paths a few times over the years. He was involved when Cineplex bought Odeon, and even before that, he acted for a number of Cineplex shareholders when they sold their shares to my partner, Myron Gottlieb, and me in the dark days of 1982.

During my last two years of law school, I wasn't really focused. By that time I really didn't care about my academic studies as much as I did about setting myself up in business. I couldn't wait to get out and exercise my entrepreneurial muscle. I graduated all right, and was later called to the bar with honours, but my heart was in creating something.

Just before I went to work for Estey for the summer, Bennett called me again.

"Garth, remember me? Malcolm Bennett?"

Of course I did.

*Employers' Digest* had gone belly-up, Malcolm said, but he felt the time was right for *Impact*, his idea for a movie magazine. After all, Toronto's first controlled-circulation magazine, *Toronto Calendar*, had just started and was doing well. Advertisers were flocking to it. If we could get *Impact* distributed monthly in every motion-picture theatre in Canada's primary markets, given free to a national audience of, say, three quarters of a million people, the magazine should have no trouble attracting advertisers and making money. The bulk of moviegoers were between eighteen and forty, perfect demographics for cigarette and beer companies.

Neither of us, of course, had the capital to launch such a magazine. Conservatively speaking, something in the order of $350,000 would be required to cover start-up costs and the deficit for a year. Malcolm was a typical ideas guy; he couldn't finance his way out of a suitcase. But could I? I had failed with the Wiesel project and with my door latches. Now, I assured myself, I was a lot wiser. I had two more years of law school. I was also married, with new responsibilities.

So I said, "Okay, Malcolm, I'm in. Leave it to me. I'll raise the money."

This, I promised myself and assured Pearl, was my passport to the life that had been gestating inside me for so many years and that I now unequivocally knew I wanted: a career in show business.

And of course, it was. If only indirectly.

Toronto, which was our prime market, had always drawn the country's largest film audiences. The city was becoming more eclectic and sophisticated at that time. The old puritanical town I had grown up in was becoming noticeably looser and more multicultural. Of course, it wasn't exactly Sodom and Gomorrah yet. You could still be arrested for drinking alcohol out of doors, the good restaurants still closed by 10 P.M., and it was so desolate on Sundays that visitors thought an air-raid warning had gone off. But there were signs everywhere that change was coming, and one of these was the growing audience for foreign and offbeat movies. Surely, I thought, the time was ripe for a movie magazine with integrity.

*Impact* was not going to be a fan magazine. I wanted it to promote movies through intelligent and entertaining articles free of any studio interference. The writers were to be freelancers. Stephen Chesley, a film fanatic, was to be editor. Gerald Pratley, who later became the director of the Ontario Film Institute, was to explore the whole world of film. Earl Pomerantz, who would go on to writing sitcoms in

Hollywood, would supply a comic turn on motion pictures each month, while George Anthony, shortly to be the movie critic for the *Toronto Sun*, would review books about the movie industry, movie stars, and the movies themselves.

First, of course, I had to get Famous Players and Canadian Odeon to agree to distribute the magazine in their theatres. A decade later those two companies would become my ruthless competitors and give me a lot of grief (though not as much as I would eventually give them!), but back then all I knew about them was that they formed the duopoly that dominated movie exhibition in Canada. That made my job simple. Apart from certain selected independent exhibitors, I had to get just two companies onside. So I went along first to see George Destounis, the president of Famous Players, at his Bloor Street office.

My first impression of Destounis was of a rotund, jovial guy, oozing sincerity and good intentions. He spoke with a quasi-Southern drawl. I knew that he had worked his way up from being an usher for United Theatres in Montreal to day-to-day control of Famous Players' operations in Canada. I was a bit surprised that, without strenuous negotiation, George gave me a warm endorsement. Yes, Famous Players would distribute *Impact* in their theatres. "Good luck, Garth," he said as he walked me to the door. Odeon, which was then owned by the British film company J. Arthur Rank, was equally agreeable.

I was suspicious. This was too easy.

Then I needed to raise the start-up money. The amount I came up with was on the high side because I wanted to print on quality stock, not on newsprint; I wanted it not only to read well but to look and feel good. I had settled on an initial print run of 500,000, and my estimate of the amount of money I needed was around $400,000 – a fair pile for a second-year law student, twenty-two years old, in 1971.

Bud Walters came along just as I needed my first angel in life. Bud, the owner of Toronto Lithographers, was a tough and feisty Italian I had met when I was researching printing costs. There was immediate chemistry between us. He was intrigued by the philosophy of the magazine, and eventually he agreed to help finance my little company by treating the value of the printing as part of his equity contribution.

I figured I could get the banks to give me a loan against projected advertising to cover general overhead, editorial, and circulation costs. To promote the magazine, I also produced my first motion picture, a momentous forty-five-second trailer designed by Ken Young of Design Workshop, to run in theatres everywhere.

*It was at this time that I paid my first visit to a major Hollywood studio. For an afternoon I wandered alone around the Warner Brothers back lot, between those memorable sound stages, the locus of so many stories, so much mythmaking, so much history, and I felt a kind of fierce determination well up in me, and I thought to myself, "Yes, this is it, I want to be here, this is a part of my life."*

Recently I got out the first issue of *Impact*, dated November 1971, and I was both surprised and pleased that it stood up so well after so long. Ken Young's design was lively and attractive. One of the articles was a psychedelic treatment of Frank Zappa. There was a story on the movie *Nicholas and Alexandra* and the Romanov massacre, printed throughout on full-bleed red pages, and Earl Pomerantz's column, "Looking at It from Where I'm Sitting," was deliberately printed upside down. I'm also proud of our February 1972 issue, which contained a strong feature on film censorship in Ontario and made an important statement in favour of freedom of expression. In those days, the province's censor board's ridiculous strictures made Ontarians look like hicks.

They were good magazines – but they lost money.

As my sales staff and I went across the country to pitch the ad agencies on the merits of what we were doing, we were given an enthusiastic reception. Account executives would say, "I'm definitely going to recommend this magazine. It's fabulous and innovative." Their dishonesty was complete. These "recommendations," if (a big if) they were ever made, led to nothing.

What I had to learn the hard way was that advertising agency executives are deeply conservative. No, it's more than that – they're sycophantic, without fibre, rigour, or balls. They seem incapable of taking risks or even of exercising their imaginations. They don't want to put their clients' dollars into anything unknown, however promising. Despite the success of *Toronto Calendar*, newsstand and subscription sales were (and are) considered a better indicator of a magazine's market penetration and reader acceptance than the controlled circulation that *Impact* offered. The ad people's argument was that though the magazine would be made available to a giant monthly audience in the movie-houses, there was no guarantee that anyone would actually take it home, read it, and pass it on.

Nevertheless, our first issue contained five pages of advertising. By the sixth issue, May 1972, I had managed to get *Impact* into theatres in every province, which meant that it was now reaching our monthly target: 750,000 copies in circulation. But advertising was growing only negligibly, and there was still no positive response from the kind of major advertisers that would break down the resistance of others.

Worse, I began to hear rumblings from Famous Players. I was told that while the brass loved the *idea* of the magazine, they were upset that the editorial content didn't directly support their films. What they wanted was more control. They complained, "You're using our customers, but you're not publicizing our movies." If Paramount had a big movie coming in, say, *The Godfather*, the studio wanted it on *Impact*'s cover.

In short, they wanted me to be a flack, a publicity organ for themselves – but that ran counter to the magazine's editorial mandate, not to mention its independence.

I was now strapped for cash. I had estimated that it would take two years to establish the magazine, but I was painfully aware that without meaningful advertising support I couldn't meet my initial projections and that I needed another $400,000 to bridge the cash drain. I asked George Destounis if Famous Players would pay me ten cents per patron for the magazine. Destounis hummed and hawed before he turned me down. I didn't know it then, but I had opened the industry's eyes to a valuable tool. Bob Yankovitch, who was then head of Paramount Canada's advertising and publicity, and Frank Mancuso, Paramount's general manager in Toronto (and eventual CEO of the parent company), had begun to talk about putting together an alternative magazine with the assistance of Famous Players. It would be only a few more weeks before I would have bled enough to be compelled to shut down *Impact*.

*How some people keep turning up, like bad pennies, like bad apples, fat and wheezing ghosts, lumbering onto the path of progress and blocking it! George Destounis is one of those people. He wouldn't help me then, and he would actively oppose me ten years later, in 1982, in my knockdown fight for a share of the Canadian movie business. The first time, he won. The second, he lost. I took pleasure in his loss. I have a long memory.*

*Impact*'s decline accelerated. Relations between Bud Walters and me became strained and, finally, he said he could no longer go on printing the magazine. I didn't blame him. I went to see Maclean Hunter about becoming a new partner. No deal.

Before I took the final step of settling with Bud and closing down the magazine, however, I plucked up all my remaining courage and called Nat Taylor.

# CHAPTER

## III

### THE NAT TAYLOR SEMINARS

*Impact* was in serious financial trouble. I had been to everyone I knew for money. I was facing my first corporate defeat – and the media was poised to cover my disaster. Nat Taylor was my last chance.

My knees were shaking when I went to see him. *Mister Taylor.* I was trying to save my business, and God himself was about to see me. *Is it any wonder that my goddamn knees were shaking?*

*Mister Taylor.* A man of wits, of quickness of mind and largeness of heart, of farsightedness and clarity of vision. He was big, the biggest, a legend in the movie business in Canada, the nearest thing Canada had to a Hollywood mogul. He had been an exhibitor, a distributor, a producer, and a TV-station shareholder. He was partners with Famous Players, the dominant exhibition chain in Canada. He owned the country's largest movie-production studio, Toronto International Studios, in Kleinburg, Ontario. He was the man who opened the first Canadian movie-house for foreign and art films. He was the guy who had come up with the idea of multiple theatres. He was a man of resource, talent, a man always ahead of the pack.

He later became a mentor, an almost-father, and a friend. But now I was a kid of twenty-two, still wet behind the ears, not yet through law school, asking for help from the great Nat Taylor. It was as presumptuous, I think, as it would have been for an American kid to expect Lew Wasserman – the chairman of MCA, the multibillion-dollar entertainment conglomerate – to bail him out.

I had no option. I was clinging by my fingertips to the edge of a financial precipice – a place I was to revisit more than once. I needed him, so I got on the phone.

"This is Garth Drabinsky. I have to see you, Mr. Taylor."

"What about?" He sounded something like George Burns. I tried not to feel intimidated.

"I want to talk to you about my magazine, *Impact*."

"Oh." Silence. "All right. Come on over."

So I went to see him.

I didn't know it then, but he would see anyone. It was his policy, but also basic to his philosophy of life. He was curious, interested, always talent-spotting. It was part of his genius.

I walked into his office on Bloor Street. It resembled a bit of California *circa* 1940, bright and airy, with a great semicircular desk made of lightly stained maple, an artefact that dominated the room. Right away, I wanted a desk like that. Memorabilia were displayed around the office: trophies, prizes, pictures of Nat with his Canadian partners Harry Mandell, Myer Axler, Raoul Auerbach, David Griesdorf, and with some of the great names of motion-picture exhibition, like Barney Balaban of Paramount.

Nat Taylor was a young and vibrant sixty-six in 1972. He was about five foot eight, smoked suffocating cigars, and had the close-cropped head of a Roman emperor. I could imagine him going to the barber and saying, "Give me a Caesar!" He exuded confidence. Although he was not unfriendly, he was not smiling.

"I've watched you," he said.

"Yes?" I just waited.

"You're a young man with a lot of guts," he went on. "In the case of this magazine, you did something I always wanted to do but never did." He paused. "You know why I never did it?"

"No, sir."

"Because nobody's going to advertise in something you give away. Nobody values anything free. So you failed. I always wanted to do it, but I always knew it would turn out to be a failure. Now, what do you want me to do?"

I was momentarily stunned. That was going straight to the heart of the matter. What did he expect? "Well, I need some money," I said, somewhat feebly. Why should he care? "I've got to keep this thing going. It's important to the industry . . ." My voice trailed away.

"I'm not going to finance *Impact*," he said firmly, closing the matter off. "I'm not going to put money into this magazine because it's never going to work."

I felt smaller and smaller.

Then he added, "Close down the magazine."

*So there it was. I had never met the man in my life, but he had brought me there to scold me, to chastise me for having the nerve to suggest I would be successful, almost because I never consulted him first. Or so I thought. But Nat was a greater man than that.*

*It turned out to be one of the seminal meetings of my life. I left with an opportunity to change my life, courtesy of Nat Taylor.*

I thought, "Oh God, defeat!" My last chance was rejecting me. Or was he?

I burst out, "You didn't bring me up here just to lecture me – just to ridicule me. There must have been some other reason why you agreed to this meeting."

Nat put down his cigar. "That's true," he said. "I've got a trade journal called the *Canadian Film Digest* that has been part of my life for the last thirty-five years. But I haven't had a proper editor since Hy Bossin died."

I saw a glimmer of light. "What are you proposing?"

"Well, forget *Impact*, close down the office, move up here, publish my newspaper, and, as an incentive, I'll give you half the company."

I really had no choice. *Impact* was as good as dead. But I had put my foot in the door of the film industry and I wasn't going to let it shut. My few months with *Impact* had taught me how little I still knew. I had had one brush with Famous Players' brass, enough to make me aware that there were controlling forces in the industry that could thwart even the experienced. Most of all there was nobody who knew the Canadian movie business like Nat Taylor. He knew production, distribution, and, most of all, exhibition. He knew where to build a theatre, how to design it, how to run it, how to book it, how to assess a film's box-office potential. He could certainly teach me what I was desperate to learn – the inner workings of the motion-picture business. So I wasted no time in saying yes to Nat's offer.

*Why did he do it? Later he would only say, "Garth was a smart kid. I liked talking to him." Then, I didn't know why either. But I seized the opportunity.*

I brought Stephen Chesley over from *Impact* and hired Barry Silver, a friend from childhood days.

*Barry has been with me, in one capacity or another, ever since. I remember so clearly that the night before Barry's bar mitzvah, his father, who had worked for so many years in his own father-in-law's deli, died abruptly, his heart just giving out. I sat with Barry for days in the midst of his stricken and brokenhearted family.*

We redesigned the *Digest* to look like the tabloid *Daily Variety*. And we prospered: the paper was important to the Canadian industry because the U.S. trades, *Variety* and *The Hollywood Reporter*, treated the Canadian market as a satellite of the U.S. market, with no concern for the burgeoning Canadian production industry.

Within a year annual profits approached $150,000. Half of that was mine. Finally, I was no longer relying on Pearl's income; although I was still in law school, I now had some meaningful money of my own.

Nat captivated and fascinated me, and in return, I think, I entertained, amused, and fascinated him. For my part, I've never known anyone more disciplined. From the year he turned forty, he refused to work more than nine months a year. He took pride in it. He brought it off, he said, by taking in partners to share the responsibilities of the business, while he spent his time travelling and, increasingly, playing golf in Palm Beach. "Sure," he said, "I could have made more money, but instead I'm alive." Nor did he believe in doing business over lunch. Instead, at half past one in the afternoon, he would say, "I'm closing up," and, locking the office door, he would go into the back room and take an hour-long nap. Every day!

His other daily ritual was tea at four o'clock in the afternoon. He'd call me up (the *Digest* office was in the basement) and say, "I'm having tea, come up and talk."

At first I just listened. Nat talked about the movies, about the movie business, about theatres, about patrons – and he talked about himself. He'd been only twelve, a tad in britches, when he started selling promotional postcards of movie stars to theatre owners. With the help of a law degree, he parlayed this early enthusiasm, and the contacts he had made, into a career as a movie buyer for the independent theatres (theatres that weren't part of a chain).

*Daily tutorials over tea and cookies! Sitting with Nat Taylor and cross-examining him for two hours every afternoon. Nat was my link to movie history. For a year I was exposed to this treasure-house six to eight hours a week, exclusively. I had him on my own. For forty weeks. A PhD in the movie business! It was my training. That's where I learned. That's where I really grasped the principles of exhibition and the economics of the movie business. The economics – and the relationships. How it really worked.*

*To my growing self-confidence, I now added knowledge.*

*It's always a formidable combination.*

When Nat Taylor talked about the old days, he would bring the Hollywood pioneers to life. Listening to Nat, I felt as if "the Jews who invented Hollywood," as Neal Gabler called them in his book *An Empire of Their Own*, were right there: Sam Goldwyn, Carl Laemmle, Jesse Lasky, Louis B. Mayer, Irving Thalberg, the Warner brothers, Adolph Zukor. To me, these men had been magicians. But Nat stripped away my illusions.

What he emphasized over and over again was that the movies were a business, always had been, always would be, and the surroundings in which they were presented were part of the package. At first the seconds-long peep shows in the penny arcades dazzled the crowds through sheer novelty. The success of nickelodeons, which charged a nickel for one- and two-reelers running up to thirty minutes and shown in makeshift theatres, confirmed the growing popularity of the movies. Even so, when Adolph Zukor (who died in 1976 at the great age of 103) opened his first theatre, he hedged his bet. In the two-hundred-seat Crystal Hall in New York, he built a spectacular glass staircase, with coloured lights shining through a waterfall. Zukor would recall later that "people paid their five cents mainly on account of the staircase, not the movies." Marcus Loew, another of the pioneers, put it more succinctly, "We sell tickets to theatres, not movies."

Loew really captured my imagination. He built a large circuit of vaudeville houses that offered a mixed program of live acts and feature films. Toronto, once an important stop on the vaudeville circuit, has three of Loew's original theatres still standing. Loew's Uptown is now the fiveplexed Uptown Cinema, and Loew's Downtown has been handsomely restored as the Elgin Theatre. Above the Elgin is the Winter Garden, the small fantasy theatre built on top of Loew's Downtown. All three theatres are stunning examples of the work of Thomas Lamb, who also designed the Pantages Theatre (which my company now owns) and who I think was the finest architect of the palatial style of vaudeville house.

Loew built some stellar U.S. theatres, too, ranging from the style of Louis XVI to replicas of Hindu temples. One of them had a Buddha in the balcony, a wall of a thousand windows, and a lost baby imprisoned in a column.

The other theatre builder and exhibitor who caught my fancy was Samuel Rothafel, better known as Roxy. He was the greatest showman of all.

It was Roxy who made motion-picture theatres into peoples' palaces, a democratic vision of royal splendour reaching its zenith in 1927, with the sixty-two-hundred-seat Roxy on Broadway. Tragically, the Roxy was torn down in 1954, a victim of the rising popularity of TV. I would love to have seen this "Cathedral of the Motion Picture" in its glory days. Roxy, a go-for-broke dreamer, described his idea this way, "I see my Theatre like the inside of a Great Bronze Bowl. . . . Everything in tones of Antique Gold. Warm. Very, very rich. Gorgeous." The result was a pastiche of Renaissance, Gothic, and Moorish themes, including the twisted columns from the baldacchino in St. Peter's in Rome and a pulpit. As for sound, it's never been rivalled – the mighty Wurlitzer. The effects were wonderful: uniformed ushers with their white gloves, a diorama of coloured lights playing over the curtain while a trio of piano, violin, and a baritone singer entertained the audience between shows.

A brilliant salesman was behind this madness: Roxy knew how to cater to his audience's every need. He found the key to customer loyalty: service cheerfully given. The *esprit de corps* of Roxy ushers was compared to that of West Point cadets. Nothing was too good for the masses: the washrooms were immaculately finished and there was even a three-bed infirmary for emergencies. It was only when I stepped into New York's six-thousand-seat Radio City Music Hall, which was inspired by the Roxy, that I was able to grasp the huge scale of Roxy's imagination, an exuberant vision that would help shape my own career in exhibition.

When the Roxy spirit came to Canada, Zukor was the key figure. Nat had met him once or twice. Zukor was a granite man with a flinty soul who wasted no time being charming; in fact he enjoyed swatting flies with a baseball bat. Once, annoyed at an editorial in the *Canadian Moving Picture Digest*, he told the editor, "I could crucify you on a cross and laugh as the blood poured from your wounds."

But Zukor was also a visionary: he saw motion pictures as having a cultural impact way beyond the novelty of the nickelodeon, and in 1912 he imported and distributed a French feature film, *Queen Elizabeth*, starring Sarah Bernhardt, then billed as the greatest actress in the world. It was successful enough for Zukor to start his own production company, Famous Players (to which he gave an uplifting slogan, "Famous Players in Famous Plays"), and to produce feature films like *The Count of Monte Cristo*. His movies were distributed through Paramount, the leading film-exchange company, with its own catchy slogan, "If it's a Paramount picture, it's the best show in town." But Zukor chafed at Paramount's terms: $35,000 paid to the producer along with 65 per cent of the net profits. Clearly, the way for a producer to maximize his profits was to go into distribution himself, or better yet, to take over Paramount. Why not? Famous Players was Paramount's largest supplier.

By 1916 Zukor had bought Paramount, after stalking it for months. He then merged Famous Players with Paramount's second-largest supplier, the Lasky Feature Play Company, and thereby controlled a primary supply of pictures to exhibitors. Finding themselves at his mercy, the exhibitors struck back. They formed their own production company, First National, and signed up Charlie Chaplin for $1 million a year, before luring Mary Pickford away from Zukor for an even larger guarantee.

Pickford had been Zukor's assurance of getting his pictures shown in the best theatres, so his retaliation was swift. He decided to control the theatres himself. In 1919 he went down to Wall Street and got $10 million from the financier Otto Kahn to capitalize what would become the most powerful exhibition circuit in the United States, and eventually in Canada as well. Zukor's pitch to the bankers was that "the largest returns of the industry result from exhibiting pictures to the public, not from manufacturing them."

In Zukor's Paramount, production, distribution, and exhibition were now merged to create a vertically integrated company that would become the model structure of the "studio system" (and later, the model I used when constructing Cineplex Odeon). With his usual thoroughness, Zukor started buying hundreds of theatres across the United States. His almost unfailing ploy was to threaten to build a bigger, better theatre opposite that of any independent who refused to sell. His rivals were left with two choices: close or sell.

Zukor had been eyeing Canada since 1916. Toronto was well on its way to becoming the largest Canadian market for movies, and one family, the Allens, dominated exhibition and distribution in the city. The Allens also had global ambitions: they had forty-five theatres across Canada and had expanded into the U.S. Midwest, with plans to build theatres in England. In addition, they held Famous–Lasky's Canadian franchise. As Nat heard it, Zukor said, "I want an interest in your circuit," and the Allens replied, "Get lost. You stay in the production business, and we'll stay in the theatre business." Then, according to Nat, they boasted that they had kept Zukor out of Canada. They had reckoned, however, without Nathan L. Nathanson.

I have a soft spot for Nathanson, a wily dealmaker. He was somewhat of a rogue, but then the movies were a rogues' business. Although N. L., as he was called, died in 1943, I feel I know him. It was he who built the Pantages in 1920. The marvellous detailing of the building clearly showed that he had a spirit larger than that of the city he lived in.

Even more significantly, Nathanson started not only the Famous Players theatre circuit in Canada but also Canadian Odeon (the purchase of which I negotiated for Cineplex in 1984). He was single-handedly responsible for the two chains that formed the duopoly that dominated Canadian exhibition for so long, and that I was to spend so much time and effort in fighting in the early eighties.

Nathanson was born in Minneapolis and moved to Toronto, where eventually he became a billboard salesman. But he soon found his niche in the motion-picture business. In 1916 he raised the money to buy the old Majestic Theatre on Adelaide Street and transformed it into the Regent, an opulent vaudeville house with its own forty-piece orchestra. He also started his own distribution company, the Regal Exchange. But he had a tough time competing with the Allens, and at one point he offered to sell his few theatres to them. Jay Allen, whom Nat liked to call the brains of the Allen empire, took one look at Nathanson's books and said, "You're going to be out of business in six months." Nat couldn't say for sure whether it was true, but rumour had it that Nathanson replied, "I'm going to stay in business and put you out of business."

In any case, when he heard the Allens' abrupt rejection of Zukor's offer, he wasted no time in hurrying down to New York and offering Zukor his own deal. He would build a circuit in Canada and split the profits of his infant circuit with Zukor in exchange for the Paramount franchise. Zukor told him to build the theatres first, which Nathanson did with financing from Lord Beaverbrook, the expatriate Canadian newspaper tycoon. In 1919 Nathanson precipitated the still-unresolved mystery of Ambrose Small. He bought Small's Trans-canada theatre chain, and a few days later Small disappeared with $1 million in cash, never to be seen again.

By the next year, Zukor was impressed enough with Nathanson's sixteen-theatre chain to do a deal. On February 9, 1920, Famous Players Canadian Corporation was given the exclusive right to exhibit Paramount pictures in Canada for a period of twenty years. It was a fifty-fifty partnership, with Zukor as president and Nathanson as managing director.

Nathanson was a charmer compared to Zukor, but he was just as ambitious and heavy-handed. He squeezed the independents merci-lessly as he built Famous Players. As Nat remembered it, Nathanson would go into a town and say to an exhibitor, "You're paying 40 or 50 per cent for pictures, what for? If you give me a partnership in your theatre, I'll give you Paramount pictures for only 15 per cent of the gross." It was a hard offer to refuse because, at that time, Paramount had all the best pictures. If the independent balked, Nathanson would use Zukor's tactic of threatening to build a theatre right next door. He didn't have to do anything to the Allens, however. Shorn of the Para-mount contract and with financing troubles of their own, they went bankrupt in 1923, and Famous Players picked up their major theatres. By 1924 Nathanson had expanded Famous Players' circuit from twenty-two theatres to seventy.

By the early twenties, the U.S. industry had shaken down to the handful of companies that would dominate Hollywood until the fifties. Like Paramount, the other companies – MGM, Fox, Warner Brothers, RKO – were vertically integrated, with divisions for production, distribution, and exhibition, and they came to be called the Majors or the Big Five. They shook hands on divvying up the exhibition business all over the continent. Each of the circuits would play the others' products where necessary and convenient.

In Canada Nathanson controlled most of the representative first-run theatres in the big cities in Canada. Every distributor needed his theatres. They were at his mercy. The independents were left with only the residual lesser-grossing films.

The oppressed independents got together and started the Exhibitors Co-op, and Nat Taylor, who by this time had made his name as a film buyer, was hired as its secretary. His job was to buy films for about forty independents, but he kept being fouled by Famous Players' monopolistic practices. Although the Canadian situation was viewed in the U.S. as an example of the Big Five's smothering of competition, nothing happened in Canada until 1930. That was the year Zukor increased Paramount's stake in Famous Players Canada to 93.8 per cent after Nathanson had gone behind his back and tried to sell his exclusive management deal with Famous Players Canada to British Gaumont. Nathanson was kicked out, and Zukor moved fast to cement American control of the company's policy and practices. Famous Players' minority Canadian shareholders protested, and it was only then the government took action. An inquiry was set up under the Federal Combines Investigation Act, with lawyer Peter White as commissioner.

The evidence was so overwhelming that, after Nat had testified for a day and a half, he remembered White saying to him, "How can they get away with all this?" And Nat replied, "Isn't that what we're here to find out?"

The outcome was frustrating. The White Commission did find that Famous Players inhibited competition, but the prosecution foundered on semantics. The Combines Act could be applied only to goods, and exhibition was defined as a service. Furthermore, the commission found that competition had not been lessened "unduly," which was taken to mean that the independents were not shut out completely. Of course not! There were far too many pictures for one circuit to play. The commission ignored the fact that Famous Players creamed the best, thus diminishing the independents' potential profits. In the end it would take more than fifty years before Famous Players' monopoly was challenged again – and then it was by me, fighting for the survival of my new enterprise, Cineplex.

Nat was fired from the Exhibitors Co-op in the depths of the Depression. He later found out that Oscar Hanson, the co-op's director, was scheming to start a new circuit with Nathanson and Twentieth Century-Fox, and Nathanson didn't want the freethinking Nat around. Nat then took the biggest gamble of his life. Borrowing $30,000 from family and friends, he bought an old store in London, Ontario, and converted it into a second-run motion-picture house, The Centre Theatre. There was, as always, a method in Nat's apparent madness. London, which had remained prosperous during the Depression, had no second-run theatre.

Back in the thirties, a well-placed second-run theatre coined money. There were so many films being released that it was the general policy to hold films for no more than a week or two, sometimes only days. After a "clearance" time, usually thirty days, the movie, which still had lots of mileage in it, could be reissued in a second-run house. Nathanson, who was now back as Famous Players' CEO (Zukor had rehired him because he was the only competent man around), took Nat out to lunch before the Centre was opened and tried to dissuade him. "Nathanson hated competition," recalled Nat, entirely undeterred. Nat opened his theatre and made his investors' money back in a year, and in gratitude they gave him a 25 per cent interest in the theatre. "You have to be on the right corner at the right time," he would say, making it sound simple. After that, Nat's stature in the industry just grew and grew.

The Centre Theatre's success put Nat in the catbird seat. Eventually, his Twentieth Century Theatres comprised seventeen motion-picture theatres, and everyone was coming to him with money. Nathanson came to him too. As usual, Nathanson was up to his neck in double-dealing. His contract with Famous Players Canada was due to expire in 1940, and he was trying to buy the company. But to cover himself, he had also set up his son Paul as president of a new chain to be called Odeon, financed by the British film company J. Arthur Rank. Nathanson offered Nat the chance to affiliate his theatres with Odeon, but Nat refused. "I liked Nathanson," Nat said, "but I didn't trust him." He much preferred Barney Balaban, who had taken over as Paramount's boss after the company went broke in the Depression, and so he chose to ally himself with Famous Players, which gave him twenty-eight of their second-run theatres to operate. Overnight Nat had forty-five theatres, the third-largest circuit in Canada.

Nathanson kept trying to make the exhibition business reflect the fact that Canada was independent of the United States. His final effort was Odeon, his hopes for which were based on the fact that his own distribution company, Regal Exchange, held the MGM franchise. MGM's strength in the forties was comparable to Paramount's in the twenties, and, trying to replay history, Nathanson flew down to New York once again, this time to see Nick Schenk, the boss of Loew's MGM. He offered Schenk the same fifty-fifty partnership he had once offered Zukor. In exchange for half the profits of the newly formed circuit, Odeon would be granted the right to play MGM exclusively. Paramount still operated the largest U.S. circuit, and when Barney Balaban heard what Nathanson was up to, he told Schenk, "If you play away from Famous Players, we won't play MGM pictures anywhere in the United States." Nathanson was checkmated, briefly. But it says something about his persistence that a summit conference was called in New York, at which the Canadian market was once again divided up. Famous Players kept the films from the Big Five studios while Odeon was awarded the residual product, films from the Little Three – Columbia, United Artists, and Universal – which didn't have exhibition circuits on which they could regularly depend to handle their releases. And that's how pictures came to be parcelled out in Canada.

*This is where I learned the lesson of leverage, never to be forgotten.*

*It's why I took Cineplex Odeon into the United States. If you're not dominant, you'll get killed; without leverage, you're held hostage by the distributors.*

Things stayed that way even after 1948, the year when the U.S. Justice Department obtained a ruling that, as far as the U.S. was concerned, exhibition must be broken off from distribution. Subsequently, the major studios sold off their theatres. But not in Canada. Paramount sold its American theatres but held on to its Canadian subsidiary Famous Players. Thus the traditional duopoly of Famous Players and Odeon continued untouched north of the border.

The Justice Department action couldn't have come at a worse time for the industry. In 1946 box-office records had been broken in North America, and average weekly attendance rose to a record ninety million. But in 1948 TV sets were being sold at the rate of two hundred thousand a month. Then came the Justice Department decision, and the major studios, having lost the theatres which were their cash cows, also lost the incentive to produce a regular supply of movies. Within ten years the audience had dropped by 50 per cent, lured away mostly by TV. The two-thousand-seat movie palaces of the twenties became dinosaurs; one after the other, the Granadas, the Tivolis, the Strands, and the Rivolis were demolished for office buildings or paved over for parking lots.

The days were gone when a movie, any movie, could fill a big theatre, except on weekends. Ingenuity was what was needed. In 1946 Nat opened the first art-house theatre in Canada, Toronto's International Cinema, run by his first wife, Yvonne, who later died of cancer. A couple of years later, Nat built another art-house in Ottawa, a four-hundred-seat addition to his eight-hundred-seat Elgin Theatre, and in doing so created the world's first dual theatre. By the time the new theatre was finished, Nat had changed his mind, and decided instead to show first-run features in both theatres.

He soon found out that twelve hundred seats could rarely be filled. He tried another refinement. He moved the flagging first features from the eight-hundred-seat theatre to the little Elgin. The experiment, which now seems logical, broke entirely new ground at the time. Ultimately, it paid off. In 1957 Nat ran into a typical dilemma when he was playing United Artists' *Witness for the Prosecution*, directed by Alfred Hitchcock, at the big Elgin, and Columbia was nudging him to replace it with David Lean's *The Bridge on the River Kwai*. However, *Witness* was still making money. Although it didn't need more than four hundred seats per screening to satisfy demand, United Artists was reluctant at the thought of it coming off. On the other hand, *Kwai* was an apparent blockbuster that Nat couldn't afford to turn down.

"Wait a minute," Nat said. "How about moving *Witness* to the little Elgin?" He did just that, after offering United Artists a more favourable split of the gross and the promise of the overflow audience from *Kwai*.

Nat's experiment at the Elgins was a success. Both auditoriums did well as he continued to juggle movies from one to the other. The two Elgins came to have the largest combined per-seat occupancy of any theatre in the country. Moreover, some distributors actually preferred to start their movies in the little Elgin. The potential weekly gross was lower, but on the other hand, the movie's run could be longer and the distributor could earn a higher percentage of the gross if the movie played at capacity.

The idea was simple and the flexibility infinite. Nat went on to twin and triple other theatres; he even built a fiveplex out of an existing theatre (Toronto's Loew's Uptown) on the theory that you could show one picture on as many screens under the same roof as was warranted – all you needed was extra prints. Or, if the public appetite was different, you could play five different films. He was also the first exhibitor to build a theatre in a shopping plaza (Toronto's Yorkdale Shopping Centre) and in an office building (Montreal's Place de Ville). In 1965 he was the first Canadian to be asked to speak at Showarama, the U.S. distributors' and exhibitors' annual convention, and he talked about nothing except the multiple-theatre concept. Everyone in the audience yawned – except Stan Durwood, an independent U.S. exhibitor who went out and started American

Multi-Cinema Corporation, which has since become one of the largest multiplex circuits in the United States.

In the movie business, an exhibitor's profits are pegged to a movie's gross.

I remember Nat sitting there at four o'clock tea and asking me, "Do you know what ninety-ten-ten is?"

Of course I didn't.

Nat beamed. "After the exhibitor has deducted his "padded" house nut, which is the sum he and the distributor have agreed he needs to pay the theatre's costs, plus 10 per cent of the gross as profit, the remaining gross is split between them, 90 per cent to the distributor."

Even with a ninety-ten deal in place, the final allocation between distributor and exhibitor is a matter of strenuous negotiation each week. The movie industry is one of the few businesses where you bargain *after* you've agreed to terms. As Nat said, "You pay for pictures based on the value of the picture at the box office. Can you tell me in advance how much it's going to take in? Not likely!"

"Fight Monday" is what the trade calls settlement day. Sometimes it takes months to settle a picture, and the negotiations can be brutal, a real yelling and shouting match. Distributors usually insist on a floor below which their percentage cannot drop, and exhibitors apply a sliding scale in their own favour to the percentage split of the gross as a run continues and audiences decline. If the distributor is a major Hollywood studio, it has the upper hand in most markets, because it can threaten to withhold future hits. On the other hand, an exhibitor with the best locations, particularly in, say, Manhattan, has his own leverage, because the distributor will lose face all over the continent if he doesn't open his picture at a prestigious New York location.

*I hated this process. Loyalty, track record, history were of secondary importance. Distributors were merely brokers. They had little emotional attachment to most of their films. Rug merchants display more feeling for their product.*

Nat never ran out of moneymaking ideas. He bought the North American rights to *Hercules*, the blockbuster Italian-made film, for his distribution company, International Film Distributors. He then sold producer Joe Levine the U.S. rights and retained the Canadian rights for free. Later Levine repaid the favour when he granted Nat the Canadian licence for Mike Nichols's *The Graduate.*

Nat also enjoyed biting off people's heads if he thought they deserved it. The Canadian cultural nationalists were always after him. At a National Film Board (NFB) symposium in the sixties, Nat was set upon by a young hothead, "Do you support a quota system for Canadian films?"

Nat replied, deadpan, "Yes, if the government will legislate people into theatres to watch them."

In 1969, when Nat had been planning a phased retirement, he had been approached by National General, a U.S. circuit then owned by the Bronfman holding company, CEMP Investments (which had been named after the Bronfman children: Charles, Edgar, Minda, and Phyllis; it was later dissolved, and Charles Bronfman channelled his investments through Claridge instead). National General had built seventeen Cinerama-style over-capacity auditoriums in Canada. These wide-screen behemoths were losing money. Nat suggested National General buy his Twentieth Century Theatres and give him a five-year contract to operate the combined circuit. When Destounis heard about it, he blew his stack. After all, Famous Players owned 50 per cent of Nat's circuit, which was about to become a competitor!

"Okay," Nat said to Destounis. "You do the same deal with me."

So he did. Nat sold his circuit to Famous Players and continued running the theatres for five years. As for National General, it was scooped up by Michael Zahorchak before he acquired Odeon from Rank.

In 1974, when his management contract ended, Nat still owned a 25-per-cent share of the Ontario drive-in theatres, which formed a part of his circuit and were 50 per cent owned by Famous Players.

Perhaps that's why Nat never got as mad as I did at Jack Bernstein, who left Nat to become the head film buyer of Famous Players. Jack would later work diligently to keep the majors from sending any films to Cineplex – without any regard for the fact that he was harming Nat, from whom he had learned everything he knew.

I remember Jack coming into Nat's office, looking, as always, as if he'd stepped out of an old Raymond Chandler movie, cigarette hanging out of the side of his mouth, hitching up his pants over a rather large belly.

"Nat, we've got a problem."

Nat never allowed his expression to change, "So what's the problem?"

"United Artists called me and they want to play *Last Tango in Paris* at the Towne." The Towne Cinema was Nat's premier downtown Toronto theatre.

"Yes. So what's the problem?"

"Well, they want 100 per cent of the box office. How do we give them 100 per cent of the box office?"

Nat didn't hesitate at all. "No problem. What's our overhead at the Towne?"

"Six thousand dollars a week."

"Okay, you tell them it's $8,000 a week. They'll be happy. They keep 100 per cent of the gross. We'll make $2,000 a week and all the profits from the concessions, which will be enormous."

Of course. How simple. Nat was "fourwalling" the theatre, renting it outright to a distributor. *Last Tango* ran a year, and Nat triumphed again.

*Wait – I've told you how smart he was, how much ahead of the pack, what he achieved in business, what I learned from him. But have I told you how I loved him?*

*I was like a son to him, and he was my mentor. Like all great men, like all great fathers, he felt only pride when the son triumphs, when the protégé outstrips the teacher. Here was a man who always yearned for the day he could make a half-million-dollar movie, a man who became excited when he built five or six new screens a year. I was building two hundred new screens a year at the pinnacle of Cineplex Odeon, creating a billion-dollar company, yet he felt nothing but pride. But after I left Cineplex Odeon, after Nat made his impassioned speech warning them against not supporting me, after that, we didn't see much of each other. I went my own way.*

*Then one day recently I said to myself, "Nat's an old man, he's eighty-eight. What if he leaves the world soon? I need to see him again." So I called him up during rehearsals of my production of Hal Prince's recreated* Show Boat.

*"What are you doing?" I demanded. You can't take too sentimental a tone with Nat.*

*"What do you mean, what am I doing?" In the same gruff, gravelly voice I remembered from years before.*

*"I'm going to have you picked up tomorrow and you're going to spend a day with me at my new theatre that you haven't seen yet. And we're going to have a corned-beef sandwich at my producer's desk in the auditorium, and I want you to watch rehearsals of* Show Boat *for four hours with me."*

*"What, you think my days are busy or something? I'll come."*

*He came up and I introduced him to everybody. We walked across the stage and stared silently out at the eighteen-hundred empty seats. After the opening night a couple of weeks later, he called me up and said, "I just have to tell you that I never could gather enough guts and conviction to do what you've done here. I could never conceive of taking on the challenges that you've taken on and have been able to succeed in."*

*This is a great entrepreneur and a guy who, during his involvement in the entertainment business, did pretty miraculous things. But he was, for a rare moment, without words, walking into the theatre and seeing the immense physicality of the place and the production.*

*Once, he called me. "You're like me," he said.*

*It was one of the great compliments of my life.*

By the early seventies Nat had only one piece of unfinished business, one idea he hadn't taken a shot at. He called it the multi-mini. He wanted to build a complex of small theatres, some with only fifty seats, to show offbeat and foreign films. He had tried and tried to get the idea off the ground, but he couldn't find a suitable location in downtown Toronto. He looked at me speculatively.

I remember the date: April 25, 1973. I would have loved to have gone to work on it right then. But I hadn't even completed law school and I was exhausted. For two years I had worked a double shift: publishing *Impact* and then *Canadian Film Digest* and pursuing a law degree. Within a couple of weeks I would take my final exams and then, I had promised myself, I would take some time off alone. Pearl was teaching until late June, and I wanted my first European adventure.

Nat wanted to talk about the multi-mini. I kept asking him about the Cannes Film Festival. Surely, I reasoned, the *Digest* should have a presence at Cannes. A lot of Canadians were going to Cannes that year – Gilles Carle was taking *La Mort d'un bûcheron (Death of a Lumberjack)*, along with its star, Carole Laure – and the more I heard about the festival, the more I itched to go. I went on and on at Nat.

He finally took the hint. "What do you want? For me to send you to Cannes?"

"I gotta go, Nat," I said.

And I did. I was in a rented Peugeot, driving along the Côte d'Azur from the Nice airport with the windows wide open, falling in love with the perfumed scents of the Riviera, that magical combination of wild rosemary, eucalyptus, sunbaked earth, and the ocean bathing the red rocks of the coast. Although I was depleted from my final law exams, when I arrived at my little hotel in Cannes, my spirits soared. The Hôtel de Paris was no big deal, but it was enchanting. I had never seen anything so carefully, so charmingly, so intimately presented, from the fresh white sheets turned down on the bed to the puffed-up pillows. In the bathroom there was a bidet, which I took time puzzling out. I felt more awake by the minute. And I felt ravenously hungry.

It was two o'clock in the afternoon. I settled on a modest little bistro near the harbour. I sat under an umbrella and ordered an omelette and frites and a bottle of Côtes de Provence, and I felt like the hero of a glamorous movie. And then, just to restore perspective and to puncture my newly found sense of my own sophistication, an American journalist sat beside me and ordered steak tartare. I goggled at the dish when it was delivered, a plate of chopped, raw, red beef topped by an uncooked egg. After mashing the ingredients together, he gulped it down with gusto. I was revolted. I said to myself, "Now I know I'm in another country."

Still, it didn't take me long to recognize I was in the middle of the ultimate movie scam. As promotion, Cannes is as brilliant as the Oscars. Everything is part of its carefully honed and controlled hype machine – the topless starlets on the beach, the exquisitely beautiful non-entities hoping to catch a major producer's eye, the gala openings, the mega-stars jetting in and out, the dutiful trek up to Roger Vergé's Moulin des Mougins (which I of course did, learning for the first time the difference between good and great cooking). And then there was business. A win at Cannes doesn't necessarily mean much across the Atlantic (exceptions being Francis Ford Coppola's *Apocalypse Now* and Quentin Tarantino's *Pulp Fiction*), but it has an impact on foreign sales. Hollywood used to consider the domestic market the most important; foreign sales were just gravy. Today, foreign markets account for 50 per cent and more of a film's total revenues.

I was astonished then, as I still am, at the large number of Canadians who show up at Cannes, particularly those attached to government organizations. For years the Canadian Film Development Corporation (CFDC), and then Telefilm, has sent over a huge contingent annually, achieving minuscule results; the size of the contingent always seemed quite out of proportion to the number of movies Canada produces.

My first Cannes was a great year for film: François Truffaut's *La Nuit Américaine (Day for Night)*, Jerry Schatzberg's *Scarecrow* with Al Pacino and Gene Hackman, Lindsay Anderson's *O Lucky Man!*, George Segal in Paul Mazursky's *Blume in Love*. Brandishing my press pass, I made it to several black-tie openings and parties, where I realized that what I thought was a very good-looking Lou Myles tuxedo was lamentably suburban compared to the casual, sunburned chic of the stars and their hangers-on.

That first experience of Cannes has never left me. After a year of Nat's tutorials, Cannes was my graduation present. I had learned the movie business from Nat, but Cannes reminded me of its magic. Every time I returned after that I would be caught up all over again in the frenzied excitement.

As the wheels screeched down on the concrete runway at Toronto's airport, I landed in the real world with a bump. I wasn't James Bond in a Lou Myles tux after all. I still had to qualify as a lawyer. I had a two-year-old marriage. A life to make.

I'd better get on with it.

# CHAPTER

## THE CRISIS BUSINESS

The phone in our bedroom shrilled at about four o'clock in the morning, sometime in late October 1976. I picked it up nervously – there's always something ominous about a phone call in the dark hours, a disembodied voice in the blackness with its message of doom – and I heard a voice I recognized. It was Jim Kennedy, a mad Irishman I knew. Three years before, he had come into the law office where I was working and plunked down a $100,000 retainer. "I want to make movies," he announced.

Now his voice was hoarse.

"Garth, the RCMP are after me! I need your help."

I thought, "So? What can I do?"

I asked him the same question.

I better come meet him, he said, giving me the coordinates of a remote intersection outside Toronto. Then his voice changed to a screech. If I didn't, he was going to come over and blow my brains out.

Pearl was sitting up in bed, an incredulous expression on her face. She remembers me carefully, delicately, putting down the phone, not saying a further word. Apparently I looked ashen, terrified. "The IRA are after me," I said, my voice quaking.

I had always thought Kennedy was unstable, if not worse, and quite capable of violence. For this I'd gone to law school? This was my grand new career in entertainment law? My father-in-law would just love it!

I had first laid eyes on Jim Kennedy in 1973, just after I had started articling. He looked and talked as if he were related to the Boston Kennedys, and he had an abundance of Irish charm. Afterwards I was told that the $100,000 he had given me came out of funds he in turn had been given by the IRA – to buy guns. Instead, he had decided quite unilaterally to direct some of the loot into movies. This was to be my first taste of the fantasy world that the idea of movies creates for some people.

Jim had a potential investing partner lined up, George Barrie, the head of Faberge. George had composed the Oscar-winning theme song for *A Touch of Class*, which starred Glenda Jackson and George Segal, and he had made Faberge into one of the hot companies of the early seventies. Cary Grant was on his board of directors; Margaux Hemingway had one of Faberge's lines of cosmetics named after her.

Jim swept me off to New York, where George put us aboard his personal Hawker Siddeley, all green and gold and smelling of Brut. George kept a piano aboard, so that he could compose on trips. We were whisked off to St. Croix, where we luxuriated in tropical splendour while George entertained us on his yacht. We lounged about. Everywhere people were doing dope. Voluptuous women seemed to come out of the woodwork. Nothing, I realized, actually got done in the way of the movie business.

*For myself, I never touched dope, never even smoked a joint. I never needed to; my highs have come from my life. I disliked the lack of focus so typical of people on drugs; I got turned off by it. My attitude is pretty rare in the entertainment business.*

Soon afterwards I had to drop Kennedy. He turned out to be all dreams and little action. But when the phone call came three years later, it appeared that he hadn't quite dropped me. Luckily the RCMP got him before he got me, and the following year he was deported from Canada as a suspected IRA terrorist.

*But I owe him something. Through him I learned my first lesson as a show business lawyer: Don't trust anyone.*

*    *    *

I had been late in getting myself articled. At first I was just too busy with *Impact* and then with Nat Taylor and the *Canadian Film Digest*. By the end of their second year, the more conscientious of my fellow students had already signed up with the firms where they would article after they graduated a year later. I was still trying to nail down an articling position in the middle of my last year, but at least I now knew exactly what I wanted: a practice in entertainment law. An indigenous film industry was starting to develop, deals were in the works, money was prying itself loose, and I wanted to find a firm that would allow me to concentrate solely on entertainment.

That wasn't so easy. There was no one in Toronto practising entertainment law exclusively. Still, the city's show-business circle was pretty small, and finally David Perlmutter, then a film producer and later a financier of films and television, suggested to me that I phone a lawyer called Dick Roberts.

My second mentor.

I knew nothing at all about Dick Roberts when I went along to meet him at Thomson, Rogers, the Bay Street law firm he had recently joined. It was also my first glimpse of Bay Street's corporate legal style. The Thomson, Rogers offices were an expansive acreage high in a downtown skyscraper, decorated in that peculiarly expensive and restrained elegance required by a firm respected mostly for its motor-vehicle litigation department. This was a world of old-boy networking, WASPish punctiliousness, tennis at Muskoka cottages, and hushed tones, as far from the beauties of St. Croix as you could get. I was already overwhelmed when I was ushered into Dick Roberts's office. I was quite unprepared for Dick.

He looked like a casting-house law lord, a tall, distinguished gentleman with graying locks and a pipe in his hand. His physical presence was imposing. But he wasn't just a prop for the firm, a lawyer-mannequin to impress the clients. He was also a Queen's Counsel, founding director of the Bar Admissions Course for the Law Society of Upper Canada, and a lawyer of some clout within the profession.

However, I may have been overwhelmed, but I'm hardly ever intimidated and never reticent; low-key, as my partner Myron Gottlieb puts it, has never been my style. I needed to be sure he really was interested in rigorously pursuing entertainment law as an off-shoot to the commercial department's activities, and I pestered him shamelessly with questions about what he was doing, who he was doing it with, and why. I'm not sure he knew who was interviewing or auditioning whom. As our conversation wound down, I laid it on the line, as only a brash student could, "I don't want to be part of the customary student rotation, three months' real estate, three months' estate planning, and so on. I don't want any of that. I know what I want. I just want to practise entertainment law."

Yes, I pitched myself hard. I wouldn't be just a passenger, I told him. I could benefit Thomson, Rogers. Nat Taylor and I were always discussing projects, ideas for this and that, and I would bring work into the firm.

Dick listened politely, although he was drawing furiously on his pipe. Occasionally a faint smile crossed his face. He didn't say all that much, but nevertheless there was a warm feeling emanating from him. Later he told me that he'd been amused by my aggressiveness.

When I let him get a word in, he explained that he had begun a small but growing practice in entertainment law. Among his clients were the novelist Margaret Atwood, whom he had represented in her negotiations with her publisher; he had helped opera star Maureen Forrester set up her personal corporation; and he was now involved in some limited-partnership film financing. It sounded fine to me. Promising, even. Then he got up, excused himself politely, and left the office.

He returned with Laurie Mandel, another lawyer in the firm, whose opinion he respected. We talked for a while longer, or at least I did. Undoubtedly I showed off some more of my recently learned Nat Taylor wisdom. But whatever I did, I seemed to go over well, because by the end of the interview, Dick suggested that I come to work for him part time while completing my last three months of law school. I would be free to work only on entertainment law.

Much later Dick told me that, after I left the office, Laurie Mandel had said, "That guy is something else!" Dick never told me whether Laurie meant it as a compliment.

Dick Roberts is the one person I never shouted at. I think that's because he never made me feel defensive. Without patronizing me, he broadened my horizons. I was unpolished and in retrospect quite unsophisticated, but he never made me feel anything but a partner. For my part, I had never met anyone as erudite as he was. He customarily used Latin in his conversation, without affectation, just as a grace note. I had never been a great reader, but I was forced to start reading just to keep up with Dick; his appetite for the written word was voracious. Among the things he taught me was my skill as a legal draughtsman. He was an elegant writer, economical with words, able to reduce complicated business notions to clear, spare writing. I don't think he taught me a huge amount about the law, and he wasn't necessarily a great business strategist or the toughest negotiator – those were my areas. But I learned about life from him.

Shortly after I returned from Cannes, Dick invited Pearl and me to dinner at his three-storey Victorian house in Toronto's Annex district. It was another revelation for me. I had always liked paintings and I did have a good eye for art, but Dick's collection knocked me out. He and his second wife, Lexie, had what was to my mind a spectacular collection of contemporary Canadian art. I had never seen so many wonderful pictures in one home, and my interest in and passion for all aspects of contemporary art took a quantum leap that evening.

*I still get such pleasure out of looking at pictures. Today in my office, behind my desk, there hangs a Michael Thompson, an exceptional oil of a young woman seated alone in a row of old-style theatre seats. Whenever I look at it, I feel elated, uplifted. The painting evokes the sort of feelings that lured me into entertainment in the first place. The young woman's face is rapt, completely absorbed by her surroundings, lost in her field of dreams, her spirit gripped by something larger than herself. The intensity of her thoughts continues to fascinate me.*

And Dick?

He was very much a father image to me, as Nat Taylor was. How he loved life! He lived it to the full, with gusto, savouring its pleasures. He loved good books, good food and wine, good art, good women. He was married three times, but it was never enough. Dick was loved by so many people. He was the guy you always wanted to have at a party. He would sing the old songs, play word games, anything that would stimulate the mind. He would walk down from the office to the Cambridge Club at lunch hour wearing his Walkman, with Shakespearean plays piped through his earphones. He studied three or four languages on his own. Lovely, lovely man.

*There is a sadness here, though, a great sadness. Years later Dick lost all his money. He had borrowed heavily to finance a lifestyle that was beyond him, and he got blown out when the value of his Cineplex stock plunged. He fell into a depression, and then, one Christmas, he attempted suicide. I was devastated. Even though it was a failed attempt, he did a lot of damage to himself. I went down to St. Michael's Hospital and spent a couple of days with him. I was willing him to pull through, to pull out of it. Dick, Dick, what the hell are you doing? I need you! I need you to live! You're such a hugely important person in my life.*

Dick pulled himself out of it, but a year later discovered he had cancer. First the bowel, then the liver. That was more than enough for him. He refused chemotherapy, refused extraordinary treatment, refused to prolong what he knew was over, and in June 1993 he gave up and succumbed. I renamed the lobby of the Pantages Theatre in his honour. About four days before the 1993 Tony Awards, for which *Kiss of the Spider Woman* was nominated in multiple categories, Dick had been in my office, lying on the couch in enormous pain. I went over with him what I would say and what I wouldn't say if we triumphed in New York. We went over all the politics behind it, the strategy, we discussed how important it was to our company, and he grimaced and writhed in pain but lay there on my couch, and I knew he was going to live just long enough to see me win the Tony. He died days afterwards. He hung on just enough, then he . . . let go.

*In his last hours, as he lay dying, he said to Lorraine, my personal bookkeeper, who looked after his books as well, "Give Garth my picture."*

*She knew what picture he wanted me to have, a Cavouk portrait of Dick.*
*How distinguished he looked in this formal portrait, his patrician face in*
*repose but full of character, so much the gentleman, so much the scholar.*
    *I miss him.*
    *I always will.*

But before all this, there I was, starting work for Thomson, Rogers. I
didn't just report for work, learn and do my business, and go home.
I can't help myself. I just can't stand idly by, letting opportunities drift
past me. It drives me crazy to see chances lost. Within a few months I
spotted what I thought was a terrible waste of financial leverage: the
way the firm's trust funds were handled.

Every law firm has a trust account into which it puts such things as
retainers, closing proceeds from real-estate deals, or litigation settlement monies. Back in the early seventies most firms kept the money
in a non-interest-bearing account to avoid the administrative
expense of allocating interest every month. On the other hand,
the bank, which didn't have to pay any interest, reaped a windfall.
Thomson, Rogers had a very healthy trust account indeed, because of
the large number of insurance claims it handled, but the money was
doing nothing for anybody but the bank. Money is a tool, a device, a
way of making things happen. And for it just to sit there . . .

I was having lunch one day with my banker friend, Wayne Squibb.
I knew Wayne's Bank of Montreal branch was a major lender to the
real-estate industry so I posed him a question. "Suppose I can arrange
to put into your bank several million dollars' worth of our trust
funds? How would you reciprocate?"

Wayne thought a minute and said, "Well, we're forever lending
mortgage money to developers of condominiums. We have to hire
lawyers to protect our interests and they're paid by the developers out
of the proceeds of the mortgage loan. That legal business is worth a
lot of money. There's no reason why we couldn't designate Thomson,
Rogers to represent us in transactions of that sort, as long as your
rates are comparable."

I rushed back to the office. Dick was away, so I went straight to Ralph Howie, the managing partner, who was also a very competent litigator. I outlined my idea to him.

Howie, a conservative thinker and an eminently decent man, was nonplussed. As soon as Dick got back, Howie telephoned him.

"Dick," he said, "who the hell is this guy Drabinsky?"

"Well, he's my law student. You may not have met him yet –"

Howie's voice rose several octaves. "Oh yes, I sure have. He's just given me a lecture on what we're going to do with our trust account!"

Dick listened as Howie related my proposal, pondered for a minute, then said, "You're damn right that's what we're going to do with the trust funds. It makes abundant good sense." So the firm deposited a significant portion of its trust funds in the Bank of Montreal and the beneficiary was Thomson, Rogers' commercial department, which began to reap the preposterous fees generated by the condominium mortgage loans sent along by the bank.

After working with Dick unofficially for much of my last term at law school, I was officially articled to him in June 1973. At that point I had to give up my daily involvement with the *Canadian Film Digest*. But I kept in touch with Nat, talking to him several times a week. He was still popping off ideas, particularly about film production. And that's how I came to meet Henry Comor, who had been hired by Nat to run his Toronto International Studios in Kleinburg, Ontario. Henry was a born hustler. He had been a radio actor in England, and he had a smooth, almost-oily voice and what used to be called a BBC accent, full of orotund vowels and clipped consonants. (His voice would play a minor role in Canadian politics – in 1987 Henry was hired as John Turner's speech coach. Turner may have spoken more clearly as a result, but it certainly didn't help him at the polls.)

When I first met Henry, I very soon came to believe that he was only using Nat, and Nat's fortune, to further his own production aspirations. But Nat was inexplicably smitten with him, and even though Henry's projects kept falling through, one lamentable failure after the other, Nat still threw him a bone: $100,000 to make *Divertimento*, a twenty-minute 16-mm documentary. Nat was convinced that documentaries were the best training ground for new directors. *Divertimento* enjoyed some theatrical life and even got some good reviews, but it recouped only a fraction of its cost.

I had a fairly good, if cautious, relationship with Henry. So when Al Bruner started the Global Television Network in Toronto and began looking around for Canadian programming, Henry got a call and he came to me.

Instant inspiration: I recommended we develop the concept of *Impact* magazine as a television series.

Global agreed to finance ten half-hour episodes at $40,000 each. We called the show "Flick Flack." Henry was producer and I was associate producer. Each episode focused on a particular aspect of film-making – scoring a film, special effects, or preparing for a role. Given the low cost per episode, I think we did some very inventive programming. Our star for one biographical segment was Clint Eastwood, who was distant but cooperative. We followed Clint with a piece on Neil Diamond, an old sixties musical hero of mine, taking us through the process of putting music to *Jonathan Livingston Seagull*. For one special-effects item, we showed how matte cinematography involved scale drawings and detailed miniature models, photographed and combined with an actor filmed against a non-reflective background. Cecil B. De Mille used this process to good effect when he parted the Red Sea in *The Ten Commandments*.

The ratings and reviews were good when the first episode of "Flick Flack" was broadcast in the fall of 1974. Only one problem: Global went belly-up. Al Bruner's idea of an Ontario-wide commercial network programmed with Canadian-made shows was just too ambitious for the times. He was also faulted for starting Global in January, in the middle of the TV season, after advertisers had allocated their budgets. After much shuffling and argument, Global was rescued by Allan Slaight of IWC Communications and made a 180-degree change in direction. Guaranteed moneymakers, proven U.S. shows, were programmed, and "Flick Flack" wasn't renewed.

It did, however, teach me some invaluable lessons – like how to handle a temperamental star. Our host was William Shatner, an expatriate Canadian, who had gone from carrying a spear at the Stratford Festival to playing Captain Kirk of "Star Trek." He was in many ways a typical Canadian artist who had upped and gone to California and given little thought to his roots (though today he's more respectful of Canada). Later I represented the comedian David Steinberg when he was in negotiation to do a series with CTV, the Canadian network. He was pretty hot then, an acerbic, sophisticated comic with a sharp edge to his personality. He had come from Winnipeg, but you would never have known he was a Canadian. Was he ever insecure! I felt he considered himself a massive failure just because he was back in Canada. I couldn't understand it then, and I still don't – I've always felt rooted here. But so many times I've met Canadians, in California and elsewhere, who don't want anyone to know where they came from. Either that or they refuse to work in Canada with talent that is as committed and enthusiastic as any they could find anywhere else, but in many cases simply lacks experience.

I soon came to realize that it was the very vulnerability of artists that so often made them unbearable, but that didn't make it any easier or more pleasant to put up with. I was quickly disillusioned when I represented these people in their negotiations. They were all high-maintenance clients.

There were exceptions, of course. One such was the great theatre director John Hirsch, a client of Dick's, whom I met in 1974 when he was negotiating his contract as head of television drama of the CBC. The first time I saw him, he sort of sidled into my office, a tall, bereft-looking individual, and I was instantly fond of him. He was a *haimisher* kind of guy, charming, warm, and sensitive. He had a reputation for being difficult to work with, but I empathized with his defensiveness and understood its source – I don't think he could ever rid himself of the horror of being orphaned by the Nazis. He was never less than passionate and challenging, and we used to talk for hours about how to develop a thriving commercial theatre in Canada. I was greatly saddened when he died of AIDS in 1989.

Dick had been as good as his word, passing along to me what show-business clients came over the transom. And quite soon I developed a reputation in New York and Los Angeles as a lawyer who knew the ropes in Canada, a country that was regarded by American film producers, who had never been here, as an unexplored and untapped (but eminently tappable) gold mine. These were the early days of the Great Canadian Movie Boom, and all sorts of strange characters, who couldn't get a hearing from the Hollywood studios, heard about the tax breaks the Canadian government was offering investors in movies and came north in a hurry. It was chaos. Films were being financed under a general tax-shelter principle, and every lawyer, dentist, and dentist's wife was taking fast write-offs in motion pictures. Movie deals were being financed on a whim. Some of these American producers coming to Canada, like David Susskind, had a track record. Others were like Jim Kennedy, inexperienced, seduced by the glamour of the business and the promise of fast big bucks.

It was a great scam and I knew it. Despite that, I was drawn irresistibly to the lure of film and this provided an opportunity.

I never set out to become a producer.

It just happened – like so much of my life.

*In 1975 my firstborn, my beautiful daughter, Alicia, came into the world at Mount Sinai Hospital in Toronto. Every parent will understand when I say this was one of the emotional high points of my life. Not every parent, however, will be lucky enough to be able to say, as I still can, that she's been a joy and a pleasure to me all her life; that she's smart and talented; that she will do great things with her life; that she's never in all her years caused me a moment's anxiety or concern about how she'll turn out. Truly a beautiful kid.*

Fast forward now to December the next year. I was in the Mayfair offices of James Mitchell, an Israeli-born British solicitor who fancied himself a movie producer. I was up to my neck in my first film production, and there I was, sitting with my head in my hands. Well, the two things seem to go together; chaotic, uncontrolled crises are to movie production what a red arse is to a monkey – one follows the other around forever, a flaming beacon of trouble.

The movie was called *The Disappearance*, and it came to epitomize the range of things that could go wrong with a movie.

First the financing evaporated. Then the director was gunned down by starfire, in this case the planet-sized ego and overweening directorial and producing ambitions of Donald Sutherland. Finally the producing team itself unravelled, and I, the junior partner in this hopeless enterprise, was powerless.

It was like a bad movie.

It *was* a bad movie.

*How did I get into this mess?*

It started, of course, much more calmly. In this case, even more calmly than usual, in fact at a stately academic pace. In 1975 I was called to the bar with honours. That same year, I authored a book based on a series of lectures I had given for the past two years at York University's film school. With Dick Roberts's help, I had made the first-ever exhaustive analysis of Canadian filmmaking from both the legal and business points of view. My book was called *Motion Pictures and the Arts in Canada*, and after it came out I was, of course, considered an instant expert. It seemed only natural that my next step would be to exploit my newfound status and practise what I had so diligently preached.

At this point I need to explain the arcane mysteries of the Canadian movie business and the sorry involvement of government in it. Along the way I'll deal with those people who call themselves Canadian cultural nationalists. Or at least some of them – those who seem to believe that a proper nationalism consists of excluding from Canada anything of real class. If you get from what follows that I believe them to be shortsighted, retrogressive, self-destructive ignoramuses, I will have made myself clear.

In 1967 the movie business in Canada was non-existent. In that year the government put $10 million into setting up the Canadian Film Development Corporation to spur local production. The CFDC would invest up to 50 per cent of the budget of a movie that cost less than $200,000 – in the days when the average Hollywood movie cost around $3.5 million. The CFDC, from its chairman on down, consisted of a bunch of time-servers who knew no more about how to make a commercially successful movie than your average man in the street, yet they demanded script approval, cast approval, and strict adherence to a set of hopelessly unrealistic Canadian-content rules.

In the early seventies the Canadian government began to offer a tax incentive to investors in Canadian films. Movies were eligible for a 60 per cent capital-cost allowance, which could be considerably enlarged through leverage. A perfect (if that's the right word) example was the financing for a movie called *Mahoney's Last Stand*, which was made in 1971. Laurie Mandel and eleven other lawyers from Thomson, Rogers had facilitated the financing of the production by putting up only $150,000 cash of the film's total cost of $577,892. They issued promissory notes covering the rest of the budget. The producer arranged the balance of the financing. In their 1971 tax returns, the partners claimed their 60 per cent capital-cost-allowance deduction on the entire cash plus note contribution of $577,892. Thus a partner who had invested $40,000 – $10,000 in cash and $30,000 by note – walked away with a reduction of taxable income of $24,000 in the very first year, with more savings to come in the following years. The icing on the cake was that under the terms of the investor's agreement with the producer, repayment of his note was only a binding obligation to the extent that he recouped his investment out of the earnings of the film.

*Mahoney's Last Stand*, like so many movies in those days, didn't generate a cent. It never played more than a few days in any theatre. It was that terrible. Even so, it was a lot better than many of the movies which were made around the same time by self-proclaimed producers with incompetent scripts, second-rate casts, and has-been directors. Many of these films were, fortunately, mercy-killed at birth and never released.

It took Revenue Canada a few years to catch up with all of this, and *Mahoney* was forced to make yet another stand, this time in Federal Court. Revenue Canada's view was that the partners could deduct their 60 per cent from only the cash portion of their investment, on the logical grounds that they were never at risk for the rest. It was the only time in my career I was gowned to go into Federal Court, as junior counsel to the stellar counsel, the late Doug Laidlaw. It wasn't even close. We got swatted out of court. At the Appeal Court, we lost again.

In 1975 the income-tax law was changed so that investors could write off 100 per cent of their cash investment in the first year, but the film had to be "certified" – that is, it had to satisfy the federal bureaucrats' rigid standards of what was considered Canadian content. Points were awarded for everything from the director and stars to the composer of the music and even the cameraman.

Raising production money was a tough enough problem, but money together with these unworkable rules. . . . The problem was, Canada didn't have anywhere close to a viable film industry and already there were two competing factions. On the one side (my side, the sensible side) were producers who wanted to create movies capable of challenging Hollywood's supremacy. This, we knew, required international stars and skilled craftspeople. On the other side were those "cultural nationalists," a strident, cacophonous bunch who believed that Canadian producers should compete with one hand tied behind their backs. All you had to do, in their opinion, was throw tax breaks at potential investors and great Canadian-content movies would automatically appear.

But who, of talent, would direct them, act in them, and make them was never discussed. These things were always assumed to be "givens."

Hah! And who, then, would watch them if they *were* made?

As Nat had said, no one would pay to see a movie just because the story was inherently Canadian. They would only pay for movies they wanted to see, Canadian or not. It's natural to want to make movies with your own voice. The problem is that Hollywood's braying is so much louder than our own. After all, it was Hollywood that made movies into the first truly mass entertainment. It was Hollywood that industrialized moviemaking. It was Hollywood that captured the imagination of people everywhere.

I don't think Canadians then understood how dynamic the Holly-wood industry was, how completely driven by the marketplace, how competitive in every phase. Hollywood has dynasties of skilled craftspeople, with access to studios whose pockets are deep enough to keep raising the ante on salaries – and on technological innovation.

In the mid-seventies, in the small film community spread between Toronto, Montreal, and Vancouver, we had only hopes and aspira-tions and tax-sheltered investors. We had pitifully few directors. We lacked major-league cinematographers, art directors, and composers. Nor did we have skilled film editors, at least none with enough expe-rience to make sure a director shot enough film covering different angles to avoid the awful possibility that there would be gaps in the story when it came to editing. And even when Canadian producers did make promising films, they didn't know how to launch them properly, how to wring the most out of ancillary markets, including TV and foreign sales.

On top of all that, there were only two technical houses in Toronto where a filmmaker could complete post-production sound editing and mixing, and neither of the two – Film House (which I later bought for Cineplex Odeon) and Pathé – was properly equipped with state-of-the-art technology. There was not a single decent soundstage in the city capable of recording a film score with a seventy-piece orchestra.

In time we could build an industry, I believed, in the same way the British did in the forties – by bringing in outside experts and integrat-ing them with Canadians. I pleaded with the government to offer tax incentives to attract master craftspeople in all areas of the industry, so they could work here with our aspiring young talent. And instead of throwing its money away on the CFDC, I said the government should subsidize education with student-aid loans and visiting craftspeople as faculty. The government was deaf. The unsurprising result: the industry languished.

Canadian producers in the mid-seventies had one more obstacle to overcome: the narrow definition of "Canadian-ness." Even Morde-cai Richler's *The Apprenticeship of Duddy Kravitz*, financed, written, and directed by Canadians, was denounced as "international" by the culturecrats because its stars, Richard Dreyfuss and Jack Warden, were Americans.

Oh yes, there was plenty wrong with the Canadian film industry. Maybe that's why I seized the first chance I could to immerse myself in it.

James Mitchell walked into my law office in 1976 and made me a proposition that I fell for instantly. It was so inexpensive! It seemed so simple!

A year before, a co-production deal had been announced between Britain and Canada, and Mitchell had wasted no time hopping an airplane to scrounge money in Canada. He was looking for a co-producer for *The Disappearance*, the film he was going to make. These co-production deals were designed to allow several countries to gang together to compete with the Americans. All elements of a production, from the stars through to the focus-puller, were pro-rated according to each country's financial participation. By some alchemy of bureaucracy, it all balanced out.

Mitchell said he had a production partnership with David Hemmings, the British actor/producer/director. The proposed cast impressed me. It included Donald Sutherland, his gorgeous wife, Francine Racette, and a brilliant supporting cast headed by John Hurt, Peter Bowles, Virginia McKenna, David Warner, and Christopher Plummer. Milena Canonero, who later created the marvellous period costumes for *Chariots of Fire*, would be our designer, and John Alcott, one of the great cinematographers (he was responsible for Stanley Kubrick's *2001: A Space Odyssey* and *Barry Lyndon*), would photograph the film. The only apparent weakness was the director, Stuart Cooper, who was young and inexperienced.

"How much do you need?" I asked.

"Just $300,000," Mitchell said. The rest of the $1.25-million budget was solid, he said.

"How solid?" I asked. I knew enough to know that solid was a word with shifting meanings in the movie business.

"Solid," he said.

Yeah, sure. I had qualms. But then $300,000 wasn't a towering amount of money. It would be an inexpensive way to get my feet wet.

I raised the money partly from Danton Films, a small Canadian distribution company owned by Daniel Weinzweig, and the balance from the CFDC – since they were giving money away anyway, I stood in line. It was the only time I ever did.

Then in mid-November – principal shooting was supposed to start in less than a week – I got a phone call from London. It was Mitchell. He was desperate. His supposedly dependable financing was teetering.

I flew to England the next day and met Mitchell in his Curzon Street offices. David Hemmings was there as well. Like so many others, I had been intrigued by the blasé character Hemmings had played in his best-known movie, *Blow-Up*. What a difference between reel and real life! He was in the terminal stages of panic and spent his time drinking in one of the quaint wine bars behind Mitchell's office in Shepherd Market.

Only a day before principal photography was to begin, Hemmings, instead of concentrating on the business at hand, took me to his house, where he played me the concept album for Andrew Lloyd Webber's *Evita*, featuring Colm Wilkinson among others (then referred to as C. T. Wilkinson). When I returned later to Toronto, I found no one had ever heard of the recording and had no idea why I was so excited. Of course, it ended up as a staggering hit under the direction of the extraordinary Hal Prince.

Mitchell was no better than Hemmings. The smooth-talking salesman I had seen in Toronto had vanished. His aplomb had fallen apart as fast as his financing had collapsed. The Rank Organisation, the largest of his investors, had failed to meet its commitments. So here I was, the minority producer, with zero experience, in the heat of production, with ineffective partners – *and I was in control!* At the eleventh hour, with a lot of cajoling from me, Rank's shortfall was picked up by Jake Eberts, a tight-lipped Canadian banker who lived in London, where he was a partner in Oppenheimer & Company. Jake, who had a terrific eye for great material, later went on to found Goldcrest Films with David Puttnam, and recently wrote a book with Terry Ilott about his film experience. The title summed up the business perfectly: *My Indecision Is Final: The Rise and Fall of Goldcrest Films.*

I should have let the movie collapse. I didn't know what I was getting into. I was now saddled with a weak director and the gifted Donald Sutherland, who thought he could wield a lot more power than me and was determined to do so. The result: six weeks of madness.

I swore I'd never repeat the experience.

How naïve!

The insane logistics of shooting the movie were determined not by the creative team but by the rules of co-production, so the whole crew shuffled off to Montreal for what seemed to be two weeks of the coldest weather in the city's history; the air was so frigid that I could see steam rising from the frozen St. Lawrence River. We spent much of the time shooting at architect Moshe Safdie's own apartment in the unusual housing complex, Habitat, that he had designed for Expo 67. Then we spent four weeks at Twickenham Studios in England, where I learned very little about the movies except that, in England, the tea break was sacrosanct. The Canadian crews had toiled outdoors for fifteen-hour days in subzero weather; in Britain, I swear we could have been in the middle of the chariot race in *Ben-Hur* and the technicians would still have stopped for tea.

But all these problems paled compared to controlling Sutherland. I soon found out there was a good reason why some of the old-time directors bullied and browbeat their stars. If they didn't, the star sensed weakness and pounced. This is what Sutherland did. He found a weak director and put him through the grinder. He immediately began rewriting the script to suit himself. The director failed to challenge him. Mitchell and Hemmings did nothing. I felt I was too inexperienced to try. So, as I said, Sutherland went on to terrorize the entire creative team. Chaos was the inevitable result.

*The Disappearance* was not one of the classics of the cinema. But it was sold around the world and received a minor release in the United States, where it garnered mixed reviews.

For me, it was a complete disappointment. I vowed that never again would I produce a motion picture without having complete control of every facet of the film's development and production.

I would have control, or I wouldn't do it.

*Well, I believed it then.*

I was getting significant press at home. Drabinsky, the baby mogul.

I confess: I liked it.

*But they don't like entrepreneurs much in Canada. And I learned pretty soon that in Canada good publicity often produces negative reactions. There are so many detractors waiting, so many of them exhaling the sour breath of envy, the mean-spirited odour of insecurity. No, they don't like entrepreneurs very much.*

Even the partners at Thomson, Rogers disapproved of all this attention. Auto insurers were nervous clients and didn't like seeing the name of their law firm in the press; my new visibility definitely clashed with their super-elegant decor.

Bill Rogers, the senior partner, pulled Dick into his office and waved a clipping at him. "What are you going to do about this?" he yelled.

"Nothing," Dick said. "I'm not going to do anything about it. The publicity is good for us. It's bringing in business."

But privately Dick knew it couldn't last. My style was too different, too flamboyant, too entrepreneurial. And I wasn't going to stop. I was only twenty-seven.

So Roberts & Drabinsky hung out its shingle.

Such grand plans! We were going to be the finest entertainment law firm in the country, and we wanted our offices to reflect our self-perceived status. We leased ten thousand square feet on the sixty-ninth floor of First Canadian Place in Toronto, for what was then the enormous rent of $16 a square foot. Albert Reichmann did the deal himself. We signed a ten-year lease with a ten-year option to renew. That lease was to become an important asset in subsequent years.

Then we went on a shopping spree. Dick and I were determined to make our offices a showplace for the very best contemporary Canadian art. With a bankroll of $150,000 we put together a collection that included works by Jack Bush, Jean-Paul Riopelle, David Milne, Guido Molinari, and Gershon Iskowitz; these were the paintings that later became the foundation of my personal collection.

*What a rush! Now $150,000 might not seem like a massive budget, but then it was plenty. We would go down to the galleries and they would pull paintings out of the stacks, rolling them out for our approval. Bush and Riopelle and Michael Snow and Graham Coughtry and Harold Town and Christopher Pratt and J. P. Lemieux. My eye was drawn to the abstract expressionists, to the colour-field realists, to the whole range of contemporary art, to paintings that were dense, layered, immersed in ideas, in constant tension, difficult pictures, pictures that would stay alive for years, pictures that were not faddish or simpleminded but complete and mysterious and profound. I remember thinking as I looked at them that this was where I belonged, in a world where art and business co-existed, where ideas could inform business and commerce nurture art. Years later, as Alicia and Marc grew up, we would wander down to the Yorkville galleries on the weekend, and go into the lofts and spend hours looking at the special pictures reserved for important buyers, and I tried to communicate to them the almost spiritual love that good pictures make me feel.*

In my next movie project, I gave the late John Candy, then a $200-a-week actor with Toronto's Second City, his first principal movie role. The rest was the usual chaos. But this time I learned plenty.

It happened this way:

*The Silent Partner*, a script about a bank teller who cunningly outwits a bank robber and keeps the loot for himself, was a thriller adapted by Curtis Hanson from a Danish novel. Hanson has since gone on to become a respected writer/director (his credits include *Bad Influence*, starring Rob Lowe and James Spader, *The Hand That*

*Rocks the Cradle*, starring Rebecca De Mornay, and *River Wild*, starring Meryl Streep). But in 1977 he lived in Venice Beach, California, hawking screenplays. *The Silent Partner* was optioned by two young producers, Joel Michaels and Stephen Young.

I liked Joel instantly. I had met him the year before, when he was trying to interest Nat Taylor in financing his $500,000 movie called *Bittersweet Love*. Nat had said no, but I struck up a friendship with Joel anyway. He was a delight, full of a zest for life. He loved to laugh. He was also a gentle man. He was eleven years older than me and always sported an elegant goatee. He had been born in Buffalo but had lived in Toronto in the early sixties, when his wife, Diana Maddox, was a member of the Stratford Festival troupe. Now they were living in Westwood Village in L.A. In a business where kissing the air is regarded as profound emotion, Joel had integrity, class, and, although he had little formal education, he had impeccable taste. A very rare individual.

Before he left Toronto, Joel gave me the Hanson script. And even as I was scurrying off to Britain to salvage *The Disappearance* before it disappeared, I was thinking about it. I wanted to work with Joel. I thought he could be my missing link. He had the grassroots production knowledge I didn't have – among other things he had spent some time as production manager with Roger Corman, the king of B movies. Our tastes were similar, so there was little conflict artistically. And we quickly became more like brothers than business associates.

Once we had agreed to proceed with *The Silent Partner*, we sorted out the credits. Joel and Stephen Young were to be co-producers, I would be executive producer. The movie was to be made in Canada and, in a reversal of the norm, we moved the story from an American city to Toronto.

We budgeted the movie at $2.2 million, which would make it at that time the most expensive Canadian movie ever. I can understand now why journalists never took me seriously in those days. They had only learned to handle small-budget movies like *Goin' Down the Road* and *Wedding in White*, or shockers like *Shivers*; and while everyone else in the country was worrying about making a movie with a budget under a million, there was Drabinsky, still a kid, announcing a movie with a budget twice that.

*Where the hell does he get off, the little snot!*

Whatever financing model we used, we needed stars and a reputable director. So I flew to Hollywood and walked with Joel into the offices of Jack Gilardi, a high-profile agent at International Creative Management (ICM), then the biggest agency in the business. That's when the frost of reality dampened our sunny optimism.

Hollywood was not impressed with Canada or its film industry, if it had one.

Gilardi was pleasant but blunt. "What makes you think you've got credibility with this agency? What can you possibly do to assure me your financing is real?"

He had liked the script, he said. But he added, "We're not going to do business. I won't submit an offer to any of my clients until the money's in the bank."

I assured him that, if a director was intrigued by the script, the money would be placed in trust within days of our pay-or-play offer. But he didn't know me. He wasn't buying it.

A classic catch-22. We couldn't get a creative package together without substantial money up front, and we couldn't raise the money until we had a creative package confirmed.

So we compromised. We found an affordable Canadian director, Daryl Duke. He was primarily a TV director, but he had made a low-budget movie called *Payday* that had shown off Rip Torn to good effect.

Then we sent the script to star after star. They all turned us down.

Finally Duke recommended Elliott Gould, whose reputation in Hollywood then was very low – he was a long way from hits like *M\*A\*S\*H* or *Bob & Carol & Ted & Alice*. But he was perfectly cast as the fall guy.

Duke and Gould were both clients of ICM, and Gilardi demanded that $500,000 U.S. be placed in a trust account with ICM to ensure that we would proceed with the film. Always the consummate pack-ager, Gilardi then offered us two other ICM clients, Susannah York and – second time for me – Christopher Plummer.

I raised the $500,000 from the Bank of Montreal, largely on my personal guarantee. Any further funds required would have to come from pre-selling selected foreign and ancillary rights and pledging the proceeds to the bank. This piecemeal, intricate, labour-intensive approach is what differentiates the independent producer, who has to hustle for capital, from the studios, with their pockets as deep as the Mindanao Trench.

We finalized our ICM package in time for Dick and me to take it to Cannes that May. We left Joel in L.A. to prepare the film.

We got lucky in Cannes. That year a new and hungry foreign-sales company called Carolco had been formed. The principals were two curious guys, as unHollywood as they come: Mario Kassar, an Italian-Lebanese who looked like a young Omar Sharif, and Andy Vajna, a shrewd, bearded Hungarian who was always suffering from psoriasis. No one quite understood where they got their money, but on the other hand no one cared either, so long as they had plenty, and they did. Later, Carolco would briefly become the leading foreign-sales company in the world and an integrated production company listed on the New York Stock Exchange. Then they got caught up in the wild inflation of the eighties, and, despite such hits as *Terminator II* and *Basic Instinct*, the company nearly went bankrupt in the early nineties. Kassar and Vajna split up. Today, it teeters on extinction.

After knocking heads for a while in Carolco's offices at the Hôtel Martinez, which overlooks La Croisette, Kassar and Vajna agreed to put up a guarantee of $1 million U.S. against our share of the proceeds from the sale of foreign rights, secured by a letter of credit issued by their bank, the Banque de la Méditerranée. Carolco would act as our agent for the world, with the exception of Canada and the United States.

We spent the entire night drafting the agreement in Dick's meticu-lous longhand and ran all over Cannes in the early hours trying to get it copied. It was executed before we left that day.

We came home riding the moon. Our bankers, however, were no closer to the moon than the ozone layer, and John Hill, the manager of the Yonge and Queen branch of the Bank of Montreal, who had gone out on a limb for me by arranging the $500,000, looked at our agreement askance. What the hell was the Banque de la Méditerranée? And who the hell were Kassar and Vajna?

Of course, we couldn't provide any references; we could hardly look into the future and tell him they would later get fabulously rich as the producers of the *Rambo* series, among others. Nevertheless, the bank ultimately accepted our letter of credit. This left us short about a million dollars.

The CFDC was prepared to advance about $250,000, but its rigid Canadian-content rules and production controls would have seriously impaired our ability to make the movie. So we turned them down.

Enter Jerry Banks, my old friend from law school, now a tax lawyer. He told me many of his partners and some of his clients needed tax shelters, and he came up with a novel structure that would give them what they wanted and satisfy the tax authorities as well.

It would work this way: We'd sell the investors a hundred units of ownership at $26,000 each. Each unit would consist of an irrevocable letter of credit and a $15,600 promissory note, personal to each investor, payable at a fixed rate of interest annually, the principal payable at the end of seven years whether or not the investment had been recouped. All the letters of credit and notes were to be discounted with the Bank of Montreal.

We were fully financed. But the administrative and legal aspects of the scheme caused our budget to rise by $400,000, to $2.6 million. And worse was in store. The interest on the notes, payable annually, had been pegged at 8 per cent. The economy was booming. I didn't know then that, before the seven years were up, the bank rate would climb as high as 22 per cent! And, as one of the personal guarantors of the loan, I would have to keep paying the bank the ever-increasing share of the differential between the current rate and the 8 per cent.

But I'm an optimist. I wouldn't have cared even if I had foreseen the rate climb. I was sure, so very sure, that *The Silent Partner* would rapidly recoup its negative cost by selling foreign rights and from the anticipated advance to be received from an attractive domestic distribution deal.

In August 1977 principal photography had started in Toronto's newest landmark, the Eaton Centre complex. As I had vowed, I was on the set every day. And right away I made an unnerving discovery. I had naïvely believed the tension on the set of *The Disappearance* was unique to that unfortunate venture; now I found out that there was going to be trench warfare on the set of *The Silent Partner* as well.

Within days I had come to another depressing conclusion: we had made the wrong choice as director. The major problem was that Duke wasn't shooting enough film to properly cover each scene. A thriller has to fit together as tightly as a jigsaw puzzle, and unless the director is a Hitchcock, who was reputed never to have shot an unnecessary frame, he needs to have lots of coverage to enable the editor to wring maximum tension from each scene. We had to make Duke shoot and reshoot. It was surely a first in production history – the money men begging the director to please, please shoot more film. It later turned out that Duke, instead of devoting his attention to our film, was worrying more about the fate of his local TV station in Vancouver, CKVU. So we went ten days over schedule and had to claw back our producers' fees to pay for it.

Fortunately we had a few superb craftspeople on the film, such as Billy Williams, the British cinematographer, and Trevor Williams, the expatriate Canadian set designer of Louis Malle's *Pretty Baby*. It was they who gave *The Silent Partner* its stylish professional look.

Principal photography ended in late September; contractually, Duke had sixty days to deliver his director's cut.

Our hopes were high when it finally arrived.

We screened it. And our hearts sank.

God help us, it was a mess. An incorrigible, hopeless mess. It was so bad that, after screening the cut, Joel, Stephen, Curtis, and I just stared at each other, stunned. We were – not to put too fine a word on it – terrified. Our $2.6-million movie had been turned into a shambles.

Our lines of credit were used up, interest costs were mounting daily. And now this.

Hadn't I sworn this would never happen again?

*In fact, post-production trauma was the norm; as my career as a producer unfolded, it became irritatingly clear that it was going to be a way of life for all my films. So be it.*

We screened the calamitous cut again and were appalled once more.

Duke came in and spent three days huddled in the editing room with George Appleby, our editor. When he emerged, he grimly handed us another cut.

It wasn't quite so bad. It wasn't calamitous. Only awful.

When Duke failed to show up at a meeting to discuss further changes, we elected to complete the film without him.

We had to find a new director to reshoot some scenes, an expert editor to recut the film, and more money.

But how?

I raised another $300,000 from the bank by more bullying and cajoling and persuading. This took our budget to $2.9 million. We recalled Elliott, photo-doubled Christopher and Susannah, and had Curtis direct three days of filming. Then we brought in David Bretherton, the Oscar-winning film editor who had cut *Cabaret*, to recut the film under Curtis's direction. And we called on Kenny Wannberg, a friend of Joel's who was music editor at Fox, to help the great Canadian jazz pianist Oscar Peterson score the film.

Considering all the obstacles, we ended up with a product that we felt was pretty good. But could we sell it?

Carolco came through with foreign sales of $1.3 million U.S., right on target. Now all we needed was a U.S. distributor.

It was now the middle of 1978, and there was no overwhelming enthusiasm among the U.S. majors for independently made English-language movies, especially Canadian ones; they were flush with product. The snide and carping attacks by Canadian nationalists on

American movies hardly helped. Only two Canadian movies, *The Apprenticeship of Duddy Kravitz* and *Meatballs*, were given full-scale U.S. distribution. Our only hope was to find a distributor who would fall in love with the movie.

In anticipation of a tough negotiating session that I surmised would soon end in a suitable deal, I booked in at the Beverly Wilshire, the comfortable, hacienda-style hotel (and home of the best, moistest coconut cake in the city) that was to be my L.A. home away from home. Poor Joel bicycled the film around from one distributor to another. "Bit violent, but I loved it," was a typical response. One day it was Peter Myers at Fox, the next day it was John Calley at Warner Brothers. Each time our hopes were raised, only to be dashed. We couldn't understand it – they loved it but then they didn't want it. Then Paramount screened the film. Michael Eisner, the company's chairman (and later CEO of Walt Disney Co.), along with Jeffrey Katzenberg, head of acquisitions (and later chairman of Disney Motion Pictures), were really turned on. Negotiations were strenuous but promising. Both parties were sure we were close to an agreement when we broke off for the July 4 holiday. We had gone through three drafts of the distribution agreement and were all set to sign the final version, but Eisner said, "We'll clean it up right after the long weekend." Too bad. Over the weekend his wife had a baby, and his mind wandered away from deals. Early Tuesday I got a call from Dick Zimbert, head of business affairs at Paramount: Eisner would pass.

I hit bottom. Eighteen months of unremitting toil and effort – not to mention the huge financial risk – and for what? Was I destined to be denied forever a successful producing role in the movie business?

The picture was released in the United States by a marginal distributor and was sold to pay TV. The reviews were good (a number of them mentioning the shocking decapitation scene Hanson had included in the final cut, in which a body was dragged over the jagged glass of a shattered aquarium, severing the head). Today *The Silent Partner* is a cult movie. A few years ago Sheila Benson of the Los Angeles *Times* called it "one of the best films of the '70s." In Canada the movie won six Canadian Film Awards, including Best Picture, and grossed nearly $2 million, a breakthrough in Canada. It recovered 70 per cent of its cost. The investors, with their tax benefits, ended up okay, but Joel and I took a bath. So it was dispiriting to learn in 1984 that a number of investors had defaulted on their obligations to pay up on their promissory notes. They were sued – successfully.

Even before the débâcle was over, I was involved in a new project. This time, I thought, I'll get it right.

Not so.

*The Changeling*, my next movie, would bring me perilously close to financial disaster.

# CHAPTER

## ON THE BRINK

*I remember snapshot images. I remember Friday, December 1, 1978, late, very late at night. I was staring out the windows of my sixty-ninth floor office, staring into the black canyons of Bay Street, staring blindly into the abyss. About forty floors below me in the same building were the lights from the offices of the Bank of Montreal, but they were hardly beacons of hope. The bank's executives and lawyers were waiting for my surrender. I had to raise $2 million before dawn or I was finished in the movie business. To say nothing of likely personal insolvency.*

*Only a few weeks later I was upstairs at Sardi's in New York, my stomach in a knot, desperately fearful of the reviews that would make or break my first foray into the theatre world of Broadway.*

*And a few weeks after that . . . another roll of the dice and construction crews were starting work in the snarl and tangle of a bizarre and ridiculous space underneath the ramp of a parking garage, and in a few weeks we would open an eighteen-screen movie complex on the site that everyone said would make us the laughingstock of the industry.*

*These things were all happening at once. Crisis as a way of life.*

*I would go home and Pearl would stare at me, shaking her head in disbelief. When she married me, at least she hadn't married dull.*

*But through it all, the drumroll of optimism kept breaking through the clattering of the naysayers.*

*I knew I could succeed. It was only a matter of time.*

*The Changeling* started off well. It was Diana Maddox who had come across Russell Hunter's literally haunting story about an important American political family with a skeleton in its closet. To ensure that the family's great fortune would be passed on intact, the sickly infant who stood to inherit it had been murdered in his bath and a healthy child put in his place. Joel bought the rights to the story and asked Diana to shape it into a thirty-page treatment. I found it mesmerizing. And it smelled right. It had been years since there had been a great modern ghost story, or at least one that didn't involve the gimmick of demonic possession. So the timing seemed terrific.

By now Joel and I had formed a partnership under the umbrella of Tiberius Productions. We were intent on staying in Canada, where we could make films using the much cheaper Canadian dollar and also avoid the huge Hollywood studio overheads.

Diana was our dramaturge. In one of those twists of fortune so common in the industry, she had once been selected as the original star of *The Boy Friend*, but she fell ill, and Julie Andrews took her place. Diana went on to join Canada's Stratford Festival and then became a respected director at San Diego's Old Globe Theatre and L.A.'s Mark Taper Forum. She is a fascinating, complex person, wildly intelligent, with an acute understanding of drama, but also dogmatic and arbitrary. From time to time her dogmatism caused some tension between Joel and me.

*The Changeling* was to be offered to the public as a tax shelter, so, mindful of the Canadian-content guidelines, we hired two scriptwriters, American Allan Scott and Canadian Christopher Bryant. They had previously collaborated on the screenplay of the impressive *Don't Look Now*, starring Donald Sutherland and Julie Christie, but the script they delivered to us bore no resemblance to Diana's engrossing treatment. We then took a shot on an all-Canadian collaboration between Diana, under the pseudonym of Adrian Morall, and Bill Gray, a Canadian-born writer who had worked for me years before on *Impact*. They came up with a suspenseful script, but it featured supernatural phenomena that would call for some very expensive special effects. A three-storey Victorian mansion was going to have to be burned down and an empty wheelchair, driven by a psychic force, was going to chase a terrified woman down corridors and stairways at unnatural speeds. These may have been everyday effects for a Hollywood studio, but they were well beyond accepted norms for Canada.

After my frustrating experiences with getting *The Silent Partner* distributed, I was absolutely determined to sew up a U.S. distribution deal with one of the majors. This meant we had to have the calibre of star no distributor could refuse. A million-dollar star.

Diana had been an acting coach to Richard Dreyfuss, and he came very close to accepting our offer. At the same time we had sent a script to George C. Scott, offering him the film's secondary role of the U.S. senator. Scott liked the script, but he wanted to play the protagonist, the widowed professor who rents the house haunted by the murdered child. He also insisted that his wife, Trish Van Devere, be given a role in the film. It was an all-or-nothing matter – and one we felt we couldn't refuse. When the late Melvyn Douglas was signed to play the senator, the package was complete.

Once again the Canadian press reacted with disbelief, almost with outrage. What was Garth Drabinsky doing now? Why was he paying an American a million U.S. dollars to star in a Canadian film?

What always gets overlooked in these arguments – which are essentially political – is the quality and reputation of the talent. I would have been hailed as a hero, apparently, if I had hired an unknown Canadian who would have done nothing whatsoever for the film, either during the financing or afterwards at the box office. Instead, I went for a terrific actor with great pedigree.

Scott's work in *Patton* had not been a fluke. He was a disciplined actor, with the superb ability to do five takes of the same scene, each one letter perfect and each one virtually identical, except for a slight nuance he introduced into each – a flare of the nostril, a twitch of the eyebrow, tiny gestures that affected the emotional tone of the scene in minute ways. Of course, we were warned that he drank savagely. His contretemps with Ava Gardner in Italy in 1966, during the shooting of John Huston's *The Bible*, still reverberated in the industry. But I couldn't see any value in these warnings. We had also been warned that Elliott Gould was trouble and Christopher Plummer was notoriously stubborn. Forewarned is forearmed. With heavy doses of tact and diplomacy, Joel and I had no trouble with any of these strong characters once we made it clear that we were independent producers who didn't have access to unlimited levels of financing. Most of them were in any case utterly disdainful of the studios, where reckless spending was the norm. I remember only one instance where Scott's temper showed. That was during a press conference on Vancouver Island where he suddenly hissed at a particularly obnoxious journalist, "I want you off the island."

Scott aside, we had managed to line up some pretty impressive Canadian talent. We were always scouring the world for expatriate Canadians who had achieved a measure of success in the industry and yet were willing to return to Canada. By this time it was well known that we were producers who refused to accept shoddy artistic compromises urged on us for political reasons, and I believe that's why we attracted such good people and why the films we made were so different from the others being made in Canada at the time.

Trevor Williams came back as set designer, and I was lucky enough to get John Coquillon, who had been working in England for Sam Peckinpah, as our cinematographer. But finding a Canadian director remained a problem. We really didn't have anyone at the time who could handle this kind of big-budget, big-special-effects, big-star movie. We ended up making a deal with Donald Cammell, a British director who had done some excellent work on *The Demon Seed*. He flew to New York to talk to Scott, they hit it off, and we were all set.

Or so we thought.

We had toyed with setting the story in Canada but rejected it. The plot demanded a heavyweight villain, someone with the political clout of a U.S. senator. Somehow a Canadian senator seemed merely venal, not villainous. So we planned to shoot the movie in Vancouver, disguised as Seattle.

By July 1978 Trevor Williams was already involved in pre-production work on the movie's centrepiece, the exterior of a Victorian Gothic mansion, and on the interior sets. But soon after Cammell was signed, he announced he wasn't satisfied with Vancouver as the location. Cammell didn't like the atmosphere. He didn't want to make the movie on a set in a soundstage. He thought it would be much spookier if the film was shot in an actual house. Now, it's much easier to control costs on a set than on location, but if we had to, the most financially feasible location was the Toronto area. Cammell and Trevor went to Oakville, Ontario, and got excited about a cockamamy little cottage on the waterfront, an unspooky building completely lacking Gothic potential. I became uneasy as I projected a ballooning budget, without enhancement of production values. I remember saying to Joel, "This is not going in the right direction."

When Cammell showed signs of wanting to tamper with the script, it was the last straw. Exit Cammell. It turned out to be an expensive dismissal, because the Directors' Guild of America decided that he had been arbitrarily fired and fined us $80,000.

Now, only twelve weeks before principal photography was scheduled to start, we were once more looking for a director, one who would stick with the Vancouver location. We were lucky. The Hungarian Peter Medak, who had directed Peter O'Toole in *The Ruling Class*, a brilliant film, became available. After rescreening the O'Toole movie, we concluded that Medak well understood how camera movement could be used to terrify the audience. Peter was only thirty-two and entirely lovable, sounding more like Zsa Zsa Gabor than a tough-minded director (it was always "dollink" this and "dollink" that), but he could also – an important point – command the respect of a powerful leading actor (the memory of Donald Sutherland was still tucked in the back of my skull).

We recreated the interior of the mansion on a soundstage at Vancouver's Panorama Studios. It was pretty spectacular. For the exterior, a three-storey facade, all gingerbread and cornices and curlicues in the Victorian manner, was built onto the front of an old house that was about to be pulled down. The physical production cost around $1 million, but it would have cost three times as much in the United States. No representative of a U.S. distributor who visited the set could understand how we were able to achieve this standard on a budget that was still almost negligible by Hollywood standards.

Never mind, by Canadian standards the budget was enormous.

To finance *The Silent Partner*, we had sold units to private investors, mainly wealthy lawyers and their clients. *The Changeling*'s budget was $5.5 million, by far the most expensive Canadian film ever made, and we knew we would never be able to raise that much by a private placement. That meant we were going to have to sell units to the general public, and this could only be done by way of a prospectus filed with the Ontario Securities Commission (OSC). I was the first to use this method of financing, which would become the model that Canadian film producers would emulate in the future. Every conceivable cost and expense had to be nailed down if the prospectus was to pass the OSC's intense scrutiny. We had to build in not only a higher contingency allowance, but all the underwriters' fees, commissions, extra legal fees, and so on. And since we were borrowing money against promissory notes secured by letters of credit, current interest payments had to be made part of the budget as well. A quick estimate suggested that our budget would now escalate to between $6.5 million and $7 million. This was out of sight in Canadian terms.

There had never been in Canada a prospectus cleared for a motion picture before, and the OSC behaved like a mother hen. Because of the growing attraction of tax shelters, the OSC was, however, happy to see the financing of films begin to be subjected to the discipline imposed by a prospectus and seemed particularly pleased that I, who had just won the Canadian Best Picture Award for *The Silent Partner*, was going to lead the way. But I couldn't do it alone. I needed an investment dealer with a substantial pool of capital to call on.

I turned once more to Jerry Banks for his help, and Jerry introduced me to someone who would subsequently become my great friend and trusted partner in every venture I undertook – Myron Gottlieb. Myron was then president of Merit Investment Corporation, a medium-sized brokerage house in downtown Toronto that specialized in institutional clients. He was certainly the youngest such president on Bay Street, and he was a fighter. Myron had founded Merit in 1977, when he and a group of associates broke away from N. L. Sandler. In the ensuing years he had established an impeccable reputation on Bay Street and a network of important relationships. According to Jerry, Myron was the next thing to a magician, and if the financing was possible, Myron would pull it off.

Imagine my surprise, then, when I met Myron and he turned out to be a boyish-faced man just a few years older than I, with a soft voice and a very sweet smile, always a few pounds comfortably overweight. He told me some time later that his uncle was Max Tanenbaum, the legendary Toronto industrialist, and this I loved. Max was never a cultured man, but he was nevertheless a Canadian financial legend. He had an instinct for making money and had amassed a fortune in real estate, steel, and the stock market. I got to know Max very well, and when I looked closely at Myron, I realized that he had a lot of Max's facial expressions, body language, and other characteristics.

We hit it off right away. Myron would eventually leave Merit and join me at Cineplex Odeon as vice-chairman and chief administrative officer, and in 1989 we would battle MCA together and go on to co-found Livent, our live-theatre company. We meshed well as partners; he's pensive where I'm passionately expressive. But in one way he's like me – he won't stop until he's got what he wants, any more than I will.

The prospectus was ready by August. It was a simple, if historic, document in movie-financing terms. The $6.6-million offering consisted of 264 units of ownership at $25,000 each. For each unit purchased, the investor had to deposit a letter of credit in the amount of $5,000 that could be cashed on closing. In addition, he had to provide an interest-bearing four-year note to cover the additional $20,000, secured by a second letter of credit. For the initial outlay of $25,000, an investor in the 60 per cent tax bracket could realize a reduction in

A year old, already a poser

McClorkin Photo Studio

Brother Shelley (left) at 3, me at 6, my father, Philip, and my mother, Ethel (Waldman)

(Above) Shelley (left), the dreamer of exotic dreams, me, and the future boss of Film House, baby Cyril

Me at my bar mitzvah, 1962

(Above)
At Camp Rockwood, near Orillia, 1964. I am in the centre of the back row.

"How Drabinsky Loves Kids." The politics of hokum: the staged picture that helped me win the Student Council presidency at my high school, North Toronto Collegiate, in 1967.

"My Three Sons." My father, Philip (third from left), with me, Cyril (second from left), and Shelley at Cyril's wedding, June 17, 1982

(Below) Pearl and me at our wedding, 1971

With Pearl and Marc at Sun Valley, Idaho

(Below) With my insouciant daughter, Alicia, at her bat mitzvah, 1988

(Above) With Alicia
and Pearl at Marc's bar
mitzvah, 1991

Mom and Dad,
a.k.a. "Fred and Ginger"

My self-assured son,
Marc, at 13

(Below) Alicia and Pearl
at home

At a rare moment of
relaxation, in Whistler,
B.C.

(Below)
Garth Drabinsky, current
edition

taxable income of $15,000 in the year of his investment. The film's earnings would be taxed as income when received by the investor, but in the meantime the investor had his tax savings available for other investments. The expectation was that the investor would recoup his entire investment before the note matured at the end of the fourth year.

By the time the prospectus was approved, Myron, true to his reputation, had lined up a raft of commitments amounting to $4.5 million, based only on the tantalizing information in the preliminary prospectus. Carolco, once again our foreign-sales representative, had generated almost $2 million at Cannes earlier in the year, out of only a portion of the foreign territories available.

Everything was looking so hopeful that I didn't watch my back.

*Why don't Canadians like people to succeed, to be first, to do something unusual or original? The stories that drifted in were hurtful and bewildering. What had I done to arouse such animosity? I was only twenty-nine! But they seemed to resent the fact that a young man could have come to the forefront of the industry so quickly, in just a couple of years, so apparently easily. But there they were, people like Bill Marshall, a co-founder of Toronto's Festival of Festivals, with their knives drawn. They wanted to discredit me, discredit my prospectus, discredit my financing, discredit my movie – I was being swamped in negativity.*

One day I got a call from Doug MacDonald, from whom I would eventually buy Film House. Doug owed me nothing – I hadn't even taken *The Silent Partner* to Film House for processing. But he was a decent man, and he loved movies and wished the Canadian film industry well.

He spoke quietly into the phone. "There's a guy by the name of Ian Brown [most recently the host of a CBC Radio public-affairs show] who's gonna call you. He's been out all over the place asking a lot of questions, and from the sounds of those questions, he's going to do an enormous hatchet job on you and the prospectus. I don't want to see this happen."

Sure enough, Ian Brown, who was then working for *Maclean's* magazine, interviewed me in the last week of October 1978. He was a pale, supercilious young man, who came in and listened to my answers with a bored expression. Then he went back to his cubicle at *Maclean's*, ignored everything I had told him, and created instead the most vivid piece of libel ever directed at me.

He didn't quite call me a thief and a cheat. But the piece was riddled with exactly those innuendoes.

I was tipped off as to when *Maclean's* was going to run the piece (November 6), so I went up to the magazine's printing plant at Yonge Street and Highway 401 late Sunday evening as the magazine was coming off the press. I got hold of a worker, who didn't know who I was, and I said, "I think there's an article in there on me. Do you mind letting me see a copy?"

As I hastily scanned what Brown had written, I felt a sickness in the pit of my stomach. The article was peppered with spiteful personal asides, "Garth Drabinsky lets a hint of joviality sprint across his resentful jowls, . . ." " 'You know,' he drawls, with the accent of a weekend New Yorker, 'this deal will be historic, . . .' " "Drabinsky is where he has always wanted to be: arrogant and unpopular, but finally in a position to make the Canadian film industry the commercial success story it has never been – or kill it. . . . He is unrepentantly belligerent."

The real damage lay not in these cheap shots but in the allegation that, unbeknownst to the investors, I was taking almost $2 million, or a third of the budget, in fees.

Drabinsky currently commands investors' attention and his fellow producers' ire because of the $6.6-million public offering of 264 $25,000 *Changeling* "units" he squeezed past the Ontario Securities Commission last month. . . . The Drabinsky prospectus raises questions in the mind of Terry Marlow, Clarkson Gordon's tax partner, who believes "*The Changeling* will be okay for the tax ruling. But how sound is the investment?" Drabinsky's fellow producers are privately "horrified" with Garth's prospectus. Citing an unproven script, George C. Scott's failure to repeat the box office draw of *Patton* and the absence of distribution guarantees, one producer feels Drabinsky "isn't giving his investors enough chance to get their money back." What he is doing instead, many feel, is taking a lot of money up front in his diverse and perhaps conflicting roles as co-producer ($225,000 with another $50,000 deferred), lawyer (a portion of $917,000 designated for legal fees) and distributor ($750,000 estimated for Canadian film rental rights alone). . . . . *Outrageous* producer Bill Marshall believes the failure of Drabinsky's movie would decimate the industry by destroying the fledgling confidence of investors.

It was easy to dismiss the article as ignorant – what script, after all, is proven before the movie's made? Moreover, the estimate of my fees was grossly exaggerated. As it turned out, Joel and I once again had to turn back the entire producers' fee of $450,000 so we could complete the picture after it went over budget. We were plagued by soaring interest rates and a falling Canadian dollar when a substantial portion of the budget was to be paid in U.S. funds. The most superficial research would have revealed how rigorously the osc had scrutinized our prospectus, particularly because film production was thought to be such a volatile business.

Even the photograph that accompanied the article was a setup. If I had been a little older and wiser, I would have seen the photographer, Brian Willer, coming, because he kept asking me to take up poses calculated to make me look as unflattering as possible.

As a personal matter, what was said about me was hurtful and obviously distressing to my family and friends. Allan Scott, one of the original scriptwriters on *The Changeling*, wrote a letter that *Maclean's* published, saying, "Garth Drabinsky's jowls are never, as you describe, resentful. I have studied them at close quarters during several script meetings . . . and found them to be zestful, insouciant, winning, waterlogged, picturesque and uncommitted, but never resentful. Of course, he's a clever fellow. It's possible his jowls took on this interesting appearance because he anticipated the hatchet job your writer would subsequently write."

The real question was, however, how badly this libel would undermine me in business and, specifically, how it would affect the sale of
units in *The Changeling*, now in full swing.

At nine o'clock the next morning, still stunned and perplexed by
the bizarre viciousness of the attack, I was on the phone to Peter
Newman, who was then editor of *Maclean's*. I had met him a few
times and thought of him as a friend; in those days he had not yet
achieved prominence as a chronicler of Canada's rich and famous
through his best-seller *The Canadian Establishment*.

I came straight to the point, "Peter, this article is going to ruin me.
It's game over for *The Changeling* underwriting."

"What can I do?" he asked. He said he hadn't seen the article
because he had been out of the country when the magazine went to
press.

Then he added the classic response of any editor against a charge
of irresponsible journalism. "You know I have to support my writer."

I was angry. "So I'll sue your magazine and you. This article is
going to cause me incalculable millions of dollars of damage."

Peter hung up but called me back shortly and said, "I've spoken to
my lawyers. We won't retract the article. We'll distribute the issue. But
I will write you a letter. What else can I do now?"

I was insistent. I said, "In that letter, you'd better attest to my
integrity, my honesty, to everything this article says I don't have. And
you can apologize and acknowledge the damage the article could
cause me. I've got to be able to read that letter to my investors."

Whether out of a sense of guilt or to sustain our friendship, Peter
did what he was told and more. He wrote me a letter that exceeded my
wildest expectations, as well as those of my lawyer, Laurie Mandel.
Essentially he cut off Ian Brown at the knees by volunteering the
admission that yes, the article did contain gross misrepresentations.
Now I had a letter from the magazine's editor that was diametrically
opposed to the contents of the article. That was at least something.

Fearing a backlash from investors, I called Joel, who was in New
York preparing for the initial four-day shoot there in December, and
asked him to come to Toronto to talk strategy. At Toronto's Pearson

airport, Joel, who is really a saintly soul, was closely scrutinized by the customs inspector and then strip-searched on suspicion of cocaine possession. Things were really deteriorating.

The article hit the newsstands and, overnight, selling stopped on units of *The Changeling*. It was now November 6 and principal photography was only four weeks away. All of our corporate lines of credit were exhausted. I had issued a $1-million pay-or-play commitment to George C. Scott, and pre-production was steaming ahead on the strength of my personal credit. Literally thousands of dollars were being spent daily at a time when the financing was in utter jeopardy. Myron came to me, his face flushed, looking shaken. "Somehow, we'll weather the storm. We'll make it happen."

He hadn't managed to sell out the issue by the required closing date. He was able to generate only about $4.5 million of the $6.5 million we needed. My anger at Brown and *Maclean's* exploded. I instructed Laurie Mandel to sue the magazine for the perfectly round sum of $10 million, then the largest defamation suit ever begun in Canada.

*The money was one thing, the hurt to my business substantial. But what I can never forgive is the malice. So why do they do it? What deep source of insecurity drives these people? Why do they like hurting others?*

*In the depths of the moment, I would wonder: When they look in their shaving mirrors in the morning, what do they see? In their secret moments, do they loathe the face that stares back at them? Or do they shave blind, terrified the razor will cut too deep, too far, if they scrutinize their image too deeply?*

In any event, the *Maclean's* article did a thorough job. The Bank of Montreal, which had issued its financing commitment letter after reading the prospectus, now became instantly anxious. Remember, this is the bank that our law firm, Roberts and Drabinsky, was still representing on condo mortgage financing. But after reading *Maclean's*, the bank refused to advance a single dollar against its commitment until all the units were sold and pledged to the bank as security. Counselled by Fraser & Beatty (who have always been a thorn in my side; they would represent MCA in their dealings with my company in 1989), the bank was intransigent. And we couldn't sell the units.

On Monday, December 4, we were to start the four-day shoot in New York. The opening shot was to be a fabulous sweeping camera move as George C. Scott's character leaves the Juilliard School of Music, from which he has just resigned as a professor, and walks on a cold, drizzly, dark December day through Lincoln Center Plaza on his way to his apartment, where he is to pack up and leave for Seattle. His wife and daughter have just been killed in a car accident, which is why he is seeking out a new life and what makes him susceptible to the parapsychological events that follow.

On December 1 Scott's lawyer called to remind me that Scott wouldn't turn up on Monday unless $1 million was in his bank account.

I was in despair. There was so much at stake. My future in film production was pegged to this movie. But the Bank of Montreal refused to advance the money. They sat on the sidelines watching, unmoved by my plight.

I had to raise $2 million immediately. The money would be repaid out of the eventual sale of the still-unsold units, for both Myron and I believed that sales would surface in late December as investors started to scurry for end-of-year tax-shelter opportunities. But that prospect was no help to me now. And I had exhausted my own personal lines of credit.

I began to make urgent phone calls. I had three possible sources. There were my cousins, the Kives of K-Tel, who had already become investors in Tiberius, the company that had to date financed a portion of pre-production. There was the very shrewd Max Tanenbaum, who was willing to lend at least $1 million, but at a hefty price. Max was a shooter. And of course there was my mentor, Nat Taylor, who was already in his Palm Beach retreat for the winter.

I needed a decision soon, instantly, right now. Our offices that Friday were crowded. Everyone was there: Myron; Jerry Banks; my younger brother, Cyril, who had just joined our firm; my personal assistant of five years, my devoted gatekeeper, and right hand, Margaret Livingston; and, well, just about everyone else who worked for us. You could hardly breathe for the tension. Pizzas poured in and cartons overflowed with hot and cold Chinese food. But I don't remember eating. All I could think of was the fast-approaching deadline.

And then the miracle happened. With a phone call to his bank, Nat Taylor lent me $1 million. By midnight K-Tel came in for the other $1 million. At two o'clock in the morning we rushed downstairs to an incredulous Bank of Montreal, our commitments in hand. We had secured the bridge capital necessary to close the public financing.

But George C. Scott still didn't have the money in his hands. Panic! The Kives again to the rescue. Raymond got the Bank of Minneapolis to open its doors on a Saturday, something the bank had never done before, and to certify a $1-million cheque for Scott. Then a K-Tel employee flew to New York and handed the cheque to Scott's lawyer.

And on Monday shooting began.

*The Changeling* opened to fair-to-good reviews and grossed $3 million in Canada, winning the Golden Reel Award for the highest-grossing Canadian picture of the year, and it grossed a respectable $15 million in the United States, where it was also sold to Home Box Office (HBO). It went on to win six Canadian Film Awards, including one for Best Picture, which was presented to me by Jack Lemmon, who was in town making the Joel-and-Garth-produced movie *Tribute*. That same afternoon, *Maclean's* settled with me, their lawyers reckoning that, once the awards were announced, they would have to cough up even more. They gave me $75,000 in settlement and agreed to print the apology Dick wrote, which he made sure was the most abject imaginable.

Later Joel and I were told by the composer Kenny Wannberg that Steven Spielberg screened *The Changeling* two or three times before he produced *Poltergeist*, because he was so impressed by the way the psychic effects had been handled, and Martin Scorsese recently requested a print to go into his personal collection of movies at the Museum of Modern Art in New York.

On the practical side, the movie was released by Sir Lew Grade in the United States, and the business it did in Canada indicated to me that it would have grossed around $25 million to $30 million U.S. had it received a major release there. It did recoup about 60 per cent of its total cost to the investors, who again in this case had enjoyed substantial tax-shelter benefits. That didn't, however, prevent a small group of investors from bringing a lawsuit charging the producers with fraud, because, it was alleged, we knew that the budget was going to be exceeded at the time we let them buy their units. The case would drag on for twelve years, until it was finally dismissed by the Ontario Court of Appeal in September 1994. For Joel and me, the emotional wear and tear was enormous, to say nothing of the legal fees.

Nevertheless, the episode closed on a happy note, with a memory of Max Tanenbaum. I loved Max. He was a larger-than-life personality housed in a hulking, bearlike frame, who treated life with all the gusto he believed it deserved. If you ever saw Max gulping a Shopsy's corned-beef sandwich in three bites, you would never have believed that he was at that time the leading Jewish industrialist in Canada. Max became in the end our biggest investor in *The Changeling*, and he was so totally supportive that I wanted to do something special for him.

So one day early in 1979 I said, "Max, I'm going to give you and Anne [his wife] a thrill. We're going to fly to England together, and you're going to come and see the scoring of *The Changeling*."

Max didn't know what I was talking about.

He was even more bewildered when we climbed aboard a British Airways jumbo jet and sat in first class. Max, who was then worth around $200 million and change, had never flown first class before. But before he could complain about the extravagance, the caviar was served. When we got to London, Joel and I checked him into the Intercontinental, off Park Lane. Max was scandalized when he learned we were putting Anne and him up in a $400-a-night room.

But he was in his element at our first English dinner together. Joel and I were jetlagged and ate lightly. Max, who loved to eat, knocked off his steak in a few minutes. "Are you finished?" he asked me, and when I nodded, he took his fork and, leaning over, stuck it into my half-eaten steak, pulled my plate over in front of him, and dug in again. When he had cleaned off my plate, he did the same to Joel's.

*What an appetite! What a man! What an antidote to the whiners, the little people!*

# CHAPTER

**VI**

## NADA, NOTHING, ZERO, ZIP

From the safe haven of hindsight I now look back on the turmoil of 1978 with some bemusement. It now seems ridiculous, amazing, foolhardy, mad – call it what you will – but within a few weeks of edging close to the precipice in funding *The Changeling*, I was teetering on the brink all over again. Around midnight on December 21, 1978, I was upstairs at Sardi's, nervously waiting for the critics' verdict on the $2.5-million *A Broadway Musical* that I had co-produced on Broadway.

I hadn't meant to get involved with a project of this size while I was still struggling to get *The Silent Partner* into distribution and at the same time up to my neck in the pre-production and financing problems of *The Changeling*. They just all happened to merge at the same time.

*Why? Partly because my enthusiasm propels me to seize an opportunity when it presents itself. But I also know that deep down I fear a window shutting, a door closing, a path disappearing. I'm afraid I'll be shut out, standing with my nose pressed to the locked door, hearing but being unable to reach the cheerful buzz of success on the other side. I'm afraid that if I fail to grasp an opportunity to do something, I might never get another.*

The year had started off well. Early in the morning of May 15 I stood beside the obstetrician, watching transfixed as he helped my son, Marc, into the world. I had been ecstatic three years before when my daughter, Alicia, was born, and I loved the child profoundly, fiercely. Still, the traditionalist in me wanted a son to perpetuate the family name and to stand beside me proudly at synagogue as I had stood so often beside my father. Now, as Marc was born, I felt completely fulfilled.

That evening, in a celebratory mood, I went to the opening of *By Strouse*, a musical revue with a cast of four that I had produced at the Theatre in the Dell in Toronto.

The timing seemed to me felicitous, a good omen – a new theatrical child born the same day as my son. The future seemed full of potential. By this time I had what I think was a realistic assessment of my own abilities. I knew that my talent and pleasure came from grasping a possibility and then exploiting the hell out of it. Perhaps, it's true, my ambition was a little too lofty for a young man not yet thirty, but I really did aspire to influence the cultural life of my own city and country, and I believed I had the ability to do it.

Getting involved in live theatre was all part of this dream. Not that I was welcomed into the small, closed world of Canadian theatre. Even before the *Maclean's* attack on me, I was having to battle the naysayers and the carpers. I was portrayed in the press as abrasive, brassy, and hard – nothing but a hustler. As my activities attracted more and more attention, I noticed that the circle of close friends who really cared about me seemed to grow smaller. The sense of growing isolation was hurtful.

*I look back on it all now with more detachment. To some degree, it was a question of style. I was "hard" in the sense that I was relentless in pursuit of an idea. I was "abrasive" when I sensed those around me giving in too easily, making second-rate compromises, fading to gray. I suppose "brassy" could be a fair description. But all my opponents saw was the push; they didn't see the main thing – the idea that this pushiness was in aid of, that this pushiness served. They missed the fact that I always demanded only the best, that I set very high standards for myself*

*as well as for my associates. And they also missed – and if it seems boast-*
*ful I can't help it – that my artistic taste was, in general, fully formed.*
*Above all, they missed what I wanted – which was to produce good art*
*for a lot of people.*

My first venture into theatrical production had been two years earlier, in 1976. It's hard now to remember how barren the Toronto theatrical scene was then. There was no Roy Thomson Hall, no restored Elgin & Winter Garden Theatres, no restored Pantages Theatre. There was an inventory of small alternative theatres that operated out of garages and warehouses and concentrated on new and experimental Canadian work; there was the O'Keefe Centre, with its overpowering dimensions; and there was the Royal Alexandra Theatre, which booked mostly touring bus and truck companies from the United States and Britain. Other than Johnny Bassett's one-year run of *Hair* in 1969, there was no locally produced commercial theatre to speak of. Indeed, a cultural vacuum existed, and for me, it represented a real opportunity.

It was then a truism that Toronto was being deprived of first-class theatre. A play would become a hit in London and on Broadway, but Toronto had to wait for years to see it, and then by way of a second-rate touring company. I wondered why. Why couldn't a local producer put together a Toronto version of one of these shows as soon as it became a critical and commercial success elsewhere? The only chance for a Canadian producer was to persuade whoever held the rights that a sit-down Canadian production would earn more than a touring production, and thus the total take by way of royalties and net profits would be greater. To do this, a show would have to be given an open-ended run in a theatre of no less than one thousand seats. And that was exactly what Toronto didn't have. The big theatres were not available. The Royal Alex was run on subscription and the O'Keefe had to keep blocks of time open for the National Ballet and the Canadian Opera Company.

Still, I refused to be deterred by such obstacles, and in 1976 I got together with Moses Znaimer, president of CITY-TV and one of its founders. He was an early proponent of the studio-free TV station and a man with an inventive and innovative intelligence. We accepted an offer from Jonathan Stanley, of the tiny New Theatre, to co-produce *Travesties*, Tom Stoppard's multi-award-winning play that was the snob hit of both the West End and Broadway. No tour for it had been planned. Here seemed a chance to prove my point. We rented the only feasible space, the St. Lawrence Centre theatre, with its eight hundred and fifty seats and zero ambience. The St. Lawrence, a publicly built space, was an aesthetic disaster. It looked like a high-school auditorium gone wrong. The whole thing was a drab grey, leaving the impression that a cement mixer had come in with the nozzle jammed in the "open" position. It was as hostile to patrons as a theatre could possibly be.

We didn't lose our entire investment, but without an open-ended run, which we couldn't get, we didn't make a profit either. Our three-week limited run of *Travesties* at the St. Lawrence did 80 per cent at the box office, but just as the box office was building to a break-even level, we had to close.

So it could be done! If we had been able to run as long as the box-office results warranted, we would have made money.

This modest success whetted my appetite. In the fall of 1977, Moses and I took out an option on the Canadian rights to *Golda*, William Gibson's play about Golda Meir, which was shortly to open on Broadway, starring Anne Bancroft and directed by Arthur Penn. We made a hurried exit when the production bombed after tryouts in Boston and Baltimore. I was left feeling frustrated and so, when I met Broadway producer Norman Kean that year, I found myself drawn into a far-more-ambitious scheme.

Norman was in many ways an archetypal small-time Broadway producer. He lived on the fringe and on his nerves. Theatre folk wisdom says that all producers are crazy, that they have to be. Why else would they gamble on such long shots as hit shows? I didn't really believe it, but Norman was the cliché incarnate. He was frenetic, compulsive, and insecure about everything, including, as it turned out, his wife, Gwyda Donhowe. This would become tragically clear a decade later when, in a jealous rage, he stabbed his wife thirty-two times, killing her while she slept. Seven hours after that he went to the roof of his apartment house, laid his glasses down on the parapet, and jumped fifteen storeys to his death. He was found by the police and his fourteen-year-old son, David. Norman had planned the whole thing meticulously: he had prepared a tape of directions to his executors, an apology to his son, and a chronicle of his despair.

In 1977, of course, I had no inkling of Norman's ultimate fate. To me, in spite of his eccentricities, he had drive, enthusiasm, energy, and a total commitment to the theatre. Sometimes he was illogical, sometimes dictatorial, and I certainly thought him neurotic. But it never crossed my mind that he was psychopathic. On the contrary, he had what I thought was a pretty cool approach to the consistently nerve-racking business of theatre. He used to say, "I like to have fun and make money, and not necessarily in that order."

*Oh! Calcutta!* gave Norman both. He had bought the rights to the notorious nude revue in the early seventies, after it had lost most of its original lustre and the intellectual pretensions given it by the British critic Kenneth Tynan, who had conceived the idea of the show, and after the contributions of some of its illustrious contributors, like Jules Feiffer and John Lennon, had been forgotten. Norman moved it into the five-hundred-seat Edison, a mildewed theatre he had recently purchased. *Oh! Calcutta!* became Norman's cash cow, bringing in a $12,000 weekly profit. He used to call it his young son's pension plan. All he had to do was keep advertising the show aggressively to tourists, particularly the Japanese, who filled the theatre each week. A nude revue, moreover, doesn't require much artistic maintenance. Every six months or so he would substantially recast it. Several famous show-business names got their start in *Oh! Calcutta!*: Bill Macy of *Maude*, Allan Rachins of *L.A. Law*, Margo Sappington the choreographer, Bruce Dern, and Canadians Richard Monette, now artistic director of Ontario's Stratford Festival, and actress Domini Blythe.

I met Norman in 1977 because Dick and I represented Hillard Elkins, the show's original producer, who wanted to make a movie of

*Oh! Calcutta!* with Canadian tax dollars. I went to see Norman about a copyright problem, and the moment I stepped into his office, I was hooked. Tucked away above the Edison's auditorium, Norman's office was windowless, airless, and piled high with scripts, programs, and brochures. My eye went immediately to the framed show posters on the walls and, most of all, to the pictures of opening nights and parties at Sardi's. In the middle of the chaos was Norman in shirtsleeves, his glasses askew, feverishly working the phones.

It seemed only moments before he had whisked me down to the Ballroom in Soho to see his production of *By Strouse.* This was a refreshing musical cocktail of songs by composer Charles Strouse, who had dreamed up and directed the revue. Strouse was one of the Broadway musical scene's heavyweights, having composed the music for *Bye Bye Birdie, Applause, Golden Boy, It's a Bird, It's a Plane, It's Superman,* and, of course, *Annie,* Strouse's then current big hit on Broadway. Songs from all of these were included in the revue. Surely, I thought, this enchanting show, with a cast of four and a pianist, would be a cinch to do in Toronto. I made a deal with Norman to co-produce it.

Later, somewhat ruefully, I realized how seductive a New York musical cabaret can be to a Torontonian and how misleading. New York has always been a night-time city, where people go out to have a good time. Toronto wasn't the same kind of city, at least not then, and there was a dearth of convivial cabaret spaces. Aside from The Teller's Cage in Commerce Court, the most plausible location was the Theatre in the Dell, the first cabaret space in Toronto. Joe and Willy de Laurentis, who ran it, were among the most enthusiastic supporters of Canadian talent and had for years headlined such performers as Tom Kneebone and Dinah Christie. I must say that, when I saw the Dell, my heart sank. It looked like the dining room of a rural golf clubhouse back in the fifties.

With my film-production experience in mind, I was determined to be closely involved with all aspects of the Toronto production of *By Strouse,* from casting to marketing, and I not only wanted Charles Strouse to once again be the director but Lee Adams, who had written the lyrics to most of Strouse's shows, to collaborate with him. The songs came from book musicals, so creating the right context for them in a revue was all-important. Charles and Lee, I discovered, were classic partners. Charles was authoritarian and businesslike, while Lee was intense and good-humoured, although there was now a slight friction between them because Lee hadn't been asked to write the lyrics for *Annie*.

The show opened to good reviews, won the Toronto Theatre Award for Best Revue of the Year, ran for four months, and covered its costs. But my real reward was getting to know Charles and Lee personally and developing a genuine fondness for Norman. He was a scrapper who got things done, even if he wasn't very elegant about it. And he'd give you the shirt off his back.

The revue's final song was called "A Broadway Musical," and it was, Charles and Lee told me, the big number from a show they were then writing that was going to be called, of all things, *A Broadway Musical*. Norman was going to produce it, and he planned to workshop the show off-Broadway sometime in the fall. (Workshopping is a relatively cheap alternative to taking the show on the road for out-of-town tryouts. Both are methods of developing and polishing a show before a paying audience, but workshopping doesn't need a full-scale production with sets and costumes.) I loved the song, so I asked to see the book, which was by William F. Brown, who had won a Tony and a Drama Desk Award for the long-running musical *The Wiz*.

The book! I know now that the book, or libretto, which in theatrical terms is a synonym for story, is all-important, critical. Then I just wanted *A Broadway Musical* to work as well as I could make it, to the extent that I understood the process (I had, after all, a lot to learn). Around that time, there had been a spate of revivals of old musicals like *Anything Goes* and *On Your Toes*, which, despite skilful updating and revision, were little more than a string of songs, some wonderful, some just turns for a star performer, linked together by a meaningless plot. Book musicals were my type of show. I loved them all, from the great Rodgers and Hammerstein musicals to Bernstein and

Sondheim's *West Side Story*. But I was bucking a trend. The hot musicals of the past two or three years had been dance-driven – *A Chorus Line, Dancin'*, and *The Wiz*.

Perhaps I was seduced by the fact that Brown's libretto dealt with the behind-the-scenes workings of show business. *A Broadway Musical* was a play within a play, the story of a white producer who takes a young black writer's serious drama about the exploitation of black basketball players and turns it into a musical called *Sneakers*. My inexperience proved a great handicap. I didn't then know, though I would later learn, that a show-within-a-show concept, with its inside-showbiz shtick, is extraordinarily hard to bring off.

Norman, Charles, and Lee came to Dick's house and played the whole show to just Pearl, Dick, Lexie, and me. It was intoxicating stuff, a private audition from Broadway heavyweights, just for us. We all loved the score and what we heard of the libretto, and I can still hum the love songs. If I was ever going to dive into producing a musical, I thought, it might as well be from a guy who was coming off one of the biggest hits in Broadway history, *Annie*. And the other members of the artistic team that were promised were formidable, all of them Tony Award winners or nominees. George Faison, the award-winning director of *The Wiz* and a former director of the Alvin Ailey Dance Company, was set to direct and choreograph the show. Randy Barselo, who had designed *Ain't Misbehavin'* and *Jesus Christ Superstar*, would do the costumes. Donald Pippin, who had won a Tony for his work on *Oliver!*, was musical supervisor. It was an impressive enough team for Dick and me to agree to raise $200,000, which was half the cost of the workshop production that Norman was going to stage. Norman was responsible for the other half. I anticipated little difficulty in assembling the money; there were many investors in Toronto interested in backing Broadway shows.

Today, a movie negative is a $40-million U.S. proposition. And you only know if it's a hit (or not) when you test the complete film at a screening in a selected market and after you tabulate the scores. By that time you're in deep. "Broadway" musicals, on the other hand, can be "stepped," first with a reading, then with a workshop, then a regional co-production. At each stage the emotional response of an audience can be tested. All this before the tremendous cost of a full-scale production.

The best hedge is not a series of out-of-town tryouts. Each move in and out of a theatre is enormously expensive, what with the attendant travel costs, per diems, local marketing costs, rehearsals in a new space with a new orchestra. Reworking a show in a first-class theatre, with an IATSE crew of forty, which is being paid for by the hour, gives you precious little time to correct mistakes. That's why Norman wanted to workshop the show instead.

We raised the financing by the now-familiar method of selling units, and we added an overcall (an agreement that the investors will come up with more money) in the event we decided to proceed to Broadway. Nat Taylor, loyal as always, was an investor. Our biggest supporter and investor was Larry Heisey, who was in every sense an angel. Larry is jovial and upbeat, and also forward-thinking: he had built a corporate career at Proctor & Gamble, then headed marketing at Standard Broadcast Sales, and in 1970 went in as president of Harlequin Enterprises Ltd., then a small public company. When Larry became chief executive officer, Harlequin was selling twelve million books a year, and when he stepped down as chairman in the late eighties, Harlequin was selling two hundred million books a year in eighteen languages. Larry was an old friend of Dick's and he had invested in my motion pictures. Now he and his wife, Annie, had agreed to host a backers' audition for several dozen of Toronto's élite by throwing a garden party at their Rosedale house. Charles and Lee played snatches of the score to a black-tie crowd. A couple of weeks later Wilf Posluns lent us the Leah Posluns Theatre in North York for a second spirited audition, and a country-club dinner given by the Young Presidents' Organization provided a perfect forum for the third. The money was in hand in short order.

Money was the easy part, I soon found out. I should have read Brown's libretto more carefully. After all, it dealt with the very problem I was up against, the trials and tribulations of a producer trying out a show before it got to Broadway. A lot of the scenes were down-right prophetic. If I had known enough to read the signals right, I would have realized right away that I was in trouble. Take the casting. George Faison, urged on by Norman, who claimed he was limited by the workshop budget, hired Julius LaRosa to play the producer Eddie Bell. I was, to say the least, nonplussed. To me, LaRosa was a forgotten figure from the distant past, the fifties TV host of the "Kraft Theatre" and a regular on "The Arthur Godfrey Show." But Faison's decision went unchallenged by Charles and Lee. I grew even more nervous when Norman cast his own wife, Gwyda, as the producer's wife. Gwyda may have been a good actress, but I was always suspicious of nepotism in the theatre. Again, Charles and Lee just nodded their approval.

After four weeks of rehearsal in a dilapidated warehouse off-Broadway, the show opened on October 18 with a cast of twenty-eight, including some exquisite dancers, at the two-hundred-seat Riverside Church on Manhattan's Upper West Side. For the four weeks of the workshop, I had had to tear myself away from the pre-production and financing problems of *The Changeling* to spend weekends in New York dealing with the developmental progress of *A Broadway Musical.* I'd see three or four performances from Friday to Sunday, and in between shows, I would huddle with the triumvi-rate of Charles, Lee, and Norman. The fights were terrible. Every ele-ment was ripped apart and examined to see whether it worked or not. Bill Brown rewrote the book daily, but he could never make up his mind whether it was supposed to be a loving homage to Broadway or a cutting satire. Charles and Lee put in new songs every week. What began to worry me was that the process never stabilized. There was no artistic focus. George Faison was simply not strong enough to with-stand the artistic egos now blazing away in intense competition. And Norman wasn't as resourceful as I had thought. He was, in fact, abso-lutely ineffectual.

Notwithstanding my concerns, the workshop was selling out, and from the audience surveys at the end of every performance, the show seemed to be well received. Suddenly, the Nederlanders, who together with the Shubert Organization dominate theatre ownership on Broadway, had a theatre for us – the historic Lunt–Fontanne Theatre would be available in December. As the workshop ended in mid-November, we decided, against all logic, to go to Broadway. Norman just didn't have the discipline to cut his losses, and neither did I.

I should have said no. But I was busy with so many things that I couldn't concentrate enough on this single, vital decision. Trouble was, I had a group of investors who were expecting to go to Broadway, who wanted to go to Broadway, who were seduced as we all were by the glamour and lure of Broadway. Hell, I wanted to go to Broadway! What would the investors say if I suddenly stopped the show at the end of the workshop? The workshop, after all, had been a reasonable success. If I had said, as I should have, "Okay, folks, this is it. The tryout just wasn't good enough. We'll start again," they would have felt cheated, deprived of "that ultimate dream, that sweet illusion," as the title song of A Broadway Musical put it.

The old pros, Charles and Lee, knew that the show was going to have to rise several notches to make it on Broadway. They didn't hesitate to say – often and loudly – that we were going to have to redo it substantially, and that was going to take more money and much more time. Over the years, I have learned the proper gestation period for a new musical is a minimum of three years. To try to solve all the problems in four weeks was absurd. We also needed a whack of money to make a TV spot, as TV had become the prime selling medium for Broadway. And ideally it was prudent to have at least an additional $200,000 in our war chest to offset any negative reviews and carry us until our marketing efforts took over.

We tackled the artistic problems first. Faison had to go. He just didn't have the vision necessary to raise the show to the required level. That put us in the market for a new director, a major one. And a new major director was going to demand not only a substantial salary but a lot of changes, and even more time to make those changes

Charles and Lee came up with the name Gower Champion as a possible director. They had worked with him on Bye Bye Birdie, and he had made the show into a dazzling amalgam of sophisticated showbiz shtick and teenage naïveté. Gower was a maker of hits. As well as *Bye Bye Birdie*, his credits included *Hello, Dolly!* and *I Do! I Do!* He'd been outshone recently by Michael Bennett and Bob Fosse, but he seemed ideally suited to our book musical. Ironically, he would go on to direct David Merrick's adaptation of *42nd Street*, the grand-daddy of all backstage musicals. Even more ironically, and tragically, he would die of a heart attack on the opening night of *42nd Street*.

Gower liked Charles's music and the show's possibilities. But he refused to be billed as director – yet. Great. I've since learned that this always means trouble, if not outright disaster. The same thing hap-pened to me later, in 1988, when Robin Phillips took over a produc-tion of *Macbeth* on the road and refused credit. A director always seems willing to get paid for his work, but sometimes, without actu-ally meaning to, gives the producer the message "Don't for heaven's sake try to connect me with this bomb." Word that the director has refused credit gets out immediately, and the show sinks several points in the media's esteem. Before you know it, you're opening a show that has already been reviewed, at least in the media's minds, and that has already generated a million preconceptions – all of them bad.

The physical production and rehearsal time needed to get us onto the Lunt–Fontanne stage was going to cost an additional $700,000, perhaps more, before we'd get to opening night. Dick and I had to go back to our investors for a further $350,000 or so, and Norman was to handle the balance. We had no trouble raising our share since, as I said, we had prudently provided for an overcall in our original financing documents.

About ten days into the transfer period, with Gower now commit-ted, Norman told me quite out of the blue that he was having trouble raising his share of the financing.

"Garth," he said, "I think we'd better close down now."

I couldn't believe what I was hearing. I yelled at him, "Norman, are you totally out of your mind? It's one thing to close the show after Riverside, but not now. We're committed to at least the $700,000. We must open this show. We must."

Norman finally agreed to fund his share personally.

All our spirits rose when Gower arrived for his first rehearsal. Momentum built and adrenaline flowed. Gower was an obsessive-compulsive, a chain-smoker like Bob Fosse. Gaunt of face and frame, he worked eighteen hours a day, then napped a couple of hours, and went back to work some more. He, Charles, and Lee were like a machine: in no time the show was reshaped, the cast upgraded through replacements. More rehearsals were added. After two weeks, the show was so improved that even Gower was pleased enough with it to say that he would put his name on it – but only as production supervisor, not as director.

Our spirits continued to soar – and so did the budget. The new bill was for another $300,000. Norman was dry.

Having embarked on this tumultuous voyage with us from the beginning, Larry Heisey came through again and split the additional financing with Dick and me. To ease the pressure, Norman negotiated deferments with every conceivable supplier, and this money was pulled away from the physical-production budget to pay for much-needed advertising – advertising that's very expensive. Today, a page in the New York Times, for example, will set you back about $60,000 U.S.

*Once again, I put my own money on the line; once again, I stood up to back an artistic endeavour with my own resources. I think it's fair to say there are very few producers who will do this.*

Previews began in the second week of December. Gower was a perfectionist. There were more changes, more rehearsals. And every performance seemed sharper, funnier, cleaner. Maybe it would work, I thought. My hopes were dashed somewhat in mid-December, when Nat Taylor brought his family to see the show and told me frankly that he didn't like it. Paradoxically, that night was the first time I felt the show itself was working, and my intuition seemed to be on target because, the day before the opening, Richard Friedman of the *Bergen Record*, which served the important New Jersey market, gave us a rave review. "Champion's choreography and the songs of Lee Adams and Charles Strouse could give this entertaining vehicle a long Broadway run." Were we excited! I was being closely monitored by the press at home, as always. The review was quoted in the *Toronto Star*, and later I learned that, in YMHA steambaths that day, the Jewish establishment was muttering that it looked like Drabinsky had himself a hit.

We felt good, even if filled with trepidation, because we knew we were absolutely dependent on good reviews to keep the show open. The advance seat sale was small, and we didn't have a war chest large enough for a post-opening advertising blitz. (One of the reasons I was determined to generate a huge advance for the Toronto production of *The Phantom of the Opera* ten years later was that I never again wanted to be completely at the mercy of the critics' whims.)

December 21, opening night, began full of great expectations. Pearl flew down from Toronto to join me. Just after six o'clock, we took a limo through choking traffic to the Lunt–Fontanne. The opening was set for 6:30 P.M., and we drew up to a sidewalk crowd thick with black ties, a large contingent of Toronto friends and investors, including Dick, of course, and Larry and Annie Heisey. John Hirsch was there, and so was Gilda Radner, who had come along with Elliott Gould. I should have felt exhilarated. As it was, I merely felt tired and anxious.

I had difficulty sitting through the performance. First-night audiences are usually a mixed group. Your friends and supporters want the show to work, while the press is invariably sceptical. The New York critics have recently changed their habits and now generally go to one of the last previews instead of opening night, and I think the reviews are fairer in consequence, particularly for musicals and comedies, which depend so much on spontaneous audience reaction for their success. But not that night. One man in particular fascinated me, Clive Barnes of the *New York Post*. For years Barnes had been the *New York Times* critic and thus the single most powerful arbiter of a show's future. His expression, I noted, did not change throughout the evening. Around him, however, the audience seemed to be having a great time. It was buoyant in its enthusiasm and gave the cast a standing ovation. I got out of my seat feeling confident.

The Broadway tradition is sadistic. We gathered at the Belasco Room in Sardi's, a happy crowd under the streamers and Christmas lights. Norman, his face set, went into the hall to call our press agent, Jeffrey Richards. Then he beckoned to me. The news was bad. Two of the three late-night TV critics had blasted the show. Then John Hirsch came up to me and shook my hand as if he were offering condolences. He knew what I didn't know and what Norman probably did, that in the high-pressure, competitive Broadway environment, there really are no last-minute miracles. *A Broadway Musical* had been deemed a dog way back when Gower refused billing, and the critics were not prepared to change their minds.

Around midnight Norman was back on the phone to find out about the *Times* review. I sat slumped in a chair at the end of a long open closet, staring at him through the coathangers. I saw his face collapse. He just kept saying, "Yes" tensely into the phone. Then he hung up and said, "Bad." Mel Gussow, the second stringer for the *Times*, had stolen from the show's libretto, "Nada, nothing, zero, zip should suffice as a four-word description of *A Broadway Musical*." When a critic uses words from the show's own lyrics against it, you know you're finished. Barnes's opinion was somewhat less harsh than Gussow's, but no different in essence, "A sorry evening in the theatre," he wrote. The *Newsday* critic's response was kinder but just as damning, "A valiant effort, but not enough to cover the rough spots." It took us five minutes to agree sadly, reluctantly, but ineluctably, that we had to close the show immediately. Neither Norman nor I could raise any more money for it.

It was time to go back into the Belasco Room and face our investors. They had left the theatre believing that we had a very significant hit on our hands. They all thought they had seen a fabulous musical.

I couldn't keep my voice from breaking as I told them simply that we couldn't go on.

"We've heard nine reviews, and eight of them are unfavourable. There's not one review we can hang our hats on. There's a history of shows that have gone on despite bad reviews and become successful. But the cost of doing that is substantial, and Norman and I just don't have the money. We have no alternative but to close the show."

It was Larry Heisey, our most generous backer, who had never wavered in his support, who supplied the evening's only light touch. He immediately called for quiet and said, "I'm sorry for the other Canadian investors who are not here to enjoy this moment of agony. It seems a shame, first, that they'll never get another chance to see the show, and second, that they're not here now to share in this glorious failure."

Then his tone changed, and he looked over at me. How rare it was, he said, for Canadians to try something like this, to dare to try something large and grand, to risk failure in the service of an idea. And he added, "How much credit Garth deserves for having done it."

How grateful I was for those words. How comforting they were at that moment of shock and sadness.

But all I wanted was to get out of there.

Pearl took my hand and we made our way to the car. We rode in silence for several blocks, my mind in turmoil and silent self-examination. Eventually I said to Pearl, "There's no way I can stay cooped up in a car right now. I just want to walk the streets of New York for a while."

We got out near the U.N. Plaza. A light drizzle was falling, a doleful accompaniment to my mental self-interrogation. I felt enveloped in a fog of incrimination and self-doubt. *What was I doing all this for? How much disappointment would I have to endure? Why must it all happen at the same time? Why must everything go wrong? How could I go back to Toronto and face the media again? The snarling, sneering press, with their baying chorus of told-you-so's? What would I say to the investors who weren't there? How would this affect my ability to raise money in the future, to take on new projects, to get on with my life? I'd had my first confrontation with the Big Apple and I had been badly defeated. It hurt.*

We walked in silence. Pearl understood.

A bleak, bleak moment, there in the rain.

At the hotel, I called my father. I knew my parents were waiting to hear the outcome. But when my father answered the phone, he was crying. While *A Broadway Musical* had been crashing, my Uncle Dave's eleven-year-old son, Earl, had been fatally injured when a car struck his bicycle. It seemed like the final straw.

I didn't sleep the rest of the night, and I flew back to Toronto in a state of shock. But as soon as the next day, I started to revive.

*I reached deep down, again, to that place I had found when I was just a kid, that place where the wellspring of my personality is stored. I reached down and I grabbed it. I had a life still, after all, and my wits, and my experience. I had a family, my wife, a daughter, and a son.*

Okay, I had lost a round. But I had *The Changeling* to work on, and I was still sure it would be a winner. I wasn't going to hang my head, I was going to look the world straight in the eye. I would do what I had to do to make sure *The Changeling* met my expectations.

And after that? Another dream. In four months' time Nat Taylor and I would be opening an eighteen-screen movie theatre complex in Toronto's Eaton Centre. My spirits began to soar again. New York was still there. It wasn't going anywhere. It would wait for me. And, next time. . . . Next time I'd triumph, I was sure of it.

# P A R T

II

# CHAPTER

## EIGHTEEN SCREENS

April 20, 1979, and Nat Taylor and I were in the basement of a parking garage, holding our breaths and counting heads, not such a difficult thing to do when you have $2 million and change at stake.

This was not your ordinary basement, but a twisting, spiralling shape underneath the parking ramp of Toronto's Eaton Centre, into which we had cunningly inserted our brand-new, never-thought-of-before, eighteen-screen multiplex movie-house.

It was opening day.

The idea had been in Nat's head the first year I met him. He had already created a twin and a triple and had experimented with a fiveplex. None of those satisfied him. When I met him, he was mulling over various possible locations for an expanded and refined version of his multiple-theatre concept. In anticipation of finding the perfect spot, he had asked the architect Mandel Sprachman, one of his protégés, to design a prototypical complex of twelve auditoriums with an average of only 125 seats per screen. Nat even had a name for this multi-mini motion-picture house. He called it a "cineplex."

As usual with Nat, there was a method to his madness, a logic underpinning his idea. Cineplex was designed to fill an important gap in exhibition that no one else seemed to have even noticed. By the late seventies the bottom had fallen out of the second-run movie market. Hollywood production was now being driven by new sources of ancillary revenues – network and pay TV – and the burgeoning video cassette retail outlets. As the window between a film's first-run theatrical release and its availability to the video market and subsequently on pay TV narrowed, the over-seated second-run and fringe houses could no longer make a go of it on their own. Studios seldom planned major re-releases of even their most successful films. Films were put on the theatrical shelf virtually upon completion of their first run, even though they might have substantial box-office life still left in them, especially if they received some attention at Academy Awards time but had been released in the first half of the previous qualifying year.

Nat understood that, while there was no getting back the monolithic audiences of the thirties, there was a way to serve the new and fragmented one. The second-run market could be revitalized by the theatre multiplex. The theory was simple enough: the way to squeeze the last dollar out of a theatrical release was to move it into a complex with, say, sixteen auditoriums, each resembling a Hollywood screening room rather than a conventional theatre. In such hundred-seat theatres, a film coming to the end of its first-run release with a final week's gross of $7,000 could still generate a healthy income. If it ran at capacity only twelve times a week, the gross (twelve hundred tickets at the 1978 price of $3.50 a crack) would be $4,200. Assuming that there were sixteen screens in all, and they were showing films that grossed equivalent amounts, the total weekly gross of the multiplex would be almost $70,000, or $3.5 million a year, a staggering amount back in the late seventies.

True, the operating overhead per seat would be slightly higher, as a cineplex would need more ushers, cashiers, and cleaners. However, those increased costs would be offset by a higher seat turnover, lower film costs, and, most importantly, greater concession revenues. Because the films' starting times would be staggered, there would be an even flow of customers all through the day, taking the pressure off the concession stands and raising their income per patron.

I didn't understand why nobody, aside from me, really believed in Nat's vision, even though he had been so stunningly right so often before. Back in 1969, when he had sold his 50 per cent share of Twentieth Century Theatres to Famous Players, he had offered George Destounis a fifty-fifty partnership in the new concept, but George laughed him out of his office. "It'll never make money!" he said. Nat's other partner in Twentieth Century, Bernie Herman, who owned City Parking and who had managed to amass a fortune from operating parking lots in Toronto, also turned him down.

But I believed. Whenever Nat discussed the subject with me over our four o'clock tea-and-cookies interludes, I reminded him of my determination to become his partner.

"I'd like to have a piece of it," I'd say. "Remember me when you're putting your financing together."

"Sure kid, I'll get to you when I get the location," Nat would say, meaning it.

At the time, exhibition seemed to me to be a safe harbour compared to production, although artistically, of course, it was not nearly as satisfying. I wanted to diversify my portfolio of risk. Exhibition's real-estate aspects appealed to my entrepreneurial instincts. I liked the idea of a cash business, because you didn't have to chase receivables. On the contrary, the money flowed in every night, and because you only settled with the distributor six or eight weeks later, you could finance the company's operating requirements with their cash. It was a wonderful form of internally generated financing.

*Still, that wasn't the true turn-on for me. Sure I loved the sound of cash registers ringing, the sheer smooth, beautiful efficiency that the business could become. But that's just money. I could see the crowds in my mind, the customers lining up each evening to come to my emporium of filmed entertainment, to come to me for their hour of dreams. Even then I fancied myself as a kind of reborn Roxy.*

I was the one who finally found the location for Nat. We were filming scenes from *The Silent Partner* in the Eaton Centre, the huge, newly

opened galleria in downtown Toronto, and at some point in the negotiations I had met Jerry Shear of Cadillac Fairview Corporation, the
developer of the centre. Shear, along with A. E. "Eph" Diamond and
Jack Daniels, was a founding partner of Cadillac Corporation, which
in 1974 had merged with the Fairview Corporation of Canada, owned
by the Samuel Bronfman family holding company, CEMP, and run by
the Bronfman frontman, Leo Kolber. At the time of the merger, it was
said that Cadillac needed Fairview's money while Fairview, considered timorous by the development community, needed Cadillac's
chutzpah. (An expression of Cadillac's expansive operating style
came from the mouth of Jack Daniels, "We want to own the world
and have an option on outer space.")

As I pitched Jerry and his colleagues for permission to film in
the complex's basement, I added, "And also, by the way, a guy by the
name of Taylor and I are looking for a location to build an innovative
movie theatre."

A little while later, in the middle of prepping a spectacular chase
scene, involving nearly a thousand extras, when I really needed dis-
traction, I got a call from Jerry.

"Garth," he said, "I think I've got the perfect place for you to build
your theatre."

"Where?" I asked.

"No more than three hundred yards from where you're shooting.
About twenty-five thousand square feet on the main floor of the
parking lot in the Dundas Street parkade. But it's not your usual space
– it's rather irregular. Check it out."

The location was terrific, steps from one of downtown Toronto's
major traffic and transit intersections. But saying it was not your
usual space was a comic understatement. It was a cockamamy space,
confused and ill-planned, about twenty-five feet high here, nine feet
high there, dominated by the curve of an adjacent parking ramp that
plunged several levels into the bowels of the earth. It was like being
below decks on a tramp steamer, which was no doubt why Loblaws,
the original proposed tenant, had dropped out. I scratched my head.

Space got a rating of one, location, a perfect ten. Still, I'm pretty good at visualizing how things could be made to fit together. Maybe it would work. I hurriedly called Nat, "I think I've finally found our location!"

Nat was disbelieving, but within hours he was down to examine the space. He brought Sprachman with him. For some time we prowled the grim concrete area, taking measurements, discussing possibilities, tossing back and forth the pros of the location versus the cons of the actual space. At the end of it Nat turned to me and said, "Garth, let's do it."

*So I was going to be in the movie-theatre business. Why? Because I was close to Nat Taylor. Because I believed his idea was a good one. Because the opportunity presented itself. Because I didn't want to work all my life and not have my money working for me. I wanted to clip coupons like the rest of the world. I had made a lot of money practising law, a serious amount of money for a young man, and I had sheltered it here and there – I had built my first apartment building when I was twenty-three. Exhibition could be stimulating, challenging.*

Obviously, before we could cost out the project, we had to come up with a workable design. With its varying heights, the space was an architect's nightmare. Sprachman met the challenge by creating a mezzanine in the area with the highest ceiling, thereby augmenting the total space from twenty-five thousand to forty thousand square feet. However, with this design approach, the maximum floor-to-ceiling height of any auditorium would be less than twelve feet.

The complications, however, had only just begun. The essence of the concept was to maximize the number of theatres, but now we were reminded by Sprachman that wherever 35-mm film was being screened, the archaic Ontario Theatres Act regulated not only the number of exits and entrances of each theatre, but the size of the projection booth. If we went with 35-mm, we would be able to squeeze in only four or five 35-mm theatres.

"So? We'll use video projection," Nat said.

But video in those days was of hopeless quality, and although high-definition TV was being touted as imminent, it didn't in fact come into production until the late eighties (and it still isn't good enough for commercial purposes).

So Nat said, "We'll use 16-mm."

Sixteen-millimetre film was used for the non-theatrical market, in schools, airbases, hospitals, and the like, and it was thus outside the scope of the Theatres Act. But this brave (or foolish, depending on the way you looked at it) decision created a whole new set of problems.

On the upside, the cost of 16-mm prints and projection equipment was substantially less than that of 35-mm. On the downside, the quality of the picture was inferior, the sound was poor, and, more critically, as it turned out, distributors were dilatory about making 16-mm prints for Canada.

Then we discovered that the twelve-foot ceiling was too low for the traditional projection from the back of the movie-house. The heads of those seated in the audience would block the picture!

Nat mulled this over for a while and then said, "So? We'll use rear-screen projection."

This was all very well, but the commercial viability of rear-screen projection had never even been tested, let alone proved. It seemed to me to be unbelievably complicated. Each projector sat in its own booth and was set up two and a half to three feet behind a glass screen. The picture was then reflected off a series of mirrors that had to be kept totally dust free to create the enlarged and properly focused image on the screen. Each time the beam was reflected off a mirror surface, the image lost about 10 per cent of its brightness. Therefore high-quality equipment (and higher-cost, though still cheaper than 35-mm) with particularly bright projection was essential. We first tried Bell & Howell, but found it unacceptable. We ended up with Fumeo and then Prevost equipment from Italy. Even then, such machinery was not designed for seventy-five hours of work each week, so for every three theatres we were going to have to hire a projectionist to babysit the machines and control the focus. One added benefit was that by using 16-mm equipment we avoided union projectionists, so the cost of labour was comparatively reasonable.

The final configuration was eighteen screens – and Cineplex made *The Guinness Book of World Records*!

The budget was the simplest thing about the project: $2.5 million. Nat negotiated $1.5 million from the Canadian Imperial Bank of Commerce and he, as chairman and CEO of Cineplex, put up 50 per cent of the remaining $1-million equity. Dick and I came in for around 30 per cent, and Harry Mandell, Nat's longtime partner, came in for 15 per cent. The rest was divided among Mandel Sprachman, Hy Ginsberg, Nat's controller and personal accountant, and the general contractor, Norman Shapiro.

While the concrete was being poured, Nat and I mulled over the vital question of programming. It was Nat's contention that art and specialty films were still largely ignored in Toronto, and now that Toronto was so ethnically fragmented, it would be the perfect city in which to program a first-run multiple-screen art house that showed foreign and offbeat films as well as retrospective series. This way, we thought, we wouldn't tread on the toes of the all-powerful duopoly, Famous Players and Canadian Odeon, by disturbing their tight relationship with the major distributors. We knew perfectly well that, if we initially insisted on booking timely move-overs of first-run product, retaliation would be swift. This had to be a slow process; we had to first establish public acceptance of the concept, then broaden our mix of film offerings. The duopoly would use every ounce of its clout to pressure the majors not to supply a competing circuit, even with second-run films using 16-mm prints.

I remember Nat saying, "Look, I'm not trying to compete with Canadian Odeon or Famous Players. I know from experience that a third circuit in Canada would drop dead – that's what happened to National General with all their resources. No, I only want to build half a circuit."

"What's half a circuit?" I asked.

"We play first-run pictures that can't play in the big first-run theatres – the art pictures, the offbeat pictures, and later, when we've established the grossing capacity of the small auditoriums, we'll add second-run pictures that still have some business left in them."

But getting access to foreign films was easier to say than to accomplish. There were perhaps two or three companies distributing art films in Canada, and then only on a limited basis. A year earlier Nat and I had set up Pan-Canadian Film Distributors to distribute *The Silent Partner* in Canada, and we decided to use this company to acquire the specialty films for our new theatre. In 1978, when I went over to Cannes to pre-sell the foreign rights to *The Changeling*, Nat joined me with Irwin Shapiro, a longtime friend of his who had for decades been a dominant force in the foreign-sales business. He was a seasoned veteran of the Cannes *marché*.

Irwin, acting as Pan-Canadian's agent, helped us buy the distribution rights to some outstanding films that year: Ermanno Olmi's *L'albero degli zoccoli* (*The Tree of the Wooden Clogs*), which won the Palme d'Or at Cannes; the Australian film, *The Chant of Jimmie Blacksmith*, which was Fred Schepisi's first film and which would be the hit of Toronto's first Festival of Festivals later that year; and a fast-moving, compelling docudrama about the public and private lives of Australian newsreel-makers in the late forties called *Newsfront*. In each instance we broke convention, because the deals required timely delivery of 16-mm prints struck off the original English or foreign-language negatives.

How was the public to understand all this? We were sure to get a lot of attention in the press, but what would they say? What could be said about a two-storey, eighteen-screen complex, with theatres that looked like screening rooms? One of them had only fifty-four seats! What would be said about rear-screen projection and 16-mm film and about programming that was limited to art and specialty films?

Too late to turn back! What we had to do was sell Cineplex as the success I once was confident it would be. *We were going to have to dance a little faster than the naysayers.* To bring it off, we needed a high-profile, aggressive approach that would show – and keep –

Cineplex in the most optimistic light. Somebody had to be found to do this.

Here we got lucky. Earlier that year, as I shuttled back and forth from New York where I was exploring new ventures in live theatre, I ran into an old friend at La Guardia. I had first met Lynda Friendly at the Beth Sholom Synagogue in Toronto when I was sixteen, and our paths had crossed occasionally since then. Seeing her again, I was immediately struck by her style. Attractive and fashionably dressed, she projected a flair that exactly matched my image for Cineplex. As we flew back together, I learned that she was now an account executive at Willhurst Communications, handling public relations and promotion for major corporations like Pepsi-Cola, the Toronto Dominion Bank, and Commonwealth Holiday Inns. I liked that she hadn't become jaded or cynical like so many people I had met in the promotion business. Her overbrimming confidence and enthusiasm were much more important than her inexperience in the world of entertainment.

As I drove her to her office downtown, we passed the Eaton Centre. "That's where Cineplex is going to be built," I said, rather grandly. (Later she said she thought I was insane. A movie-house in a parking garage?) I said I didn't exactly know when we'd be ready to hire her, but at the very least I hoped she could come and work on publicizing the Cineplex opening with us.

By the fall I convinced Nat that we should hire Lynda's firm to prepare an outline and analysis of just how to present this new house of movie entertainment in such a way as to excite the media and public rather than confuse and bewilder them.

The first press conference in September confirmed my confidence in Lynda. With what I would come to know as her customary efficiency, she staged a terrific presentation at the Eaton Centre building site for the more than two hundred media and industry people. The centrepiece was a large-scale model of Cineplex, a vividly coloured hub that curled away in tunnels to different theatres. We used the conference to detail the innovations we would introduce in an exhibition business that had grown complacent, even contemptuous, of its customers. Cineplex was to reverse this trend: we were determined to be a user-friendly exhibitor.

Some of our innovations are commonplace today, found in many theatres, but back in 1979 they were breakthrough concepts. For example, tickets would be colour-coded to help guide patrons to the right auditorium. Throughout the complex there would be customized rich red carpeting with the Cineplex logo woven into it. A computerized ticket system, the first of its kind, would allow for same-day advance-ticket purchasing. You could buy a ticket at 11 A.M. for the 9 P.M. show.

And no more sticky floors! Following the example of Disneyland, we wanted the theatres squeaky-clean, so we would clean all the auditoriums between shows.

For some time motion-picture theatres had relied on inordinately overpriced concession stands to boost box-office profits. Lynda, who had been trained in hotel management, had specific ideas for expanding our concession business. Cineplex was not only going to offer the usual assortment of candy bars, colas, and popcorn. It was going to have a two-hundred-seat Common Room run by Mickey Firestone, one of the great caterers in the city – real food, real coffee, real comfort, real ambience. For this purpose we set aside a cheerful eating-and-meeting area in a large, bright-windowed space overlooking the Bay/Dundas park.

*I still hankered for the lost splendours of the Roxy, but how to instill grandeur in a poky little space? How to create glamour-in-a-box? And at seventies prices? Colour and style helped. But I wanted more. And so I created a space in the main lobby to exhibit the works of young Canadian artists who didn't have ready access to gallery space. Some of them were offered for sale. Did anyone notice? It didn't matter. They would in time.*

Nat and I carefully picked the films for our opening. While Cineplex was designed to showcase art and specialty films, we were concerned not to be seen as too esoteric, so our opening line-up was eclectic. Along with *The Chant of Jimmie Blacksmith, Newsfront,* and

*The Tree of the Wooden Clogs*, we were going to show *The Shout* by Polish writer/director Jerzy Skolimowski, Allen Moyle's *The Rubber Gun*, the Russian movie, *Queen of the Gypsies*, a Hungarian comedy, *Rain and Shine*, and the French/Italian/Irish co-production, *A Purple Taxi*, starring Phillipe Noiret, Charlotte Rampling, Peter Ustinov, and Fred Astaire. In the second week we scheduled a revival of The Who's rock opera, *Tommy*, to show off our innovative, sophisticated new M-4 sound system as the ultimate sonic environment to date. And all this in a city that up to then had only two or three cinemas dedicated to specialty films.

The booking schedule allowed us to emphasize Cineplex's unique ability to respond quickly to public demand. That's why only eight films were selected for the first week, with *Tommy* added in the second. If one of the films got hot, we could expand its booking to other screens, and if a film slumped, we could move it into a single smaller auditorium.

It was time to let the world know about our new baby. I've never believed in sitting on my hands when it comes to advertising and publicity: in this kind of business, shyness is a deadly disease. The best way to get word of mouth rippling throughout all segments of a market – whether for a new building or a new entertainment experience – is to create a gala invitational event, supported by a saturation radio, TV, and newspaper buy. If the campaign is designed with imagination, this immediately establishes the importance of the venture and casts it into that elusive not-to-be-missed category.

Lynda was responsible for implementing my strategy, which was to deliver a one-two punch a couple of days before we opened the doors to the paying public. We had the customary opening ceremony in the early afternoon, with a fat list of dignitaries, from the Ontario minister of culture and the mayor of Toronto on down, and we all made self-congratulatory speeches. But in the evening we threw a huge party for upwards of eight hundred guests, including a carefully "random" assortment of local celebrities and tycoons, such as the industrialist/publisher Ken Thomson and the chairman of the TD

Bank, Dick Thomson (no relation), both of whom were intrigued but who manfully managed to control their enthusiasm. All shades of opinion were represented.

There was no shortage of cynical hecklers, mostly distributors, who were looking down their noses at "Taylor's Folly" and openly predicting a speedy failure. One press wit described Cineplex as "a colour-coded sardine box," a harbinger of the harsh criticism of the small theatres that would rain down for many years. Another termed the physical environment "sleekly functional and innocuous." But Nat and I were not put out by any of it. We believed implicitly that we were the wave of the future. And that Friday, April 20, 1979, when the cinemas opened, we felt positively triumphant.

Still, on the opening day I couldn't eat. I did nothing but study the audience profile and, of course, the hourly grosses. I've always had a mania for monitoring these, because they represent the moviegoers' true pulse. Once an hourly trend is established for a picture, it's easy to predict daily and weekly figures. For ten hours Nat and I watched the audience pour in. When the ticket sales surpassed fifteen hundred, we were ecstatic. It seemed our advertising and publicity thrust had worked. The public was coming.

The next morning I was sitting with Nat in his office reviewing the box office figures and Nat was wearing a grin as wide as Cinema-Scope. All he said was "Tremendous," his favourite expression. And tremendous it was. We had budgeted the first week's total box office at $21,000, or 6,000 patrons at $3.50 a ticket. If we kept up the opening day's grosses, we would come damn near budget expectations. And we did. In fact, we were dead on.

However, the high soon wore off. Within six weeks it was clear that, while the retrospective programming had worked, we were still too reliant on art films. What we made from exhibiting foreign films, we lost in distributing them. Because we used 16-mm film, it was hard for us to get a continuous supply on a timely basis. As a Canadian distributor, we had little opportunity to further exploit our rights, because 16-mm film had minimal theatrical play and it was still early days for Canadian pay TV and video. It cost us up to $25,000 U.S. for

the Canadian rights to a film, and more to make the prints and advertise the film. That meant we had to gross $70,000 at our own box
office to justify the cost of the rights plus the cost of prints and
advertising. A $70,000 gross for a foreign film was a big deal in
Toronto, and it was tough to sell outside Toronto – even Vancouver
had little appetite for foreign films.

I suggested to Nat that since *Tommy* worked pretty well, we
increase the proportion of retrospective programming. The first
breakthrough was delivered by Stanley Kubrick's *Dr. Strangelove*. In
its first week, *Strangelove* took in about $7,500, compared with the
$2,000 to $3,000 gross of one of the foreign films. And this was on
only one screen with a hundred seats. A bonanza! Suddenly the
weekly box-office gross for the complex soared from $20,000, once
nearly touching $40,000. We were making a lot of money at forty
grand a week. And the Cineplex practice of staggering starting times
was beginning to affect concession sales, which grossed well beyond
budget levels.

Naturally there were numerous start-up problems. Focusing was
one. Sometimes subtitles of foreign-language films, and even heads of
the actors, were cut off. The computerized box office broke down. We
were plagued by distorted sound caused by the inconsistent sound-
striping of 16-mm prints. Overall, though, the public was buying
Cineplex. It was clean, fresh, and comfortable. And just as we had
thought, we had the single greatest location in Canada. Hundreds of
thousands of commuters flowed by our theatre every week via the
escalator that descended into the Eaton Centre *en route* to the Yonge/
Dundas subway station.

What happened next was, I suppose, inevitable. Cineplex's
momentum carried us into discussions with the major distributors
about transferring to Cineplex the first-run films that were being
taken off downtown Toronto screens prematurely by Famous Players
and Canadian Odeon.

Canadian Odeon, the weaker of the two, was vulnerable in downtown Toronto. From midtown south to the lakeshore, they had only
six screens. Since this was Toronto's prime zone, Canadian Odeon

had to be judicious in allocating screens to its suppliers. Sometimes this meant that a hit had to be taken off long before what should have been the end of its run, so that another distributor's film could meet its scheduled release date. A distributor might be miffed and, occasionally, might switch allegiances and move his films for a short time from Canadian Odeon to Famous Players and vice versa. There were even instances when the naturally volatile relationship between distributors and exhibitors turned explosive, but the duopoly's division of product basically held.

In 1977 Mike Zahorchak had bought the Canadian Odeon chain from J. Arthur Rank. Mike was something of a rough diamond, an ambitious Czech immigrant with street smarts and garish taste, particularly in the area of ornamental art and antiques. He had owned a couple of drive-in chains in Hamilton and Montreal, and the National General Cinerama theatres, which were built in Canada in the late sixties. From the time he bought the chain until 1982, Zahorchak was blessed with the most incredible luck. Industry insiders didn't give him much of a chance of making a profit from his Canadian Odeon acquisition, but Fox had a falling out with Famous Players and gave Zahorchak's chain access to George Lucas's breakthrough *Star Wars* and the pulp success *The Other Side of Midnight.* The cash flow from these two films helped retire much of the $28 million he paid for Canadian Odeon. Over the next few years his luck, already ballistic, went into orbit: Columbia and Universal, which routinely played Canadian Odeon theatres, released *Close Encounters of the Third Kind, Slap Shot, Airport '77, The Deep, Smokey and the Bandit, Kramer vs. Kramer, The Electric Horseman, Blue Lagoon, Alien, All That Jazz, The Rose, Animal House, Jaws II, The Deer Hunter,* and the most successful picture of all time, *E. T. – The Extra-Terrestrial,* all of which generated spectacular grosses throughout the circuit.

Zahorchak had joined George Destounis of Famous Players in chuckling over what they saw as our Mickey Mouse operation. He brushed us aside, and to show how secure he felt, he decided in June 1979 to pull *The Deer Hunter* off his downtown Varsity screen only eight weeks after it had won the Academy Award for Best Picture and when it was still grossing something around $20,000 a week.

Bill Soady, who then ran Universal Pictures Canada, the distributor of *The Deer Hunter*, was furious. "There's no way that I'm going to allow you to take the best picture of the year off in downtown Toronto." he said. "I'm warning you, Mike, if you take it off, I've got a 16-mm print of the film and I'll book it at the Eaton Centre."

Zahorchak said, "Fuck you. I'm taking the film off."

Nat was in his element. He had seen it all before. He took Soady's 16-mm print and ran it at the Eaton Centre, and the movie grossed almost $12,000 in its first week. The grosses of the entire complex skyrocketed to nearly $50,000.

*For the first time, I began to smell blood.*

Some time later both Famous Players and Canadian Odeon maintained that I had planned to challenge them all along, that from the moment we opened Cineplex in the Eaton Centre, I had my sights set on building a third circuit. That's both true and untrue. I was a complete novice in film exhibition. The technical difficulties of constructing and equipping the Eaton Centre Cineplex had been daunting. It wasn't until the theatre had been open for three months that it became even feasible to think of building another Cineplex. And by then, Nat and I knew that the nature of Cineplex had to change. The box office was clicking along with our specialty films and retrospective series, but it had become obvious that the real upside lay in moving over first-run films like *The Deer Hunter* and adding more strategic locations to form that "half circuit" Nat had talked about.

We began to analyse our next move, but in truth it didn't take much analysis: looking at a map of existing movie theatres in the primary zones throughout Canada was like looking through Swiss cheese. Canadian Odeon had only 249 screens to Famous Players' 388 screens, and its coverage was spotty: strong in Montreal, only 50 per cent as strong as Famous Players in Toronto, weak in Western Canada. In many critical zones in the seven key Canadian cities (Toronto, Montreal, Vancouver, Winnipeg, Ottawa, Calgary, and

Edmonton), Zahorchak didn't even have enough screens to service his primary distributors' needs, and the distributors were frustrated and angry when, as with *The Deer Hunter*, Canadian Odeon took off a film that was still doing good business in its most recent week at the box office. So Zahorchak had left himself open to attack, as vulnerable as a tethered lamb.

But so was Famous Players. Both members of the duopoly had grown fat, complacent, and lethargic over the years and hadn't kept up with the shopping-mall boom in the new suburbs. How did we know? Because developers were now calling us! Famous Players and Canadian Odeon never attempted to forestall our expansion.

The Eaton Centre model proved highly attractive to developers. Famous Players and Canadian Odeon demanded column-free spaces spanning fifty to sixty feet by eighty feet to a height of thirty to thirty-five feet, but we had shown it was feasible to build theatres within more conventional mall dimensions. Building costs for the developer were thus reduced significantly. That was the magic of our new techniques.

*And that's when the Canadian exhibition war of the eighties began in earnest.*

Like a couple of generals, Nat and I planned strategy. We would continue to pursue first-run move-overs in Toronto, but in addition to that we would build Cineplexes where the other two chains were weak.

First, though, our armies needed more ammunition. We would have to refinance the company and bring in more equity.

Myron Gottlieb and I did a private placement for $2.5 million, made up of ten units, each worth $250,000. Our new investors included Jack Daniels, Eph Diamond, Jerry Shear, lawyer/developer Rudy Bratty, the financier Andy Sarlos, Max Tanenbaum, and Myron.

Our war chest filled, we started to stake out our territory. Peterborough, Ontario, was a typical target. This small-but-important regional centre was underscreened. Distributors often had to delay releasing a film there in the lucrative summer and Christmas seasons, in some cases until weeks after its national launch. We planned a sixplex for Peterborough, reckoning that we would not only get move-overs on a timely basis, but also that we'd fall heir to first-run films from distributors anxious to enjoy the seasonal movie boom.

We were modelling the new theatres closely on the Eaton Centre, but changes were being incorporated all the time. While we still used 16-mm film, we had introduced conventional front-screen projection in the new Cineplexes – we weren't building in parking garages any more and fourteen- to sixteen-feet ceilings were adequate. A typical space was that offered to us in Olympia & York's Esso Centre in Calgary. Columns divided the space every thirty to forty feet, but ceilings were about fourteen feet high. Awkward for traditional movie-houses, but a snap for us.

The opportunities were everywhere. We built a fiveplex in Kanata, Ottawa's brand-new Silicon Valley. We built a sevenplex in Eaton Place in downtown Winnipeg, nine screens in Edmonton's Principal Plaza, and ten screens in the Royal Centre in downtown Vancouver.

*Nat was gleeful at our success, at our chutzpah, at being proved right. I felt suffused with energy, eager to get on with it, hungry for growth. I had the scent of conquest in my nostrils. We were going to take them on. We were going to grow big, bigger; we had an opportunity to become . . . enormous.*

*How could I resist?*

# CHAPTER

### Turning the Wheel

*In 1981 I turned down a fortune. And then I turned down a second.*
  *Did I do right?*
  *This is how it went:*

To tell the story, I must move away from Cineplex for the moment. True, I was up to my eyeballs in getting the company going, but I was also still heavily involved in film production. Joel Michaels and I had completed *The Changeling* by the end of 1979, and right away we began preparations to make a film of Bernard Slade's Broadway smash hit *Tribute*.

I hoped *Tribute* would be a breakaway film for Michaels/ Drabinsky. Our first two films had deliberately exploited the suspense genre, and both had sold well in foreign markets. I was ready to do something more serious.

*Tribute* had come to us through a call from a Hollywood producer named Larry Turman. He and his partner, David Foster, had been signed up to produce *Tribute*, which Paramount had acquired on their behalf. But the studio had decided to put the project in turn-around, which means that the film rights were for sale to any producer willing to reimburse Paramount for its costs to date. Turman, a silky-smooth Hollywood type with an extra-casual manner, called me to see if I would finance the production.

Our company, Tiberius, was still financing films on an *ad hoc* basis. We had developed neither the infrastructure nor the pool of capital needed for a production company that expected to proceed on an orderly basis from one project to the next. We were still living from hand to mouth. For the third time, therefore, I found myself the catalyst around whom the development and packaging of another tax-shelter movie was taking place. *Tribute* was to be sold to investors via a prospectus, just as *The Changeling* had been.

We put the elements together carefully. We were fully aware that Slade's *Same Time, Next Year* had been first a hit on Broadway and then was made into a hit movie starring Alan Alda and Ellen Burstyn. We of course wanted to engage Slade, an expatriate Canadian living in L.A., to write the screenplay, and Jack Lemmon to repeat on film his *tour de force* performance as the charming schlemiel of a Broadway agent who is facing death from leukemia. It had the essential elements of a great film story. The movie had a chance of winning an Oscar.

*And I admit it, I was imagining myself holding an Oscar.*

Of course, there was the usual groundswell of criticism from the Canadian nationalists about my choice of vehicle. If I were going to choose a play written by a Canadian, why couldn't it have been an obscure and unknown one rather than a Broadway hit? My answer was simple enough. While the Canadian film industry was gradually gaining international recognition, it was still a minor player. We simply couldn't put together the expertise needed. We had no core of reliable screenwriters, and, unlike the British experience, there was little cross-pollination of writing and craft between our legitimate theatre and our moviemaking. And, in general, Canada didn't have the stories, the mythic tales, that would bring the public to the box office.

*Tribute* started off well. Turman, whose career as a producer began in 1967 with Mike Nichols's breakthrough movie *The Graduate* starring a then-unknown Dustin Hoffman, proved reasonable in negotiations. A deal was cut quickly, and Slade was put to work on the screenplay.

I hadn't yet met "Bern," as Turman called him. I knew however that he was fifty years old, that, after getting his start with the CBC, he had become one of Hollywood's most successful writers for TV and the movies, and that he was the author of two stage hits. I soon found out that he was also unbelievably arrogant.

Talk about chutzpah! The first draft of the screenplay was delivered, stamped FINAL DRAFT!

Joel, Turman, and I were together in Hollywood when the draft arrived, and we were appalled. There were gaping holes throughout the script in the plot, in characterization, and in dramatic transitions. A meeting was set up around the Bel Air Hotel pool, with Joel and me, Turman, Foster, and Bern.

Slade walked in looking as if the most he could spare us was five minutes. He began to seethe, and I swear his blood pressure must have risen twenty notches as he started to look over the notes Joel and I gave him. I had thought Slade's success would have made him resilient in the face of criticism. Wrong. Instead, I had the feeling we had mortally wounded his ego, and when he finally left the meeting, I wondered whether we'd ever see him again. We did. Eleven times. That's how many drafts it took before he delivered an acceptable script.

What surprised me was how Turman had let Joel and me, the outsiders, play the heavies with Slade. Naïvely, I thought Turman would be, if anything, even more determined than we were to get an excellent script. I came to believe that Turman and Foster, like so many others in Hollywood, had managed to amortize one perfectly-timed hit over a professional lifetime; they were mostly brilliant at playing studios off against each other as they locked up development deal after development deal. It took me a while, but I finally realized that Turman would never come on strong to his friend Bern. It simply wouldn't be in his long-term interests.

Jack Lemmon, by contrast, was both affable and completely straightforward. We met him in the huge bar of his spectacular house in the Bel Air Hills. It was made of beautiful woods and upholstered in leather and boasted every whisky made on earth. Through an absolutely humungous window, it provided a breathtaking view of the golden, sunsplashed California hills marching toward infinity. Jack used his bar as the late Jackie Gleason did – as a prop for his endless one-liners.

The part of Scotty Templeton, the acid-tongued agent whose wisecracks go sour when he learns he's dying of cancer, had been written for Jack's return to the Broadway stage after an eight-year hiatus. Superficially, Scotty and Jack were alike: they both met life with a gag and a quip but were nice guys underneath. In Scotty's case, you had to dig a little deeper to find this out. Theatre audiences had loved Scotty, and Jack's stage performance had won him a nomination for a Tony. Not that he needed affirmation. In twenty-four years of filmmaking, Jack had given a remarkable range of performances from *Mister Roberts* to *Some Like It Hot*, *The Apartment*, *Irma La Douce*, *The Odd Couple*, and *The China Syndrome*.

I found Jack easy to get along with. He was warm and emotional, with a ready laugh. He basked unabashedly in his stardom, but he was always approachable and sympathetic. At our first three-hour-long meeting, peppered with Jack's jokes, I explained to him that our budget was capped at $8 million Cdn and that, because we wanted to hire two more stars to complement him, we were asking him to drop his upfront fee significantly and, instead, participate in the back end. In effect, we gave him more points, a percentage of the net profits. He was immediately agreeable. Why not? He knew that on Broadway *Tribute* had returned its money to its investors by opening night. Could the movie be expected to do less?

With Jack's okay we were then free to offer the role of Scotty's twenty-two-year-old son to Robby Benson, the new teen idol who had just come off *Ice Castles*. Not perfect casting, but then Matthew Broderick, who would have been perfect casting, hadn't yet surfaced. For Scotty's wife, we did get perfection in the beautiful Lee Remick, reuniting her with Jack for the first time since they had made *Days of Wine and Roses* together in 1962.

Once more, because of the Canadian-content rules, we had to engage a Canadian director. In this case the Canadian turned out to be American-born. Bob Clark, a landed immigrant, had shown great promise in 1979 with *Murder by Decree*, a Sherlock Holmes caper starring Christopher Plummer, James Mason, and John Gielgud. Still, those three are models of restraint compared to Jack Lemmon, whose exaggerated mannerisms have been knit into his character so tightly that they can be separated only by a director filled with empathy and sure of his authority. In this regard, Clark's value was unknown. So to protect ourselves, we imported the superb American film editor Richard Halsey, who had won an Oscar for cutting *Rocky*.

We knew only too well, from previous sad experience, that a film editor often makes the difference between a good and a mediocre film. But however good he is, he can't make bricks without straw. He can't produce good work without enough coverage – enough camera shots from different angles to cover every editing possibility. Halsey was thus our point man on the production. In those days directors didn't have the comfortingly instant feedback of onset video. Halsey would assemble the rushes – the film shot daily – and assess whether the footage was adequate to create the essential moments of comedy and dramatic intensity and whether it would allow for proper transitions between scenes. If not, he would tell the director and the producers and the necessary reshooting would be done the next day before the set had been struck.

But we weren't done casting yet. A Canadian director wasn't Canadian enough for the Alliance of Canadian Cinema, Television and Radio Artists (ACTRA). The union squawked, loudly and publicly, about my decision to cast three American actors in the lead roles. Under the Canadian-content rules, I was allowed only two Americans before going to ACTRA for immigration approval for the third. They were balking at my casting of Lee Remick.

I was enraged. Why should I have to justify my decision? Why was I obliged to defend the integrity of the casting in the first place? It was, after all, my reputation, my name, and my neck – not ACTRA's. But of course none of that mattered to them. In 1990, when U.S. Equity challenged Cameron Mackintosh's casting of Jonathan Pryce as an Eurasian in *Miss Saigon*, I felt just as angry on Cameron's behalf as I had on my own. As far as I'm concerned, the unions (or associations, as they prefer to be called) don't create the shows that provide employment for their members; they're not necessarily that interested in the aesthetic qualities of the play or musical or film; they have little regard for the audience that will pay to see the show. All they care about is jobs for their boys and girls.

I felt particularly incensed, because in the past three years I had produced *The Silent Partner* and *The Changeling*, which provided hundreds of jobs for Canadian actors. Surely I had proved by this time I wasn't just a one-off producer but that I was trying to help to build an industry that would benefit us all.

But ACTRA didn't give a damn, and ultimately I was forced to call them on it. I could just as easily make the film in New York, I said, and still conform to the Canadian-content rules, though by doing so I would have to deny dozens of jobs in Toronto to the International Alliance of Theatrical Stage Employees (IATSE) crews and to many ACTRA members in secondary and cameo roles. At the very tense ACTRA hearing that was called to decide the matter, I went on the attack. I criticized what I said was the negative collectivist mentality that always seemed to pick the wrong issues to fight.

In the end ACTRA was not prepared to endure the embarrassment of a Canadian production moving out of the country because of its own pigheadedness. And they certainly didn't want their fellow craftspeople, IATSE, dumping on them as well. So Lee Remick was given clearance and we started work.

But the experience left me with a bad taste in my mouth that has never completely gone away and a conviction that actors' associations are often fatally shortsighted.

*Tribute* was otherwise a happy experience. It came in more or less on time and budget and, best news of all, I had in hand a distribution deal with a major, Twentieth Century-Fox, where my old friend Norman Levy was now vice-chairman. I had met Norman while he was still at Columbia, before he and Alan Hirschfeld and Sherry Lansing all moved to Fox after oilman Marvin Davis bought the studio.

Fox paid nothing in advance for domestic rights, but committed millions of dollars for prints and advertising, thus ensuring that the film would be properly launched. Fox also agreed to allow us, the producers, to participate in the distributors' gross from the very first dollar. The U.S. pay-TV rights were sold to HBO and Time Life bought worldwide syndication rights.

Anticipation was high when we previewed *Tribute* at the Capri Theatre in Phoenix (which, coincidentally, would in four years become an asset of Cineplex Odeon). Norman Levy was there, along with Sherry Lansing, the bubbly head of Fox production. Jack Lemmon came, of course. Bob Clark, Joel, and I were all there.

During the last scenes of the film, when Jack is being roasted by his friends during a superbly cut montage, ending with Robby and Jack embracing on the stage, the audience cried uncontrollably. When the screen went dark, there was tumultuous applause. Even this didn't prepare us for what was on the rating cards, which had been handed out to the audience. *Tribute* had scored higher than *Kramer vs. Kramer*, the last huge hit produced and distributed in 1979 by Columbia during the Hirschfeld–Levy regime.

After the screening, we all left the theatre feeling terrific. The next day Sherry Lansing persuaded Norman to acquire the foreign rights to *Tribute* for an advance of $2.5 million.

But then I made one of the greatest mistakes of my career. A week later Joel and I met Norman in his office on the Fox lot, and he rocked us by offering us $5 million U.S. for Tiberius Films' entire interest in the movie.

Though I should have, I didn't even hesitate. I had seen those cards in Phoenix. I did some quick arithmetic. *Kramer vs. Kramer* had grossed $100 million U.S. in the United States. If we grossed only half of that, our points would be worth double Norman's offer. Anyway, Joel and I weren't in the business just to cash in. Not after spending eighteen months on a project. We were committed to making movies. If it was a failure, so be it.

I riffled through the reasons in my head, like a croupier shuffling cards. And we turned Norman's offer down.

*I should have remembered: preview audiences had responded well to* A Broadway Musical. *Preview audiences are a special breed. Preview audiences can often be wildly wrong.*

Considering the enthusiastic response at the preview, Fox decided to "platform" the film with a Thanksgiving release, giving it an exclusive opening at one theatre in each of the three leading North American markets. In New York it was at the Coronet, a major showcase on Manhattan's east side. A comparable strategic theatre was planned for L.A. and Toronto. Then, in January, Fox proposed to spread the picture wider and wider, building to a full saturation release in time for the Academy Award nominations in February.

Everything seemed to be falling into place. The Canadian première was one of the truly memorable and stellar evenings of my life. It was given in aid of the Canadian Cancer Society, and the current prime minister, Pierre Trudeau, was my guest. I didn't even mind when he made the front pages the next day instead of Jack Lemmon. I was just delighted to be making a splash in my own home town.

Opening night in New York was rather different. Joel and I checked the box-office grosses by the hour, and our hearts sank. That first day we grossed only $6,000, a paltry amount in light of Fox's lavish pre-opening advertising campaign; we had expected $10,000 or even $12,000. As I learned only too well at Cineplex, the first day of a movie's release usually tells the entire story. There are movies that start big and maintain the momentum for successive weeks, as word of mouth builds. Some start limp and build because of word of mouth. Others, like the Stallone exploitation collection, start huge and decline every day, until they have exhausted the market. And finally there are movies like *Tribute* that start out limp and, alas, stay that way.

*Tribute* bombed.

Our timing was off by a couple of years. In 1982 Debra Winger would die of cancer in *Terms of Endearment*, and that movie would be a $150-million U.S. hit. But in 1980 cancer was still taboo. Even though *Tribute* was funny, poignant, and schmaltzy, and even though Jack Lemmon was a lovable star, nothing could overcome audience resistance to the subject matter. Every review seemed to begin, "This is a movie about a man dying of cancer. . . ."

Norman Levy had a well-deserved reputation as an expert marketer, but he and his ad-pub team of Dick Ingber and Irv Ivers never did come up with the handle for an effective advertising campaign. Every concept had misery and suffering written all over it. The best artwork they could generate was a picture of Jack Lemmon hugging Robby Benson. We should never have okayed that ad look. Scotty wasn't supposed to be a bundle of human warmth. Rather, he was riddled with contradictions – a man who would send strippers to friends on their birthdays, would purport to mistake the boss's wife for a party girl, and would play tricks by phone. That he was finally a sympathetic character is a paradoxical triumph.

There were some consolation prizes. Jack Lemmon was nominated for a Canadian Genie Award and an Oscar, but won neither. Joel and I garnered twelve more Genie nominations, but we would be thwarted in our bid to win a third successive Best Picture Award. Eventually, NBC bought the film for $1.5 million U.S., and finally, *Tribute* recouped 95 per cent of its cost.

I came away from the experience disappointed and frustrated all over again by the way raising money for a movie from the public in Canada created artistic obstacles in the way of the movie's success. If we were to continue in production, we had to make an ongoing financing arrangement with a studio. So Joel and I went to Norman Levy.

Our relationship with him was flourishing, despite the *Tribute* débâcle. By the time we approached him, we had already refinanced Tiberius by means of a convertible debenture in which industrialists like Max Tanenbaum and Ted Rogers, through Rogers Cablesystems, participated. With a strengthened balance sheet, I was able to assure

Norman that Joel and I would continue to develop and deliver moderately budgeted projects. He was impressed enough to offer us a six-picture deal with Fox.

Joel and I came away delighted. Although I still couldn't completely sever the cord of tax-shelter financing with the Fox deal, no Canadian working in Canada had yet concluded a deal of that size with a major Hollywood studio.

Under the agreement, Fox would distribute in all media throughout the world a maximum of six films to be produced over four years. The films would be budgeted at less than $10 million each, and Fox was required to advance a minimum of 30 per cent of the negative cost (the cost of producing the movie) against 100 per cent of foreign receipts and 50 per cent of domestic receipts. Usually a producer isn't cut in on a share of the receipts until the distributor has recouped his costs, but as with *Tribute*, our share of the distributors' gross receipts was calculated from the first dollar. Fox was also granted an option to participate as an investor in one or more of the six films for up to 50 per cent of the budget.

Distribution is the Achilles' heel of the English-Canadian industry. It's not hard to see why. Compare Canada with Spain, for example. Spanish filmmaker Pedro Almodovar can make *Tie Me Up! Tie Me Down!* for under $1 million, and he has a Spanish-speaking audience of fifty-seven million to tap into. Whatever money he makes outside Spain is therefore just gravy. The inspired Quebec filmmaker Denys Arcand has a similar cultural advantage; he can make movies like *Jesus of Montreal* and *The Decline and Fall of the American Empire* with complete assurance that his tiny home market, along with those of France and the former French colonies, will produce enough at the box office to enable him to recoup.

But the English-Canadian filmmaker not only has a tiny market (eighteen million), he also has to compete for that market with the overpowering U.S. majors, not to mention every other English-language moviemaker in the world. You can't take much more than $3 million or $3.5 million, from all sources, out of Canada. Any Canadian film with a budget of more than an inordinately modest

$3 million simply has to penetrate the United States and other foreign markets to have any chance of earning its money back. To reach this larger audience, the movies must be as good as – if not better than – the other two hundred or so English-language movies released world-wide each year.

*Ah, the first temptation of Garth. . . . Armed with this multipicture deal and a vision of what I could do within reach of the deep well of Hollywood talent and money, I was sorely tempted to pull up my roots and move to L.A. I was also nagged by the thought that I would never be able to break through completely on my terms in Canada, that I would never be able to bring off the movies of which I knew I was capable, that I would be hamstrung and hogtied by the tangled web of Canadian-content rules. It definitely hurt me, staying here. I never did get to the stage where I had control over my own destiny.*

The first film to be financed under the new Fox arrangement was *The Amateur*, a movie about terrorists, starring John Savage, Marthe Keller, and Christopher Plummer. The screenplay was adapted from a novel by Robert Littell and told the story of a CIA computer technologist driven to avenge the heinous murder of his fiancée at the hands of a German terrorist group. The timing was just right: it tapped into the public fascination with the wave of PLO terrorism in Europe in 1981. Canadian-born Charles Jarrott (who had directed *Anne of the Thousand Days*) was set to direct. We had planned to shoot on location in Zagreb, but the city turned us down on ideological grounds (later, of course, Zagreb became a killing field for real, as the savagery of the Balkan civil war raged through it). Ultimately, we found the necessary locations in Vienna, Munich, Washington, and Toronto. The budget was $9.5 million.

Everything was going well. Prospects were good. The movie would likely make money. Our partners would be pleased. We would prosper.

But it didn't satisfy me creatively.

I think it was during the fourteen-week shoot in the dead of winter in Austria that I realized how completely soulless this kind of moviemaking was for me. *The Amateur* was an exploitation film, made purely for commercial reasons, empty of ideas or passion or creativity (except for the creativity of craft). Yet as a hands-on producer, I still had to stay right on top of every detail.

*I shuttled back and forth between Toronto and Vienna, and in the drone of the jets and the silent night of intercontinental space, I stared blindly down at the black ocean below and kept asking myself, "Why am I making this film? What am I doing? Is this what I want from life, some bitter story of revenge and intrigue?" I grew more and more depressed. I checked into the Intercontinental in Vienna and sought out the services of the hotel's masseur, hoping vainly that soothed muscles would bring inner peace, but the doubt remained, as insistent and persistent as the deep throb from the hip joint above my bad leg.*

*In all this time, with all these movies, we had come within, say, 20 per cent of recouping the negative cost. Nothing was ever a disaster but nothing was ever a breakthrough. Even my fees got plowed back. I said to Joel, "I can't do this any more. I'm not getting any satisfaction from any of this. We're not working with the best people in the business. They're good, but they're not where I want to be." If I had been able, say, to produce a movie like* Schindler's List, *a movie that dealt with fundamental, raw emotions in a true and honest way (the kind of movie I had wanted to make when Wiesel's* Night *first came to my attention all those years ago), that for me would have been perfect, creative nirvana. But I never could achieve that pinnacle. I never got there in film. Whereas I have got there in the world of live theatre. And very quickly.*

Joel was as exhausted as I was, and by the time we finished the film, neither of us was thinking rationally. At any rate, that's my excuse for what followed.

Within days of completing principal photography on *The Amateur*, a screenplay arrived in our office. It was from Carolco, the Mario Kassar–Andy Vajna partnership that had been our foreign-sales agent for *The Silent Partner* and *The Changeling*. By this time Carolco had become a fully fledged production company, and Kassar and Vajna first asked us to co-finance and then to produce a film for them – *with their money!* – to be called *First Blood*. The Canadian director Ted Kotcheff was already lined up, and Sylvester Stallone was to star.

Joel and I dutifully read the script, and when we were done, we stared at each other. It was another exploitation theme: this time a war veteran runs amok after he tries to track a Vietnam buddy, only to find the man has died.

*When the need for a decision came to me, I looked at the paintings in my office and my home, losing myself in the tranquil pools of creative endeavour that they represented, and I knew what I should do.*

"All I see is trouble," I said.

So soon after coming close to freezing to death in Eastern Europe, I just couldn't face risking life and limb on a twelve-week shoot in the wilds of British Columbia. Not to mention the problem of having to deal with the artistic demands of a Hollywood powerhouse like Sly Stallone. Not for that kind of film.

Carolco offered us a $400,000 producers' fee and generous net-profit points in the movie. Net-profit points are usually called turkey-points in the trade, because only very rarely does a film ever make any net profit after the studio and the stars get what is coming to them out of gross film rentals, but in this case we would have done unbelievably well, because Carolco was also offering us the right to produce any sequels.

But we were weary of exploitation, weary of empty stories, weary in body and mind.

So we passed it up.

Didn't pass up much, did we? Only the chance to produce one of the most phenomenally successful series in the history of motion pictures – *Rambo I, II, III*, and *IV*. Total worldwide rental gross for the series topped $1 billion U.S.

The very next week I did it again. Norman Levy called me and said, "Why don't you help out Harold Greenberg? He's short about $400,000 to finance a film called *Porky's*." He said Bob Clark, who had directed *Tribute*, had been hired as the director.

I read the screenplay. Then I turned to Joel and said, "Do you really want to put up $400,000 to do a movie about four horny guys in Florida?"

So we turned down *Porky's* too. It grossed over $100 million in North America. The two sequels also racked up substantial grosses.

*Turning point! Clear turning point, ninety-degree bend in the road of life. When a guy turns down two mega-hits in a week, because in his own mind he prefers to look upward at the stars rather than downward into empty exploitation, he has to do some serious soulsearching. If First Blood was what the masses were thirsting for, or the crudeness of Porky's, then clearly Joel and I were out of touch.*

*I would have made my fortune if I had done First Blood. And in spite of my emotional bond to Canada, I would have had to move to L.A. I would be living in Bel Air today as an independent producer. I would never have been involved any further in the Cineplex saga. I would have missed all that. I would have missed a chance to build a great company. On the other hand, I would also have missed the treachery of my financial partners in Cineplex and the heartbreak of Black Friday. And I would also have missed what I am doing now.*

*So, over the years, my feelings have gone both ways.*

Joel and I, however, weren't always immune to the temptation of commercialization. After seeing a rough cut of *Porky's* in Norman Levy's office and realizing that it was set to become a huge hit, we did our own teen flick, *Losin' It*, about the experiences of four Californian teenagers rock'n'rolling down to Tijuana, a town dreamt of by every young American in the sixties who had grown up with J. D. Salinger's *Catcher in the Rye*, a town filled with sleaze, whorehouses, and dope. Curtis Hanson, who had written *The Silent Partner*, was set to direct, and the budget was a modest $4 million U.S. because we were able to shoot it with a non-union crew in Calexico, California. The downside of the location was the 110°F heat.

Our major achievement in a minor film was casting Shelley Long (later of "Cheers") and the magnetically handsome Tom Cruise in his first starring role. I remember we went into an editing suite on the Twentieth Century lot and I got the editor of *Taps* to cut me twenty frames of this young guy, Cruise. All I looked at was twenty frames and I knew at once – this kid's going to be a huge star. We had been trying to cast the main roles, and up to then we hadn't been able to find the person we wanted. We needed a really young matinee idol, and now we had found him. (I notice with amusement that in his interviews these days, Tom doesn't say much about his role in *Losin' It*!)

We signed Tom for $40,000, with a two-picture option (which unfortunately never got exercised) at the same amount. Today, of course, he commands about $10 million U.S. a picture, but he hasn't changed at all: on the set he's still totally supportive, no trouble, and willing to do everything he's asked.

It was a blow when Norman Levy screened the movie and told us that he didn't think it was particularly commercial. He wasn't perceptive enough in this instance to take a Tom Cruise movie and make it into a hit and preserve the options on Mr. Cruise. *Losin' It* lost it at the box office too.

Meanwhile, over at Cineplex, things were hopping.

My spirits may have been taking a beating over film production, but I cheered up every time I looked at what was happening to Cineplex. From 1979 to 1981, as I plunged from one movie to another, Cineplex was growing dramatically from Montreal to Vancouver.

Once we got going on our major expansion plans, developers had started to come to us. As our track record improved, along with our equity base, landlords frequently offered us turn-key deals – they assumed the entire cost of leasehold improvements, even to equipping the theatres. By 1981 we had opened, or made plans to open, about a hundred and forty-six screens in seventeen Canadian locations, a tremendous amount of growth. But we were still small and vulnerable compared to our competition, Canadian Odeon and Famous Players.

Expanding at such a furious pace was changing the nature of Cineplex. I was determined to make it into Canada's premier movie-theatre circuit. The opportunity was there: I could see clearly that the exhibition business in Canada was steeped in inefficient, decades-old business practices; worse, it was managed by exhibitors who let themselves be dictated to by the Hollywood majors, which have never cared about the significant differences between Canadian and American audiences.

Still, Nat and I couldn't run Cineplex by ourselves any more; we had to build a management team.

The people I picked were young. I stole Cary Brokaw from Fox, where he was running the Boston branch of Fox's theatrical distribution arm, and he became my right-hand man. (Cary later turned to film production; one of his credits was as producer of one of 1992's hottest movies, *The Player.*) Chuck Wysocky came from the American Multi-Cinemas chain in the United States as my senior operations man. Barry Silver, my longtime colleague and friend, became general manager of Canadian theatre operations, while Lynda Friendly's mandate was broadened to include supervision of all marketing and communications.

The need for a fast-thinking and fast-acting team was never so clearly illustrated as by our problem with the Carlton Cineplex. This ten-screen complex was built into an office high-rise on the site where Odeon's huge downtown Toronto flagship, the Carlton, had once stood. I was delighted to have a theatre there, because if ever a motion-picture theatre had tugged at my heartstrings, it was the Carlton, which Rank had built just after the war in a wonderfully anachronistic style. I still remember how a mighty theatre organ rose from the floor prior to the screening of *Lawrence of Arabia* when I saw it there as a boy.

We opened our Carlton Cineplex in 1981 with a program of massappeal action flicks similar to those the Eaton Centre was playing. To our amazement, these movies were a bust.

What was wrong? We finally concluded that we had miscalculated the neighbourhood audience. The specialty-film audience we had initially discovered at the Eaton Centre, only a few blocks from the Carlton, was being ignored, because the Eaton Centre was now being programmed with the higher-grossing, mass-appeal, move-over product. This specialty audience was still out there, but it had nowhere to go. Our path seemed clear: we closed the Carlton for a refit, renamed it the Carlton Cinemas, and opened it as an art house in November 1981.

Lynda took the lead in giving it a new style. She pioneered the up-scaling of concessions by installing a European café that served cappuccino and espresso, Perrier, freshly baked muffins and pastry from Dufflet, Toronto's top patisserie. Over the next eight years, the café concept would become a primary feature of the Cineplexes we opened in the more sophisticated areas and would become one of our most praised innovations.

But while we were building, our competitors were waking up and beginning to probe for our weaknesses. They easily found the chink in our armour – our reliance on 16-mm film. We had always had problems getting 16-mm prints quickly enough. Now Famous Players and Canadian Odeon began to lean on the distributors to stall – sometimes for as much as twelve weeks – before they brought them into Canada. And very often the distributors wouldn't bring in enough copies. This meant that, by the time we got a movie, the public's attention had flickered and died. It was too late to capitalize on its initial advertising launch and on whatever favourable word of mouth it had generated and had remaining.

As a consequence, every 16-mm booking of a move-over had to be essentially a new launch to reintroduce the movie to the paying customers, with Cineplex having to pick up the advertising tab because the distributors refused to lay out much for what they thought would result in minimal incremental returns.

If we didn't act forcefully to reverse the situation, it would become critical. As we expanded, we had more screens to book, more seats to fill, and our pipeline to move-over films was being choked off. We were beginning to hurt all over. We were not achieving our box-office projections. The TD Bank and our investors were growing impatient. Still, as the product-supply issue became more clearly defined, my adrenaline kept surging. I warmed up to the challenge.

Obviously 16-mm film would prove to be our downfall if we continued to depend on it. As long as we couldn't use the more readily available 35-mm film, we were providing the distributors with an easy and unassailable reason for giving in to the pressures of Famous Players and Canadian Odeon.

On a hunch, in August 1981, I asked Barry Silver, "Has there been any change in the building codes that might affect our ability to convert to 35-mm?"

To the chagrin of both of us, it took Barry only a few hours to discover that, in Ontario at least, the antiquated Theatres Act had been superseded by the Ontario Building Code, which at last recognized 35-mm film as fireproof. Similar changes in other provincial building codes had already occurred; the standards were no longer nearly as rigid.

"You mean we can install 35-mm projection in our booths and start running it tomorrow?" I demanded, to be sure.

"That's it," Barry said.

After meeting with Nat and the Cineplex board, I issued the watershed directive to buy as many Ballantyne, Prevost, and Zeiss Icon 35-mm projectors as were available.

"Let's do it," I said, echoing Nat's familiar phrase. The chase was on.

The cost of retrofitting the circuit with new 35-mm projection equipment would be about $2 million, but we had to spend the money to protect our already-substantial investment. We had to get move-overs faster, and that meant eliminating any excuse the distributors might have to refuse to give them to us.

The duopoly struck back immediately. Zahorchak and Destounis refused to let the distributors move over a film to a Cineplex screen immediately after a first-run engagement, though most of them wanted to.

They not only stopped move-overs to our theatres in the same film zone, but they also, in order to thwart us, went much further. They insisted that no film could be moved over to a Cineplex house in the same metropolitan area until all first-runs everywhere in that area had come to an end.

For example, they would open a film in ten or twelve theatres, each in a different Toronto zone. As audiences dwindled, the film would be kept running on a single suburban screen, excuse enough for the chain to tell the distributor, "As long as we're advertising this film in Toronto's newspapers, you're not to make the film available to Cineplex."

Our retort was simple. We told the distributors, "We can give you five runs for this film today. Take off the single Famous Players and Canadian Odeon run and make more money with us."

They refused.

The main threat they faced was that any distributor who breached the rule would suffer by being given poor locations all over the country for subsequent releases. Retaliation was threatened: *thou shalt obey, or else. . . .* It was, without doubt, flagrant restraint of trade.

Famous Players and Canadian Odeon would never have gotten away with it in the United States, because it was exactly what the Sherman Anti-Trust Act of 1890 had been enacted to prevent. Yet in Canada, American distributors were conspiring with Canadian exhibitors to put an infant Canadian venture out of business. Talk about cutting off their noses to spite their faces! They would have made much more money by creating competition and bidding up the price of films if they had fed Cineplex, but the combination of comfort with the status quo and fear of reprisal was too persuasive for them. They stood pat.

Soon we were in a state of open warfare.

*And I didn't have the time to deal with it properly, not really. I couldn't concentrate. I was being ripped apart, run ragged, shuttling between my law offices and the Cineplex offices. One minute I was fretting about bookings, or the theatre construction program, or box-office revenues, and the next I was wrestling with the multiple problems of movie production, my other clients, and my life. It couldn't go on.*

*I was making too many bad decisions. There was a flaw in my decision-making process. I thought to myself, "Am I turning the wheel, or is the wheel turning me?"*

Halfway through 1981, I finally sat down with Nat, Dick, Joel, and Myron. With my heart in my mouth, filled with uncertainty and doubt, I decided to shut down my end of the law practice; my filmmaking career was in any case winding down. I wanted to see Cineplex Corporation assimilate Pan-Canadian, the distribution company, and Tiberius Films. The existing and separate shareholder structures would be folded into Cineplex, operations would be rationalized, and the new corporation put on a sounder financial base. Nat would remain as chairman of the board, and I would succeed him as president and CEO. Nat was now seventy-five; he'd been the stalwart of Cineplex for three hectic years, and he handed over responsibility to me with considerable relief.

This decision provoked complicated emotions. I remember feeling sad and regretful that I was closing down my compatible law partnership with Dick, even though we wouldn't lose contact, because he was to become Cineplex's secretary-treasurer.

*But my doubts vanished when I looked ahead. I was going to build a major Canadian corporation. Under my direction, Cineplex would become a force to be reckoned with in its industry, a major player, a cultural heavyweight, a North American presence. I couldn't wait!*

# CHAPTER

## THE INDOOR DRIVE-IN

It was the third week of November 1982, and I was in Harry's Bar in New York's Helmsley Palace Hotel. A waiter brought me a phone. Myron Gottlieb was calling from Toronto. No matter what the provocation, Myron never actually sounds upset; he just delivers the news, good or bad, in his usual soft monotone. The guy could be announcing the presence of a band of international terrorists in his living room and he would sound just the same.

But at least he got right to the point. Andy Sarlos had called him, Myron told me, and said, "Myron, Garth's gotta go as president of the company."

Not exactly what a person wants to hear.

But was I surprised? Not very much.

I had committed myself totally to Cineplex when I took over as president the year before. My every waking hour and what money I had was tied up in the company, and it was in deep trouble – it was, in fact, on the verge of bankruptcy. Five months earlier, in June, our audited consolidated financial statement showed Cineplex to be $9.3 million in debt. Interest rates were rocketing as the recession took hold. Our cash flow was shrivelling. Famous Players and Canadian Odeon had been largely successful in keeping the studios from sending films to

Cineplex. The TD Bank, our banker, was on our case day and night. It was the bank, I was sure, that was agitating for a change in Cineplex's leadership, and Andy Sarlos and his partner, Barry Zukerman, who both sat on Cineplex's board, were accommodating them.

What a great pair they were! Sarlos, a shrewd Hungarian with a gut instinct for survival, was renowned for his flair in the money markets. At the market's peak in 1981, he was running a portfolio of assets that was approaching $1 billion. Zukerman was a cocky McGill graduate and ex-TD officer, who was so shortsighted that he had to press his nose almost onto a document before he could read it. They had their own investment fund, HCI Holdings Ltd., and just then were also heavily dependent on the TD Bank's goodwill. Who wasn't, in 1982, dependent on a bank?

Cineplex could easily be put on solid footing. All I needed was time. In July 1982 we had opened the Beverly Center Cineplex in L.A., our first complex in the United States, fourteen screens on the top floor of an eight-storey shopping centre. It was an immediate success and demonstrated that Cineplex had a future in the United States as well as in Canada. Not only that, it provided hard evidence that it was the difference in the laws of the two countries that was responsible for the Beverly Center being able to outperform comparable Canadian outlets at the box office. In the United States, the Sherman Anti-Trust Act forced the distributors to give all exhibitors in a given geographical zone an equal opportunity to book a picture. I had no trouble booking Beverly Center. But in Canada there was only the ineffective anti-combines legislation that Nat had tried to invoke years before in his fight on behalf of the independent distributors.

When I took over as president of Cineplex, I knew I was going to have to fight this discrimination in Canada. But first I had to get the company properly organized and consolidated. To a bank, the Cineplex balance sheet was not a pretty sight. We had a little over $1 million in equity and were deeply in hock to the banks and to our investors. Our shareholders had contributed $6.5 million, but mostly in the form of loans instead of equity; the company was burdened with having to pay interest on these shareholders' loans.

Myron and I knew the only recourse was new equity from a public issue to pay down our loans. In May 1982 we amended the corporation's articles and began the process of filing a prospectus to sell shares, with an eventual listing on the Toronto Stock Exchange (TSE). We knew this would take at least six months.

*In hindsight, I don't know if we chose the wisest course. There's no doubt we needed refinancing, and a public offering seemed to provide the best solution. But some of our original backers, including Eph Diamond, voted against the whole idea and got out. Eph pleaded with Myron and me to reconsider going public.*

*"Taking Cadillac public was the worst decision of my career," Eph told us. "Forget the glamour. The public company will become an albatross – the regulations, the restrictions, the horrendous amount of time required to run a public company will distract you from the actual management of the business. Your productivity will be diluted. Analysts, investment bankers, securities commissions, and shareholders will consume more and more of your entrepreneurial time and drain you emotionally."*

*I should have listened to him. Seven years later Eph's words rang in my ears as I struggled against those very forces in my fight to hang on to Cineplex Odeon.*

*But at the time I felt I had no option. Some of our other shareholders, like Jack Daniels, Andy Sarlos, and Rudy Bratty, were entrepreneurs caught in the crunch of 1982's deteriorating economy and ballooning interest rates. Their balance sheets were inverting as they fought off their own banks. They welcomed the idea of Cineplex going public because it gave them the expectation of cashing in their investment at a time when money was excruciatingly tight.*

Our timing was terrible. Just as we issued our preliminary prospectus, Canadian corporate profits began to plummet and the TSE composite index took a plunge. We were turned down by our preferred underwriter on the grounds that the corporation's business was outside conventional norms and that our rocky start had given us a deplorable track record, which would not attract national institutional support. I didn't have the heart to disagree.

We had to fall back on Myron Gottlieb, an investor and share-holder, and his Merit Investment Corporation for support. Merit agreed to sell 770,000 units at $5.00 a unit, each unit consisting of one common share and a share-purchase warrant entitling the holder to purchase a further common share at $5.50 until June 30, 1983, and at $6.00 until June 30, 1984.

Then, at a critical moment, Max Tanenbaum, who had been such a good friend and staunch supporter, had a stroke that left him incapacitated and unable to manage his business affairs. A bitter public battle began among the members of his immediate family. We worried about Max, and then we became victims of the indecisiveness of the committee that had been appointed to deal with the vast Tanenbaum holdings. In the midst of the family squabbles, two of Max's four sons were appointed to the Cineplex board, but neither of them were particularly sympathetic to our problems.

The most difficult problem of all was the bank. The TD Bank was our major lender. In the hopeful days of early 1980, Dick Thomson, the urbane chairman of the TD, had actively wooed Nat and me. He and his senior vice-president, Ernest Mercier, had invited us to lunch in the bank's private dining room, on the fifty-fourth floor of the TD Centre, and asked to become our major lender. Of course, I was thrilled – being courted by a banker was something new for me. But it all fitted in so neatly. The TD had a 25 per cent investment in the Eaton Centre, which had been built by Cadillac Fairview, and Cadillac Fairview was our landlord for half of the leaseholds in our growing circuit.

By June 1982, however, our debt with the TD Bank had mushroomed as we rushed to finish our expansion program, including opening Beverly Center.

Now they were on my case. There was a "gang of four" assigned to harass me. They sent me nagging letters every week. No matter how I tried, I couldn't get them to take into account my difficulties in getting films from distributors.

I could feel the noose getting tighter as I kept yelling, "I can't put asses on the seats if I can't get product!"

My relationship with Famous Players and Canadian Odeon had soured completely. Nat and I had gone to visit Mike Zahorchak of Canadian Odeon and his son Bob shortly after I took the reins of Cineplex, in the hope of coming to some accommodation. Nat was doubtful, but I insisted, and off we drove to the outskirts of Toronto where the Zahorchaks had their bizarre offices, which resembled a turn-of-the-century home in the Balkans, with heavy, elaborate furniture and velvets and brocades in rich, bright colours.

The Zahorchaks *père et fils* managed to restrain themselves from toasting our arrival.

I was direct and to the point. "Listen," I said. "I'm going to do everything I can to change the conditions of exhibition in this country."

Since this didn't seem to make much of an impression, I added with a certain bravura, "You'll find I'm a very formidable foe."

This, too, seemed to leave them unmoved, so I slammed my fist down on the table and shouted, "If I have to, I'm going to crush you. But it doesn't have to come to that. All you've got to do is cut me into the business, let me have my reasonable share, enough to let me live, and we can get along together."

*Yeah sure, Garth, and didn't Moses ask Pharaoh to be reasonable, just before calling down the plagues?*

Mike looked at me and said blandly, "What are you talking about? What do you want from me?" He wasn't going to give up a morsel. He was sure Cineplex was quickly reaching the end of its resources.

I wasn't sure I entirely disagreed with him.

The deal that resulted in Beverly Center had come over the transom back in 1980, when I got a call from an L.A. developer, Sheldon Gordon. The motion-picture world is small, and Cineplex's innovations were giving rise to a lot of comment in the industry – much of it derogatory. Competing exhibitors regularly attacked Cineplex's tiny auditoriums as uneconomical. There were, they said, too few seats to justify the cost of prints, an allegation we refuted convincingly by the high grosses we achieved with film distributed by our own Pan-

Canadian Films and when we got any move-over with some life left in it. For example, three Eaton Centre screens totalling four hundred seats had showed a first-run of a Pan-Canadian release, *The Secret Policeman's Other Ball*, and grossed $31,000 in its first week, while in Calgary, a smaller market, the movie had grossed $32,000 in three theatres with a total of three hundred and fifty seats. In 1982 these were impressive grosses.

Sheldon Gordon told me he was building an eight-storey shopping centre around some oil derricks (a common sight in L.A.) at the corner of La Cienega and Beverly Boulevard.

"Absurd!" I thought, but said nothing.

Floors two to five, Sheldon said, were to be parking. This made sense; in many areas of L.A. you can't put parking underground because of the fear of earthquakes. There would be a Hard Rock Cafe and a California Pizza as well as other restaurants and food emporiums on the ground floor; floors six and seven would be retail. And then he said, "I want you to build a theatre on level eight."

I almost asked, "Are you crazy?" but I bit my tongue and said nothing. Still, "crazy" had been the standard response of every other U.S. exhibitor Sheldon had canvassed. American Multi-Cinema, General Cinema, Pacific, Mann, United Artists had all turned him down. This was not especially surprising. The column-free spans were too small for building conventional theatres, and the location seemed a loser, sandwiched as it was between Westwood and Hollywood, the two most important film zones west of Manhattan. Any upstart exhibitor was going to have trouble getting film: he would be cleared from two zones, not just one.

But even as he talked, I could see the answer: the original Eaton Centre format. We would play first-run art and specialty movies and move-over runs from Westwood and Hollywood Boulevard. Those screens were in such demand that first-run films were customarily taken off when still grossing $20,000 to $30,000 weekly. The demand was unceasing. Every filmmaker wants his movie to open in the backyards of the fellows who run the studios. They want visibility, and this means a lot of turnover. These egotists need to be massaged constantly with the biggest lettering on the marquees and the most prestigious theatre locations. The Westwood demographics in particular are dynamite: one square mile of high-density retail, nestled between Beverly Hills, Brentwood, and Bel Air, drawing on the UCLA campus of between fifty thousand and sixty thousand students.

There were other plusses too. A Cineplex in Beverly Center would also benefit from being in one of the two top markets in the world for film promotion, the other being New York. L.A. is still a company town; there's an awareness and appreciation of motion pictures there that can't be found anywhere else. The moment kids go to public school in L.A., they know they're living in the heart of the motion-picture world. And the grosses! Westwood customarily had the highest single opening-week's gross anywhere.

Nat pointed out something else about the Beverly Center idea. We would really be building an "indoor drive-in." It's L.A.'s worst-kept secret that it's choking on its traffic; there is gridlock everywhere. In a neighbourhood chronically short of parking, Beverly Center would have four floors of it, free to customers.

So I flew off to L.A. with a strong feeling that I had possibly lucked into a gold mine. Sheldon's plans in hand, I went to take a look at the three oil derricks on their triangular patch of dirt. After poking about a bit, I turned to the developer.

"I'll do it," I said. "I'll build you sixteen screens with twelve hundred seats at the top of your crazy mall."

"Are you sure?" he said, his eyes lighting up and his jaw dropping. "You're not worried about Westwood?"

"No," I replied. "I've got the formula."

Sheldon Gordon subsequently ran into financial trouble and was rescued by the powerful Detroit real-estate billionaire Al Taubman, arguably the most astute and imaginative shopping-centre developer in the United States. When I learned of Taubman's involvement, I felt apprehensive, because I had never heard of him. So I did some homework in a hurry. Back in the late seventies, together with his cronies Henry Ford II and Max Fisher, he had successfully bid against Mobil

Oil and Cadillac Fairview for the Irvine Ranch property, a mega-mega development project in Southern California. Among his other prime real-estate and shopping centres were Chicago's Woodfield Mall and the prestigious Short Hills Mall in Milburn, New Jersey. (In the late eighties, Al would make one of his more glittering acquisitions – Sotheby's, the art auction house.)

My introduction to Al Taubman was like the man himself: blunt. He called me to say, "I'm flying to Toronto, because if you're going to be one of my tenants, I want to see if you're to be taken seriously." He was also precise, "I'll meet you at the Eaton Centre at two thirty on Tuesday afternoon. My plane will bring me in."

I did more homework. I found out that Al was a joint-venture partner with United Artists Theatres in about a hundred and forty screens, many of which were in Taubman malls. He apparently had showmanship in his blood.

Al flew into Toronto in his Falcon 10 (which our company was to buy from him four years later) and was whisked by limo downtown to the Eaton Centre, where I was waiting. He exuded an air of "I know it all, don't ever question me, this is the way it is." He was an imposing figure, a big man, well-groomed and well-dressed in an habitual black suit, a cigar clutched firmly in one hand. He seemed to be a listener, but he left little room for debate.

Al was fascinated by the Eaton Centre Cineplex. He gave it a thorough inspection. Then he turned to me and asked, "Are you confident this will work at Beverly Center? Are you absolutely sure about this?" Then, before I could answer, he shook his head and said, "I don't know, I don't know. But I've got no choice. I need you. I need you to be in this project. I just don't know whether you're gonna blow your brains out or not."

I had my answer ready. I told him all about Cineplex and what it meant to the future of exhibition. I must have half-persuaded him. Before he left, he looked at me appraisingly and delivered his verdict, "I like this kid."

Al spent exactly one and a half hours in Toronto before flying back to Detroit. I know because I clocked him.

Beverly Center was to be the new showcase for our evolving design philosophy. Halfway through its construction, I realized that it would be more effective to have fourteen rather than sixteen theatres. I could create two larger theatres of 140 and 120 seats respectively from four smaller screens, still intimate when compared to the average conventional auditorium size of 400 seats. These two would have Dolby stereo sound, as would a couple of the other auditoriums. The major innovation was the introduction of a common projection booth that served all fourteen screens. Another was a synchronized projection system that allowed us to play one movie simultaneously in as many as six theatres using the same print running through six different projectors. This technological advance offered distributors an increased box-office gross without incurring any additional film-print costs.

It was in L.A. that we first began relating our Cineplex colour schemes to the demographic characteristics of the market we were serving. L.A. was influenced by Mediterranean hues, so we chose pastels. And, hankering as I always was for the Roxy touch, we used generous amounts of marble in the foyer for the first time. Even the poster holders and marquee identification symbols were elaborate compared to the Canadian Cineplexes. And Beverly Center was where, at Dick's suggestion, I started to commission works of Canadian art to give our theatre complexes a unique character. The art was a major part of it. I saw an opportunity to link two obsessions: my belief in the unmatched quality of contemporary Canadian art and my desire to create a fresh and vital environment for our patrons. In this case I engaged Vancouver artist Gerald Gladstone to create a lobby mural, *Life Force*, to be the first permanent installation of a work of art in a Cineplex theatre.

Beverly Center was a milestone project because it established the style I wanted to achieve in all our theatres.

The challenge of building a theatre eight storeys in the air proved a formidable one, and Beverly Center ran over budget. The TD Bank was now really turning up the heat, so in June I set up a meeting in Detroit with Al Taubman and Bob Larson, who was president of

Taubman Construction, and put all my cards on the table. I asked for an $800,000 U.S. line of credit to be extended to Cineplex by Taubman Construction. I reminded Al that Cineplex had almost $2 million in the theatre and that I was the only exhibitor to have had the unwavering conviction and confidence to commit to his centre. "In short," I said, "we need each other." A deal was struck.

The TD Bank was now monitoring our account daily and refused us further credit. We were already "dragging" our rent payments. Two weeks before Beverly Center's opening on July 14, 1982, Leo Kolber and Bernie Ghert, chairman and president respectively of Cadillac Fairview, called me in L.A. I had spoken to Ghert before, but this was the first time I had exchanged words with Kolber – and the words we exchanged were not what you would call amicable. Kolber threatened to close down Cineplex and terminate all our leases if the rent arrears were not paid immediately.

*This conversation set the tone for my subsequent relations with Leo. Ironically, only one year later, he became my partner.*

I must have said something right, though. I didn't know it then, but Kolber also sat on the TD Bank's board and had the ear of its chairman, Dick Thomson. He must have whispered something favourable about Cineplex, because Thomson subsequently gave instructions that we were to get a further $500,000 credit – but only if Nat, Myron, and I personally guaranteed the funds. Not that we had any alternative. Beverly Center had to open on schedule, otherwise the rumour-mongering Hollywood distributors would immediately turn any delay into our defeat as they met over lunch at their favourite restaurants, Jimmy's in Beverly Hills and The Palm on Santa Monica Boulevard.

I barely had time to take a deep breath before Myron gave me bad news about the Cineplex prospectus. The Ontario Securities Commission's first review of the preliminary prospectus zeroed in on our significant working-capital deficit of $3.5 million. The OSC would allow us to proceed only if we brought down that figure substantially.

I did have one ace in the hole left: my relationship with Twentieth

Century-Fox and the six-picture deal I had made with Norman Levy a year earlier. What I intended to propose to Levy and Alan Hirschfield was that Fox lend Cineplex $3.5 million. The security would be an assignment of all rights to *The Amateur* and the pay-TV rights to *Losin' It*. The downside for Fox was negligible. I'd get a five-year loan that bore no interest for the first two years. The sweetener for Fox would be a five-year option to acquire 25 per cent of Cineplex at nominal cost.

A good deal for them, but hell, this was Hollywood, and I had to prostrate myself to even get a hearing. As I've said before, I liked Norman Levy very much. He was one of the best marketing men in the industry, and his meticulous attention to the micro aspects of the business really impressed me. Moreover, unlike most studio executives, he knew all about Canada – its media, its socio-economic structure, its politics, its theatres. Best of all, he was on my side; he too wanted to break the duopoly's hold on Canadian exhibition.

But still, as I've said, this *was* Hollywood, and he had to demonstrate his power. His attitude was "Drabinsky will have to wait until I'm ready to see him. He needs this loan badly." I sat for hours in Norman's reception lobby in the Skouras Building, Fox's administration hub, watching his two secretaries discharge their responsibilities as non-scheduled visitors paraded in and out of his office. But Norman did finally make the deal.

The drafting of the Fox loan agreement was handled by the outrageous Buddy Monasch, then head of Fox's business affairs. Monasch, an ex-family-law attorney, was not to be outdone by Levy. He kept me waiting even longer than Norman did – but this time I was sitting right in his office. I was trying to conclude a deal to save my business, and he was on the phone trying to set up his social schedule for the week.

*Hollywood!*

The only light moments for me were when I met the tall, glamorous Sherry Lansing in the halls. She'd always give me a big hug whenever I met her. "Hi, hon," she'd say, and give me a kiss on one cheek and then the other. This didn't get me any further with the loan agreement, but it did make me feel as though someone there appreciated me.

Every day the pressure in Toronto was building. For me, it was all the money in the world; for them, it was little more than a tip to a carhop. But I couldn't blame Fox's management too much. This was Hollywood's twilight and, like certain other studios, Fox had become the new plaything of a financier, in this case, Marvin Davis, an oil-man. It was pathetic to watch. When Davis telephoned from his jet that he was flying in from his Denver oilfields, the whole studio ground to a sickening halt. "Marvin's comin' to town. Cancel all meetings." It was as though everyone were waiting around for the Pope to arrive so they could genuflect.

Finally, just before Beverly Center opened, Norman telephoned me to say that he had obtained Marvin's agreement to my proposal and I had better come and see "the big guy."

He wasn't kidding about his boss's size. We were ushered into Marvin's huge and garish office, and I was confronted by a six-foot-seven, three-hundred-pound bear. He was hunkered down behind his desk and didn't bother to stand up to greet me. All he did was cast me a baleful glance and ask, "Do you really think you can pull this off, kid?" He gave a great windy sigh. "Is there really a future for Cineplex Corporation?"

What did he expect me to say – no? I felt a mix of indignation and contempt. But I projected nothing but confidence. "I've got my own money on the line and a lot of investors behind me," I said. "I won't let you down."

Marvin grunted. "Okay kid, go get 'em."

I had my $3.5 million. Finally, the prospectus could go ahead.

Buddy Monasch later told me how Marvin had made up his mind on the loan. Marvin had called up his "good friend" Leo Kolber at Cadillac Fairview and asked, "Leo, what do you know about this guy Drabinsky?"

And Leo said, "I don't know him, but he's in a mess. He's got real difficulties. He owes us money, he's slow to pay, and today, I wouldn't touch him."

Davis hung up, turned to Norman Levy, and said, "Okay, let's back Drabinsky."

The capper to this story would come a little more than a year later, in the fall of 1983. We were in the midst of our first rights issue, which would yield an additional $3.5 million in equity. By this time Cineplex had retired about half of the Fox loan, and it was a propitious time to get Fox's commitment either to exercise its option for 25 per cent of the corporation or sell it to someone else. Myron, with the help of Tim Hoare of the British investment banking firm of Laing & Cruickshank, had assembled a group of British institutions that offered Fox $2.10 a share for its entire stake in Cineplex. Fox agreed, was repaid its loan in full, and netted a handsome profit of $2 million on its one-year investment.

But before selling the shares, Davis called his good friend Leo Kolber again. By this time CEMP had bought an interest in Cineplex, and Leo said, "Drabinsky is a fabulous guy. We're backing him. We're investing in his company. He's pulled off a minor miracle. Stay in the company, Marvin, you'll have a great time and you'll make a lot of money."

Davis hung up the phone, turned to Levy, and said, "Fuck him. What does Leo Kolber know? Sell the stock."

All this within twelve months! If Davis had hung on for just two more years, he would have made between $15 million and $20 million.

It's a perfect example of the irrational psychology of the business mind. Davis made the loan while I was on the ropes. I weathered the storm, his bet paid off, and the future was ripe with opportunity. Then he refused to ride the crest of the wave.

Back in July 1982, however, when Davis okayed the loan, success still seemed a long way away. The financial pressures were so great in Toronto I turned almost with relief to the staffing of Beverly Center. The latest Cineplex was the newest entry in the industry's most competitive location. I moved in two of my most aggressive young executives, Neil Blatt and Cary Brokaw. Neil, a former booker for Fox in

Kansas City, had the kind of chutzpah I thought would be just right for Hollywood, while Cary was a seasoned Cineplex hand who understood my way of thinking. Their first job was to put together a judicious mixture of first-run art films and timely move-overs; the list included *Quest for Fire, Chariots of Fire, Don's Party,* and the Monty Python picture, *The Secret Policeman's Other Ball.* To reinforce matters and to prepare the way for possible litigation, I had written a letter to the distributors, with the help of U.S. counsel, telling them that I was prepared to go after them with all the weapons provided by the Sherman Anti-Trust Act if they attempted to behave in the same way they had in Canada – blocking our access to motion pictures. Significantly, no distributor ever denied us timely move-over product.

Our opening party was held two days before the public opening of Beverly Center. You would have never known from the happy expressions on our faces how close we had come to not being able to open at all. Bob Larson, the gregarious president of Taubman's company, gave a great speech, Mayor Tom Bradley welcomed us to L.A., and then we had the film-cutting ceremony and unveiling of the Gladstone mural. But so far as the motion-picture industry was concerned, it was the Eaton Centre all over again. Every exhibitor in L.A. had come along to see us fall flat on our faces. They knew, of course, about the difficulties Cineplex was having in Canada and the word was, "Better see this now 'cause it isn't going to be here next week."

Opening day found Nat and me in our customary position – on a bench in front of the box office. We were nervous. The shopping centre was only 40 per cent rented. Would the public find their way to the eighth floor? Would they really want to come to movies on top of a parking lot? To our delight, hordes of people streamed out of the elevators, and, by nightfall, the line-ups wrapped around the perimeter of the floor.

It was the next evening that almost gave me a heart attack. Saturday evening, 9 P.M., every seat in every theatre was sold – and the fire alarm for the Beverly Center began to clang incessantly.

We had to evacuate every auditorium! Hundreds of people stampeded out of the complex. I thought I was going to kill myself.

As it turned out, it didn't matter. We had projected a $44,000 U.S. box office a week, but at the end of the first week, the theatre had grossed $56,000 U.S., nearly 30 per cent over expectations. And it never stopped. During the week of American Thanksgiving, Beverly Center boasted a $100,000 U.S. gross, the highest on a per-seat basis in North America! It was proving to be a truly exceptional theatre.

As I flew back to Toronto, I was ecstatic. Al Taubman was too. He was now firmly in my corner (and within a year he'd prove it, handsomely). I now had hard evidence that Cineplex could be a very profitable circuit in Canada if it were given access to films. Beverly Center's average per-seat-per-week sales were $42 U.S. against approximately $16 Cdn for the entire Canadian circuit.

The difference was clearly my access to films, assisted by the strong anti-trust laws in the United States. My point was proved. In a similar business climate in Canada, Cineplex would work beautifully. Surely, I thought, the bank and my investors would now understand what I had been trying to tell them.

Nothing changed.

By September 1982 I was being squeezed unmercifully in Canada, while Beverly Center's grosses soared. Although our public issue was fully subscribed, the TD Bank was becoming more and more impatient, and Famous Players and Canadian Odeon were betting that the doors would close forever by Christmas.

Once again, I looked for a lifeline. This time it was an unlikely source for me – the federal government. The Combines Investigation Act must be made to work for us. Dick Roberts found an expert lawyer to advise me. W. E. Stewart McKeown had worked for the Restrictive Trade Practices Commission and was now in private practice in Toronto. McKeown's advice was succinct, "Get down to Ottawa and stay there until you get results."

So off I went, boiling with fury.

*Why was I so bloody angry? Because in the United States, where I was just another foreigner, I was protected by an enlightened, effective law that kept potential violators in check and encouraged entrepreneurship. In Canada, in my own country, a country that needed to encourage its entrepreneurs at every juncture if it ever wanted to move beyond a branch-plant economy, I was being frustrated by an inadequate, badly drafted combines law.*

*My attention was now fully focused on trying to make the provisions of this asinine law work.*

*And when I'm focused, I can be relentless.*

It was September 2, 1982, when I first met Don Partridge, the point man at the combines investigation office. I liked him right away. He was a genuine fellow who seemed very concerned about the rights of the little guy. He had spent the last six years reviewing the business practices of the Canadian film industry without being able to put a sufficiently strong case together, and almost before I started talking, he was nodding his understanding.

When I finished, he told me some good news. The loophole through which the distributors and Famous Players had escaped back in 1930 was now plugged. In 1976 the Combines Investigation Act was amended to include services as well as goods, and a more recent amendment to the act had established a tribunal to hear cases brought pursuant to the act – the Restrictive Trade Practices Commission. Partridge underlined section 31.2 of the act, which defined "the refusal to deal." Under this section, an application could be made to the commission for an order against the major film distributors, ordering them to accept Cineplex as a customer and directing them to supply commercially valuable motion pictures to Cineplex on the usual trade terms.

Armed with such a ruling, I would be able to compete on a zone-by-zone basis. This meant, first of all, that if Famous Players or Canadian Odeon didn't have a theatre in a particular zone, Cineplex would have a right to the film's first run in that zone and the right to play it simultaneously with other theatres owned by the competition in other zones. Second, even if the competition had theatres in the same zone, Cineplex would have the right to compete, and the best terms offered to the distributor would determine the winner. And third, the moment one of the other exhibitors vacated a zone by taking off a first-run engagement, Cineplex would have the right to move the picture over to one of its theatres in that zone on competitive terms.

Later that day I was introduced to Lawson Hunter, director of investigation and research for the Combines Investigation Act. He was a lawyer who looked like a Harvard Business School professor, complete with granny glasses. He looked as polished and distinguished as Partridge was practical and down-to-earth. They made a great team.

Lawson amplified what Partridge had told me about the way the act actually worked. It didn't matter, he said, who was really the driving force behind the apparent conspiracy – that is, whether the distributors were keeping films from Cineplex because they wanted to or whether it was pressure from the exhibitors exercising their market power with the distributors. In my mind, there was no doubt that it was the exhibitors who were to blame, but, as Lawson told me, the structure of the act allowed only one approach, and that was an action against the distributors.

"Now," said Hunter to me, "we need your help in assembling the necessary evidence before we can make a section 31.2 application, based on the distributors' refusal to deal."

"You've got it!" I said. "My organization will work seven days a week to get you all the evidence you need – and fast."

I thumped the table and said, "I'm like a patient in the last stages of cancer. If you don't start an action in the next two months, it won't matter, because the company will be bankrupt and whatever opportunity you have to open up competition in the film marketplace will be lost for another fifty years."

"We need to get all our ducks in a row," Partridge said, and he sent me to see the minister of consumer and corporate affairs, André Ouellett. "Political will is essential to the case," Partridge explained. "Things could get messy and the publicity could get ugly. Movies are hot potatoes. The U.S. Congress is constantly being lobbied heavily by the Motion Picture Association of America to intervene on the distributors' behalf whenever their interests are threatened anywhere in the world, and you can bet it will be lobbied to death in this case.

The heads of various companies might even threaten Canada with scorched-earth retaliatory tactics." (This is exactly what Martin Davis of Gulf + Western did several years later when Marcel Masse, minister of communications, tried to block the sale of the Canadian branch of Prentice-Hall, the publishing firm. He threatened to close the subsidiary down rather than be dictated to.)

My timing couldn't have been better. My film-production activities had given me a high profile in Canada, and the Liberal government approved of my efforts in attempting to build up the production and exhibition sectors of the industry. So Ouellett was quick to assure me, after my passionate speech to him, that the cabinet would support any action taken by the combines department. He seemed to be well aware that the case would generate national publicity and would give the combines guys much greater credibility with other challenges they were expected to make later.

Compiling the necessary evidence was a labour of love. What pleasure to assemble instances of distributor hypocrisy and double-dealing!

When it became clear the government was serious, the distributors began to get antsy. But they had nowhere to run. They attempted to defend their actions in denying first-runs to Cineplex by asserting that our auditoriums were too small to justify an early run of a picture. This was easy to deal with: the success of Beverly Center and selected instances throughout our Canadian circuit strongly refuted this argument.

Of course I told the TD Bank that I was now working closely with the combines investigation department in a last-ditch effort to get pictures on Cineplex screens, but they were unimpressed.

At one point a credit officer of the bank wrote an internal memo, plaintively asking something to the effect, "what trouble are they getting us into *now*?"

I was working against the clock. The bank wanted out and they were impatient. I was on the phone almost daily to Partridge and Lawson, urging them to hurry.

"The bank's going to close me down," I said.

By late 1982 a lot of loans were going bad. Third World countries and major oil companies were defaulting all over, but nobody was calling their loans. Typically, the banks targeted the smaller business loans because they knew they could collect those with fewer repercussions. Big corporations and Third World countries could tell the banks to stick it. We couldn't.

At one point in these anxious months, Doug Bassett of Baton Broadcasting told me how his father, the imperious John Bassett, Sr., had handled his bankers when they called the loan on his newspaper, the *Toronto Telegram*. The elder Bassett, for whom I've always had a great deal of affection, was a tall, patrician, acerbic man with a commanding manner. He walked into the bank chairman's office and put the keys to his office on the desk. "You want the business? Go run it."

Dick Thomson had lobbied Nat and me to become Cineplex's bankers, and now he wanted to shoot us down.

I was in Doug Bassett's office one day and I asked him to call Dick and ask him why he was so intent on putting me under.

I heard Dick's reply, "Garth's not going to drive around in a Mercedes 450SL on my money."

*This drives me up the wall, these accusations of extravagance. They've dogged me all my working life. This thing with the car drove me nuts. Here's the problem: I had polio. I can't drive a standard-shift car. Most of the great sports cars of the world are standard shift, so I can't drive them. From the beginning, the only car I could find that looked like how I wanted a car to look and felt like how I wanted a car to feel was a two-seater Mercedes automatic, and that's the car I've driven all my life. I love that car. So it costs more – that's the way it is. I work so goddamn hard, I've got to be able to enjoy something.*

*The reality is this: I have only one hobby – my art. My only investment outside my company shares has been in art; I spent all my money acquiring what I consider a wonderful collection of paintings. True, the collection holds substantial value today, but I bought these works in the first instance because I love them. I look around my office now, at Livent.*

*It's hardly palatial, just comfortable. The reality is, I just don't leave myself a lot of time to be indulgent.*

*I live to get things done.*

By November the TD Bank had totally given up on me. Our debt-to-equity ratio was now five to one; we were wallowing in debt. But the bank couldn't run an exhibition business; they didn't have the expertise. They needed management to work out the repayment of their loans. That's where Andy Sarlos and Barry Zukerman came in, and when Myron phoned me in New York with the news that Sarlos was trying to depose me, I thought I knew why – they were both members of our board, and the bank was using them to put me on the rack.

I had – and have – some sympathy with them. The pressure of business, of being in business extremis, sometimes make people behave in certain ways they might not otherwise prefer. Despite our differences, I had always enjoyed listening to the savvy Sarlos. He had quite correctly predicted to me the disastrous economic slide of 1981-82 – but then, he inexplicably refused to act on his own predictions, never being able to bring himself to really believe the market would crash. I've never held a grudge against Andy for his actions against me at Cineplex. Some years later he was big enough to ignore our history, see my talents, and come back as an investor when I set up my present company, Livent.

After I got Myron's call, I rushed back to Toronto and met Sarlos and Zukerman at Myron's house the following night. I was fighting mad. "You'll have to see this company in bankruptcy before you see me resign," I declared. "If I go down, so does the company!"

The meeting ended with an agreement that a full board meeting must be called as soon as possible, which turned out to be in the middle of the week. I had little time to rally my troops. Of the ten-man board, I was sure of six votes: mine and Myron's, Nat Taylor's, Dick's, and those of Jack Daniels and Rudy Bratty. Sarlos and Zukerman had the Tanenbaum brothers, Howard and Larry, and worked hard on Jack and Rudy, but those two remained resolute in my defence. Indeed, when Jack heard that Sarlos wanted Zukerman to be the president, he blew up, "That's a ludicrous idea. Barry knows nothing about the business!"

At the board meeting, I spoke without notes for ninety gut-wrenching minutes. I explained the history of the company, how we had grown, and what we had accomplished. I stressed that this was not the time to change management, on the eve of the very government initiative that would keep us alive.

The atmosphere was tense, but the vote went with me, six to four, and Sarlos and Zukerman resigned from the board. Their defeat, however, only made the TD Bank more determined to wipe Cineplex out. In the first week of December it asked the management consulting firm of Woods Gordon to prepare to put us into receivership.

By now I was calling Don Partridge and Lawson Hunter at their homes every night.

"You have to get this action started, you've got to give me some room to breathe, because otherwise we'll be finished in a matter of days. I'm not bluffing. The bank wants this company in receivership right now, and if this happens, then Famous Players and Canadian Odeon will have achieved their objective of killing Cineplex."

For the first time, even I could smell the possibility of defeat. I was so low I just wanted to hide. Lynda Friendly had organized a Christmas pizza party for our staff of forty people, and I remember she kept coming into my office, where Myron and I sat in misery, chivvying us to pull ourselves together. "For the sake of everyone's morale, you've got to join us."

But we just couldn't.

On December 16 the TD Bank asked that certain of the company's bridge-financing loans guaranteed by the principal shareholders (that is to say, me, Myron, and Nat) be repaid as a first step toward putting Cineplex into formal receivership. This was no time to vamp. My distress calls to Ottawa grew more frequent. Five days later Don Partridge, bless him, took the final draft of the papers required for the section 31.2 application to his department's Christmas party, where Lawson Hunter signed them. Indeed, 'tis (or 'twas) the season to be jolly.

The official announcement was made on December 22, and the next day it was banner news in the *Toronto Star*: "COMBINES ACTION LAUNCHED ON BEHALF OF CINEPLEX CORPORATION AGAINST THE MAJOR DISTRIBUTORS."

The TD Bank was stymied, at least briefly. It was now in an embarrassing position. Should it be seen as putting a Canadian company out of business on the eve of a great battle with the big, bad Americans?

As for me, I was alive.

Wasn't that enough?

*When you're alive, there are always possibilities.*

# CHAPTER

## THE DUOPOLY DOO-WOP

The news of the combines action against the distributors won Cineplex only a short reprieve. The TD Bank still had us under the gun, and from what we could see, its fingers were quivering eagerly on the trigger. Myron and I reckoned we had only nine days, until January 1, 1983, not only to come up with a debt-restructuring plan that would satisfy the bank but also to inject at least the $2 million the bank was demanding in new equity.

*So much for the holidays!*

Some weeks before, having announced its intention of calling its loan, the bank had commissioned a report on our operations from the management-consulting firm Woods Gordon. It was delivered in mid-December and contained no surprises as far as I was concerned. Indeed, it supported a lot of what I had been telling the bank all along about the reasons for the doleful state of our fiscal health. Not only that, but Woods Gordon was optimistic about Cineplex's management being able to turn things around.

The bank, however, believed it knew better than its hired experts. Arthur English, the TD executive handling Cineplex's account, rejected the report, calling it "long on hope and short on fact." He then directed them to submit a second, much-tougher assessment of Cineplex's management and of the corporation's viability.

In this climate, the idea of restructuring our loans with TD was toast.

I remember speculating to Myron that the bank might have decided to force Cineplex into liquidation during the anti-combines fight, reasoning that Canadian Odeon or Famous Players might bid higher than they otherwise would for Cineplex's assets just to rid themselves once and for all of the ongoing aggravation called Drabinsky.

Our cash flow was stabilized temporarily by heavy Christmas moviegoing, but the holiday season wasn't the best time to find people in their offices, let alone find them willing to consider major investments – especially as the 1982 recession was rolling unchecked into 1983.

Desperation drove us. We worked round the clock, meeting with shareholders and likely lenders. Every banking day we met with the bank's representatives to report progress. Each session was remarkably unpleasant. We would stare across the table, wondering at the level of animosity, astonished at the level of personal feeling; we were deeply aware of their rancour.

We started off proposing a modest refinancing, and then slowly upped the ante.

The bank was hard to break down because it was convinced we had nowhere to turn. Max Tanenbaum, our biggest supporter, had been immobilized by his stroke. I couldn't go back to Nat Taylor; he had already done all I could reasonably ask of him in the past year, and after all, he was approaching eighty.

It was Al Taubman who finally came through for us. After the TD Bank had called its loan in November, Myron and I had flown to New York over the American Thanksgiving holiday to talk to Al about our difficulty repaying the loans he had made to us for the completion of Beverly Center.

We met in Al's Manhattan *pied-à-terre*, a sumptuous apartment in the Pierre Hotel with as fine a collection of twentieth-century art as I've ever seen. I walked in an admiring daze from Matisse to Picasso and then on to Rothko, Pollock, Hofmann, Motherwell, and Giacometti.

*As usual when confronted by great paintings, I felt both calmed and energized. There's something in a truly fine painting that trivializes anxiety and minimizes despair: art is by far the best restorative.*

For his part, Al was his usual black-suited, terse self.

We proposed that he salvage his debt position by becoming an equity investor in Cineplex. Al listened to us carefully and reserved judgement.

Three weeks later we were summoned to a second meeting at Taubman Corporation's headquarters in Bloomfield Hills, just outside Detroit. This was a full-dress performance with Al, his son Bobby, Bob Larson, and a horde of legal and financial advisers. (Still, while we had their attention, we didn't have all of it. Even as they listened, Al was scurrying back and forth to an adjoining boardroom where other associates were drawing up plans for his new Detroit World Football League team with fellow franchise-owner Donald Trump, who that morning had signed standout running back Herschel Walker to a multimillion-dollar contract.)

At the inception of the meeting, I made it clear that Cineplex was close to becoming history. A direct capital transfusion was essential if the TD Bank's hostility was to be neutralized. We had something on our side: Taubman was eager for us to stay alive – he didn't want anything to jeopardize the continued smooth-running of the Beverly Center Cineplex, which had proved to be such a successful magnet for attracting prospective lessees to the shopping centre.

It was a long, bruising, difficult meeting. The Taubman people were tough negotiators. In football terms, we spent four hours inching to the twenty-yard line. Then Al called a time-out to huddle with his son and his other associates.

When we got back together an hour later, he put forward an ingenious idea. If a refinancing package that included new equity could be worked out that met with the TD Bank's approval, Taubman would buy the Beverly Center Cineplex for $4.3 million, $3 million in cash, and $1.3 million worth of debt forgiveness. We would continue to run the theatre for a management fee. We would apply about $850,000 of the funds received to pay down the bank and use the rest for working capital. There were incentives in it for us, too: Taubman would give us an option, open until September 19, 1983, to buy back a 50 per cent interest in Beverly Center, plus the possibility of buying a 50 per cent interest in all of Taubman's other theatre properties, including his joint ventures with United Artists.

We had a deal – as long as the TD Bank went along and allowed the sale of our most valuable asset, the Beverly Center complex.

We set up a meeting between Bob Larson, ourselves, and the bank for early January, by which time we hoped that the rest of the package would be in place.

Our next move was tackling the $3.7-million debentures (fixed-interest bonds) and promissory notes held by Rogers Cablesystems and other investors. These, of course, appeared on the Cineplex balance sheet as debt.

We proposed to convert this debt into equity by issuing approximately 370,000 new convertible preference shares. The preferred shareholders would be guaranteed a dividend as long as they held the shares, and could at a later date convert their shares to equity. The debt holders had little choice: either they accepted a refinancing package that would appease the bank or they would watch their investment go down the tubes when the corporation went into receivership.

The last necessary element of the refinancing was to raise $2.25 million in new equity. Myron and I came up with $1.8 million of this by pledging personal property: our houses, our shares in other companies, and our art collections.

*My paintings! I risked my art for the bank! I risked my solvency, the house my family lived in, everything! The two of us risked everything we owned to bail out a company of which we owned only a fraction, because the other large shareholders couldn't or wouldn't put in another nickel.*

*It was probably nuts. It was certainly brave. And it worked.*

Once the whole refinancing package was in hand (although not yet accepted by the bank), we turned to cutting the corporation's expenses. I went to see Jim Bullock, president of the shopping-centre division of Cadillac Fairview, who later became CEO when Charles and Edgar Bronfman sold the company to JMB Realty Corporation of Chicago. (Jim is now the head of Laidlaw and on the board of Livent.) What I wanted was some rent relief from our major landlord until success in the combines action enabled Cineplex to compete in the exhibition market. Bullock, showing both astuteness and friendship, agreed to defer rent on all Cadillac Fairview's leases for a year. Other landlords followed suit. We had saved at least $1 million from our current expenses.

This was going to be my only chance to save Cineplex, so I set about trimming any remaining fat from the corporation. I took the lead by agreeing to draw no salary at all until Cineplex's cash flow turned positive. Rather than firing at least four top executives, I asked all salaried staff to take a one-third cut in salary and benefits, on the understanding that, when the company was once again solvent, it would be made up to them. *No key employee turned away from me. Their loyalty was heartwarming.*

Finally, I asked my brother Sheldon and Marty Shimkofsky, an accountant I often used as a troubleshooter, to find seven thousand square feet of cheap, functional office space. No more could we afford an imperial view of the city from the Cadillac Fairview tower. Instead we moved to a much-more-modest space on King Street opposite Roy Thomson Hall and lopped $400,000 off our annual rent.

This was the totality of the package we took to the TD Bank in early January. Arthur English and his cohorts confessed to some amazement at what we had accomplished.

But the bank still refused to bless the restructuring.

*My hands still sweat as I remember that tension-ridden meeting in mid-January. Those blind, smug people with their shuttered minds and that smothering blanket of condescension. How I loathed them at that moment!*

English led off for the bank with a swipe at me. "We'll allow the sale of Beverly Center," he said, "but we're not yet prepared to accede to new operating terms with the current management." In other words, the bank would continue to monitor the account day to day, even after the refinancing package was in place, and would remain in a position to call the loan at any moment. On top of all this, they still wanted me out. *Such chutzpah!*

But they were playing with bigger men now. Bob Larson, a bright, incisive executive widely respected in business and political circles in the United States, said, "No deal. That leaves a gun pointed at management's head. We want a settlement of all issues that everyone agrees to live with. These guys have earned the right to see this thing through."

Then he added, "And if this whole matter isn't resolved in the next fifteen minutes, our offer to buy Beverly Center is off the table, and I don't care what happens to Cineplex, the bank, or anyone else!"

I couldn't believe it. *He was playing poker with my life!*

He got up from the table and started to leave the room. I swear my whole life passed before my eyes – the cliché is true! – in the few short seconds it took the bank to throw in the towel. Arthur English caved. "The bank will go along," he said. Not gracefully, of course, but it would go along.

There was one more small piece of petty malice. The deal called for Taubman to issue a letter of credit, which he arranged with the Manufacturers' Bank of Detroit, of which Al was a significant shareholder. The Manufacturers' was a correspondent bank of the TD Bank, which raised no objection to the notion of a Manufacturers' letter of credit until the day before the scheduled closing. Then the TD suddenly reversed its decision and refused to accept it. One of the bank's officers gave me the news gleefully, ending her phone call by asking, "How are you going to close the deal now?"

Myron didn't waste a minute. He called the international division of the Royal Bank, with which we had a relationship through our production/distribution activities, and – within four hours – the Royal agreed to discount the letter of credit so we could close at the appointed hour. I didn't actually see the faces of the TD bank officers when they got the news, but I have always wished I had.

Beverly Center turned out to be the key element in our plan to save the company. I had gone out on a limb to build a Cineplex in a location everybody else had turned down, and the gamble had paid off gloriously. Our success with Beverly Center had attracted Taubman's respect, and the Taubman money had saved us.

As a postscript, on October 17, 1983, Cineplex entered into a new option agreement with Taubman, whereby Cineplex was given the right, on or before October 1, 1984, to buy back 100 per cent of the Beverly Center Cineplex for $4 million U.S. We exercised this option.

*You think it was over? No! Misery comes in threes, it's said, and the TD Bank was only misery number one.*

*Number two was caused by someone I had thought was a friend.*

Mandel Sprachman had been taught just about all he knew about theatre architecture by Nat Taylor, when Nat was multiplexing theatres in the sixties and seventies. Cineplex had used Mandel exclusively for the first four years of its existence, when we were building at a frenetic pace. He had been one of the first shareholders in Cineplex and, as its exclusive architect, he had reaped hundreds of thousands of dollars in fees from the first 150 screens we built. He had done very well by us. A little loyalty wouldn't have been misplaced.

Like everyone else at Cineplex, Mandel knew how difficult 1982 was for the company. There was an agreement that he would get paid an hourly rate for whatever time he put in drawing up plans, and that ultimately he would get a percentage of the cost of the theatre – but only if and when it was built. Mandel was a slightly built, bearded, nervous guy, very low-key at meetings, always sucking on his pipe. He was sometimes hard to read, but he never seemed to have difficulty living with this agreement.

In spite of it, though, early in 1983, he billed us a percentage of the estimated cost of theatres yet to be built. And it was a big bill: $600,000. On an hourly calculation, we reckoned we owed him $200,000. Still, we weren't worried. We made no big deal of the bill. Mandel was family. We could work it out.

Imagine my chagrin, then, at a time when I was still in the middle of tidying up the mess of the last few months, when I got a call from his lawyer, Jules Berman, a senior partner at a firm called Minden Gross.

He had barely introduced himself when, in his grating, unpleasant voice, he demanded Sprachman's full $600,000 immediately.

I challenged the basis of the claim and told Berman that, if we couldn't come to an agreement, he could go ahead and sue.

"I don't sue," he said.

"What do you mean, you don't sue?"

"I don't sue," he repeated.

Three days later he called again. "If you don't pay up within the next twenty-four hours, I'll petition your company into bankruptcy."

My blood pressure zoomed. Our stock was still below $2 and still suffering from the constant Bay Street innuendoes that our days were numbered. Despite our restructuring, our relationship with our creditors was shaky. All we needed was something like this to jeopardize our recovery.

Berman was well aware that Cineplex couldn't afford any more negative publicity. He knew, experienced bankruptcy lawyer that he was, that just the threat of bankruptcy proceedings would damage the corporation – possibly irreparably. I might have succeeded in overturning his petition, but by that time Cineplex would be kaput. He was going to use the notorious inequity of the Canadian bankruptcy laws to wring out an extra $400,000 for his client.

I couldn't win with the economic climate the way it was, and Berman seemed determined to ruin us if he had to. Even though it was a corporate liability, I couldn't load any more debt on to the books. Myron and I personally guaranteed a $500,000 payment to Sprachman over the next six months.

*But don't think it didn't rankle!*

Even that wasn't enough: after the deal was made, Berman called Jerry Banks, who was acting for us in the matter, and said he was going to renege on the agreement unless we paid more money up front. Jerry was curt. Back off or I'll report you to the Law Society, he said.

As for Sprachman, I haven't spoken to him since. I haven't

forgotten – and won't – that he and his lawyer gave me perhaps the most abhorrent experience of my business career.

And, for the record, none of the complexes for which he extracted his pound of flesh were ever built.

Then along came misery number three: the Ontario Securities Commission.

On February 17, 1983, after the TSE had opened trading for the day, HCI Holdings Ltd., the financial-services company controlled by Andy Sarlos, requested a delay in the trading of its stock, pending an announcement that it was writing down the value of its Cineplex holdings by $1 million. Although Sarlos and Zukerman had resigned from the Cineplex board the previous November after their failed coup against me, HCI had held onto its stock. The implication of this announcement was that the write-down was necessitated by the dire financial condition of Cineplex.

There was, of course, a valid explanation for the write-down, other than our poor financial health. Back in the hair-raising month of December, when Myron and I had put everything we owned on the line to rescue Cineplex, we asked Andy for something in return. After all he was a substantial shareholder, who wasn't putting up another nickel, but who stood to benefit greatly by our further investment in the company. So we asked him for an option to buy HCI's stock in Cineplex for $2.50 a share, $0.25 more than the shares were selling for on the open market – but much less than the per share amount (original cost) at which it was carried on HCI's books. It seemed fair. We needed the stock to attract new equity shareholders. ($2.50 was a reasonable price at the time. The Tanenbaum people gave us a similar option for their 1.1 million shares.)

Andy willingly gave us the option we requested on HCI's 1.2 million shares. Now the time had come, because of the option, for HCI to take the write-down. But because there had never been a legal obligation to report the option, HCI's request for a delay of its stock opening was the first the Ontario Securities Commission heard about it.

The commission issued a cease-trading order on Cineplex's stock

the same morning, claiming that the corporation had not fully dis-
closed its financial condition on February 4, when it filed the required
statement of material change on the closing of the Taubman/Beverly
Center transaction. There was, in fact, nothing wrong with this statement, which had been prepared on the advice of counsel. To save face,
however, they made us file a so-called clarification of the material-
change statement that, I swear to God, differed in no significant
respect from the original press release. Once we did that, trading in
our stock was permitted to resume. Another heart attack was nar-
rowly avoided.

*Thank God misery finally stops at three!*

By February 1983 things were just beginning to go our way. By the
end of March they were really looking up. The U.S. distributors were
very conscious that they were under the Canadian government's
scrutiny, and they started letting us have some move-overs with
some life left in them. We were also beginning to make sales from
Pan Canadian's valuable film library to the newly established pay-TV
services. The result was that revenues rose to $7 million for the first
three months of 1983, and for the first time in its short history,
Cineplex showed a net profit: $104,000.

All during this time I kept urging the government to get on with
the combines action. I calculated I had six months at most to crack
the duopoly's hold on the market, so I was on the phone daily to
Lawson Hunter and Don Partridge in Ottawa.

I wished I could do it myself, but I couldn't. The exasperating part
of the whole combines matter was that, by Canadian law, I had to
work indirectly through the federal government. It was intensely
frustrating. I was enveloped in the stultifying bureaucratic fog of
official Ottawa.

The Restrictive Trade Practices Commission had set May 4 as the
date for a pre-hearing conference, with the formal hearing to start on
May 30. With the filing of the application, Lawson Hunter, as director
of investigation and research, had spelled out to the six Hollywood
majors – Columbia, Fox, Universal, MGM/UA, TriStar, and Buena
Vista (Disney) – and to the Canadian distributor, Astral Films, the

allegation that they had supplied movies to Famous Players and Canadian Odeon to the "exclusion of Cineplex and others." Although the distributors were just beginning to mend their ways by throwing a few bones in Cineplex's direction, they continued blatantly to favour the duopoly in the way they allocated their new releases and in the way they still refused most move-overs to Cineplex until they were virtually not worth showing. After all it was so comfortable. Famous Players took the entire output of certain distributors and Canadian Odeon took the rest.

If a distributor so much as hinted that it might now lean more toward Cineplex, all Famous Players or Canadian Odeon had to do was say, "Play Cineplex and we'll pull your film from our theatres everywhere else." And, as the duopoly overwhelmingly dominated Canadian exhibition, the distributors perforce had to submit.

To build up the file for the government's case, Cineplex began to go on record with bids in writing for every picture. Sometimes we caught the distributors red-handed. In one case we had information, which we passed on to Don Partridge, that a distributor was telling an exhibitor what bid to make to ensure he got a certain film.

I felt confident we would win. The only question was when. In the meantime I had to find ways to boost the box office so as to keep us alive until the hearing. I gathered together my senior executives to chew over the problem. Box-office figures showed that Friday, Saturday, and Sunday accounted for 75 per cent of our week's gross. Somehow we had to fill the theatres in midweek. We agreed that we had to offer a price break of a sort that Famous Players and Canadian Odeon would never consider.

The duopoly didn't have to bother with price breaks, because they automatically got all key-city runs of the major pictures. In the United States, on the other hand, circuits routinely discounted tickets – but in a hit-or-miss sort of way. I wanted something much simpler and more dramatic: a single discount day somewhere in the middle of the week, so that the weekend grosses wouldn't be hurt.

It was Lynda Friendly who picked Tuesday and set the price at two dollars (the regular movie price was then four dollars). Thus was born "Two-Dollar Tuesday," a perfect new slogan with a real ring. We sprang the scheme on the competition by breaking with our advertising blitz only a couple of days in advance of our first discount Tuesday, to ensure that they wouldn't be able to react. A typical Tuesday gross at Eaton Centre at that time was $4,500, or approximately eleven hundred patrons. The first Two-Dollar Tuesday exploded, drawing a line-up several blocks long. It was a stunning success. Grosses doubled, patrons increased fourfold, and the gains at the concession counters were staggering. About 80 per cent of concession sales are profit, and they aren't included when figuring out the percentages paid to either the distributor or the landlord.

Nor did we have any negative fallout. The box office for the rest of the week blipped but then remained steady, and, within weeks, Two-Dollar Tuesday had become a well-beloved feature of every Cineplex in the country. We achieved a first in the history of our industry by using spot TV in each market to advertise our new pricing strategy rather than to plug a particular film.

In Ottawa, meanwhile, the legal battles were heating up. Famous Players and Canadian Odeon tried and failed to be added as parties to the May 30 hearing. They argued unsuccessfully that their rights would be affected by the commission's decision. The Hollywood studios had by this time lined up most of the major law firms in Toronto and given them instructions to delay the hearing for as long as possible. On May 3 Warner Brothers and United Artists, in a last-ditch stand, applied to the Federal Court to quash the May 30 hearing, arguing that the phrase "commercially valuable motion pictures" could not be defined. We, of course, armed the government's lawyers not only with a list of such pictures, which were quite simply all the major first-run releases, but also an explanation of why an exhibitor needed to get them on screen in a timely fashion if he was to be able to make any money.

On May 13 Mr. Justice Addy dismissed the distributors' application almost contemptuously, and, within a week, their united front fell apart. Ironically, in view of later events, it was Universal (owned by MCA) that broke ranks first, acknowledging that it had been party to business practices that would never have been tolerated under U.S. anti-trust law and that it had done so only because it was threatened with retaliation by Canadian Odeon.

The duopoly had lost, even before the actual hearing. The distributors immediately began negotiating with Lawson Hunter, who was prepared by Dick and me with drafts of what would be an acceptable settlement for us. The government might have been leading the action, but Cineplex was the principal player. We would have the responsibility of making the settlement work, so we had to be sure that the wording was clear and unambiguous. Hunter and his staff consulted us all the way, asking, "Can you live with this? Are you comfortable with this clause?"

During the final evening's negotiations, Dick, Myron, and I were linked up on a conference call with Lawson Hunter, Brian Findlay (the government's very able counsel in the matter), Don Partridge and the staff of all the departments involved on the one side, and the various legal counsel for the distributors on the other, as each distributor's undertaking to Lawson Hunter was drafted and redrafted.

At 4:30 A.M. on June 3, we got our agreement. It was complete.

As of July 1, 1983, the distributors undertook to drop all practices favouring Famous Players and Canadian Odeon. Before any film was licensed by an exhibitor, the distributor was to ask all eligible exhibitors in a geographic area to submit bids for it, and then license it on a zone-by-zone, theatre-by-theatre basis. This put all exhibitors on an equal footing. Most importantly for Cineplex was the part of the undertaking that spelled out how, on completion of a film's first run, the distributor must make it available immediately for a second or move-over run to another theatre in the same zone.

As Hunter said in his press release later that day, "After fifty years of complaints, market forces will now determine which theatres play a picture rather than any long-standing agreement." I felt as if I had finally climbed Everest – after twenty long months of using all my determination and ingenuity to fight off defeat in just about all of its many manifestations.

One irritant remained: the bank. As late as May, even as the combines action was reaching a climax, the TD Bank was still on our case, although other investors already understood what had happened and what the decision would mean for our financial health. For example, Myron had arranged a private placement of two hundred thousand treasury shares of Cineplex with AGF at $2.50 a share. Bob Farquarson's AGF was a shrewd institutional investor with enough imagination to see the effect the success in the combines action would have on the price of our stock. But Woods Gordon, which was still, at considerable expense to us, babysitting Cineplex for the TD Bank, remained sceptical to the end. We had given them a seven-month education, but they still didn't understand the workings of the movie-exhibition industry. Nor did the TD Bank, which stood by and allowed Woods Gordon to suck tens of thousands of dollars in consulting fees out of us when we were fighting for our survival. It wasn't until the end of July that Myron and I were able to persuade the bank to call off their minders. By that time even they could see we were not only stable but beginning to generate positive cash flow.

In spite of the bank, a sense of euphoria lingered. Exhibitors had been trying for fifty years to smash the duopoly that had locked up the Canadian market, and I had done it for them.

Later, after Cineplex bought Canadian Odeon and the distributors once again began to divide their films between the two major Canadian chains, it would be said that I had restored a duopoly as soon as it suited me. Not true. If a third circuit were to be started in Canada today, it would be able to bid for movies on an equal basis with Cineplex and Famous Players, its right to do so ensured by the undertakings made to Lawson Hunter, which are still in effect.

I had done what no one else in the motion-picture business had done. It was truly an unalloyed triumph.

*Hey, a little hubris is pardonable.*

# CHAPTER

## XI

### ADIOS ODEON

You would think the phone would have rung after my long struggle for the combines victory. You would think someone from Cadillac Fairview, my largest landlord, would have called to congratulate me. "Nice work, Garth," you'd think they'd say. "Well done. We're delighted." After all, twelve months earlier its chairman, Leo Kolber, had personally been making my life miserable because Cineplex was behind in its rent. Now all rent was current, and we were in a position to become a more and more important tenant. We were growing fast, and they must have known it. A phone call would have made good business sense, as well as being simply courteous.

But no. Silence.

*I mean, it's not as though I were sitting by the phone, like a sheepish schoolboy waiting for his dream date to call. So screw it. If Kolber wouldn't call me, I'd call him. It was time we met each other.*

I picked up the phone.

"Leo," I said, "we've never met, but I want you to know I think you're an asshole."

"Why?" He didn't sound surprised.

"Why? Because you were the first person to call and demand money a year ago when I was desperately trying to get Beverly Center open. Now I've not only stabilized the company, I've changed the economic climate of the whole industry in this country – and I don't even get a phone call from you! I don't get it and I don't like it!"

Leo said, "Let's have a meeting."

I went to see him three weeks later. I obviously knew a lot more about him than he knew about me. He had been with Charles Bronfman for twenty years, guiding CEMP through any number of deals. I had done my homework on the Bronfmans, too. Charles was the youngest son of "Mr. Sam" Bronfman, the founder of Seagram Corporation, the biggest liquor business in the world and the owner of such labels as Chivas Regal, Mumm and Perrier Jouet champagne, Barton & Guestier, Myers's rum, Famous Grouse, and The Glenlivet. The family fortune had been made bootlegging during U.S. Prohibition. Mr. Sam consolidated his empire as a ruthless dynasty, cutting his brother Allan's children out of Seagram's in favour of his eldest and flamboyant son, Edgar, who until 1994 ran the U.S. side of the business before turning it over in turn to his son Edgar, Jr., and the publicity-shy Charles, who was in charge of the Canadian operations. (As Edgar, Jr., moved into a position of power, he began taking Seagram's more and more into the entertainment world, as much through a massive investment in Time Warner as anything else.)

Leo Kolber had long been involved with the Bronfmans. He was there when Edgar tried to buy MGM, an attempt at diversification that was shot down by Mr. Sam. "There are cheaper ways to get laid than buying MGM," the old tyrant had said. And Leo had masterminded the sale of CEMP's control block of Paramount stock to Gulf + Western that had enabled Charlie Bluhdorn to take over the studio. He had also been an investor in Toronto's CITY-TV.

Leo's office was on the fourth floor of the Cadillac Fairview south tower in the Eaton Centre, the same building Cineplex and I had left only six months earlier. It was palatial.

Leo himself was a small, balding man, dressed in a blue suit that looked a couple of sizes too big for him. As he came toward me, cigar in hand, the right side of his face suddenly contracted alarmingly and seized up. I found this tic, this sudden, unexpected spasm, disconcerting.

Tic aside, Leo was all smiles that first meeting. He had the oily smoothness of a professional powerbroker, which is what he was; Prime Minister Trudeau had made him a senator in 1984 because of his ability to raise money for the Liberal Party. We sat together on the couch in his beautifully appointed inner sanctum and I took him through Cineplex's whole roller-coaster ride. His close attention encouraged me to tell him everything – and more.

As I reached the end of Cineplex's short and tumultuous history, I pointed out that I had achieved an almost-level playing field and I was going to have to take advantage of it. First I was going to have to bid aggressively for motion pictures, and that was going to cost a lot of money, and second I would set out to renew my challenge to the duopoly, specifically Canadian Odeon, by building new Cineplexes in those areas where it was weakest. I intended to exploit its vulnerability.

Leo paused after I finished and then he said, "But you didn't come here just to talk about this without asking for anything. What do you want?"

"That's all I wanted, Leo," I asserted. "Essentially a little respect from my pivotal landlord."

Leo pressed me further. "But what are you going to do for money?"

"I'm not quite sure," I said, which was true, if disingenuous. It was only a month after the combines victory, and Myron and I were still developing a financial strategy. But money is where money is. So I added, almost without thinking, "Now that you're asking, I could use $5 million."

I don't know where I got that figure. But it sounded right.

Why? I hadn't fought for twenty months just to remain a little guy in the Canadian exhibition business. For the past three years I had had in my mind to take Cineplex to the top, and I was more determined than ever to do so. If I was to take advantage of the new climate I had helped to create, I had to have more equity.

Leo was obviously intrigued, and I left his office feeling good. He was going to discuss the matter with Jimmy Raymond, his longtime partner, and Charles Bronfman.

When I told Myron the way the meeting had gone, he was wary. He had a cautionary tale to tell me about Leo and the ways of CEMP. A few years earlier, in 1979, he and his close friend Ned Goodman, an investment counsellor, had won a bitter proxy fight and taken control of Campbell Chibougamau Mines, a company listed on the Toronto and American stock exchanges. At the time Kolber and Raymond asked them if CEMP could become a passive investor, and CEMP pledged its unwavering support of management. This was typical CEMP behaviour. Charles Bronfman's great desire was to be detached from the day-to-day rough and tumble of business, so management was not a hallmark of the organization he controlled. But, of course, a certain type of investor is never entirely passive, and gradually Leo and Jimmy withdrew their pledge of support of Myron and Ned. In a management showdown, CEMP voted against them, and Campbell was spun off into two corporations. Myron and Ned had fallen on their feet, ending up with Corona Corporation, which became one of the top gold producers in Canada. Nevertheless, the way the CEMP pair had behaved still rankled.

*I should have listened! For all their financial muscle, Charles Bronfman's chosen agents were as nervous as Victorian maidens fiddling with their frocks at their first ball. And just as flighty. Their tendency was to fold at the first sign of trouble. Pass the smelling salts, Charles! We're outta here!*

At the next CEMP meeting, Myron and I met alone with Jimmy Raymond. It was difficult not to be charmed by Jimmy's infectious enthusiasm. A little leprechaun of a fellow, with a huge, waxed handlebar mustache, he took great pride in his appearance. And he also had a sense of humour, a rare commodity in the hushed and reverent world of big money. Once, at a Cineplex board meeting, one of the directors congratulated Jimmy on his threads, and Jimmy, without missing a beat, replied, "Rented."

Jimmy, though he considered himself the world's greatest deal-maker, was in fact one of the world's greatest nickel-and-dimers. He couldn't help himself. He couldn't stop negotiating until everyone else was worn out. Even after a deal was done and the lawyers had gone home, he would still come back and try to remake it on even better terms.

The most difficult thing about doing business with CEMP was dealing with the Bronfman family lawyer, Michael Vineberg. He was a nice enough person, a chatty, social sort of guy who basked in the Bronfman's aura, delighting in his secondhand power. His father, Philip, had been the family's senior lawyer for a generation, inheriting the role from his uncle, Lazarus Phillips. Perhaps because of that, Michael also had his irritating side. He behaved as though he had been anointed, not hired, which was grating. But he was very slow to stand up to his clients. I later came to understand that his lack of assertiveness was a reflection of how little power he really had.

By August 1983, Jimmy and Myron had begun to negotiate a $2.5-million CEMP investment in Cineplex. Jimmy wanted CEMP's investment to be in the form of a convertible debenture that would pay current interest. This way he could hedge CEMP's investment. We resisted. I wasn't excited about new forms of debt on Cineplex's balance sheet – we had been trying to reduce debt, not increase it. For us, an equity investment was preferable. Myron was already lining up equity financing elsewhere; for some time he had been in negotiation with Ned Goodman, then senior partner at the investment firm Beutel Goodman, to buy some or all of the 2.9 million shares optioned by Myron and me at the time of our refinancing. Beutel Goodman actually went further. Not only did they undertake to purchase these shares for their managed accounts, but they came up with an offer to underwrite a rights offering to raise much-needed new equity.

Only when this surfaced did Jimmy Raymond drop his demand for convertible debentures and agree on CEMP's behalf to buy a million shares of the total block that was for sale. It was less a vote of confidence in us than in the market savvy of Beutel Goodman. He seemed to be saying, "If Cineplex looks that good to those guys, we'll piggyback."

The share purchases were completed in October. Two months later the corporation completed a rights offering, whereby

$3.7 million of new equity was raised. CEMP became the owner of a substantial chunk of Cineplex.

*I've waited for years to straighten out the snarled records of the dealings between Cineplex and the Bronfmans. Ever since CEMP originally invested in Cineplex, the media have insisted that the Bronfmans bailed out Cineplex in 1983, saving us from bankruptcy. This story, once it made its way into the press, seemed to take on a strange life of its own. It was unkillable; despite our best efforts, it went on existing somewhere in the media memory banks (somewhere in those caverns there must be keepers who feed raw innuendo to rumours to keep them alive). Every time the story surfaced again we would stomp on it, but it had as many heads as Medusa had snakes, and it survived.*

*So here, for the record, are the facts: Leo Kolber, Jimmy Raymond, and CEMP were no white knights, which is how the press characterized their investment in Cineplex. CEMP came in only after Cineplex's cash flow turned positive, and after the combines matter was settled, and after AGF had come in with $500,000; CEMP participated in an equity share purchase on the same terms committed to by Beutel Goodman and then added to their position in a subsequent rights issue.*

*They came in because we were in a growth mode, not because we needed help. They came in to let us make them money, not to save us.*

*I also savoured the irony of Leo Kolber, a member of the board of the TD Bank, becoming a personal shareholder in Cineplex.*

That was the year we started to boom. Our net income for 1983 would turn out to be $760,000 on revenues of $29.5 million, compared to a loss of $15 million on revenues of $20 million a year earlier. We would also reduce our debt by $4 million and triple shareholder equity to $7.6 million.

As I had told Leo I would, I moved quickly to exploit the new conditions that prevailed after the July 1 combines decision, and I chose as the battlefield Toronto's rich downtown zone.

Famous Players had twenty-four screens in that zone, while Canadian Odeon had only six. Little Cineplex, however, had eighteen screens at the Eaton Centre, ten at the Carlton, and, as of Labour Day

1983, it was going to have six more at Market Square in the heart of the brand-new St. Lawrence Market development, only a couple of blocks from the lake. Market Square had dropped in our lap after both Famous Players and Canadian Odeon had passed on the site. Once again, they failed to see me looking over their shoulder. Naturally, the good old TD Bank had ridiculed the Market Square location as "off the track."

Market Square was the first complex designed by David Mesbur, the architect I recruited to succeed Mandel Sprachman. I had not been able to find a Canadian architect who truly understood movie-theatre design and decor, but David was both talented and willing to learn. He could convert everything I told him into plans, sketches, and models, far faster than I thought possible. Market Square was nearly state-of-the-art for its time, with larger screens, 35-mm and 70-mm projection, and Dolby sound.

I wanted to open this new location with the Cineplex banner flying high, and I had already prepared myself to bid aggressively for the new fall releases. I waited for the distributors to send out the bid letters, as they had undertaken to do. Columbia, one of Canadian Odeon's traditional suppliers, was the first distributor to bow to the new order. It sent out bid letters for its two big upcoming films, Lawrence Kasdan's *The Big Chill* and Lewis Gilbert's *Educating Rita*.

A bid letter is the equivalent of a mini-prospectus for a film: it includes a plot synopsis, the genre of film, the cast, and the credits and biographies of all the major participants. It also spells out the terms on which the distributor is prepared to license the movie, the most important of which is the percentage of the box-office gross to be paid to the distributor. There are, as well, a raft of subordinate matters to be dealt with: the amount the exhibitor is being asked to advance (to be recouped from the distributor's share of box-office receipts); the number of weeks the exhibitor is willing to play the film in each proposed theatre and the number of seats in that theatre; and the "house nut," the individual theatre's running expenses (which are taken off the top of the box-office receipts before any money goes to the distributor). Finally, the bid letter specifies the name and number of non-competitive theatres in any geographical market that the exhibitor will allow to play the picture at the same time.

What the distributor wants, of course, is an early commitment from the exhibitor for the best screens which are likely to gross the most. Of course, the distributor wants to exact the best possible terms. The exhibitor, in turn, must be sure of a winner before he commits to pay a large advance and a high percentage of the gross.

My bookers and I were sure of *Educating Rita* after we screened it in July, but *The Big Chill* wasn't available for screening. As is often the case, the movie wouldn't even be delivered to the studio until just before its release date. We were going to have to "blind bid" the movie, which meant gambling a non-refundable cash advance. To this day blind bidding remains the most contentious issue between distributors and exhibitors, and it's not hard to see why: it's like gambling on a horse race without knowing the form or being able to see the horses. In fairness, though, in this case I wasn't bidding blind: my espionage ring in Hollywood told me that the word on *The Big Chill* was terrific.

My strategy for Market Square was simple. Canadian Odeon had in the past offered Columbia only one run in downtown Toronto for each of their releases. I instructed my bookers to offer Columbia two runs in downtown Toronto for *Educating Rita*, one at the five-hundred-seat International Cinema (which we had acquired four years earlier to shore up our midtown presence) and the other at Market Square on two screens totalling nearly four hundred seats. I insisted they offer the maximum terms and cash guarantees suggested in the bid letter. For *The Big Chill* (I was already infatuated with its wonderful musical score), they were to offer Columbia two screens at Market Square to play day and date (at the same time) with any Canadian Odeon theatre in the downtown core. Once again, they were to agree to Columbia's maximum terms.

These were bids, I reckoned, to call any balky distributor's bluff. Columbia was going to be extremely careful in awarding the first picture under the new system. We had another ace in the hole, too: Jim Spitz, the head of Columbia distribution, was sympathetic to us. I was also sure that Canadian Odeon was not going to be eager to raise the ante in the early stages of the bidding wars.

So I bid high and I won big time. *Educating Rita* was awarded to the International Cinema, and both it and *The Big Chill* were awarded to Market Square. We also won the bids for both pictures in many other locations across Canada, and Cineplex was thus able to prove its first-run grossing potential immediately. The movies opened through the roof, and we grossed hundreds of thousands of dollars in the first week. A few weeks later my old friend Norman Levy at Fox awarded Cineplex numerous runs of *Blame It on Rio*, a comedy caper that became another of that season's hits.

My strategy to undermine Canadian Odeon was working: I was eating into their runs and thereby diluting their box-office returns. True, the cost of taking film from them was high, but the success of the movies we won paid us back a thousandfold by raising Cineplex's profile in the eyes of the distributors and the public alike.

In the best traditions of our free-enterprise system, I was now stalking Canadian Odeon, but, before going for the jugular, I had to show them that I was prepared to slug it out in those zones where they had formerly been king. To give an example: Canadian Odeon's number-one grossing theatre in Toronto was the York 1 and 2 in the yuppie epicentre at Yonge Street and Eglinton Avenue. I had always wanted a Cineplex in that area, and one day, as I drove by the city transit system's bus station at the Eglinton subway, I found the solution. As I raised my eyes above the bus station, all I could see was – air.

*Build a castle in the air! Well, why not?*

*I had done it in my dreams often enough, if only metaphorically. Why not do it for real?*

"Why not," I thought to myself, "float a theatre above the bus station?" There's got to be a way to lease those air rights, I reasoned, and thus avoid buying a half-acre of some of Toronto's most expensive land. And once we had the lease, there had to be a way we could use the space – isn't that what technological development is all about?

I had to find out who had developed Canada Square, the office-retail development next to the bus station. And then, as I parked the car, I remembered. It was an entrepreneur called Gerhard Moog. Surely he would control the air rights?

So I went to see him. Moog was a colourful character. He was a sailor and he looked the part and more – he resembled everyone's image of an old salt, weathered and worn, with crinkly eyes and leathery skin, just the way Gregory Peck looked, lashed to the back of Moby Dick. The most notable feature of his otherwise commonplace office was the collection of model sailboats that scudded around the perimeter. He was immediately intrigued when I told him I wanted to lease twenty thousand square feet of air rights over the bus station. He had wanted, he told me, to build a second office building over the bus station, but engineering difficulties, coupled with the high cost of such construction, had held him back. Now, on the other hand, if I were willing to take on the basic construction of the theatre. . .? Then together we could plan for the highest and best use of these air rights.

Moog was a hard bargainer, but after six months I had a long lease at low rent. The next step was to assemble an investor group to finance the $3.5-million project. I wanted to protect our balance sheet, so a limited partnership structure was adopted. The participants comprised the principals of CEMP and some close friends of theirs.

That was by no means the hardest part. The structural complexities of the building were many and varied. To support a concrete shell rising six storeys above the surface, we had to drive pylons forty feet into the ground, while working around trolley-bus wires and power lines of up to ten million volts. Scary stuff.

By this time, however, Peter Kofman, then all of twenty-five years old, was our resident engineer. Peter was a graduate of the University of Waterloo who had started his career climbing telephone poles for Bell. But he had a quality that drew me to him – he couldn't refuse a challenge. In 1983 he joined David Mesbur to form Cineplex's own inhouse architectural-engineering team. Between them, they could assess any new lease opportunity within a day or two. Over the years Peter has become another younger brother to me; he's bright, ambitious, dedicated, available twenty-four hours a day – a sensational guy.

The eight-screen, seventeen-hundred-seat Canada Square complex took two years to build. We finally opened it at Christmas 1985. It was a spectacular success right away, generating a box-office gross of $3 million in its first year. It also featured a superb café and was the first theatre in Canada to offer THX, a sound-enhancement system developed by George Lucas.

Canadian Odeon was building too, shrugging off Cineplex's challenge and telling others that I would blow my brains out if I kept on bidding so high for films.

I knew better. I had knowledge from industry participants that Canadian Odeon was on the ropes.

In May 1982 Michael Zahorchak had died suddenly, and Canadian Odeon's leadership was divided among a troika of Chris Salmon, its staunchly British president, Michael's eldest son, Bob, who was still in his father's shadow, and Wally Partridge, a soft-spoken chartered accountant from St. Catharines who managed Michael's estate.

Moreover, on closer examination, the theatre chain was less coherent than it appeared. It had been cobbled together from three disparate chains. There was Zahorchak's own Niagara regional circuit; there was the Canadian Theatre chain he had bought from Fairview Corporation when they ignominiously left the exhibition field in 1971; and there was Odeon itself, the J. Arthur Rank chain that, with Famous Players, had formed the original duopoly. In 1978 Michael had startled industry observers by paying almost $28 million for Odeon or, more correctly, for Odeon's share of the duopoly's films, Odeon having been allotted the minor studios' movies in the famous 1947 carve-up of the Canadian market. There was speculation at the time about whether Michael would get enough hits from such studios as Columbia, Universal, and Fox to service his then 283 screens at 152 locations.

In fact, those were buoyant years for Zahorchak. He had an annual pre-interest, pre-tax cash flow that fluctuated between $12 million and $17 million. After Michael's death, however, the business began to change. The chain had gone increasingly into debt building new theatres. From 1982 to early 1984, Canadian Odeon's long-term bank debt rose from $20 million to $30 million. Revenues, moreover, were being nibbled away by our successful bids for major motion pictures. Worst of all, Fox and Columbia were in flux, and movies from them were slow in coming. By the end of 1983, Canadian Odeon's bankers, the Bank of Montreal, were getting restive, as the company headed toward a pre-tax loss of more than $6 million over the winter. The industry knew that Canadian Odeon was really haemorrhaging.

In January 1984 I set up a meeting with Wally Partridge, Bob Zahorchak, and the family's lawyer, Gordon Cooper of Goodman and Carr, to explore the possibility of our taking over Canadian Odeon. The last time I had met Bob was when Mike was still alive – when Nat and I had gone to Odeon to ask Mike to give Cineplex breathing space – and we had been treated with contempt. Now the tables were turned, and I went straight to the point. "I've got the backing of the Bronfmans and I'm going to continue to build theatres. I'm going to bid like mad for product. And," I added, "I understand your bankers are very upset and that you're going to have to sell your company. I'm a buyer." Their faces didn't change, but I knew I had shaken them.

Several weeks later I was having dinner at Joe Allen's restaurant with Lynda Friendly and Myron Gottlieb. Seated at the next table was David Fingold. I had never met him, but I knew of him. He and his brother Paul were partners with Canadian Odeon in six locations spread through Ontario and Quebec.

We chatted about inconsequentials and left it at that. The next day David called me. Paul and he wanted a meeting. The Fingold investment in Canadian Odeon had gone sour; the company had stopped paying dividends. The Fingolds asked me if I thought I could turn the circuit around. I said I thought I could, but added, "It's unlikely that the Zahorchaks will sell to me, since they believe I'm the source of all their afflictions."

The Fingolds had a suggestion.

"We'd be prepared to front the deal," David said. "The Zahorchaks would sell to us. There's no open hostility between us. But before we go in too deep, we have to know if you can arrange the financing." Myron and I assured them that financing would be no problem.

We made our plans in great secrecy. The buyer of record would be Fobasco Ltd., a company controlled by the Fingolds. If Fobasco's offer was accepted, Cineplex agreed to take over its position as purchaser and also to buy the Fingolds' interest in the six Canadian Odeon theatres for $1.4 million – five times the Fingolds' share of the average annual profits thrown off by these theatres between November 1, 1978, and October 31, 1983 – in the form of 510,000 Cineplex shares. We added a sweetener. The Fingolds would be paid a consulting fee of $1.2 million over the next eight years.

The negotiations were between Partridge and Zahorchak on the one hand and the Fingolds and Al Gnat of Lang Michener, their lawyer, on the other. Within a few weeks the deal began to take shape. The purchaser would pay $22 million cash and assume the now-$35-million Canadian Odeon debt, which had been taken over from the Bank of Montreal by the Royal Bank in early 1984. The deal would be structured in such a way as to give the Zahorchaks the best possible tax break.

In retrospect, the total purchase price was a flea bite compared to the value of the assets we were buying. But Cineplex was going to need a substantial injection of new equity to close the deal, so I had to get the Bronfman group's agreement before giving the Fingolds the green light.

I knew this deal would appeal to Leo. We had had dinner together at the Courtyard Café in Toronto's Windsor Arms Hotel about three months after CEMP had made its first purchase of Cineplex stock and the 1983 rights offering of common stock had closed. That evening Leo was fired up, and his instructions were simple and direct, "I want you to build me the biggest entertainment company in the world." *Sure, Leo.* Now, I was in the process of doing so.

The Zahorchaks accepted the Fingolds' offer. They had to. There was no other potential buyer, and they had few alternatives. Only one hurdle remained: would Mary Zahorchak, the family matriarch, back out of the sale if she knew Cineplex was the real buyer? Nobody believed Fobasco knew enough to operate Canadian Odeon, and, as the Fingolds moved toward closing the deal at the end of May 1984, there was widespread speculation in the industry that Cineplex was the real buyer. For my part, I managed to look wide-eyed with innocent ignorance. Buy Canadian Odeon? Me? Surely not! I vehemently denied any such thing any time I was asked.

The transaction would be paid for with a variety of instruments: $12 million cash, a five-year promissory note for $5 million (secured by a mortgage on two Edmonton theatre properties), and a $4.3-million tax refund that would be forthcoming as the result of creating a new, shortened tax year for Canadian Odeon. (Immediately following the new year end, we would file a tax return applying for the loss for that shortened year against the taxable income of Canadian Odeon from previous years.)

The missing link was a $12-million bridge loan until September, when our planned second-rights offering would produce a sufficient amount of new equity to repay it. With Leo's exhortation to go out and create the biggest entertainment company in the world ringing in my ears, and Jimmy Raymond always making public statements about how he hoped CEMP's financial clout and real-estate connections would help Cineplex expand, I thought getting the loan from CEMP would be a cinch. Not so. CEMP balked.

Ironically, it was the other branch of the Bronfman family that came to our rescue. For years Myron had been nurturing ties with Hees International Bancorp, the merchant banking firm owned by Edper, the holding company started by Edward and Peter Bronfman, Charles's Toronto cousins. Edward and Peter had amassed a spectacular fortune after Mr. Sam had turfed them out of the Seagram empire. They and their associates, the astute and inventive Jack Cockwell, Trevor Eyton, Tim Price, and Bill L'Hereux, were gentlemen in every sense of the word, responsive, quick to give a decision on a proposition, and fair. In forty-eight hours Hees had committed itself to providing Cineplex with the $12-million bridge.

When Myron informed Jimmy that interim financing had

been arranged and told him the fees involved, Jimmy asked, "Who's doing it?"

"Hees," said Myron and watched Jimmy's face fall.

Within twenty-four hours Jimmy called back and insisted that CEMP provide the $12 million after all. This was the first time I encountered the Bronfman family rivalry, and it worked in our favour. Fortunately the Hees group backed off gracefully when we told them we were going to take the $12 million from CEMP.

In September, CEMP was repaid from part of the $16.25 million we raised from our second rights offering of 5.7 million, 8.33 per cent, convertible preference shares at $3.00 a share.

The signing was scheduled for May 31. I was very tense during that last week of May, waiting for the other shoe to drop. Any significant delay could jeopardize the agreement. The Zahorchaks' need to sell, for example, might become much less urgent if, in the intervening weeks, Canadian Odeon lucked into a blockbuster, and I knew that Columbia had *Ghostbusters* in the pipeline.

The moment I was dreading came as the Zahorchaks were assembled to sign the final documents.

My phone rang. It was Al Gnat, calling me from the Lang Michener offices, where the Zahorchak family had gathered. "They won't go any further until they know who they're dealing with," he said.

I looked at Dick and Myron, who were with me. "We have no choice," I said. "Tell them the truth and I'll pray."

Gnat hung up. I put the phone down slowly and stared at it, daring it to ring again. Time crawled by. Dick and Myron said nothing. We all just waited. I sat unmoving, but my heart was racing. The deal of a lifetime, as I now desperately thought of it, was slipping through my fingers. I knew it. I could smell it.

What was happening at the other end? The Zahorchaks, when they learned who the buyer was, had abruptly left the Lang Michener boardroom to huddle with their advisers.

I didn't know that, but it wouldn't have made the wait any worse. It couldn't possibly have been any more tense.

The family returned to the boardroom twenty minutes later. Mary, the one with the clout, had made up her mind. She wasn't going to risk any further deterioration of the family assets. At the rate Canadian Odeon was losing money, a later offer might be for much less. "They'll complete the deal," chortled Gnat when he phoned.

I almost ran the few blocks to Lang Michener's offices. When I got there, I walked over to Mary and shook her hand. Hard feelings were put aside. We talked privately for a while, and I assured her I would preserve the Canadian Odeon name and continue Michael's trailblazing effort to build a powerful national theatre circuit.

On June 28, 1984, Cineplex officially took over Canadian Odeon. The flea had swallowed the camel. In one stroke little Cineplex had grown by 200 per cent, from a circuit of 143 screens in 21 locations to a national theatre network of 446 screens in 185 locations. *Maclean's* would later put me on the cover with the headline "KING OF THE SILVER SCREEN." Ian Brown didn't write the piece.

*I knew the accolade was not bestowed without a certain amount of cynicism, though. I knew I was perceived as a renegade, a spoiler, brash and pushy. Why, I had been nearly bankrupt only eighteen months ago! This wasn't the way the conservative Canadian business establishment did things. I was an anomaly – not the most comfortable thing to be in Canada.*

*Ah, to hell with them, though. I loved it.*

I wasted no time stamping Cineplex all over Odeon. The first Friday after the takeover, I ran our first Canadian Odeon ads under the Cineplex banner, and we immediately set to work creating a name and logo for what was going to be, I was determined, the largest and most prestigious circuit in Canada.

My first order of business was to take a tough look at our acquisition, to find some way of plugging Canadian Odeon's substantial losses and to pay down a large chunk of the debt we had assumed. I intended to dispose of those theatres that had become redundant in the combined chain. But first I had to see exactly what I had bought.

A ritual then began that I followed religiously in all subsequent acquisitions. I assembled Cineplex's SWAT team – Lynda Friendly,

Barry Silver, Peter Kofman, and David Mesbur – and invited along three of the Zahorchaks' representatives: Barney Regan, Ron Emilio, and Dave Allen. I was surprised to discover that the Canadian Odeon trio were seeing many of their own theatres for the first time!

Every weekend for the next eight weeks we set off (in the chartered TD corporate jet – *there* was a reversal of fortune!) on a safari into the wilds of Canadian Odeon's far-flung circuit. The tours were eye-openers and depressing. Most of the theatres were positively decrepit. The décor, if you can dignify it with that word, jarred the eyes: orange and green were the dominant colours, set off by shabby, gold-flocked wallpaper. Maintenance was slack. Carpets and curtains were mildewed. The washrooms were dirty. For the first time I got a comprehensive idea of just how much heart had gone out of the movie business since the fifties, when TV had reduced the industry's cash flow to a trickle.

I, however, was still a romantic about exhibition, haunted by the ghosts of showmen like Roxy and the practical visionary, Marcus Loew. Times might have changed, but I knew people hadn't. I was convinced that audiences were tired of watching films in run-down theatres operated by disgruntled staff. I was sure they could be wooed back time and time again by an exhibitor who provided some Roxy-style service, even in much simpler surroundings. I would say as much in 1987 when, as the only Canadian ever to be asked to address the National Association of Theatre Owners, I urged my colleagues to open up their pocketbooks and upgrade their theatres with verve and imagination. This was, I told them, the most important tactic they could use to lure an audience distracted by pay TV and videocassettes back to the movies.

Even if I couldn't aspire to Roxy's buildings, I could use him as an inspiration. My aim was to make sure that patrons always knew they were in a Cineplex theatre. New Cineplexes were equipped with more-comfortable seats, and colour themes were chosen for the walls and carpets to reflect the demographics of different regions, something we had begun in Beverly Center. I resorted to marble extensively for the floors. Sure it was a touch of luxury, but it was also practical. Marble lasts for generations, whereas carpeting has to be replaced regularly – a point that was wonderfully reinforced for me later when I walked up the two thousand-year-old stone steps of Jerusalem's Citadel, built by King Herod, and saw for myself how well they had worn after all those years. We also had to set in motion a massive refurbishment plan for Canadian Odeon's theatres.

In October 1984 I contacted David Burnett. He was just leaving his position as curator of Contemporary Canadian Art at the Art Gallery of Ontario to set up his own consulting business with his wife, Marilyn. I engaged them to organize and coordinate Cineplex Odeon's art program. As Cineplex grew, so the art program grew, and over the next five years we gave commissions to fifty-five artists, selecting Canadians exclusively, even for the theatres in the United States. The challenge we gave to the artists was to create large-scale works that would have prominent positions in lobbies where hundreds of thousands of people would see them. I didn't dictate themes to them because I didn't want to compromise their individual ideas. I told them to create art that was right for the space. All I said was, "Tell me in your painting how the world of motion pictures has influenced your work."

For me, good service was the final touch we could offer. Movie exhibition had been in the doghouse – or, more accurately, had *been* a doghouse – for so long that there was a depressing dearth of skilled and motivated people to run theatres. I knew we would have to train and nurture staff over time to get the kind of service I demanded, so Cineplex developed its own program. The staff of each theatre was thoroughly indoctrinated with the Cineplex standard of service, all the way from the ticket seller making eye contact with the patrons to the maintenance crews keeping the theatres spotless. Managers were instructed to wear tuxedos on weekends, and we designed uniforms for the ushers – complete with Roxy's white gloves.

I established a clear chain of responsibility. Regional managers were instructed to write detailed reports every other week on each of their theatres and send them to senior management. We signed up an agency to do random quality checks on how the theatres were running, the same agency used by the Four Seasons hotel chain to check on the standards of service in their establishments. The mandate we gave them was simple: check everything, the treatment of patrons, the cleanliness of the theatres, the focus of the picture on the screen, *everything*. They were also to conduct stringent and unexpected financial audits, even including opening the safe and counting the day's receipts. Their reports and audits would be summarized under twenty headings and sent to senior management. Finally, most theatres would be visited at least quarterly by a senior officer of the corporation.

*If genius is an infinite capacity for taking pains, well, I was going to be a genius.*

I also wanted to be flexible, open to any new idea. An example came when we were touring Canadian Odeon's theatres in Vancouver. Lynda, Barry, and I were exhausted by the time we got to the Scott Delta 72, a typically tawdry fourplex about twenty miles southeast of the city. I remember wandering outside into the gloomy dusk and suddenly feeling hungry. Lynda went back into the theatre to get me a diet Coke and some popcorn, and when she came back, she was almost yelling with enthusiasm.

"You've got to try this popcorn! It's got real butter!"

"What do you mean, real butter?" I asked sceptically. "Everybody gave up on real butter years ago. We don't even use real butter at Cineplex. It's too expensive. Everyone uses that lousy, rancid, artificial oil."

Lynda insisted. "I'm talking real butter. They just told me inside that this is one of the last Canadian Odeon theatres using it, and that it's going to be phased out after this week."

I was so hungry I could have eaten anything. But as I crammed the popcorn into my mouth, I could tell at once it was different. Different – and a lot better.

I turned to Barry. "How fast can this be on sale in all our theatres?" Without waiting for a response, I added, "Get it done by October, whatever the cost. Pass it on in our pricing. The patron won't care. It's that good."

Lynda ran with the idea and produced a national advertising campaign headlined, "WHERE'S THE BUTTER? WE'VE GOT IT!" The slogan was splashed across ads and the yellow T-shirts worn by Cineplex's concession staff. And shortly afterward, my brother Sheldon, who at that time was managing our purchasing department, came up with the clincher – the Cineplex popcorn bag. Not only was the traditional cardboard container expensive, each one costing between thirteen and forty cents depending on its size and shape, but it took up a lot of space in the green garbage bags that added greatly to our cleaning costs. One day Shelley came triumphantly into my office. He showed me a bag that was leakproof and nearly crackleproof and cost a fraction of a cardboard container. The bag was also thick enough to take printing in bold colours, an invaluable marketing tool. Patrons actually left our theatres with their uneaten popcorn, carrying their bright red bags, neatly rolled up! When I took into account the new theatres we were planning and the imminent expansion of our audience, I reckoned the bag would not only save us about $5 million annually but would spur our concession sales. The bag and the butter were smash hits, and, in fact, the bag can now be found in almost every theatre and stadium in North America.

By the end of 1984 it was time to change the corporation's name and logo. Cineplex was now flexing its muscles, and the business community was finally giving us some respect. We were ending the year on an upbeat note. The asset base of the corporation had increased to $103 million. Shareholders' equity had increased fivefold to $39 million, and revenues had tripled to $87 million. Net income for the year was $12 million. Most significantly for the future was that, with the absorption of Canadian Odeon, we had seen our share of all first-run mass-appeal releases grow to an even split with Famous Players.

The name came naturally: Cineplex Odeon. I had promised Mary Zahorchak to keep Canadian Odeon alive, but I would have done so anyway. The word "odeon" (Greek for theatre) had long ago become synonymous with movie-houses, and it would have been idiotic of me to drop it. As for the logo, it was based on the shape of the Greek amphitheatre, a series of facing Cs that came together in a triple sphere. I picked the contemporary colours of blue and purple. To me, they suggested majesty and power; the logo itself gave Cineplex Odeon an image of impregnability.

*When I first saw that logo flashing on a screen, its rings and spheres rippling with energy, I felt a great welling up of pride. I had done this! This was my doing!*

*And I thought to myself, "Watch out, Famous Players, here we come!" In a few short years, Cineplex Odeon would dominate Canadian exhibition forever.*

*Canada? Why stop there?*

# CHAPTER

## FLYING HIGH

I was sitting by my pool one hot Saturday morning in July 1985 when the phone rang. The caller was Joel Reader, an investment banker with the New York firm of L. F. Rothschild, whom I had recently come to know.

Reader came right to the point. "I believe Henry Plitt's ready to meet with you," he said. "I think he's prepared to sell you his circuit."

When I hung up, I didn't move for a long while. I knew right away that I was on the point of a radical transformation in my life and in the life of the company I was building. "Something's coming, something big," I thought. *Somewhere a relay clicked that engaged a gear that started the machinery to turn the biggest goddamn wheel of my life. I had known Reader was going to call – he had presented me with several financial packages on Plitt seven weeks earlier, and of course I had expressed interest. But now . . . well, it seemed to be happening so fast.*

*Was I ready for the turn of the Great Wheel?*

After I had successfully consolidated Cineplex Odeon at the end of 1984, I started getting calls from Wall Street bankers. I clicked with one of them right away. Roy Furman of Furman Selz Mager Dietz & Birney, one of the investment bankers most knowledgeable about the entertainment industry, was a Harvard graduate whose advice I came to trust. Roy's an effervescent, enthusiastic character, effusive, but also loyal, supportive, and always ready with cogent advice. I've known him for eleven years, and one of the many things I like about him is that he's always quick to tell me when I'm getting off track.

After our first lengthy meeting, at which I expounded my ideas about the future of the exhibition business, he had one of his analysts follow our stock. Institutions based in the United States began nibbling at our shares. Cineplex Odeon was flagged as a company on the march, hungry to grow as the eighties roared back from the recession.

The combination of easy money and declining interest rates was fuelling a boom in leveraged buyouts paid for by junk bonds. Corporate raiders were swallowing companies, zapping them off as though they were little more than electronic blips on a video screen. Everything was for sale. So I wasn't surprised when, in June 1985, Reader arrived in Toronto to see me.

Joel was my introduction to the high flyers of the high-flying eighties, and I was fascinated. He must have been still in his thirties, but he looked as if he had stepped right out of a Cagney–Raft gangster movie. His hair was greased back with a part down the middle; he wore pinstriped suits and, although I didn't actually see them, I remain convinced to this day that he wore spats. He wasted few words, "I have an acquisition for you – the Plitt circuit!"

My eyes popped. Plitt was the fourth-largest movie-theatre circuit in the United States. It had been spun off from Adolph Zukor's mighty Paramount chain when it was dismembered by the consent decree that forced the studios to sell their theatres. Plitt owned some six hundred screens in more than two hundred locations, but the numbers were less important than the markets he covered. The circuit was in twenty-one states: it controlled 70 per cent of the screens in Chicago, the third-ranked American city for movie attendance, and it was well represented in most of the top-twenty cities, with key theatres in San Francisco, Los Angeles, Minneapolis, Atlanta, and Houston.

Plitt was in trouble, however. In 1984 its income had been $11 million U.S. on revenues of $168 million U.S., but 1985 was a different story. Exhibitors aim to at least break even for three-quarters of the year and make their profits from July through September. But here was Plitt going into the summer with a $5-million U.S. loss on revenues of $111 million U.S. By the end of its financial year in October, Plitt would not fully recover its lost ground and would record a $1-million U.S. loss on shrinking revenues of $165 million U.S.

The reason was simple. Henry Plitt, who had bought the circuit in the seventies from ABC Films, which in turn had bought it from Paramount, was over his head in debt. In 1983 his aggressive expansion plans had split his board of directors, and he'd had to buy out some disgruntled investors. He held on to two-thirds of the equity in the circuit only by leveraging the company's assets. For two years running, in 1984 and 1985, L. F. Rothschild, one of the largest underwriters and market-makers of junk bonds, succeeded in placing a total of $72 million U.S. for Plitt at an annual interest cost of 15.25 per cent. Henry was now paying nearly $11 million U.S. of interest annually, and the circuit's survival depended on its maintaining a healthy cash flow.

But Plitt was also getting hit by the jittery state of the Hollywood studios. Starting with Kirk Kerkorian's takeover of MGM in 1969, Hollywood had been crippled by corporate raiders. Louis B. Mayer's legendary studio, once the pride of the old studio system, with stars like Greta Garbo, Judy Garland, and Clark Gable, had been eviscerated. In the eighties Kerkorian, helped by Michael Milken, who virtually created the junk-bond vehicle, bought United Artists. United Artists! Founded by Charlie Chaplin, Mary Pickford, Douglas Fairbanks, and D. W. Griffiths, United Artists was another wonderful piece of Hollywood history, but it had been brought to its knees by Heaven's Gate, Michael Cimino's multimillion-dollar fiasco. Kerkorian picked it off, gutted it, and merged it with the shell of MGM. Meanwhile, Twentieth Century-Fox had been taken over by Marvin Davis (who later flipped it to Rupert Murdoch). And in 1983 Coca-Cola confounded the pundits by overpaying unbelievably for Columbia Pictures, which it subsequently flipped, at a sizeable profit, for $5 billion U.S. in 1989 to the Japanese giant, Sony Corporation.

This kind of questionable wheeler-dealing – the great Hollywood assets treated as playthings by speculators without a millimetre of celluloid in their veins – was convulsing the whole industry. The studios were no longer primarily moviemakers; they were merely wannabe moneymakers. A shiver in the money markets could turn a whole studio upside down. Each studio shake-up, for whatever reasons, resulted in numerous lower-echelon executives playing musical chairs as they followed their protectors from studio to studio. Each studio shuffle would disrupt personal relationships with directors, actors, writers, producers, the whole gamut of above- and below-the-line personnel. The few movies that made it through the system were poorly promoted. After a shake-up, a studio's new regime would have little interest in marketing and promoting the movies, good or bad, that had been made by their predecessors. As a consequence, the studios' creative people were put through an emotional meat grinder and their output sputtered to a halt.

For an exhibitor with allegiance to a particular studio in the middle of the shake-up, it was a disaster. Few quality movies were produced or, at any rate, few came down the pipeline.

*I sat there by the pool and brooded. I wanted to go for Plitt and yet I didn't. If I did, I knew my life would be unalterably changed. I was comfortable for the first time in several years. After winning many battles, I was enjoying financial security and peace of mind. I saw no obstacle to Cineplex Odeon becoming within a very short time in Canada the cash cow I had originally envisaged. Did I want to roll the dice again and perhaps lose everything?*

But the lure of expanding Cineplex Odeon in the United States was ultimately irresistible. We already had Beverly Center and two grand old movie houses in the Hollywood zone, the Showcase, which became Woody Allen's favourite house in L.A., and the Fairfax, which we had meticulously restored so as to preserve its glorious twenties design and decor.

America was the promised land, where the huge profits lay. My scalp tingled.

Moreover, I knew I had a team of executives that was capable of assuming the management of Plitt. I had assembled a cadre that was now running five hundred screens very smoothly, and I was sure could run a good many more.

On the other hand, the United States was a new frontier for us, and we couldn't expect to absorb an asset the size of Plitt without pangs of indigestion. How many times had I heard of Canadian companies that had ventured into the United States and been sent home in a brown paper bag? Even Cadillac Fairview lost huge sums of money by investing in Dallas office towers. The men who ran these giants were not fools. What made me think I would do better?

The only way to answer that was to find out. Let's see whether a deal could be done that made financial sense.

I got up from the pool and went to call Henry Plitt. We arranged to meet the following Monday in L.A., and I asked Myron to come along with me.

Henry Plitt was about sixty-five, and he had the reputation of a gunslinger, perhaps because he had been a general in the Israeli army and, several years after that, the hard-hitting general manager of the old United Paramount circuit. He came from an older generation, but we had something in common: we were both enamoured of the past splendours of exhibition. We just saw the future differently. Henry was still so swept up in the grandeur of the twenties and thirties that he believed that properly equipped, palatial, Cinerama-style theatres would nuke the oncoming VCR onslaught. At the time we met he was obsessed with SHOWSCAN, a sophisticated film and projection system that he and British cinematographer Douglas Turnbull had developed and which he was sure would revive the theatre industry. I, on the other hand, prior to the Canadian Odeon acquisition, had been trying to revive moviegoing with small, luxurious, intimate screening rooms in the multiplex format. As I came to realize, we were both right, and by the end of the eighties the best of the new Cineplexes were a hybrid of the two types.

Henry's office was on the second floor of a Century City office tower a block from the Plitt flagship: a twin theatre with two spectacular auditoriums of eleven hundred and eight hundred seats.

It wasn't a particularly friendly meeting. Henry was low-key, even reserved, and he seemed to approach negotiations with disdain. But he wasted no time telling us what he wanted: $65 million U.S. plus our assumption of the $72-million U.S. junk-bond debt. $137 million U.S.!

Ten minutes later Myron and I retreated to an adjoining office to huddle. Obviously, we had a lot to think about. We were going to have to devise some way to absorb the high-interest junk bonds so they didn't have a negative impact on our balance sheet and cause our stock to nosedive.

But our first order of business was the cash component of the deal. We looked over Henry's figures; he had been very persuasive about the real-estate values of several of his "non-contributing properties" that were up for sale. They were listed in his books as being worth $11 million U.S., but he had recently had them appraised at $35 million U.S., and this was what he wanted us to pay for them. This was the hook, in an otherwise marginal deal, that could make it attractive.

When we returned to Henry's office, we were joined by Plitt's chief operating officer, Jim Sorensen, and the heavy bargaining began. Henry hung tough on every point. Finally I said, "Okay, if you think this extraneous real estate is really worth $35 million, it's yours for $35 million. We'll pay you the $30-million cash balance of your $65-million asking price, $12.5 million now and $17.5 million by way of a six-year promissory note."

At this, Henry cocked his head and looked at us with more interest. We had his attention – we were proposing to buy his circuit for less than 10 per cent of the purchase price in cash! This was good leverage, and leverage was a game he well understood. He indicated he would go along.

Back in Toronto, I called a board meeting at the offices of Goodman and Carr. This would be one of the most significant board meetings in Cineplex Odeon's short history. We were embarking on a giant expansion in unknown territory. Everyone had to be on side.

I put my case forcefully. The exhibition industry in the United States, I started off, was atrophying, and conventional wisdom said it was a terminal case: videocassettes and the five-hundred-channel universe were going to turn out the lights on every marquee in the country. Exhibition, which had come to be looked upon as a get-rich-quick business, was now a get-something-while-you-can business. Since the consent decree, exhibitors had treated their patrons like cattle. Instead of watching the store, the typical theatre owner spent his mornings planning his estate and his afternoons on the golf course. One thing he didn't do was reinvest his cash in the business and demonstrate his commitment or care for his audience. I contrasted this to the Cineplex Odeon ideology, which was to make our theatres user-friendly. Everyone was talking about how service was the great growth industry of the future. Well, we were incorporating service into our company's basic philosophy.

There was another advantage: the acquisition of Plitt would give us further muscle in Canada. Distributors would think carefully before picking a fight with Cineplex Odeon if it meant alienating the Plitt chain as well. With a box-office gross of more than $300 million, the combined companies would have considerable financial heft.

The board didn't argue the deal's virtues. How could they? The cash requirements of only $12.5 million U.S. made it irresistible. Still, there were some reservations about whether we were wise to acquire 100 per cent of Plitt. In the end we agreed that the prudent course was to keep Plitt's $72 million U.S. of junk bonds off our balance sheet by finding a U.S. partner. This way the whole Plitt debt, including the $17.5-million U.S. promissory note, would be on the newly formed partnership's balance sheet and not on Cineplex Odeon's.

I was now thrust into the world of Wall Street, and for the first time I began to see how the game was played stateside.

I turned to Roy Furman to identify several investor groups for us as potential partners. Among those he scouted were such corporate raiders as Ivan Boesky and Carl Icahn. The massive insider-trading scandal and the subsequent racketeering and government investigation had not yet broken around Boesky's head, but even in the mid-eighties, he was among the most hated and feared arbitrageurs on

Wall Street, and he was subsequently incarcerated. Icahn, for his part, was known for his "short-term, fast-buck, turnover approach," cutting a savage swathe through corporate America as he gobbled up Phillips Petroleum and TWA, which he turned into an investment vehicle for building a powerful position in U.S. Steel.

Cineplex Odeon, perhaps fortunately, was too small a fish to attract the arbs' interest, and in any case I had what was for me an aberrant moment of Canadian caution. Cineplex Odeon didn't need someone who wanted to churn things up. We wanted a partner who would be quietly in for the long haul.

Furman introduced us to Odyssey Partners, a private-investment pool managed by Jack Nash and Leon Levy (formerly senior partners at Oppenheimer & Company), Lester Pollock (formerly of Loews Corporation), and Marty Rabinowitz, a tax lawyer. I think the way Cineplex had absorbed Canadian Odeon so efficiently particularly impressed Odyssey. So did the upside of the Plitt deal, with its considerable leverage.

The negotiation took a single day. Cineplex Odeon would retain unfettered operating management of the venture. The equity would be split fifty-fifty. We would only be obligated to advance $2.5 million U.S., the balance of the cash component, while $10 million U.S. would be put up by Odyssey.

So, for a mere $2.5 million U.S. cash I had managed to wrap up about $100 million U.S. of assets. Best of all, we didn't have to issue a dollar of new equity to finance the acquisition. Now that I look back, this was the most creative piece of financing that I've ever been part of – better even than the Canadian Odeon structure.

The Plitt deal brought me another great acquisition: Ira Mitchell. Ira, a Wharton School graduate, had been a real-estate consultant to the Plitt organization, and when I asked him why he hadn't signed on exclusively with Plitt, he answered, "These people just don't excite me. I need my juices turned on." When I outlined my plan to weed out Plitt's weaker locations and capitalize on its key markets, making Cineplex Odeon the major force in North American exhibition, Ira didn't hesitate. "Let's do it," he said. Ira became my human

*Michelin Guide*: he knew every interstate freeway intersection, every DeBartolo, Taubman, and JMB shopping centre; he seemed to know the location of every lonely 7-11 in the Prairies.

We were going to close with Plitt by American Thanksgiving 1985. That gave me just enough time to kick the tires of six hundred theatres. With Ira's help, I put together a newly configured SWAT team and we set off around the United States in private jets, helicopters, and limos.

The old real-estate dictum "Location, location, location," as applied to movie theatres, seemed to translate to one word: mall. As I helicoptered over the developing exurbs and suburbs, I was witnessing the incredible extent of the malling of America. Often malls were being built into the countryside, clearly in the hope that the city would catch up and settle around them. Each mall typically featured a motion-picture theatre – usually in the mall's worst location, another example of the exhibitors' myopia. They were so anxious to get into these new malls that they gave the developers the upper hand in negotiations. Worse, in their indiscriminate rush, the exhibitors grossly overscreened certain zones, particularly in Arizona, Texas, and much of the Southeast, putting twenty to twenty-five screens in a zone where the rational number would have been twelve to fifteen, plenty to accommodate all the first-run pictures in release over a six-week span.

By overscreening, the exhibitors gave away another negotiating advantage, this time to the distributors. Film rentals skyrocketed and profits dwindled. At Cineplex Odeon, I vowed, we would not go into any market where we weren't in control. As for the competition among multiplexes, I took a certain satisfaction in surveying the bland insipidity of many of the new multiplex cinemas. We'd show 'em *our* aesthetics, *our* architecture, and make 'em sit up!

I loved the helicopter portion of these inspection trips. Each segment was carefully orchestrated in proper military fashion. In each district the landing strips were all pre-arranged by Plitt's regional vice-president or supervisor to reduce the time required for each tour. I got a lot of surprises, some of them to do with food. After a swing over the alligator-infested swamps of Gulfport, Mississippi, we landed in Baton Rouge, Louisiana, and I had my guts ripped out by some real Cajun cooking. On the Rio Grande border in Texas, I downed several racks of hickory smoked ribs, my first taste of real barbecue.

There was one trip over Florida that, in light of later events, was significant. We were helicoptering from Jacksonville to Gainesville and on to Ocala, and late in the day would reach Orlando. Looking down, I saw an empty expanse of superb land just southwest of Orlando's downtown core.

I peered down at it. "Who owns that?" I asked.

"Universal Studios," Ira told me. "There's four hundred acres down there. Lew Wasserman assembled it in the late seventies. He wants to build a movie studio down here, and ultimately a studio tour like the one Universal runs in Hollywood."

"So what's happening with the land right now?"

"Oh, it's going nowhere," Ira said. "The project's on hold."

*On hold, was it! If only I had known. . . . No shiver of premonition passed through me, not a tiny hint that those empty four hundred acres would help overturn my future! No hint that in a few short months I would be skimming over those same acres again, this time with my new partners, planning the project that would damage my relationship with them and trigger the awful events of 1989.*

*Orlando! It helped turn the ruler of the Black Tower, Lew Wasserman of MCA, into the Beast that Ate Drabinsky.*

With Plitt well on its way to being assimilated, I was cheerfully hurtling along the fast lane, *the passing lane*. And then, one day in August 1985, I got a call from my assistant, Margaret Livingston. "Bill Soady is calling you from L.A.," she said.

Soady was an old friend. He had gone from head of Universal Film Distribution in Canada to head of Universal's North American distribution operations. When I reached him, he asked, "Garth, what do you think about building a theatre at Universal Studios?"

"On the lot?" I asked, my mind doing somersaults. I knew Universal's real estate very well. A huge block of land and buildings in Burbank, two miles north of Mann's Chinese Theater, just off the Hollywood Freeway, the home of the country's most popular studio tour, as well as being the headquarters of MCA.

I pulled my mind back to the phone. Soady was still talking. "Ted Mann [the owner of Mann Theaters] was gonna do it, but it looks like he's bowing out. He designed a fourteen-screen complex of about seventy-two thousand square feet, and their preliminary cost estimates have come in at $7 million U.S. They're real nervous!"

I said nothing. There was a pregnant pause.

After a few beats, Bill added, "If you like, I could set up a meeting with you and Sid Sheinberg, MCA's president, and Frank Price, who's now running Universal Pictures."

"Go ahead," I said. "Set up the meeting."

When I told Ira, he nodded. He knew about the Mann situation and had lobbied hard with Larry Spungin, head of MCA's real-estate division, to give Cineplex Odeon an opportunity to bid. Now, it was all coming together.

Bill Soady's call reminded me of something I had been brooding about on and off even before I started negotiations with Plitt – the reintegration of exhibition and distribution. Since the consent decree, which had broken up the studios' vertical integration, the exhibitor had been the industry's orphan. With the rise of TV, cable, pay TV, and videocassettes, theatrical exhibition was no longer accorded the same status by the distributors, who had a "devil take the hindmost and you're the most hind" attitude toward the exhibitors. Their reasoning was an example of classic shortsighted self-interest: Why should we leave a window of twelve months before releasing a video? Why don't we cut it to six and get the money in the till as soon as possible? What do we care about the damage done to the exhibitors in the process?

Obviously I had a big stake in changing this attitude. But how? The only way distributors could be persuaded to protect and enhance theatrical revenue was to give them a direct interest in exhibition. The consent decree still stood, but the Reagan government was notoriously *laissez-faire*, and deregulation was the ideological flavour of the month. Surely one of the big capital-rich studios could be persuaded to test the climate by investing in exhibition – and thus begin to reverse the deleterious effects of divestiture?

Earlier that year I had approached Columbia with this idea. It had plenty of available cash, since it was part of the huge Coca-Cola empire. I was predisposed toward Coke and felt in an indirect way part of the Coke family, not only because of my uncle Harold Waldman's Coke franchise in Saskatchewan but also because Cineplex Odeon had an exclusive and very favourable supply arrangement with Coca-Cola, an arrangement that had won the blessings of Donald Keough, Coke's worldwide president. It wasn't a big windfall for Coke, but it represented a major advertising presence, since the Coke logo was plastered all over our theatre lobbies.

My talks with Coke had started well. I met Keough and Coke's Cuban-born chairman, Roberto Goizueta, who was clearly dazzled by show business, at their fortress-like Atlanta headquarters. It had been Goizueta who had been behind the purchase of Columbia, for which he paid almost $800 million, about $30 above the going share price. When I suggested that Columbia buy an equity interest in Cineplex Odeon, Coke rose to the bait and I was sent off to see Fay Vincent, then chairman of Columbia Pictures (later to become Commissioner of Baseball) at Columbia's Fifth Avenue offices in New York. Vincent was interested enough in my idea to send me on to Guy McIlwaine, Columbia Pictures' president in Hollywood. Guy was Mr. Smooth. He had recently moved to Columbia from International Creative Management (ICM), then Hollywood's super-agency, and hadn't yet produced anything of much merit. He wasn't discouraging about Columbia's taking down some Cineplex Odeon shares, but he wasn't exactly encouraging either.

I flew back to Toronto feeling that a deal was possible. Then things ground to a halt. I think if Columbia had just been a studio, we could have come to an agreement. Instead, calls and letters and memos started whizzing back and forth between Atlanta, New York, and L.A., and complications multiplied. What I was to learn was that Coke's corporate interests came first, and Coke had more than 90 per cent of all theatre accounts in the United States. If Coke got into bed with Cineplex Odeon, rival chains might switch to Pepsi – Coke's nemesis.

In contrast to this entanglement, MCA, as far as I knew, had no conflict about owning a theatre chain. I couldn't help anticipating that the lease I was going to negotiate with MCA for a Cineplex Odeon complex at Universal City might lead to something greater.

The day before I was to meet Sid Sheinberg, I drove Neil Blatt, the Beverly Center's film buyer, and Mike Bisio, whom I was then promoting to the job of our head U.S. film buyer, over to the Universal lot in the San Fernando Valley. The lot is just over the Hollywood Hills from Hollywood and Westwood, where rival-owned theatres cluster cheek by jowl. The planned structure was to be built on a two-acre pad beside the Universal amphitheatre.

My executives thought I was crazy.

"Garth," said Mike, "what are you doing building a theatre just two and a half miles from Hollywood? How are we going to book it, when we'll be up against the Chinese and the Egyptian and the Pacific Dome?"

He warned me that, because Cineplex Odeon had no theatres in Westwood, one of the prime theatre locations in the country, our bargaining position with the studios was already pretty weak.

*But I could see my way through that. It's one of my knacks, I think, to see simple answers to complicated questions, simple solutions to intractable problems.*

*The answer, so often, is the bold stroke.*

In this case, there was a big population to be tapped, and there was no reason why Universal Cineplex Odeon shouldn't play day and date with any theatre in Hollywood, or Westwood, or with the whole Valley, and come out on top.

"Look guys," I said, "I heard the same bullshit when I was about to build Beverly Center. I said then, and I say now, look at Hollywood!

It's run down, it's full of drugs, prostitution. Its theatres are dirty and smelly. Westwood is classier, but parking is almost non-existent! Once we get this place opened, it will become the most sought-after theatre in America."

They remained, it's fair to say, unimpressed.

The next day I was off to MCA. I felt like David walking out with his slingshot to meet Goliath. MCA's nickname is The Octopus. Its tentacles stretch throughout showbiz, from Universal Films to the MCA record label to book publishing, theme parks, and merchandising. The movie-business's pioneers were extravagant, lavish, boastful, and high on glamour; MCA is as uptight as a Wall Street accounting firm. Its employees are dressed in regulation dark suits, white shirts, and sober ties. The corporation's headquarters is an imposing sixteen-storey Black Tower set down in the exotic palm-strewn landscape of L.A. on a parcel of land worth around a billion dollars (which could have been transformed, during the halcyon days of the late eighties, into billions more, if only MCA had had the foresight to get it rezoned before prohibitive restrictions were passed by the municipality).

The ruler of the Black Tower was Lew Wasserman, the ultimate powerbroker in the disintegrating Hollywood system. Wasserman had started out as a movie-house usher in Cleveland, then caught the attention of Dr. Jules Stein, the ophthalmologist-turned-talent agent who founded MCA in 1924. MCA rode change brilliantly, Wasserman was always moving forward into new areas of exploitation as they became revealed. In the early fifties Wasserman made a pioneering deal that gave James Stewart, then one of the most bankable stars, a percentage of his films' net profits rather than an irrationally large upfront salary. If the movie was a hit, everyone won; if it flopped, the studio didn't have to pay Stewart an astronomical upfront salary. From this deal flowed a series of ever-more-complicated payment permutations that would make agents bigger and richer than the stars they manipulated, and would end up with agents like the McIlwaines and Begelmans running the studios.

Wasserman was also a master politician. He had been the agent for a second-rate movie actor named Ronald Reagan, and he turned that into a synergistic relationship if there ever was one: Reagan, as president of the Screen Actors Guild (SAG) in the forties, helped Wasserman expand MCA into movie production, and Wasserman returned the favour by helping Reagan's political career.

Wasserman always fended off political interference with his empire by assiduously cultivating Washington officials. Robert Strauss, for example, the former chairman of the Democratic Party, sat on the MCA board.

I went to see Bill Soady first, at his office on the fourteenth floor. MCA offices were white and sparsely furnished, their austerity set off only by the priceless antiques collected by Stein. Bill then walked me over to the executive dining room, which was next to the Universal commissary. Lew Wasserman didn't attend. I admit I was disappointed. I had a hankering to see the agent who had helped guide Ronald Reagan to the presidency, not just of SAG but of the United States. Instead, I sat down with Soady, Frank Price, and Sid Sheinberg.

*Sid Sheinberg! I didn't see the icy side of him, not then. I didn't see the ruthlessness.*

Sid had been a Texas lawyer before he had come to L.A. to teach constitutional law at UCLA, and he retained a certain good ol' boy charm, being apt to start conversations with "Sir!" his Texas drawl making it sound like "Suh!"

I don't know how we got onto the subject of Saskatoon, but before I knew it, Sid and I were practically family. His younger son was going to marry the daughter of Dr. Morris Claman, who with his eight brothers and sisters had lived only a few blocks from my father in Saskatoon. In fact, Dr. Claman's oldest sister had married my father's first cousin.

Bill Soady later told me, "You and Sid were in each other pocket's before the soup was finished," and it felt true.

Not so with Frank Price, however, a dour fellow who had had a hot streak at Columbia when he oversaw *Tootsie, Stripes,* and *Gandhi.* Wasserman had hired him away as his head of production, but now he had gone cold. I didn't know it then, but he and Sid were on the outs.

At first, he didn't say too much.

I said plenty, though. And as I launched, with my usual enthusiasm, into savaging the Mann theatre plan, I could feel the tension mounting between Frank and Sid. I attacked the whole idea of a four-thousand-seat complex that had hallways only twelve feet wide, far too narrow to handle weekend crowds. Frank kept interrupting me, and Sid kept coming to my defence. I felt I was somewhere in the Gaza Strip!

In the end, though, my message got through: the Mann proposal was inappropriate for a theatre that, if it was to succeed at all, had to become instantly, obviously, gloriously a landmark.

I ended lunch on a bravura note.

"Let me redesign the theatre," I said. "It'll take me no more than a week. And, by the way, I'd also like to review the terms of your deal with Mann."

Sid smiled and in his customary style said, "Suh, I will see you in one week."

I rushed back to Toronto with Mann's plans and pored over them with David Mesbur and Peter Kofman.

It was easy. I could feel it taking shape in my mind, everything that was needed, the showplace of the industry. I could see a two-storey complex, with eighteen screens and at least six thousand seats, auditoriums ranging from two hundred to eight hundred seats. Twenty-five-foot hallways. The entrance to feature a breathtaking thirty-five-foot-high foyer, a floating staircase, and a domed ceiling with a painted *trompe l'œil* effect, complete with twinkling stars reminiscent of John Eberson's original atmospheric theatres. And there would be great spaces for major works of art: Harold Town would be perfect; a great painter and a movie buff from way back. At least four massive concession stands and two Parisian-style cafés, and the façade would be ablaze with a brilliant marquee.

"You've got one week to design it," I told David.

He stared at me and grinned.

I loved that.

*One week! Why not? Take on a dare and then do it, and then do it again, only bigger and better and faster.*

*We would build them the best goddamn theatre in America, the best goddamn theatre there was.*

# CHAPTER

## XIII

### SUPPING WITH THE DEVIL

I knew we would double in size when the Plitt deal closed, and I needed to bolster senior management. So, while the Plitt discussions were still underway, I made a pitch to Myron. Our styles fitted so well together. I reminded him that his shareholding levels were now comparable to mine and that he had a significant interest in the long-term growth of the company.

"I need your full-time involvement," I said. "Together we can do wonders with this company."

Fortunately for me and the company, Myron acknowledged the challenges would be exciting and agreed to give up the presidency of Merit, where he had an important roster of clients, and come over to Cineplex Odeon as chief administrative officer. (He was already a director and vice-chairman of the board.) And so we came to the cementing of one of the most enduring and fruitful partnerships in Canadian entertainment.

Then we settled down to work.

We had already begun to outline our future strategy in a "Black Book," which contained a complete analysis of the combined resources of Plitt and Cineplex Odeon and their respective upgrading and expansion programs. It also set out the projected cash flow for the next three years – projections that turned out to be grossly underestimated in light of later events, in that they couldn't possibly have reflected the torrid pace of our U.S. conquests, including those in New York City. One of our people who had been influential in preparing this essential tool of our business was Robert Topol, our most skilful number cruncher. Robert was born in Tbilisi, Georgia, and came to Toronto via Israel. He worked for a while for BASS Ticket Agency (later called Ticketmaster). I hired him in the early eighties when he was still a kid, not very polished, but hungry for advancement. He was quick and savvy, a sponge for the business, an acute analyst. Most importantly, he was loyal and he became an essential part of our team.

I waited around just long enough for David Mesbur to finish his drawings for the new Universal complex and then I raced off again to L.A. I had the plans under one arm, the Black Book under the other; I was prepared for any eventuality. Who knew?

Once more to the Black Tower, to Sid's office. I spread the plans and the projections out on his table. He was stunned by the scale of the enterprise I was proposing, given the short time I'd had to prepare for it. My $14-million U.S. plan for the Universal theatre was double Mann's cost, but that wasn't what impressed him most. The most telling blow was my announcing to Sid that we were going to take a mere eighteen months to prepare working drawings, obtain building permits, and complete construction, so that the complex would open on the July 4 weekend of 1987. Moreover, I was prepared to accept terms at least as favourable to MCA as those of the Mann deal, in spite of the much-larger commitment.

Sid then took me next door to meet the fabled Lew Wasserman, the King of Hollywood. I had heard all the stories, listened to the rumours, heard him described (at its kindest and most low-key) as "tough and formidable." What a letdown! He looked . . . ordinary. He was then about seventy-two and wore what I later found was the Wasserman (and MCA) uniform: a blue suit, white shirt, blue tie, and a pair of huge, black-rimmed glasses. True, weekends in Palm Springs had given him a golden orange tan that complemented his perfectly groomed white hair, but the only real hint that his seven million or so

MCA shares were worth anywhere from $250 million to $500 million U.S. on any given day was the gold Rolex on his left wrist. But I could tell he was used to power: his desk was totally clean. Otherwise, he was an unexciting individual.

His manner that day was aloof, uninvolved. Still, in his soft-spoken way, he did ask me about Cineplex Odeon. "What plans have you charted for your corporation?" he said.

I, of course, launched into my usual spiel about the sad state of U.S. exhibition and the need for new and imaginative approaches that called for a change in the ownership of theatres. His expression didn't change.

*Well, why not go for broke?*

I handed him the Black Book, and for the next ninety minutes we leafed through the pages together, Wasserman throwing in the occasional probing question.

At last he said, "Now what are you going to do with the company?"

I played innocent. "What do you mean?"

"Well, would you consider taking in an investor?"

*Would I? This was getting interesting!*

But I took my time and then said, as blandly as I could, "I hadn't thought about it."

We danced a little more in a will-you-won't-you gavotte, and then the meeting ended. Clearly, he was interested. And I . . . I was over the moon. But I was determined to show him that I was in no way dependent on the mighty MCA.

Before I left, I said, "Let me get through the Plitt acquisition. I have a partner in that deal who'll have to be properly dealt with before I can entertain any new proposition."

I arranged to get back to Sid in December, and then I floated out of the Black Tower and back to the two-storey Century City condo I had retained. *I had been courted by MCA and Lew Wasserman, a man of mythical power in my industry. I hadn't felt so high since the pinnacle achievement of the combines victory in 1983. In fact, I've rarely, if ever, felt such euphoria.*

The Plitt closing brought me down to earth fast. This was my first experience with American horse-trading. Plitt and his lawyer, Mickey Rudin, must have tried to change the deal a dozen times before we finally closed. This Rudin was a character. Hollywood is full of them, of course, as full of human cartoons as it is of hopeful starlets. But even by Hollywood standards, Mickey Rudin was a caricature. He was something of a star, as lawyers go – Frank Sinatra was among his clients. He was short and feisty, an overweight guy in a signature bow tie. His only negotiating style was to scream. At least three times I threatened to leave the table, taking my team of lawyers along with me.

I, however, was intransigent – screaming never impresses me. As far as I was concerned, the $137-million U.S. deal had to close just the way Myron and I had negotiated it in Henry's office three months earlier. To me, only minor deviations were allowable.

Allen Karp led the Goodman and Carr lawyers. I watched him carefully during those weeks, and I was impressed by the way he handled his end of the negotiations. Although he lived directly across the street from me in Toronto, I had hardly known him before this transaction. Allen was a short, balding man of forty-something, who had been sidelined by a heart condition a couple of years before. Now, however, he seemed fully recovered. What interested me about him was that he had some experience in the movie-theatre business, having represented Mike Zahorchak when Mike bought Odeon. He had, I thought at the time, administrative strengths that showed up well when he was coordinating the real-estate, tax, and corporate components of the Plitt deal. Six months later I would persuade him to trade in his partnership with Goodman and Carr for a senior vice-presidency at Cineplex Odeon.

During his internship, I worked with him closely. I encouraged him to ask many questions. His mandate was broad – to learn everything he could about the exhibition business, a business that until then he had known about only from the perspective of a lawyer. I didn't care if he needed eighteen months to groom himself; ultimately, if he was going to be useful to me, he had to learn it all.

*Little did I know what I was doing. I failed to understand that Allen's ambition exceeded his commitment to me.*

But this was 1985 and events were galloping along. The Plitt deal finally culminated on a happy and propitious note. We closed in L.A. the night before American Thanksgiving. I remember looking out of Myron's suite in the new wing of the Century Plaza Hotel at Plitt's twin theatres opposite the hotel. Taylor Hackford's *White Nights*, starring Mikhail Baryshnikov and Gregory Hines, was opening even as we were executing the final documents. I went over to the floor-to-ceiling window and looked down at the line of people winding round the perimeter of the complex. It was a portent of the success of the whole deal: *White Nights* would break house records at the Plitt twin – *our twin* – for the next four days.

Toronto now became the nerve-centre of the fastest-growing theatre chain in North America. Following our usual pattern, our people had quickly moved the fiscal and operating control of the Plitt circuit to head office, striking budgets for every location and introducing economies that eliminated some $3 million U.S. annually in general expenses.

Going through Plitt's books gave us an interesting insight into the way the exhibition business operated in the United States. Plitt, for example, had always underpriced itself compared to the competition, and we reckoned that its consumers wouldn't resist a half-dollar increase on the top ticket price of four dollars. This would substantially boost Plitt's operating income.

Plitt was also running a Reduced Admission Ticket (RAT) program, but it was ludicrous compared to Cineplex Odeon's well-focused Two-Dollar Tuesdays. Under Plitt's useless scheme, corporations, unions, charitable organizations, and God knows who else were offered blocks of tickets for any day of the week at roughly 50 per cent of face value. No attempt was made to control these tickets from being resold for a marked-up price that was still lower than the one being charged at the box office. The RAT program (aptly named) was widespread among U.S. exhibitors, and it had two obvious defects. First, theatre management received more from the commissions they earned by selling RAT program tickets than they did for running their theatres efficiently and cleanly. So guess where they applied their efforts? And second, a policy so widely abused undermined the integrity of the industry's ticket-price structure in the United States. As Cineplex Odeon grew larger, I became the industry's most vocal advocate in the fight to get rid of these RAT programs.

Plitt's public identity was also a major problem. To be blunt, it had none. Some theatres still retained the name of whatever company Henry had bought them from. The exterior signage and newspaper advertising had no consistency of image. This was easy to fix, and I struck fast. Within days Cineplex Odeon's logo, with its concentric rings, began to appear all over the United States, on Plitt theatres and in all media advertising.

Plitt was barely masticated, let alone digested, when Myron and I set off for New York on December 8, 1985. Our destination was MCA's offices at 445 Park Avenue.

We were the first to arrive in the boardroom. Big mistake – it made us look like courtiers, which gave the upper hand to Sid Sheinberg and Lew Wasserman, who swept into the room with two subordinates. The first of these was MCA's chief financial officer, Hal Haas, a chain-smoker with a pronounced limp (one foot was damaged in the Second World War), a devoted lieutenant of Lew. The other was Luis Rinaldini, a young hot shot from MCA's investment bank, Lazard Frères. His only role, as far as I could see, was to impress his clients.

We spent the next few hours going over an analysis of the projections in our Black Book. After our numbers seemingly stood up to everybody's scrutiny, Lew rose to his feet and cleared his throat.

"MCA," he intoned in a churchly manner meant to be portentous, "has to be extremely careful about its investments because, of course, an investment from MCA is perceived by the business community as the ultimate accolade."

*Sure, I thought to myself, we're about to be blessed. But I held my tongue.*

Just as well. Before we had time to tug our forelocks, Lew stuck the knife in. If MCA proceeded, he said, it was not going to pay Cineplex Odeon a premium, but instead would buy the shares at the price they were selling for that day – $9.75. He said that this was common practice for a transaction of this size, because the shares would no doubt go up when the deal was announced.

The next stage was for Hal Haas to visit our Toronto offices to perform the necessary due diligence on us. I rather expected him to bring along a bureaucratic horde of accounting types to pore over our corporate books and records with a microscope and to grill our financial people. Instead, he came alone for his scheduled three days of examinations. He left after one, saying that was all he needed to confirm our financial health.

*Our accounting was A-1! Imagine that! Only three years later, in one of their many inept attempts to embarrass me publicly, MCA would describe our accounting by using that dread word "creative."*

By Christmas I was exhausted. I took my family to the Cable Beach Hotel in Nassau for a much-needed rest. I wanted to walk the powdery sands, pink and blinding white; I wanted to paddle my feet in the azure Atlantic waters, warmed by the gulf to the temperature of tropical lassitude. But of course my mind never stopped racing. Sid Sheinberg had gone off to Fiji to stay with Dino De Laurentiis, who owned a hotel there, telling me casually, "I'll call you either from Fiji or from my beach house in Malibu immediately on my return, which will probably be on New Year's Day."

"Fine," I answered as coolly as I could. "Here's my number in Nassau." I was in a holding pattern for ten days, an uncommon position for me.

*I hate holding patterns. I hate enforced idleness. To tell the truth, I'm not even very good at vacations – to me, vacations cut me off from my real world. Their only virtue is that they give me a chance to reconnect with and focus on my wife and kids.*

*Sailing I love. Sailing between Anguilla and Grenada on a sleek Fin-
nish Swan can be a wonderful experience, and I've sailed the whole area,
exploring the islands and poking about their coves and reefs with a great
group of guys, my regulars, Lenny Gill, my brother Cyril, and Robert
Topol (when they're not seasick!), Alan Adelkind, my godfather's son
and an Olympic-class sailor, and Peter Kofman.*

*We do sometimes laugh a little, drink a little good wine, get caught
up on sleep. But idle vacations often just give me time to brood.*

*And when I brood I remember the pain in my hip and the struggle
in my life to deal with my leg, and emotions of uncertainty and insecurity ricochet around in my head, as volatile as rumours of fire in a
crowded theatre.*

Sid telephoned on New Year's Eve, as he said he would, and in his
engaging Texas style, he said simply, "Suh, I'd like to talk to you in
L.A. in two or three days about MCA proceeding with an investment
in your company."

Yes! I saw the brass ring within my grasp. Three New Year's Eves
ago I had my back to the wall and the company was toppling into
bankruptcy. Now – and I knew it was going to happen – I was about
to make the biggest deal a Canadian entertainment company had
ever made.

So stick that up your exhibition palaces, Adolph Zukor!

Since the beginning of the motion-picture industry, Canada had
been exploited like a colony. Those Canadians who had tried to make
a living in the business were at the beck and call, the whim and the
politics, of the Wall Street financiers and the Hollywood bosses who
controlled the studios and thus the product.

Now, incredibly, Cineplex Odeon appeared to be turning the
tables.

*How was I to know I was supping with the devil?*

We held a board meeting immediately on my return from Nassau.
The directors were all enormously exhilarated. Jack Daniels, who
always liked to be close to power, positively glowed. "It'll be good to
sit down with shareholders like those," he said.

Leo Kolber and Jimmy Raymond were equally ecstatic. The Bronfman group, as our largest shareholder, had been given a special in-depth session on the prospective deal and how it would undoubtedly affect our stock, and I was the golden boy all right.

*I was definitely flying closer to the sun. And they were definitely on the ground, looking up.*

Before we went back to L.A., Myron and I had a chore to do in New York. A deal with MCA wasn't feasible unless we owned 100 per cent of Plitt. So, a mere thirty-five days after setting up the partnership with Odyssey to jointly buy Plitt, we were now going to have to ask them to back off.

The negotiation had to be handled delicately and without mentioning MCA. The Odyssey guys were a gentlemanly lot, and, while reluctant, they agreed to walk. Their only condition was that we delay the closing of the deal with our "new investors" until late in May. Otherwise they would be hit by a capital-gains tax that applied to flips executed within six months. Of course, we were happy to accommodate them. In the end Odyssey made a profit of $9.5 million U.S. on their original investment of $10 million U.S., a spectacular return for the length of time their money was tied up.

I've often since wondered what would have happened if Odyssey had balked and MCA had backed out. Cineplex Odeon would have grown at a slower pace, but it might have prospered longer. No doubt I would still have been completely in charge. But, back in 1986, my entrepreneurial energies were far too revved up for such introspection. We were a hot corporation in a sizzling market. Money for buyouts was flowing everywhere, as easy to get as beer in a tavern. With the formidable backing of MCA, Cineplex Odeon would be the envy of all other exhibition companies. And a deal with MCA was just waiting to be consummated.

Myron and Allen Karp came with me to L.A. Again we were out-manoeuvred. We arrived at the sixteenth-floor boardroom first and were caught dunking bran muffins in coffee when the MCA entourage swept in. I could swear I heard a distant roll of drums. Lew, Sid, and

Hal led the party, followed by George Smith, their tax man, who was a fair-haired (if balding) and tight-lipped Washington lawyer, and, of course, the self-described "great one," Luis Rinaldini. (Sid had by now confided to me in all sincerity that he considered Rinaldini a genius – but then this was the mid-eighties, and any thirty-year-old guy on Wall Street was a genius. I was never so underwhelmed.)

There was one new person in the entourage: Charles Paul, commonly called "Skip." I could see right away that Sid had chosen Skip to be his protégé. He was in his late thirties, with that just-out-of-the-sauna flush. As I was later to learn, Skip Paul was the company executioner, who smiled or snarled on cue for either Sheinberg or Wasserman.

But few doubts assailed me that January day. Our side was all piss and vinegar, and theirs was filled with what passed for sweetness and light at MCA. Sid talked about his new Italian threads, Lew ogled us owlishly through his horn rims, and Rinaldini bit his nails over in the corner.

MCA never liked to buy less than a 50-per-cent interest in any company. If push came to shove, it always wanted to be in control. But Investment Canada was standing firmly in the way of any foreign company wanting to acquire more than 33.3 per cent of the votes in a corporation that owned what were defined as Canadian cultural assets.

Sid fired the opening salvo. "Subject to structuring the deal to comply with Canadian law, we are prepared to purchase up to 50 per cent of the shares of your company."

*"Okay, fine," I thought, as I sat quietly taking notes. So far nothing unexpected.*

Then he went on, "We desire to use our shares in lieu of cash, which of course you have the option of holding or selling."

I knew that was typical MCA; the company seldom used cash in its deals so it could maintain a very conservative balance sheet that showed huge shareholders' equity and minimum debt. I had no problem with that.

"One other wrinkle," Sid added, "is that we'll insist on a mechanism whereby we can maintain our percentage of equity by topping up any time your company issues additional shares."

Also consistent with MCA's philosophy. Still no problem.

"What about the price?" I asked.

Predictably, Cineplex Odeon shares had risen since the December 8 meeting and were now selling for $11.50. Lew had said originally that MCA would not pay over the market price of December 8, which was $9.75. Now Sid began to test the waters and offered a lowball price of $9.00 a share.

I knew right away that we weren't going to conclude a deal at that meeting. We would need more time for horse-trading. We couldn't sell at $9.00 a share, even if we wanted to, because the Ontario Securities Commission doesn't permit the private placement of stock for a discount of more than 15 per cent of its current market price. Of course, Sid knew this too. It was all just part of the game.

So I said, "We're going to think about this overnight. We want to do business with you, but we are just too far apart on the price." I stared at the other side. "Sid, there's got to be some room for give and take if we're going to make this thing happen."

We looked at each other with poker faces. No one gave anything or blinked. Finally, we agreed we'd meet at lunch time the next day.

Our team went back to my condo to deliberate. "This has huge implications," I said to Myron. "At what point do we walk away? How tough can we be in negotiating with Wasserman?"

We decided to consult Roy Furman in New York and Jimmy Raymond, who was in Montreal at the CEMP offices. Roy was upbeat. He was astonished, he said, that we had managed to get as far as we had. He felt a deal was clearly within reach. We then patched in Jimmy in Montreal. After much discussion, it was decided that we would put $10.25 on the table. And rather than being defensive in our tactics, we would move to the offence. So I called Sid and suggested that tomorrow's meeting be only a foursome: Myron and me, Sid and Lew. No advisers.

The next day Lew and Sid walked into the boardroom with that irritatingly lofty air I had come to associate with MCA. "You're shit, we're great, now let's negotiate" is what it said. They thought they were tossing us live grenades.

I began with a long statement about the prospects and values that would flow to each of our two companies as a result of an association. But, I said, if we were to do business together, the perceived value of our stock was critical. Since MCA was to be a shareholder, surely it would want the signal to the public to be one of unequivocal support. I set the price at $10.25.

"Oh, come on fellas," complained Wasserman. It was a phrase he would use incessantly when he was perturbed. "We're not going to overpay. When we met the first time in L.A., your stock was only $8.00." He and Sid just looked over at each other and then Sid counteroffered $9.50.

Time-out. More phone calls.

Twenty minutes later we returned and, taking a deep breath, I said, "We'll split the difference at $9.80."

Lew and Sid left the room and returned five minutes later. We shook hands on the deal at $9.80. Lew managed a frosty smile. Our advisers were then asked to join the session and were given their instructions. Speed was now the priority. The deal had to be wrapped up with alacrity, and secrecy had to be total, because just one leak could make Cineplex Odeon stock surge. If that happened, the agreed share price would be lower than the maximum allowable discount of 15 per cent.

We returned to Toronto early in the morning, arriving in the middle of a raging snowstorm. Skip Paul, Luis Rinaldini, and George Smith, who had come with us, went to get a few hours sleep at the Four Seasons. At ten o'clock that morning, we all assembled in Goodman and Carr's offices downtown.

By now there was a platoon of lawyers involved: ten from Goodman and Carr, two or three from Wachtell Lipton, MCA's New York lawyers and one of the top mergers-and-acquisitions firms in North America, and another squad of suits from Fraser & Beatty, MCA's Toronto lawyers, who were smugger than they should have been – they had, to quote Churchill's wonderful put-down, plenty to be modest about.

We needed them all. This was a mammoth deal, at least for a Canadian company. It took seven days working round the clock to complete. I spurred on the lawyers without mercy, never leaving Goodman and Carr's offices, snatching a little sleep from time to time on the couch in the law office's lobby. I went ape if anyone took a dinner break longer than forty-five minutes. I knew only too well how short a lawyer's attention span is. There could be no hiatus, no delay, in completing the documentation. I was paranoid that the deal would be unravelled by lawyers running off at tangents.

For sheer obstreperous obstruction, MCA's lawyers Wachtell Lipton were in a class by themselves (as I found out even more painfully in 1989). This was my first introduction to one of their team leaders, Pamela Seymon, humourless and machine-like, always turned out in dull greys without even the slightest hint of colour. Her style reflected that of her client – she was unwilling ever to yield a position, displaying an intransigence that frequently brought the negotiations to a standstill.

It took us forty-eight hours just to get the first draft on paper. And then the shouting and screaming really began, because the other side came to that draft assuming that everything was up for renegotiation. The deal I thought I had made kept changing shape. Skip Paul turned out to be insufferable as he tried to remake the essential elements of our agreement. As for Luis Rinaldini, he simply vanished on Day 3 for thirty-six hours. We never found out where he had been, but he returned as abruptly as he had left, glassy-eyed and looking as if he hadn't slept.

Every time I discovered that the drafts were no longer reflecting the spirit or intent of the agreement I had struck with Wasserman and Sheinberg, I called Sid and laid it on the line. "You sent Skip Paul up here and now he's trying to play hero. Rinaldini's worse. He just disappears. I won't tolerate changes to the deal. This isn't the way to begin this relationship."

I had to make this identical call on four occasions during the week.

Finally, on January 15, 1986, about two hours before dawn, Cineplex Odeon and MCA executed the historic document. Under the terms of the agreement, MCA was to be issued 10,883,042 shares of a new class of Cineplex Odeon stock called subordinate restrictive voting shares (SRV). MCA would pay $106.65 million by way of the issuance to us of 1.5 million of its common shares, which were then trading at about $50.00 U.S. After the purchase of the Cineplex Odeon shares, MCA would own approximately one-third of the equity of the corporation and would be entitled to one-third of the votes. MCA would be allowed to nominate four members to our board of fifteen.

MCA was also given an option to buy, within forty-two months, a further 10,883,042 SRV shares at a formula price, but in no event less than $9.80 per share, and thereby increase its stake in Cineplex Odeon to a maximum of 50 per cent of the equity. To satisfy Investment Canada, a fundamental condition was attached: while MCA, under the topping-up provision, could acquire more shares, it would never get more than 33.3 per cent of the votes. Still, despite the condition, MCA thought highly enough of its investment that it exercised its option by May 1986, ending up with a total of 21.7 million Cineplex Odeon shares.

A sterling vote of confidence in our future together, I thought at the time – MCA was buying into Cineplex Odeon's management because Wasserman and Sheinberg were convinced that the value of their equity would increase substantially.

Several aspects of the deal pleased and reassured me. MCA agreed not to sell or dispose of any of the SRV shares for two and a half years, except under certain limited conditions. One of these conditions was if I were no longer CEO of Cineplex Odeon. In light of the 1989 blow-up, it's important to note that MCA was given the right of first refusal to purchase any U.S. assets we wished to dispose of, such as the theatres, but was precluded from trying to acquire effective control of the company or from making a takeover bid for the shares of our corporation for ten years.

There were two financial conditions. We had to use the proceeds of our intended sale of the MCA shares to immediately retire Plitt's $72 million U.S. in junk bonds, which we gladly agreed to do since they bore interest at 15.25 per cent, far higher than the market rate of about 9 per cent.

We also had to list Cineplex Odeon common shares for trading on either the New York, American, or NASDAQ exchanges within two years of the date of closing. MCA believed, and I must say I agreed, that any company MCA had a major interest in would have greater visibility and recognition if it had a U.S. listing.

I felt I had made the deal of a lifetime. But then Skip informed me that neither Lew nor Sid wanted to be nominated to our board. This wouldn't do. I was so upset that I got on the phone immediately. "Sid, if you or Lew were to come on the board it would send the right signal to the investment community. If you don't, you're sending just the opposite message." Sid conceded and became a Cineplex Odeon director.

I've often been asked since what I really knew about MCA when I made the deal. After all, I had no experience in dealing with a corporation of its size and complexity.

Whenever I'm asked this, it hurts.

*Why? Because I made one major, devastating, and ultimately self-destructive mistake – I never did my own rigorous due diligence, my own exploration of MCA's history and culture, before signing. I was carried away with the size and grandeur of my dealmaking and forgot one of the most fundamental rules: watch your back! Thus I never really understood MCA's imperial mind-set. I never looked at what had happened to other companies MCA had acquired, and so I never realized that, once Cineplex Odeon was safely in its fold, MCA would attempt to turn me into just another colonial governor with minimal autonomy.*

I had hoped that big MCA and little Cineplex Odeon would be synergistic. But by the time we linked up, MCA had lost much of its hunger. It seemed to be no longer interested in innovation or new ideas. It used its might in lieu of its wits. After all, its huge wealth never stopped growing incrementally from securely invested capital.

Here's an example: Sid Sheinberg had discovered Steven Spielberg, as he told everyone within hearing distance as often as he could.

"Well then why, Sid," I remember asking him, "didn't you lock him into Universal forever, after *Jaws* and *E. T.*? Why is he now making films for the competition? For projects where Steven, and not another studio, controls the rights, why ever let him out of the fold?"

No answer.

But what would I have cared in 1986? Cineplex Odeon shares increased sharply in value after MCA's investment in January of that year. By the end of 1985 our revenues had doubled again to $162 million, net income had tripled to $12.5 million, and shareholders' equity had increased to $52.3 million, while total assets stood at $143 million. Operating cash flow had increased fourfold in three years to almost $29 million.

A mere five months later, by the end of May 1986, after the Plitt consolidation and the MCA transaction, Cineplex Odeon's equity soared to $274 million and total assets reached $530 million. As for the circuit, Cineplex Odeon had 1,176 screens, 395 of them in the key locations that made Cineplex Odeon into a blockbuster in the exhibition business.

The future looked secure. No, more than secure – glorious. True, my old friend Norman Levy's words kept reverberating in my head, "This may be the way to build an empire, Garth," he had said, "but the problem is that you might wake up one morning and find you're not the Caesar of the empire you built."

*But who wanted to listen to prophecy?*

# CHAPTER

XIV

## SIEGE

This was a thrilling time for me. Cineplex Odeon had become massive and massively profitable. We were gobbling up theatre chains the way the Starship Enterprise gobbled up parsecs. The grand theatre at the Universal lot was nearing completion. My entrepreneurial energies were at their height. I felt invincible.

Even the TD Bank acknowledged the error of its ways. The bank officers who had given us such a hard time in 1983 sent me a huge cookie with a note that said, "It is we who should be eating this humble pie!"

"That showed some class," I thought. I confess, I was feeling smug.

Then came the Imperial Six, a delicious, small *frisson* of pure malicious pleasure.

*It is a small story that is not a small story in the end. It began with the chance to do some damage to a company that had done damage to me, but it turned into my future, a lifeline, a slender golden thread to which I clung all through the dark days ahead, and which, in the end, took me where I am today.*

The Imperial Six was Famous Players' flagship theatre in downtown Toronto. It was housed in one of the few evocative old vaudeville palaces still surviving. When it opened in 1920, it was a magnificent thirty-six-hundred-seat auditorium with a spectacular domed ceiling. In the early seventies, it had been carved into six screens and decorated with carny garishness by Mandel Sprachman. The location, however, was strategically superb, right across from the Eaton Centre, which housed Cineplex Odeon's eighteen screens. In other words, Cineplex Odeon and Famous Players were going head to head at one of the busiest intersections in Toronto.

In May 1986 I lucked into a chance to lease the land on which half the Imperial Six stood. To me, it was irresistible. When I thought of how Famous Players had tried to kill Cineplex in its early days, I didn't hesitate to grab the opportunity.

It was Dick Roberts, then the secretary-treasurer of Cineplex Odeon, who started the ball rolling. The weekend before the 1986 annual general meeting, Dick received a telephone call, out of the blue, from a Windsor, Ontario, lawyer named David McWilliams. This is the value of the old-boy network: Dick and David had sailed together at the Royal Canadian Yacht Club when they were both striplings of twelve. Later, after their careers in the army during the Second World War, both had gone through Osgoode Hall Law School. Since they had been called to the bar, they hadn't seen much of each other. But David remembered Dick, and when he needed help, he called.

"Dick," he said, "I've got an elderly client who owns half of the Imperial Six Theatre and has been leasing it to Famous Players."

Dick was mystified. "Wait a minute, David. How can anybody own half a theatre?"

So McWilliams began his explanation of the odd history of the ownership of the Imperial Six Theatre. It had all started with N. L. Nathanson, the wily theatre impresario who founded Famous Players. In 1918 his company, Eastern Theatres, was planning to build a large vaudeville house in downtown Toronto. Nathanson decided (in order to save money) to locate the main part of the theatre building on Victoria Street rather than on busy Yonge Street, where land was relatively expensive. But because Yonge Street was, and is, a magnet for the public, Nathanson purchased a narrow strip of land fronting on Yonge Street which would create a passageway linking that main thoroughfare to the theatre on Victoria.

Problems initially arose because an important piece of the Victoria Street property was occupied by a family-owned lumber yard. Although willing to move the lumber yard, for some reason the family was reluctant to sell the property outright. Nathanson must have desperately wanted this parcel of land, because he agreed to enter into a lease for the lumber yard – a long-term lease which could be perpetually renewed by Eastern Theatres by giving notice every twenty-one years.

The resulting theatre property was a strange one. Eastern Theatres owned both the south half of the land on which the theatre stood and the narrow strip leading to Yonge Street. In between, the land on which the north half of the theatre was located continued to be owned by the family, who received rents according to the 1918 lease and its subsequent renewals.

Nathanson named his new vaudeville theatre the Pantages, in honour of Alexander Pantages, a vaudeville circuit operator based mainly on the west coast. Pantages had led a fascinating life. He was born in poverty in Greece in 1871 and had stowed away on a ship to South America when he was only seven years old. He travelled extensively in his early years and finally made his fortune in the Klondike Gold Rush – not by panning gold, but by operating a successful amusement hall in Dawson City. Pantages returned to Seattle and built a profitable vaudeville circuit. In order to ensure a steady supply of top acts for his new theatre, Nathanson decided to name it after Pantages.

As the years wore on and the value of Toronto real estate skyrocketed, the lease payments on the north portion of the property on which the Imperial Theatre sat stayed more or less constant. During that time, the property had been passed down through the family to a woman now living in Michigan named Edna Rakas, who was receiving a constant, but not substantial, flow of income from Famous Players.

And then, in 1981, it happened. Every twenty-one years, Famous Players had to give timely notice to the owner of the lumber-yard property to renew the 1918 lease at a minuscule rent by current standards for another twenty-one years. This had been done faithfully in 1939 and 1960 – but in 1981, *Famous Players forgot to send the notice.* As a result, the lease expired. And this is where David McWilliams came in, as the lawyer for Mrs. Rakas.

Through 1981 and 1982, McWilliams attempted to negotiate a new long-term lease with Famous Players, but they could not agree on the value of the property. A short-term lease was then arranged to permit both Famous Players and Mrs. Rakas some breathing room to obtain valuations of the land and attempt to determine an appropriate rent. Negotiations dragged on into 1986. The short-term lease was to expire in May 1986.

McWilliams told me later that he thought that Famous Players never told their American parent company, Gulf + Western, about the screw-up with the Imperial Theatre lease until the spring of 1986, just before the short-term lease expired. At that point, the Famous Players' team with whom McWilliams had been negotiating suddenly disappeared and were replaced by a hot-shot "consultant," who flew to Windsor from somewhere in the southern United States to put an ultimatum to McWilliams and his client.

"Either sign a new long-term lease at the rent we specify, or we'll close down the theatre and you'll have nothing," the hot shot told McWilliams. The demanded rent was one-half what Famous Players had been paying on its short-term lease and well below what McWilliams felt was the market rent.

"That's absolutely outrageous," replied McWilliams, "perhaps I should call Garth Drabinsky and see if he'd be interesting in leasing this property."

The hot shot laughed. "Drabinsky won't be interested in half a theatre. Here, I'll give you his phone number."

"No thanks," McWilliams said calmly, "I already have it."

So McWilliams called Dick at home that weekend. "I can't get

Famous Players to pay what my client thinks the property is worth, either by way of rent or by buying her out," he told Dick. "They are really playing hardball. I'm sick of their arrogance. They say nobody else will be foolish enough to pay me a nickel for half a theatre. My question is, would Cineplex Odeon be interested?"

Dick came to see me to relay McWilliam's strange story. When he repeated his question, I bounced right out of my chair. "Interested?" I cried, "get your friend down here right away!"

I couldn't meet McWilliams the next day, Monday, because of Cineplex Odeon's annual general meeting, but I asked Dick to make sure he was in my office first thing Tuesday morning.

The possibilities, I thought, were mindboggling. If I could make a deal with the owner of half the land on which the Imperial Six was built, and then close the theatre down, I would with one stroke dominate exhibition in downtown Toronto. The distributors who supplied Famous Players – Paramount, Warner Brothers, Disney, and MGM/UA in particular – would no longer have access to the most visible downtown launching pad for their pictures. But there Cineplex Odeon would be, right around the corner.

I reckoned that the Eaton Centre Cineplex Odeon might pick up incrementally as much as $2 million a year at the box office.

This deal was worth *plenty*.

On Monday Cineplex Odeon held what was surely our most upbeat annual general meeting ever. But I was so excited I could hardly maintain my focus. I was too busy working out in my mind how to handle the negotiations with David McWilliams.

Dick led David McWilliams into my office at 9 A.M. on Tuesday, and I listened carefully to what he had to say. His client, Mrs. Rakas, owned a large rectangle of land facing Victoria Street and linked by a narrow passageway to the main theatre entrance on Yonge Street. She did not own the link, Famous Players did, but that link led to her half. And her property contained, as well, the Victoria Street entrance, the only other access to the sixplex. Should Cineplex Odeon lease Mrs. Rakas's property, Famous Players would be left with the Yonge Street passageway leading nowhere, as far as they were concerned,

A formal portrait, by
Cavouk, of my mentor,
Dick Roberts

(Below) With my other
mentor, Nat Taylor,
*Mister Taylor*

Cavouk

Edward Gajdel

With David Hemmings in rural Quebec, on the set of *The Disappearance*

With my longtime friend and colleague, Joel Michaels (left), and director Bob Clark (centre) on the set of *Tribute*

A moment with the irre-
pressible Norman Jewison

(Below) At a party in
1977 for *The Silent
Partner,* with stars Elliot
Gould and Christopher
Plummer and my wife,
Pearl, among others.
Taken before principal
photography began.
A disaster-filled produc-
tion, but not a bad movie.

Joel Michaels, George C. Scott, and me during the filming of
*The Changeling*

With Jack Lemmon on the set of *Tribute*

A private conversation with Bob Redford at the dinner B'nai B'rith held in my honour in New York in 1989

With Paul Newman

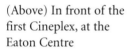

(Above) In front of the
first Cineplex, at the
Eaton Centre

(Left) By Al Hirschfeld

(Above) With Allen Karp (second from left), now president of Cineplex Odeon, Lenny Gill of Echo Advertising, and Lynda Friendly. This is when Allan and I were still amiable colleagues.

(Left) Leo and Sandra Kolber

(Above) Hollywood powermeisters Lew Wasserman (left) and Sid Sheinberg of MCA.

(Left) Shirley MacLaine presenting me with the International B'nai B'rith Award in New York in 1989

and the south half of the theatre on Victoria Street with no access. They would have no way to get customers into their theatre, and thus no way to do business.

McWilliams also explained that the Famous Players lease with Mrs. Rakas had expired the preceding Saturday, so they were now illegally occupying the premises – they were what the law calls overholding tenants.

He had barely finished his presentation when I said, "What do you want?"

He looked a bit flustered and then said, "Well, I've asked Famous Players for around $185,000 a year, about double what they've been paying, and they turned me down."

I did some quick mental arithmetic. My first thought was what McWilliams was asking was still not excessive, considering all that Famous Players had at stake. I couldn't believe their bad judgement. How could they be stupid enough to take any chance at all on losing such an asset! Complacency, I guessed. Cineplex Odeon could pay the figure named out of the increased box-office revenue that would inevitably accrue to the Eaton Centre – at least until Famous Players had found a new location downtown – which could take years, and it would be neither cheap nor easy for them to accomplish.

*In this game of mental chess, I was already four or five moves ahead. Already I could see the pieces falling into place. This was going to be special!*

"You've got it!" I said.

McWilliams now looked bewildered. "Got what?"

"Got the rent you asked for. Now get your client on the phone and tell her she's got a deal – but it's got to be signed up today."

"Wait a minute," said McWilliams, "I only came to see if you were interested. I'll have to go back and get my client to give me instructions. It's a very important matter to her, because this rent is what she lives on. She's away at her summer house in Northern Michigan and both she and her husband are quite elderly, so it will take a few days. Besides, she won't do anything without the approval of her son and daughter."

I wasn't going to wait several days for a family conclave, not for this. I was too hot to complete the deal. "Get them all on the phone now," I insisted. "Tell them the score."

David was looking as if he had been hit by a truck. Dick led him to an office so he could phone his clients. I knew that Famous Players was not going to take this lying down. I had to call in my litigation team.

In 1982 Cineplex had faced its first serious piece of litigation, which not surprisingly also involved Famous Players. I had made a deal to build a theatre in the new Rideau Centre development in Ottawa. During construction, the developer, who was edgy about our financial condition, changed his mind and made a deal with Famous Players. I was outraged, and determined to make Famous Players and the developer pay for our damages, so I went to Dick. "I need the best litigation lawyer in Canada." Dick thought for a moment and wrote down three or four names. "Start at the top," he told me.

The first name on the list was Ron Rolls of Fasken & Calvin (now Fasken Campbell Godfrey). I never got any further.

Ron is a legend in Canadian legal circles. A fierce and commanding counsel, Ron had for many years directed the civil procedure section of the Ontario Bar Admission Course. A generation of lawyers (including me) had learned the arcane minutiae of pleadings, motions, and appeals from his spare and precise lectures. Ron had co-written the two most respected legal texts on civil procedure in Canada – you could not do better than employing the guy who had written the book! So Dick and I went to see Ron Rolls.

In person, Ron is tall and balding, with a formal and curt air. His analysis of problems is unfailingly insightful, his advice to the point. I knew that many people found Ron intimidating – but we hit it off immediately and became good friends. Ron's interests in cultural and artistic matters paralleled mine – we have on several occasions admired each others' art collections.

Soon after we began work on the Rideau Centre case, Ron introduced me to Mark Hayes, who became my other legal guru. Mark was, in 1982, just a new articling student at Faskens, but he had some of the same cockiness which I had displayed when I was in the same position some years earlier. Over the next few years, Mark would take over most of my contentious legal work and become a close and trusted adviser.

Ron and Mark are brilliant legal tacticians and many times proved their ability to work with lightning speed in dealing with fast-breaking developments. Whenever I smelled trouble, I knew where to go.

As Dick led David McWilliams down the hall in search of a telephone, I spied Mark at the other end of our office reviewing documents relating to another case. I pulled him into my office and unfurled what became known as our "treasure map" – a blueprint of the Imperial Six showing the three separate pieces of land. I explained to Mark what Famous Players owned and I pointed to the middle section. "And the lawyer for the woman who owns this piece is down the hall and wants to lease it to us!" A huge grin spread across Mark's face. "What do you want to know?"

I shoved a copy of the expired 1918 lease into Mark's hands and pointed him toward an empty office next door. "Sit down and read this," I told him, "I want to know in ten minutes when and how we can take over this property and shut down the theatre."

Exactly ten minutes later Mark, Dick, and I reconvened in my office. I looked at both of them. "Well guys, assuming that we can get a lease from Mrs. Rakas, how much notice do we give Famous Players?"

Dick interrupted. "Notice be damned!" he said. "If we give them notice, they'll stay in possession, and we'll have to take them to court. They'll still be there, and we'll still be litigating years from now, until they've exhausted every conceivable right of appeal, right up to the Supreme Court of Canada."

Mark agreed. "You have a legal right to re-enter without any notice at all," he explained. "Just to be safe, we can get written authority from the landlord to re-enter on her behalf. Then they'll have to go to court to get us out – even if they win, we can appeal and stay there for quite a while."

I looked at both of them with a smile. All we had to do was march in and take away our competitor's most important theatre! But we had to move fast – and the sooner the better.

David McWilliams returned to say that he had discussed our proposal with his client, who had tentatively agreed to the terms we had proposed. Mark then raced back to his office to draft the necessary documentation. I told him it had to be done in four hours – no excuses!

I got on the phone to the pilots who flew our company jet and put them on standby. The nearest airport to where Mrs. Rakas was summering was Traverse City, Michigan, and I asked McWilliams to have his client there that same evening to sign the documents.

"My God!" he said. "She's already nervous enough! This thing has been stalled for four months, and now I've got to ask her to drive sixty or seventy miles to sign a deal the very day I first laid eyes on you. She's too old for this. She's not used to acting this fast."

Under his breath, he added, "For that matter, neither am I."

Still, he did it all, bless him. Over the telephone, he got the agreement of all the family, and Mrs. Rakas said she would meet us at nine o'clock that evening, at what turned out to be a beautiful log-cabin fishing lodge on the shores of Lake Michigan. Mark Hayes came back around six o'clock with the sheaf of documents that Mrs. Rakas was to sign (lawyers *will* work fast if you push them hard enough). Then Dick, McWilliams, and I piled into my two-seater Mercedes to drive to the airport.

I drove at my usual unhurried ninety miles an hour, steering wheel in one hand, cellular phone in the other. I didn't know it until later, but McWilliams had a heart condition and was popping digitalis pills like jellybeans, as he had been doing all day.

We got to the lodge only minutes ahead of Mrs. Rakas and her husband. It was clear that he was unwell and that they were both troubled and confused by the helter-skelter pace at which things were happening. She was naturally suspicious, wondering aloud whether there wasn't something wrong with the deal if it had to be closed so fast. In fact, she even seemed suspicious of David McWilliams.

I put on one of my most impassioned performances that night for this intimate audience of two. I explained how Famous Players had tried to put me out of business for years, and I reminded her how they had treated her, holding her to ransom for months by refusing to negotiate and by continually trying to make her believe she had no alternative. By contrast, I said I hadn't even tried to negotiate with her, because I knew that the lease was her sole source of income – I accepted her terms right off.

When I finished, Mrs. Rakas was silent. She still seemed over-whelmed, but David McWilliams was obviously supporting every-thing I had said. And Dick's avuncular presence was clearly reassuring.

I don't think I've ever watched anyone make every letter of their signature with as much intensity as I watched Mrs. Rakas sign all the necessary documents. It was midnight when we finally parted – with mutual expressions of esteem – and the three of us started back to Toronto, but I had in my hands not only a binding lease to the prop-erty, but also my landlord's power of attorney to deal with Famous Players, which was now in the untenable position of being a tenant without a lease.

While we were jetting to Michigan to close the deal, Mark Hayes, at my request, was taking a stroll through the Imperial Six to check the layout. It was a half-price Tuesday (Famous Players having been driven to copy Cineplex Odeon's ticket-pricing strategy) so Mark got in cheap. Still, the ushers looked puzzled as this well-dressed young man made a tour through the complex, looked into the washrooms, studied the lobby and the entrances to each of the six theatres, and then walked right out again.

The next morning, I met in my office with Myron, Dick, and Mark Hayes. Mark repeated his opinion that, with Mrs. Rakas's power of attorney in hand, we had the right to take possession of the Imperial Six if we did not cause a breach of the peace. At first, I wanted to move in on Friday afternoon, in order to ensure that Famous Players would not be able to get into court until the following Monday, but Mark disagreed. "Your only chance to get in," Mark argued, "is to ensure that Famous Players doesn't get any advance notice. A huge team of people will be involved in this and you can't keep a lid on it all forever. I say go in tomorrow morning."

That made sense. But it would mean that I couldn't be there in person as I had meetings scheduled in Los Angeles. So Myron and Mark got the job of planning and carrying out the takeover, which was set to take place at dawn on Thursday.

The coup was like a comic opera. At 6 A.M. sharp on Thursday morning, law students from Faskens served notices on George Destounis, the president of Famous Players, and on Larry Pilon, its general counsel, that Cineplex Odeon was taking possession of what was now its half of the Imperial Six. There is a lawyer in Toronto who still delights in telling the story of how a surprised Destounis arrived at the door of his home in his pyjamas, wiping sleep from his eyes, to see her proffering a sealed envelope from Fasken & Calvin.

At the same time, Myron and Mark were driving up to the Victoria Street entrance of the Imperial Six at the head of a procession of about twenty cars and trucks carrying security guards, locksmiths, surveyors, carpenters, and plasterers, all equipped with the tools of their trade, plus two-by-fours, plywood, and chainlink fencing – a virtual army that filled almost two city blocks. Just before the final assault, Myron, who was enjoying himself immensely, had called together the assembled masses. None of them knew what they were there for, only that they had been ordered to meet at an appointed spot just before 6 A.M. Myron unrolled the treasure map, pointed to the northern rectangle of the Imperial Six building, and said, "As of today, this belongs to us." The entire crowd of more than a hundred people, many of whom had been involved with Cineplex in the dark days when Famous Players had tried to crush us, burst into uproarious laughter.

At exactly 5:55 A.M., Mark Hayes called the police on a mobile telephone and told them "We've taken possession of the Imperial Six Theatre, and we're changing the locks." Mark was concerned that there might be some kind of silent alarm which would send dozens of police cruisers speeding to the scene. The sergeant who took the call showed how concerned he was. "They're out of business, are they? I'll make a note."

Then, at 6 A.M., just as the entire battalion of Cineplex Odeon raiders left their vehicles and started to cross Victoria Street towards the entrance to the theatre, a very untidy-looking old guy suddenly walked up to the door and opened it with – I kid you not – a coat hanger. We discovered later that, even more amazingly, there was no security system whatsoever in the theatre, and the week's payroll was sitting on the manager's desk in an unlocked office. Incredible!

In any event, Mark hurried towards the old guy and shouted, "Excuse me, what are you doing?" The surprised man said, "I'm the cleaner," whereupon he was unceremoniously sent home. At 3:30 A.M., Los Angeles time, I got a call from Myron, who quoted Macbeth: "I have done the deed."

It took our team only twenty minutes to board up the Victoria Street entrance, fence off the link to Yonge Street, put on new locks, and construct a wall of wooden studs and plaster board between Famous Players' portion of the theatre and ours. Cineplex Odeon executives manned newly installed telephones. Notices were posted in the windows saying, "Attention Former Tenant: if you wish to retrieve your chattels, etc. . . ." At about half past six, a panicked and dishevelled Famous Players' theatre manager arrived, took one look at the barricades and the notice, and spent the next hour in the public telephone booth across the street.

At this point, the operation went kind of overboard and, more than any other single incident in my career, gave me a reputation for ruthlessness, if not viciousness. The walls and the security guards had been suggested by Mark Hayes, who insisted that we secure our property immediately so that Famous Players could not get back in. Mark told us that we might have to demonstrate to a court that we had effective possession of our property. However, unbeknownst to Myron and Mark, two of the security guards hired for the operation brought their Doberman guard dogs with them. The next day, the Dobermans' snarling jaws were splashed all over the newspapers.

They were like a red flag to the Toronto media, which had already set me up as a bully-boy, and it would become a trademark Drabinsky story, quoted in almost every piece ever written about me since.

Moreover, the aftershock quickly spread to New York and L.A., where Lew Wasserman got a call from Martin Davis, the chairman of Gulf + Western, which owned Famous Players. Davis called me a Nazi.

*It was a bum rap. I had nothing to do with the Dobermans, and if I had been around, I would have vetoed the dogs before they ever left their kennels. Myron and Mark should never have allowed this to happen.*

Around half past eight that morning, the first upper-level movie executive rolled by the theatre, lowered the tinted window of his limo, and poked his head out. He was from Twentieth Century-Fox and his anxiety was intense. Famous Players was playing Arnold Schwarzenegger's giant hit, *Predator*, on three screens. The three prints of the film were locked inside. In no time, Fox was phoning Myron, begging him to give them the prints. The only trouble was that they were in Famous Players' half of the building, and only Famous Players could give Fox back their prints.

It didn't take long for Famous Players to try to strike back. At noon Ron Rolls called Mark Hayes at the theatre to say that an emergency court hearing had been scheduled for that very afternoon. Famous Players was trying to get an injunction to get us out again! Mark raced back to his office to prepare.

That afternoon Famous Players' motion was heard by Justice Alvin Rosenberg, an acknowledged real-estate law expert. Justice Rosenberg decided that Famous Players had not shown enough justification for an emergency injunction and adjourned the entire matter until Monday morning. I was ecstatic. The first weekend for *Predator* was gone for sure.

On Monday morning the lawyers convened in front of Justice Rosenberg. Counsel for Famous Players made an impassioned plea for the return of our part of the building, calling our entry "stealing a march in the night." The judge listened carefully, then took a short break. When he returned, Ron Rolls noticed that he had already written out his reasons – without even needing to hear our argument! Ron leaned over to Dick Roberts, who was sitting nearby. "Dick," he said, "it's all over."

And indeed it was. Justice Rosenberg methodically dealt with all of the slender legal reeds grasped at by Famous Players. Most telling was his comment that Famous Players had not even asserted a theory which would allow it to remain in long-term possession of the entire theatre while Cineplex Odeon had a lease of the Rakas property. Now the deed was done, completely and finally.

But now, unexpectedly, I found myself second-guessed by my newest shareholder, MCA. I hadn't consulted Sid Sheinberg in advance, because I didn't want to put him in a position of being tempted to tip off Paramount. MCA was tied up with Paramount in various joint ventures – for example, United International Pictures in the area of foreign distribution and the recently formed USA TV network. Now Sid phoned, not to congratulate me but to chew me out, complaining at a high-decibel level that I was disrupting MCA's cosy relationship with Paramount.

I waited till Sid finished his diatribe. Then I said, "Sid, don't you remember that you're a major shareholder of Cineplex Odeon? Is your relationship with Paramount more important to you than ours?"

Even as I asked, I felt my suspicions grow. Barely a month after our partnership had begun, I was having reason to doubt MCA's allegiance.

The obvious thing for Famous Players to do was to sell me its half of the Imperial Six. They couldn't get in to their half of the building because the structure had been designated a historic site, so its façade couldn't be altered. That meant they couldn't put a new entrance on Victoria Street. Nevertheless, Gulf + Western decided to fight. George Destounis and Larry Pilon were abruptly terminated, and Walter Senior was parachuted in as Famous Players' new CEO, with a new operating mandate that included making it difficult for us to use our half of the building. I hunkered down for a while, and, as I had predicted, the box office at the Eaton Centre Cineplex Odeon really took off.

I bought out Mrs. Rakas's interest that December for $4 million, hoping that this would show Famous Players I was in the Imperial to stay. Still no movement.

So in April 1987 I announced I was going to renovate my side of the building and open a nine-hundred-seat theatre by the end of the year under the theatre's original name: the Pantages. My architectural and engineering team had investigated several ways of creating a multiplex but, in the end, the most feasible idea proved to be to turn the theatre's original balcony into a single auditorium of nine hundred seats, using the entrance from Victoria Street and the elegant and spacious lobby with its two spiral staircases. All of these were located in our half of the building.

Famous Players reacted as if stung by a giant hornet.

Walter Senior rushed into print, crying "dirty pool." When we filed for a permit with the city's building department, Famous Players lobbied unceasingly with city councillors and officials in the public-works department, and the issue of our permit kept getting delayed. However, we did get a demolition permit and went as far as we could with that, but Famous Players had guards posted along the line dividing our respective properties. If one of our workmen so much as dropped a hammer over that line, a guard was there to call the police.

Our building permit didn't come through until mid-November, which gave us about four weeks in which to do three months' work if we wanted to get the new theatre open for the Christmas season. Even then, Famous Players didn't let up; it hired its own private fire inspector to make a report that said the dividing wall between our properties was not fireproof. The Toronto fire marshal didn't agree.

We were now racing toward our deadline, December 10.

I had planned a gala opening with a preview of Oliver Stone's new film, *Wall Street*. It was to be Cineplex Odeon's Christmas party for all its employees, and the invitation list also included everybody in the local industry who did business with us.

At the theatre itself, all was chaos. David Mesbur and Peter Kofman were directing three shifts of workmen. On December 7, everyone seemed optimistic. We should make the deadline by a nose. *I had never missed a schedule theatre opening.*

But Famous Players was not finished. That same day, it appealed the issuance of our building permit. Under provincial law, the building permit was stayed by the commencement of an appeal. Work was halted for an entire precious day.

But Ron Rolls and Mark Hayes stepped into the breach once more. After a frenzied late night of drafting and revising affidavits and papers with me and Peter Kofman, an emergency appeal to lift the stay was heard the next day by Judge Drew Hudson. Noting that our lawyers had moved with "lightning speed," Judge Hudson agreed that it was appropriate to lift the stay of our building permit, allowing construction to continue and the theatre to open. But before we could throw our hats in the air, the judge, apparently misunderstanding the approval process, added that our opening was contingent on approval from the Ontario fire marshall.

When I heard this, I could smell trouble – political trouble. Until that point, the only authority we had to satisfy had been the Toronto fire marshall, who had been working with us every step of the way and had approved the work which we had done. But now, the Ontario fire marshall was in on the act, and we would have to bring his staff up to speed. Sure enough, on December 10, the day we planned to have a private party in the theatre to celebrate the opening, the Ontario fire marshall was on site with more fire inspectors than there were workmen. My antennae were up and, anticipating problems, I instructed Lynda Friendly to make alternate arrangements to move the party in the event of trouble.

All I could do was will everything to be ready. The party was set to begin at seven o'clock. The caterers, along with the band, started arriving at six o'clock. Already our guests were lining up outside and the TV cameras were there; the media had once again been monitoring the clash.

I was going crazy, and so were the fire inspectors. Finally they all huddled together, and one of the inspectors came back to me to say, "We're sorry, Mr. Drabinsky, we can't let this theatre open for any purpose. The exits have not been entirely finished and we are concerned about the fire rating of the dividing wall between the two properties."

This was a perfect example of a public official overreacting to the glare of publicity. There were at least a dozen ways to empty the theatre in the case of emergency. No member of the public was at risk. All that was required was a rational exercise of official discretion. So much for Christmas cheer.

I had been running on adrenaline and nerves for the past forty-eight hours, and I felt utterly deflated. I said to Lynda, who had been supervising the party arrangements, "I'm leaving. I need to meet with Mesbur and Kofman," and I headed for an unfinished fire exit.

But Lynda caught up with me and said, "You can't. There are four hundred people outside. You have to go out and explain."

She stuck a mike in my hand, and I found myself saying in front of the whirring cameras, "Ladies and gentlemen, we have been instructed not to open tonight. There'll still be a party, but the movie will be screened at our Varsity theatre and refreshments served at Mövenpick. I'm sorry for any inconvenience." I was disgusted. I had twenty-four hours before *Wall Street* was to open to the public.

As they left, the officials of the buildings department told me, "There's no way in the world you're going to get everything done by tomorrow."

I felt a bubble of anger and I said, "Watch me! Make sure your inspectors are here by 5 P.M. sharp tomorrow. This theatre is going to open."

I rolled up my sleeves and went to work with Kofman, analysing what we had to do. The key was drywall. So I called up Marco Muzzo of Marel Corporation, widely known in the construction trades as "the Drywall King of Toronto." I had helped him out twice when he desperately needed a Cineplex Odeon in Toronto and then in a Montreal development in which he was a principal investor.

Marco's a great guy, in more ways than one – his weight once topped two hundred and seventy pounds. He's a bear of a man, a workaholic who started as a plasterer's apprentice and built a major real-estate and development company. It was the Erin Mills deal that gave his career its topspin, as it had for Rudy Bratty and Jack Daniels. I liked him enormously.

"Marco," I said, "I'm in the fight of my life right now. If I lose to Famous Players, the spirit of my company is going to be broken. I may never get this theatre opened again if I don't get it open tomorrow."

*Well, it felt that way.*

Marco was his usual calm, competent self. "What do you want me to do?" he asked.

"I need five hundred sheets of drywall delivered to this theatre within the next two hours, and I need every drywall labourer that you can find from Hamilton to Oshawa."

Marco came through. I was now running on empty, but I became the site superintendent, and for twenty-three hours I worked non-stop alongside the workmen. Throughout the day I placed urgent calls to the offices of the premier and the mayor to ensure that no public official was planning an early Christmas holiday at my expense. We did two weeks of work in twenty-three hours! The new Pantages may not have been ready for the Christmas party, but it opened to the public on schedule the next day, much to the chagrin of the Famous Players employees who had planted themselves outside the theatre all day waiting to gloat over my failure.

The Pantages turned out to be ideal for prestige pictures like *Wall Street, The Incredible Lightness of Being,* and *Die Hard,* all of which played there in the next few months, but something about it still kept nagging at me. All the time I had been watching the renovation, I had realized that it was a compromise. And God, how I hate to compromise!

*A couple of weeks before Christmas, I stole into the Famous Players' half of the Pantages, which was, of course, empty, and I saw that, despite the tasteless carve-up of the space, the original seventy-foot fly tower and articulated domed ceiling were both intact. And suddenly a picture flooded into my mind, a full-blown image of the theatre as it had been in*

*its heyday, with its glitter and its gilt. If I stood very still I could hear the*
*music of the orchestra and the roaring of the crowd, and I was almost*
*overwhelmed by a fierce longing to have a live theatre of my own. It was*
*my moment of epiphany.*

  *I had suppressed this longing all the time I was building Cineplex*
*Odeon, but here it was, stronger than ever.*

  *This time, I knew I was going to do it.*

Remember, this wasn't the first time I had wanted a legitimate theatre.

  Back in the late seventies my co-production with Moses Znaimer
of Tom Stoppard's *Travesties* could have run substantially longer if I
had been able to extend its stay or to find another house to which it
could be transferred. Neither solution proved possible. I became
acutely aware that Toronto had no transfer houses – theatres large
enough to profitably accommodate commercial productions for
open-ended runs.

  It was so frustrating! In the late seventies there was more theatrical
activity in Toronto than in any other city except New York and
London – far more than in Chicago, Los Angeles, Boston, or San
Francisco. Alternative theatres that depended more on government
subsidies than on box-office revenue were presenting productions by
the score. But there was no large, seventeen-hundred-seat centre
where a producer could present an open-ended engagement of an
original world-class production and recoup his investment. As mentioned, the O'Keefe Centre was committed to the Canadian Opera
Company and the National Ballet of Canada for most of the year. The
Royal Alexandra Theatre had extremely successful subscription seasons and wouldn't allow a long run to interfere.

  The answer, I thought, was the Elgin & Winter Garden complex,
which was a block south of the Pantages on Yonge Street. Most of the
dozen and more vaudeville theatres that had once existed in Toronto
had either been torn down or, like the Uptown and Imperial Six,
multiplexed into cinemas. But there still remained the Elgin & Winter
Garden.

  I had first seen the theatres in 1978, when Moses and I were planning to produce *Golda* in Toronto. I pitched Famous Players to make a deal with us. They had to put up the building and half the cost of restoration in return for an agreed rent and a piece of the equity. Moses and I were to put up the remaining money required for the reconstruction. As I recounted in an earlier chapter, *Golda* flopped in New York, but even before that, Famous Players had turned us down.

In 1980 I tried again to get the Elgin. I made a formal offer to buy it from Famous Players for $3.5 million. Famous Players again refused. I think George Destounis saw me as too much of a competitor, despite the fact that I was prepared to sign a covenant that I wouldn't use the theatre to show movies.

Both the Elgin and the Winter Garden are exceptional theatres and part of the city's theatrical heritage. They had originally been built by Marcus Loew, the legendary financial wizard of a continental circuit of vaudeville theatres. He commissioned Thomas Lamb to design and build "Loew's Yonge Street and Winter Garden Theatres" – a double-decker complex, originally containing a 2,149-seat auditorium on the ground floor and another 1,410-seat auditorium seven storeys above the street. Lamb spared no expense. Both theatres had expansive proscenium arches, opera boxes, a projection booth, and balconies. It was a rare gem.

Those who attended Loew's Yonge Street Theatre on opening night in 1913 were greeted by an elegance, style, and opulence that until then had been the exclusive experience of the privileged classes. The decor was in the neo-classical style first employed by the distinguished eighteenth-century Scottish architect, Robert Adam, and revived one hundred years later as "Adam and Empire." White Corinthian columns lined the main entranceway, which was finished with scagliola, friezes of reclining cherubs, and gold leaf. The grand hall's mirrors were reminiscent of Versailles, and lavish paintings evoked the great days of Pompeii and Herculaneum. Victorian murals abounded; Edwardian colours, including gilt and red brocade, gladdened the eye.

The downstairs auditorium, which resembled New York's New Amsterdam Theatre on 42nd Street, the site of Loew's corporate headquarters, was more formal, characterized by elegant and graceful ornamentation made up of elaborate plasterwork resplendent in bright colours. The upstairs Winter Garden Theatre was designed in the "atmospheric" tradition to give patrons the sensation that they were actually sitting in a lovely treed and flowered setting, underneath the canopy of a tranquil "sky" – a veritable "roof garden" theatre. Garden murals decorated its walls, while supporting pillars were fashioned in the shape of tree trunks from which sprang a profusion of flowers, foliage, leafy boughs, and garden lanterns.

Admission to the downstairs theatre ranged from ten cents to thirty-five cents. There were no reserved seats; admission was on a first-come-first-served basis. Patrons of the classier Winter Garden Theatre paid a premium price to purchase reserved seats. A continuous program of up to a dozen vaudeville acts was presented downstairs, along with a silent newsreel and a silent motion picture. The Winter Garden had only one show each night, its starting time staggered with the downstairs theatre to enable the producers to attract two audiences with one show, nearly doubling box-office receipts. Jugglers, tumblers, hypnotists, mind readers, magicians, illusionists, chorus girls, comedians, and musicians hurried up and down nine levels between the two stages, through an intricate network of staircases, corridors, and passages to display their talents for both audiences.

Just a year before the talkies revolutionized motion pictures, public tastes had veered away from vaudeville. As audiences declined, the upstairs Winter Garden Theatre was closed and, for the next sixty-two years, became a ghost. Few knew of its existence. The grand, winding staircase that led up to the Winter Garden disappeared from view. The downstairs auditorium became a movie-house, developing a reputation first as the showcase of celebrated motion pictures (*The Wizard of Oz* and *Gone With the Wind*) and then, as its box-office grosses continued to wane, as a sleazy, single-auditorium movie-house playing violent and soft-porn films. In March 1978 the theatre was rechristened the Elgin in an attempt to change its image and regain its reputation as a respected first-run movie-house.

I had been entranced, as I meandered up and down the stairways and through the two auditoriums and the countless service areas that made up the venerable old edifice, by the possibility of restoring them to all their early-century glory.

Then the Ontario Heritage Foundation (OHF) got into the act and persuaded the province that the Elgin & Winter Garden was a cultural treasure worth preserving. The province subsequently bought the theatres for $4.5 million and did a deal with the City of Toronto, obtaining permission to sell the air rights to raise at least part of the money the foundation needed to restore the building. At this point, they called for tenders for the operation of the theatres.

I thought my best chance to be appointed the theatres' operator was to form a joint venture with Concert Productions International (CPI), which was primarily a rock promoter, but also operated the BASS Ticket Agency. In November 1981 our partnership got the nod from the province over our two competitors, Ed Mirvish, who owned the Royal Alexandra Theatre, and Peter Peroff of Toronto Truck Theatre. We signed a forty-year lease at $1 a year in exchange for a bank-generated commitment to advance about half the estimated restoration cost of $9 million. The investors for my share were a number of the original Cineplex shareholders, who were still solvent, the market crash of 1982 being still in the future.

I thought I had come up with the perfect political balance. I envisaged the smaller Winter Garden as the longed-for transfer house for Canadian plays that had succeeded in the non-profit theatres. The Elgin would be a commercial house where shows could run on an open-ended basis. It all sounded irresistible to me.

However, for the next eighteen months I became mired in a morass of red tape, weighted down with the Kafkaesque absurdity of provincial bureaucracy. I wrangled constantly with the stupefyingly inept politicians, their sycophantic appointees, and the unctuous civil servants who made up the so-called Restoration Committee, and who supposedly represented the interests of the province and the OHF, but in fact did little but delay and frustrate progress on the project.

Throughout these months, detailed plans were drawn and redrawn with the dispatch of a snail on Lithium; naturally, the restoration budget soared from the original estimate of $9 million to more than $19 million. Why? Because the province, in its unrelenting demands for changes and upgrades, revealed its true agenda – it wanted a functionless historical monument, rather than a functioning theatre for a sensibly sized investment.

The province's employees and appointees were utterly devoid of a knowledge of theatre basics. For example, I pointed out what should have been obvious: both existing stages were inadequate for contemporary productions – they were neither deep enough nor wide enough to provide the necessary stage and wing space. Fortunately, a small parking lot, with an entrance from Victoria Street, was located behind the stage, and, after my urging, the province agreed to let me pick this up to make the necessary expansion possible.

But then they wouldn't allow the expansion to go ahead. After the lot was acquired, the province's representatives decided to leave the stage as it was and to use the new space for dressing rooms and rehearsal facilities – a typically ludicrous solution, because these facilities could be readily located elsewhere. Mandel Sprachman offered one of his feckless solutions: excavate under the link that joined the theatres to their Yonge Street entrance and put the dressing rooms there. Of course, they would be too far away to be of any use. I had the proper solution, the only one: excavate under the orchestra of the downstairs theatre, as we later did with the Pantages, and locate the dressing rooms and other necessary facilities there, in close proximity to the stage.

I was on a suicide mission, a bobsled to hell. The province's financial contribution was fixed under our agreement, which meant that cost overruns caused by their grandiose delusions had to be funded by our joint venture. By this time, because of market conditions, my shareholders had withdrawn their support; Cineplex, to which I was now devoting all my energy, was having its own travails. I was forced to part company with the province.

My final involvement with the Elgin & Winter Garden was in 1987, after Andrew Lloyd Webber's *Cats* had completed a successful two-year run in the Elgin, which had been patched up as an interim measure just enough to permit the run. (This long engagement, by the way, reinforced once again the faith in Toronto theatre's economic viability that I had first embraced wholeheartedly ten years earlier.) The provincial government was spending what was now reputed to be the staggering sum of $40 million renovating the two theatres, when the Ministry of Citizenship and Culture once again called for tenders to operate them. I said I would be interested, but only if they agreed to adopt my suggestions for correcting the dimensions of the downstairs stage. Once more they stubbornly refused to excavate under the orchestra. As a result, today's Elgin & Winter Garden is a typical loused-up example of government waste; the Elgin is a beautiful fifteen-hundred-seat theatre with an inadequate stage. Someday, it will have to be corrected.

Another phase of what might be called my apprenticeship in live theatre came about when I was persuaded by David Silcox, who was then director of arts administration of the City of Toronto, into acting as chairman of the Toronto International Theatre Festival, called Onstage '81. The idea was for the festival to take place during a three-week span that May.

With a straight face, Silcox told me I could count on the wholehearted support, moral and financial, of the three levels of government, all of whom he assured me were emotionally committed to the festival's success. Although I was still practising law at that time and was heavily involved both in film production and the early expansion of Cineplex, I couldn't turn down the chance to become more closely involved with the theatre community.

When I came on the scene, the usual blue-ribbon board of topline businessmen and bureaucrats were already ensconced. Naturally they had all been appointed either for their money, their political connections, or for having done well in some other endeavour. None of them, it soon became lamentably clear, had the slightest intention of devoting enough time to their duties as directors of the festival or to even learn what in the world it was all about. Some of them knew pathetically little about the theatre. If they went at all, it was to the star-laden foreign-produced road shows at the Royal Alexandra and the O'Keefe. They said they wanted a glitzy festival that would attract large crowds and culturally enhance Toronto's reputation, but the sad truth is they had no idea what they wanted. They were aimless, waiting for someone to give them some advice about artistic vision or fund-raising strategies. Alas, I've found these attitudes all too prevalent among the members of every arts board I've ever had anything to do with in Toronto. I suspect the situation is no different in other cities.

As well, the board was huge – an invitation to play politics at the expense of taking action. Prominent were directors of Toronto alternate theatres: Paul Thompson of Theatre Passe Muraille, Tom Hendry of Toronto Free Theatre, Bill Glassco of Tarragon Theatre, and Ken Gass of Factory Theatre Lab. They wanted the festival to represent their own brand of shopworn, leftover cultural nationalism.

I knew better. I quickly realized that the festival would have to be staged on a much-more-ambitious scale if it was to have any chance at all of firing everyone's imagination and attracting both national and international attention. I was determined to make the first festival such a standout that it would become a permanent annual event. I wanted to create a frenzied, "must-see" buzz throughout the theatrical community, to dazzle the city and the world, and to cultivate a new Toronto theatre audience that was larger, more sophisticated, and more devoted than any that had existed before.

I went to work with Shane Jaffe, the festival's chief administrator and artistic director, an energetic man whose theatre mind was also adept at handling all of the festival's mind-boggling logistics. Shane and I wanted to attract the world's best theatre troupes, companies whose excellence would give lustre on the whole enterprise and whose fame would stimulate the kind of media attention that would attract patrons.

Of course, this meant not only spending substantially more than the original budget allowed, but also resulted in my stepping on a lot of toes. The local alternative theatres thought of the festival as an opportunity for the aggrandizement of their own companies. As people like that usually do, they feared that if better-known groups were imported, they would be upstaged. "Our festival is being taken away from us" was the chronic complaint. Commercial theatre creates paranoia among the non-profit theatre sector, a fear that the crowds attracted to large-scale events diminish audiences for smaller theatres. They fail, then, to understand that commercially successful productions cultivate new audiences and reawaken the idea in a broader segment of the population that theatre can be an exciting, challenging, and satisfying way of spending their leisure time.

Regardless, I plowed on.

The foolishness of the small-theatre paranoia was revealed when Onstage '81 finally opened. During those three weeks in May, a thousand performances of more than a hundred productions were presented. There were twenty-seven international companies, nineteen companies from elsewhere in Canada, and seventy from Toronto alone. Thirty-eight locations were used, including every available theatre and hockey arena in the city – even the Toronto Islands, where a British company staged an environmental show called *The Tempest on Snake Island*.

Ironically, the most popular hit was a Canadian play staged by Toronto's Necessary Angel theatre company – *Tamara*, a four-hour environmental show by two Torontonians, John Krizanc and Richard Rose. The structure was original: each performance was played to a maximum of fifty people, and the premise was that fifty patrons had been invited to dine at the mansion of the Italian poet and patriot, Gabriel D'Annunzio. The play began immediately upon your arrival at Strachan House on Queen Street West, which had been decorated to look like a villa in Mussolini's prewar Northern Italy, *circa* 1927. A black-shirted Fascist policeman demanded to see your papers. Of course, you didn't know what he was talking about, so he would lead you to the box office where you would pick up your tickets/passports. "These are your papers," he would inform you. "Do not let me find you without them again."

At the beginning of the play, each member of the audience had to choose a character to follow. Since the play took place throughout the house, and sometimes outdoors, audience members could be frequently seen scurrying after one of the performers. As the maid confessed her secrets in the kitchen, you could smell the pungent aromas of spices, vegetables, and sauces as she cooked in front of you. You would feel embarrassed as actors portraying lovers lost themselves in passionate embraces less than a foot away from you. You could even find yourself in the way of a pistol pointed at a closed door. At the intermission, audience members were encouraged to chat and share information about the intrigue that was really going on and to put together the pieces of the story. This was total interactive theatre.

*Tamara* was a hit after the first previews, and it became the most sought-after ticket at the festival. Later Moses Znaimer bought the rights and produced it in New York at the Park Avenue Armory, where it played from November 1987 to the summer of 1990. In L.A. its engagement at a Legion Hall on Highland Avenue ran ten years, ending in the summer of 1993.

None of the imports, impressive as they were, had that kind of impact. They included Everard Schall, considered to be Germany's Laurence Olivier; he was married to Bertolt Brecht's daughter. Schall's one-man show was the festival's hit among the theatre professionals, while a young unknown from Britain, Alan Williams, gave the North American première of his satire on rock and roll, *The Cockroach Trilogy*. JoAnne Akalaitis, who went on to succeed Joseph Papp as head of the New York Public Theatre, came with her troupe, Mabou Mines. Other world-famous companies included The Scottish Traverse Theatre Club; Israel's Habimah Theater; Britain's Shared Experience; John Jory's Actors' Theater of Louisville; and, from Italy, Teatro Stabile dell'Aquila. And behind the scenes, in workshops, seminars, and lecture series, people from every walk of theatrical life and from every theatrical community came together in celebration.

Toronto was electrified. Suddenly it found itself transformed into North America's largest movable stage. Onstage '81 was a triumph; it was on everyone's lips. Radio stations and television programs were singing its praises. Newspapers heralded it in their editorials. "There hasn't been as much excitement among playgoers, performers, producers, and even critics since the first, heady days of the Stratford Festival," lauded the *Toronto Star*.

Onstage '81 achieved all its cultural objectives and more. But, alas, it lost money, failing in the end to break even by about $750,000.

When it was all over and the hoopla began to fade, did the board then say, "Let's get together and lick the deficit?"

Like hell. What they said was, "Who, us? You're the chairman, Garth. You fix it."

Within days, every creditor whose account had remained unpaid got me on the telephone to ask me what I was going to do about it. I was being pilloried in the newspapers for the unmitigated financial disaster I had brought upon our righteous community – pilloried by the same newspapers that only weeks before had been singing the festival's praises. I was abandoned.

Well, there's always a way out for an inventive mind. At about this time the movie industry was abuzz with the story of Francis Ford Coppola having provided financial assistance to Kevin Brownlow for resuscitating, out of archival fragments and remnants, a classic silent film, Abel Gance's *Napoléon*, which had premièred in Paris in 1927. Here was the apotheosis of the silent film as art, a work that was way ahead of its time. Thirty years before the advent of Cinerama, *Napoléon* introduced three-screen Polyvision on a colossal triptych screen during its climactic last twenty minutes, almost all of which were spent portraying the clashing armies who met in the battle of Marengo, Napoleon's crucial battle for Italy. Toronto's newspapers described the film as "an awesome moment in motion-picture history" and "an event of memorable proportions."

Coppola had had his composer father, Carmine, write an orchestral score for sixty musicians to highlight the four-and-a-half-hour film's many visually enthralling moments and was about to stage it in

Radio City Music Hall in Manhattan. I conceived the notion of there-after bringing it to the thirty-two-hundred-seat O'Keefe Centre for a week. Opening night would be a $250-a-seat gala to raise the money necessary to liquidate the festival's deficit. With Lynda Friendly's usual determination and organizational help, I campaigned hard to get the support of the media and to attract corporate sponsors – successfully in both cases. American Motors Renault alone put up $250,000. I spent what seemed endless hours on the telephone per-suading some of the creditors to accept tickets to the gala for their accounts. An imposing list of special guests attended the gala, includ-ing Prime Minister Trudeau. It was an overwhelming success and enough was raised to clear the slate.

There's one more episode in my adventures in live theatre that I want to describe here.

In late 1987 I got a call from Christopher Plummer. I like Christopher; he had starred in three of the motion pictures I had produced: – *The Disappearance*, *The Silent Partner*, and *The Amateur* – and I consider him one of the most honourable and talented indi-viduals I've worked with. His call was to tell me that he and Glenda Jackson were starring in a stage production of *Macbeth*, but the proj-ect was *in extremis*. Somebody had to step in to salvage it. He hoped it would be me.

From what he said on the phone, the production was hexed – con-forming to the legendary superstition about "the Scottish play," as actors sometimes call it. The producers, Fran and Barry Weissler, had raised a million dollars. The director was Long Wharf's associate artistic director, Kenneth Frankel, and, from a technical standpoint, the production boasted what were supposed to be Broadway's best: costumes by Patricia Zipprodt and a set designed by Tony Walton. Walton I knew; his work I considered generally outstanding. Here, however, he had conjured up a single-set moonscape, littered with plastic rocks. It was godawful. Not only was it a visual disaster but it was also a hazard to life and limb. No one knew this better than

Christopher, who had aggravated an old knee injury trying to sword-fight on the uneven stage.

I flew to New Haven to see a performance, during which Christopher limped around painfully. I concluded that the only way to redeem the situation was to scrap everything and start over. But this was impossible, given the short amount of time Glenda and Christopher had available before they had to leave for distant parts to fulfil other commitments. I had already set up a new theatrical division of Cineplex Odeon under Edgar Dobie, who now heads the North American operations for Andrew Lloyd Webber's Really Useful Group (RUG).

The Weisslers asked Cineplex Odeon to get involved by putting up a cash advance against the Toronto rights to the show. I agreed, provided I could also contribute artistically. I also insisted that, if Cineplex Odeon were to participate, Robin Phillips, who by good luck was available, be engaged to replace the director. Robin is a wildly gifted director who had a considerable impact on Canadian theatre as Stratford's artistic director in the last half of the seventies and, more recently, as the artistic director of Edmonton's Citadel Theatre.

Robin duly stepped in, summoned Daphne Dare from London to redesign the set, recast the show to the best of his ability in the time available, and quickly won the support of the cast, even that formidable intellect Glenda Jackson.

Prior to the show's arrival in Toronto, I launched my usual omnipresent advertising campaign, and *Macbeth* broke Canadian box-office records for a legitimate dramatic work by selling out the O'Keefe Centre for two weeks and grossing $1.5 million. On the road, it continued to play to mixed reviews, but it didn't really matter – the show was a hit at the box office. Shakespeare's classic is ineluctable, and the combined star power of Christopher Plummer and Glenda Jackson was impossible to resist.

New York was another story. Although we augmented the Broadway budget, Robin, who is nothing if not true to his convictions, refused to allow himself to be billed as director, just as Gower Champion had refused to take credit for his work on *A Broadway Musical.* He would only settle for a billing as artistic consultant because, he insisted, the production was not his from the outset. As if that weren't enough, he finally had to withdraw from guiding the production to New York because of his pre-existing contractual obligations to direct *King Lear* and *Twelfth Night* at Stratford. Then Zoe Caldwell's engagement as Robin's replacement led to an unfortunately timed negative story about the history of the production in the *Sunday New York Times* a week before the opening. The criticism had nothing to do with Zoe's merits as a director, only with the fact of the change.

The critics were more influenced by this story, I think, than by what they saw and heard on opening night. To put it mildly, they contained their enthusiasm toward everything in the production except Glenda's performance (which won her a Tony nomination).

With all this as the background, you can understand why, when I was unlawfully prowling around Famous Player's half of the Pantages building that December 1987, I began to feel an all-too-familiar prickle of excitement on the back of my neck. I looked up at the huge dome and imagined how it would look when it had been masterfully restored and was once again a deep green embroidered in gold. Then I went through the whole building, seriously rediscovering it. The theatre had an airy elegance, and underneath the grime of the 125-foot-long passageway that linked the Yonge Street entrance to the theatre was a riot of decoration, faux marble, Ionic pillars, cross-vaulted ceilings, and an astonishing palette of colours. The Pantages, I realized, could be restored to become a very sophisticated people's palace indeed. It could be one of the most beautiful theatres in North America.

Once on this track, my mind raced ahead. A new house needs a blockbuster to establish it in the public consciousness. The O'Keefe Centre benefited greatly over the years by the fact that it opened in 1960 with the Broadway tryout of *Camelot.* The equivalent blockbusters of the eighties were Andrew Lloyd Webber musicals, and his latest mammoth hit in London was *The Phantom of the Opera*. How about opening the Pantages with a Canadian production of *Phantom*? Might as well have large-scale dreams while I was at it.

*I told you, once I get an idea, I can't be deflected, I don't easily take no for an answer.*

But first I had to buy out Famous Players. I knew they had to be hurting by now; the question was whether their pique still outweighed their business sense. I had my half of the building up and running, but they could do nothing but pay taxes on their half. Any construction they undertook would disturb my theatre patrons, and they knew I would slap an injunction on them if this happened. While I was sure they would never sell me their half if I wanted to use it to compete with them by showing motion pictures, they might deal if I promised not to do that.

I decided to go right to the top and flew to New York to meet with Martin Davis. I knew he would take some handling. Sid had been saying for months that I had to somehow soothe his feelings. "He hates your guts," Sid told me over and over again. "Every time your name comes up, it's nothing but pain for Lew Wasserman and me."

Davis was yet another Wall-Street-financier-turned-movie-industry-pundit. He had succeeded the notorious Charles Bluhdorn as the head of Gulf + Western and had thus inherited Paramount Pictures. I had met him once before, when Leo Kolber and I had tried to get him to sell Famous Players to Cineplex Odeon, and I had the impression that he couldn't quite grasp or believe that he was running a conglomerate expansive enough to include companies that sold insurance and others that grew pineapples.

Davis didn't say much when I saw him; he had a habit of silently sucking on his pipe. I did my best to make the deal palatable to him. I began by trying to help him understand where I was coming from. I explained how I had not sought the theatre out. Rather, his people had screwed up badly, and it was handed to me. Famous Players had deliberately and with premeditation tried their best to put me out of business, I said, so when I was handed a chance to strike back, I of course took it.

"I don't want to continue a war with you," I said. "If you agree to sell me your half of the Imperial, I'll promise not to run movies in it and I'll apologize for any embarrassment I've caused you. I'll use the occasion to publicly acknowledge your great contribution to the future of Canadian culture and ensure that Ottawa takes appropriate notice of this sale."

He could also see, of course, that by selling the theatre to me he would staunch the bleeding my manoeuvre had caused him – plus he would get rid of a humiliating symbol of his managers' grievous error. In any case, he seemed to like my proposals, and we shook hands on the deal. As I left his office, I noticed on his desk a piece of acrylic with the phrase "Assume Nothin'" carved on it. I laughed all the way home. He should have given that advice to his own guys at Famous Players when they tried to take advantage of Mrs. Rakas.

*So you can see that a small story about a serendipitous opportunity became a turning point in my life, in far more ways than I could have guessed at the time.*

The deal closed in March 1988. Walter Senior and I met for breakfast at the Courtyard Café, in the now-defunct Windsor Arms Hotel, the morning of the closing. He said in his usual sarcastic tone, "Now you've got the theatre, I suppose you're going to put *The Phantom of the Opera* in it."

I smiled and said, "Walter, you never know."

# CHAPTER

## I'LL TAKE MANHATTAN

We were growing explosively. Analysts loved us. And though there were uneasy signals from the board (the Martin Davis thing with Paramount and the Imperial Six left a bad smell with the MCA contingent), we were doing what we had set out to do: fulfilling Leo Kolber's direction to build a great entertainment company.

Not long after we had concluded the deal with MCA, Skip Paul was telephoning to suggest a Cineplex Odeon foray into New York by buying Loew's theatres. New York is the single most critical city in the world for movies, and Loew's was the city's premier circuit. Universal didn't have – but badly wanted – access "in first position" to a circuit in the city. For my part, I knew that Cineplex Odeon had to have a prominent New York circuit if it was to enjoy a dominant position in exhibition in North America.

But this vast, volatile city can make or break you overnight, as I had found out to my sorrow in 1978 when *A Broadway Musical* had opened and then closed ignominiously the same night. So I shouldn't have been surprised that New York would proclaim me a champ one day, only to have its mayor chewing me out the next while the press castigated me as "Darth Grabinsky" of "CineOdious."

But I'm getting ahead of myself. We still had to breach the city's walls.

If an exhibitor has to be situated anywhere in New York, it's in Manhattan's Silk Stocking district. This skinny little stretch of Upper East Side real estate between Central Park and the East River is, after Universal City and Westwood, the best location for movie-theatres in North America. These few blocks have demographics that are a marketer's fantasy: the rich, the famous, the yuppies, the tastemakers, and the wheeler-dealers. Manhattan is still the hub of sophistication and opinion, home of the major media companies, the top financial institutions, and advertising agencies. Hollywood may make the movies, but New York sells them to America – and to the world.

In 1986 Manhattan was still severely underscreened, which meant it was an exhibitor's heaven. The circuit with the best locations can, and does, wring major concessions from the distributors, not only for New York itself but for the rest of the country as well. If you control the top locations in Manhattan, you can make a better deal with distributors for, say, the highly competitive zones in the U.S. Southeast and Southwest.

Loew's had 222 screens in prime locations throughout metropolitan New York and New Jersey. Just the year before, the circuit had been bought jointly by Jerry Perenchio, a former MCA agent, and TV producer Norman Lear for $158 million U.S., or 6 times cash flow. Now Loew's was on the block for $325 million U.S.

The price was too steep. Nat Taylor had taught me that ten times cash flow was the maximum that should be paid for a theatre. When we crunched Loew's numbers, we found the asking price much too exorbitant to even consider a deal for the circuit.

But even as we reluctantly turned away, we had to confront the volatile nature of the theatre market. The Hollywood studios were going back into exhibition, thanks to the Reagan administration's lax attitude toward vertical integration. MCA had already bought into Cineplex Odeon, and Paramount had paid $220 million U.S. (12.2 times cash flow) for the 360-screen, Westwood-based Mann theatre chain.

So when I heard that RKO's 97 screens might be for sale, I moved as fast as I could. The name was irresistible: RKO was the studio that had produced so many memorable movies of the thirties, among them the Fred Astaire and Ginger Rogers musicals. In the late forties RKO had been bought by Howard Hughes, the archetypal studio owner, who, before he became one of the world's most famous recluses, used his position of power to carry on his sexual pursuits of the movie stars.

RKO had been one of the casualties of the 1948 consent decree that broke the studios' grip on the industry; subsequently, the circuit declined as it went from owner to owner. In the early eighties, a couple of real-estate lawyers, Al Schwartz and Mike Landis, had bought the circuit and expanded it to include some of Manhattan's top screens, including the Paris, the Plaza, the Sutton, the Beekman, and Cinema III in the Plaza Hotel.

Schwartz and Landis were asking $180 million U.S., which after converting to Canadian dollars was $20 million more than MCA had paid for its shares in Cineplex Odeon. There was little room to manoeuvre the price down. The price worked out to be 14.6 times their current cash flow, still too much. After depreciation had been factored in, RKO would barely earn an accounting profit, and I knew analysts would be on Cineplex Odeon's case, pointing out that RKO was a continual drag on our earnings.

So why did we make an offer?

The superficial answer is that we were sure we could easily enhance the chain's cash flow using Cineplex Odeon's much stricter management style. RKO had a lot of latent potential in it then, which with insightful management could be exploited and maximized. For example, the company owned a twin in Fresh Meadows, Queens, a true neighbourhood movie-house, where the teenaged Donald Trump had gone to the movies on Friday nights. Every distributor wanted to get into one of the two thousand-seat theatres because the potential gross during an opening week was $75,000 to $100,000 U.S. I went one better than that – I converted the complex into seven screens, and when the renovated Fresh Meadows opened in 1988, it grossed $4 million U.S. in its first year and generated $1.5 million U.S. in cash flow. For the relatively modest investment of $9 million U.S., I had created a superb new jewel worth – based on 12 times cash flow – $18 million U.S.

But the real answer as to why we bought RKO was this: we had no alternative. We had to have New York. We needed the clout it gave us with the distributors. MCA wanted it for Universal. Prices were rising around us. We needed to protect ourselves.

RKO's Al Schwartz and Mike Landis (their company combined their first names, ALMI) were most disagreeable people. Schwartz was a showbiz lawyer and Landis a former bankruptcy expert; both loved to grandstand outrageously. They fussed and fretted about every detail, and when we got to the actual negotiation, it was like wrestling alligators.

Like Plitt and Canadian Odeon, RKO had been built on leverage, and Cineplex Odeon would have to assume its $97.3-million U.S. debt. In addition, we needed about $80 million U.S. in cash. Our plan was to use the 1.5 million MCA shares that remained from the stock MCA had used to buy Cineplex Odeon. MCA shares had been worth $50 U.S. each at the time of the transaction. Since then, their price had fallen 16 per cent. If we were to sell them now, we would lose $8 million U.S. – at least on paper. We offered Schwartz and Landis the stock at the lower value, on a condition that they lower the price of RKO by the same amount. After all, the expectation was that MCA's stock would rise again. In the end they agreed.

At this point Sid Sheinberg had to be brought into the negotiations.

Landis took less than an hour to enrage Sheinberg as they argued and nit-picked over how long they would have to hold the MCA paper before they had the right to register it with the Securities and Exchange Commission (SEC) for resale. But it was their general attitude of senseless carping that so offended Sid. He finally took me into the hall and said, "I don't want to do business with these guys. I can't stand them. Life is too short."

I had to remind him that we were trying to capture an asset that was significantly underutilized and we had a solid plan to improve its cash flow. What's more, I could finally provide Universal with a primary position in New York. Sid listened and in the end agreed. I was pleased, because it showed that, at that stage of our relationship, he still trusted my business judgement.

As for the "odd couple," they agreed to remain MCA shareholders long enough for Sid to be comfortable with the deal. We finally bought the circuit for $169 million U.S.

RKO was our biggest acquisition in 1986, but with the ever-capable Roy Furman as our investment banker and constant adviser, we also mopped up some other strategic circuits. One of them, the forty-eight-theatre Septum chain in Atlanta, cost us $7.5 million U.S. and gave us control of 50 per cent of the pivotal Atlanta market. We also consolidated our Chicago position, paying $14.5 million U.S. for the fifty-one-screen Essaness circuit. Then, in November, I got a toe-hold in the fourth-largest North American market, Washington, D.C., when Cineplex Odeon bought the seventy-six-screen Neigh-borhood chain for $21 million U.S. Neighborhood also provided us with an extended presence into the rich Virginia suburbs. And just before Christmas, we bought Sterling Recreation Organization's (SRO) ninety-nine screens in the Seattle–Tacoma area, a top-notch movie market, for $44.5 million U.S.

The year ended spectacularly. Our asset base had risen to $632 million U.S. from a little more than $100 million U.S. the year before. Shareholders' equity, boosted by the MCA transaction, had increased to $228 million U.S. from $37 million U.S. a year earlier. Net income had increased by 250 per cent to $22.5 million U.S., and revenues had nearly tripled to $357 million U.S. It was true that, due to our rapid expansion, our bank debt had risen as well – to $318 million U.S. – but thanks to Myron's astuteness with our North American banking con-sortium, our average interest costs were 9 per cent and our cash flow far exceeded the amount required to service that amount of debt.

Early the following year, 1987, I pieced together the final compo-nents in Cineplex Odeon's complicated Manhattan theatre structure by buying the biggest little circuit in the business. The Walter Reade chain was known as "the ego circuit," because it had the "Bloomie's" theatres – the Baronet and Coronet across from Bloomingdale's department store – the giant eleven-hundred-seat single-screen Ziegfeld at 54th and Sixth avenues, and the Waverly Twin in Greenwich Village.

This small acquisition demonstrates how complicated and interlocking relationships are in the movie industry, and how tricky they make doing business.

Walter Reade had been bought only the year before by Coca-Cola, which then, through its subsidiary TriStar, bought Loew's screens in New York. Coca-Cola and TriStar were beginning to have a disproportionate market position in Manhattan, which would undoubtedly draw the Justice Department down on TriStar, and Coca-Cola was skittish about tainting its unblemished image in Washington. They were therefore happy at the prospect of unloading Walter Reade.

For our part, buying Walter Reade would allow us to shed some competitive RKO theatres in Manhattan that had only short-term leases remaining, while augmenting key zones and adding other new zones with the upscale Walter Reade theatres, which included several freehold interests.

It was just like a game of Monopoly! What could I give TriStar to persuade it to let Coca-Cola sell Walter Reade to me? I negotiated an interesting swap. Loew's needed a superior Long Island location and I had just the theatre, the newly expanded and renovated Roosevelt Field eightplex, which grossed $130,000 U.S. a week. So we bought Walter Reade for $32.5 million U.S., paying $22.5 million U.S. cash and 650,000 common shares of Cineplex Odeon, issued to Coca-Cola, for the remaining $10 million U.S. In turn, I sold Roosevelt Field, which was listed on our books at $10 million U.S., to Loew's for an initial price of $17 million U.S., with an adjustment to the purchase price based on a multiple of its 1987 cash flow that ultimately yielded a total sale price of $25 million U.S. In effect, we laid out zero dollars in the transaction. Manhattan was now completely secured, and we even had Coca-Cola as a 1.5 per cent shareholder.

Understand, once I went into the United States it became a race against the clock to conquer markets and achieve sufficient heft to protect our buying position so the majors couldn't dictate to us and drive our costs through the roof. So that I could tell them, "If you don't play ball with me in these markets at these film terms, you don't get my theatres in New York, you don't get the juggernauts in Chicago and L.A. and later Seattle." I needed a critical mass in the relevant markets in order to achieve this dominance.

I guess the first time I really realized the muscle I was now wielding was when I screened Oliver Stone's movie *Platoon*.

When I first ran a print in my screening room, alone at two o'clock in the morning, I had been stunned by the movie's compelling images of men at war and by the melancholy soundtrack, based on Samuel Barber's "Adagio for Strings" that had been used as a dirge at Franklin Roosevelt's funeral. As soon as I could the next morning, I called Arnold Kopelson, the film's producer and my longtime friend (he had sold foreign-territorial rights for my film *The Disappearance*), and gave him my snap assessment that *Platoon* would win Best Picture and a host of other Academy Awards. The film was already booked into my Canadian theatres, because Orion, its distributor, automatically placed its films with Cineplex Odeon in Canada. I offered Orion every one of our U.S. flagship theatres, our large single-screen houses like the North Point in San Francisco, the McClurg Court in Chicago, and the Century City in L.A.

But Orion was unsure of the film's potential, and so had set a limited-platform release, calling for the film to open in just a few select cinemas at Christmas, increasing the run in January if warranted. I knew this was a mistake even before the movie opened in December to virtually unanimous raves. Orion's folly was confirmed the day the movie opened at Cineplex Odeon Canada Square in Toronto, where the first day's gross was $11,000.

That night, while most exhibitors were on their way to Florida or Mexico or the Caribbean, I was on the phone to Oliver Stone and Arnold Kopelson, yelling at them, hectoring them, badgering them, demanding that they increase the runs over the Christmas season. The next morning I took part in a conference call with Orion.

Orion resisted. They couldn't place ads in time, they said.

"I'll open the film wherever and whenever you want, so long as it's now," I said. "Give me the prints! I'll open even without saturated advertising from you – the public wants this movie and you must give it to them!"

My persistence paid off. *Platoon* went wide over Christmas, was heralded on the cover of *Time*, and became the season's runaway hit.

In March came the Academy Awards.

Arnold asked me the day before the ceremony, "What can I do to say thank you?"

"You can say thank you," I said, "on national TV, when you pick up the Best Picture Award."

And that's what he did – in front of a billion or so TV viewers.

*I admit it. I was in the theatre that night with a gleeful smile on my face. I took some credit. Why not? I was due.*

I had taken New York, and it seemed that New York was taking to me. I was getting favourable press for Cineplex Odeon's clean floors and washrooms, refurbishment policies, and, of course, popcorn with real butter. The icing on the gingerbread was our renovation of the Carnegie Hall Cinema, which, as the name suggests, is tucked under the main stage of Carnegie Hall. Back in 1891 it had been a recital hall, and when we reopened it in June 1987, it had been restored to all its original glory. The plasterwork ceiling was rebuilt and regilded, and the three hundred seats were upholstered in rich burgundy. Naturally, we offered cappuccino and espresso in the theatre's intimate lounge. We arranged for a gala opening; Christopher Walken was there and so were Paul Newman and Joanne Woodward. Everyone bubbled over with congratulations, particularly Ed Koch, the outspoken mayor of New York, who declared, "Garth Drabinsky is wonderful!" That's a direct quote. Remember it when you read what happened only a few months later.

My next move brought New York's self-proclaimed intelligentsia down on my head. I needed a theatre on Manhattan's Upper West Side to challenge Loew's enormously successful sixplex at 84th Street and Broadway, so I leased the nearby Regency, a four-hundred-and-fifty-seat single-screen theatre. This was New York's last true repertory house, showing only film classics. Its audience had been declining steadily since the advent of the VCR, which had siphoned off the rep audience, and I reckoned it could be turned into a gold mine as a first-run house. What I didn't realize, however, was that the Regency was treasured by some of the most vocal, influential, single-minded, and unforgiving people in New York.

One morning the manager of the Regency called me in Toronto, sounding flustered. "Mr. Drabinsky, there's a mob scene going on outside the theatre."

"A mob scene?" I was puzzled.

"Yes, and a lot of people and a lot of TV cameras."

I snapped on CNN. According to a hyperventilating local newsman, there were two hundred people protesting the Regency's change of policy. They included Isaac Asimov, Arthur Penn, Celeste Holm, James Ivory, Tony Randall – and a name from the distant past, Lillian Gish!

In no time the news was flashed on network TV and national public radio. The *International Herald Tribune* carried the tale to 164 countries. *Garth Drabinsky was wrecking New York's most beloved theatre!* Community boards protested, and the city council tried to bring in a resolution saying that only film revivals could be shown at the Regency.

I couldn't believe it. I was being crucified for turning a rat-infested theatre into a comfortable, clean, marble-walled cinema with new sound and projection systems. It wasn't as though I were destroying a venerable tradition, either: the theatre had run revivals for only eleven years!

So I dug in and got stubborn. The next thing I knew, the *Village Voice* was challenging me.

"What will Darth Grabinsky, as West Side wags call him, do next? He has the opportunity to become a New York folk hero, he can follow the example of Coca-Cola, another large corporation that once decided to give the public what it didn't want – millions of dollars later Classic Coke was reborn. That lesson should apply to classic films."

That made me think. I didn't enjoy being the most colourful businessman to hit New York since Rupert Murdoch.

At this point I got help from an unexpected source: Woody Allen. He hadn't been out demonstrating, but he had, according to Orion Pictures, actually been fretting about the issue.

*God! Here I was, contributing to Woody's angst!*

Would I meet him? Orion asked.

Would I? I loved the guy and his movies! The meeting was to take place at his midtown-Manhattan office on fashionable Park Avenue.

When I arrived, I was shown into a dimly lit art-deco suite, which I gathered was his editing and production office. Woody sort of edged toward me and we nervously shook hands; then he cleared his throat. I felt like I was in the middle of *Annie Hall.* He eased into the discussion gently. He explained he had been elected as spokesman by those luminaries, the now-disenfranchised patrons of the Regency. Wouldn't I reverse my decision and restore the previous policy at the theatre?

I was flummoxed. I found myself on the one hand plunging into an account of the delicate economics of the exhibition industry and, on the other, reminding him how he insisted that his films play at Cineplex Odeon's beautifully refurbished Showcase Theatre in Hollywood. Woody was polite, but he wouldn't budge from his point.

After an hour I came up with a compromise. Cineplex Odeon also owned the 572-seat New Carnegie, beside the Hard Rock Cafe on West 57th Street between Seventh Avenue and Broadway, and I knew it wasn't competitive as a first-run theatre. I offered to turn it into a revival house. I would renovate it, rename it, and bring back revival enthusiast Frank Rowley to book and run it.

For the first time, Woody Allen smiled and offered me another handshake. Before I knew it, I was out the door.

I kept my word. Later that year the New Carnegie was renamed the Biograph after the Chicago movie-house where the FBI gunned down John Dillinger in 1934, just after he'd seen Clark Gable and Myrna Loy in *Manhattan Melodrama*. I was careful not to go to the opening. Instead, Frank Rowley, the manager, helped Myrna Loy hold the scissors and cut the ribbon. The glitterati nodded their approval.

But I wasn't a good guy in New York for long. I committed my second act of heresy at Christmas 1987. I raised the price of New York movie tickets from six dollars to seven dollars. The cost of doing business in New York was staggering. Security, utilities, maintenance, taxes, and labour were higher than anywhere else, and escalating all the time. And I had had to renovate some of the most dilapidated theatres on the continent. Not only that, movie tickets in New York were a steal. In the past ten years, tickets to a Broadway musical had gone up by 250 per cent, and so had tickets to a Yankee game. Off-Broadway show tickets had gone up by 300 per cent, and tickets to the New York Philharmonic went up by 350 per cent. In the same period, by comparison, movie tickets had risen only 100 per cent.

I was on holiday in Antigua when the row blew up that December; Pearl and the kids and I were enjoying the Caribbean sun at our villa on Mamora Bay. Then the first telex came in. It was Lynda. "This is a crisis. They're killing us in New York. The people are going crazy over the seven-dollar ticket."

Sigh. Back to CNN.

It was freezing in New York, and there was Mayor Koch standing in front of our Baronet Theatre, urging New Yorkers to boycott Cineplex Odeon.

"They're ripping us off!" he cried. "What you're hearing is a primordial scream of rage!"

This was followed by a lot of witty name-calling, like CineOdious and Cinebucks.

"Let him rant away," I thought, "but aren't his priorities a little out of whack? Surely New York had more important fiscal and social concerns than the seven-dollar movie ticket?" In any case, CNN informed me, the weather was due to sink to about 15°F in a few days, when the picketers would no doubt retreat to their warm Cadillacs.

In fact, Koch would eat his words soon after. One night the manager at our exquisitely refurbished National Twin Theatre on Broadway overheard Koch say, "This is a really beautiful theatre. I guess
this is why Drabinsky has to charge seven dollars. I didn't completely
understand the issue." *Why is there never a camera around when you
need one?*

That wasn't the end of my heretical notions. I was, after all, the guy
who introduced on-screen advertising into Canadian movie theatres,
for which I was excoriated all over again.

The reaction from some newspapers, especially the *Toronto Star*,
was so hysterical, so over the top, that at one point I successfully got
an injunction (only reversed on appeal at the eleventh hour) enjoin-
ing them from running yet another of their diatribes against me and
Cineplex Odeon – the court agreed with me that the commentary
went way beyond fair comment.

Now, of course, screen advertising is a routine part of exhibition
and is another significant revenue stream for exhibitors.

I was barely back from Cannes, in June 1987, when Lew Wasserman
almost died on the operating table, setting off a buzz of rumour and
speculation. Early stories said a surgeon had left a sponge in his
stomach cavity; it was later revealed that he had bitten down on a
glass thermometer after a routine operation and almost bled to
death. His illness sent ripples of apprehension through Hollywood
that reached Toronto. I think I realized for the first time how much
MCA *was* Wasserman. His departure would have a widespread
impact not just on the film business in general but on Cineplex
Odeon directly.

MCA stock went a little wild. The word went out that the company
was ripe for a takeover bid; the favoured candidate was Sony, which
was known to be shopping for a Hollywood property. (In fact, Sony
later bought Columbia, and Matsushita ended up with MCA.) It
made me nervous. MCA was a difficult partner, but at least I knew
who they were. What would I do with Sony?

At once Myron and I started trying to negotiate an amendment to our original agreement with MCA. In the event of a takeover, we wanted an option to obligate MCA to sell its Cineplex Odeon stock back to the corporation. Lew and Sid wouldn't go that far: they would only accept a sell position if the takeover was a hostile one. Even so, they later told us they had been reamed out by the MCA board for agreeing to this. (For my part, I think they should have been grateful to us for adding a dash of toxins to their poison pill.)

However, Lew recovered well enough to come to the opening of the Universal City Cineplex Odeon over the American Independence Day weekend.

It was the world's largest theatre complex, with eighteen screens and six thousand seats. The final cost was $18 million U.S. ($4 million U.S. over budget, in part to accommodate the rigid seismic building standards in L.A.).

Only ten months before, all of Hollywood had turned out at the groundbreaking. There I was, with Lew Wasserman, Sid Sheinberg, Steven Spielberg, and, once more, Mayor Tom Bradley. And we mustn't forget Frankenstein and Red Sonya and Conan the Barbarian and dozens of other Hollywood characters, real and imaginary, some of them with toy pneumatic drills in hand. It was quite an event.

I had chosen July 1 for the opening to ensure that the maximum number of peak summer releases would be available to us. The line-up would include *Innerspace, Spaceballs, Full Metal Jacket, Beverly Hills Cop II, Predator, Dragnet, Roxanne, Harry and the Hendersons*, and *The Secret of My Success*.

The opening required a graduate degree in logistics. I estimated as many as fifteen thousand people were going to arrive to buy tickets. Each film had to be scheduled so that in case of a sellout, the overflow crowd would be able to find at least one other suitable movie. Each washroom had to be cleaned every fifteen minutes; each concession stand had to have lines of pre-poured Coke and mountains of pre-bagged popcorn; and the Parisian-style cafés had to have staff trained to prepare and serve the yuppie treats, quiche Lorraine and pasta primavera.

We knew we had to open with a bang big enough to attract public attention in this movie-hyped town. Lynda got together with Lenny Gill, the ebullient South African whose Toronto company, Echo Advertising, had a reputation for innovation. Together they came up with a terrific idea, a contest called The Magnificent Movie Poll, sponsored by KPWR Radio and the Los Angeles *Times*. The contest invited Angelenos to send in nominations for their favourite movies of all time. More than twelve hundred films were nominated, and the eighteen most popular were selected for screening at the Universal Cineplex Odeon the night before the complex officially opened. Celebrities connected with many of the eighteen films were on hand. I felt I was in a time warp seeing Charlton Heston (*Ben-Hur*), James Stewart (*It's a Wonderful Life*), Robert Wise (director of *The Sound of Music*), and some of the munchkins from *The Wizard of Oz* walk into the exhilarating seventy-foot-wide skylit lobby.

The atmosphere was like a circus.

And the $250,000 U.S. radio and television advertising buy didn't hurt either.

The first week's gross was $350,000 U.S., and Universal City Cineplex Odeon instantly became the highest-grossing movie complex in the world. The first year's statistics were mind-boggling: box-office gross of $12 million U.S.; concession revenues in excess of $4 million U.S.; operating cash flow of $5 million U.S. In June 1989 the total complex broke all existing box-office records by grossing – in a single week – $450,000 U.S., almost $300,000 U.S. of it coming from a single movie, *Batman*. Distributors were clamouring for the theatre. It was in a class by itself.

There was one more stellar moment for me that year. In August I was honoured by the Montreal World Film Festival as its first Renaissance Man of Film.

*For once, they came to praise me, not to bury me.*

Christopher Plummer made the presentation speech, saying, "Garth Vader has elicited awe and buckets of slimy green admiration in the business."

That was good enough for me!

The turnout at lunch was evidence that I had reached a position of some influence in the international movie business. Columbia chairman David Puttnam was at the head table. So were Sid Sheinberg, Pierre Trudeau, Norman Jewison, Michael Caine, Allan Gottlieb (the Canadian ambassador to the U.S.), Leo Kolber, Jack Valenti (president of the Motion Picture Association of America), Jean Furstenberg of the American Film Institute, Royal Bank chairman Allan Taylor, and – at my personal invitation – Dr. Robert Salter of Sick Kids Hospital in Toronto.

By the end of 1987 it was clear that our aggressive expansion plan had paid off. Cineplex Odeon's net income had soared to $34.5 million U.S. on revenues of $520 million U.S. Total assets had reached $925 million U.S. from $632 million U.S. a year earlier. The trading record of Cineplex Odeon's shares was also stunning. From the first quarter of 1985 to the first quarter of 1987, the stock had climbed from $4 to $22.

Our debt, spurred by the rapid buildup of the circuit, had climbed to $470 million U.S., but 50 per cent of it was fixed for ten years and was thus insulated from any gyrations in the financial markets north or south of the border.

Cineplex Odeon now had nearly seventeen hundred screens. By the time our expansion and refurbishment program would be complete in 1990, we would dominate fourteen of the twenty key markets on the continent. No one, not even Adolph Zukor, had ever been so powerful an exhibitor. At that point our annual cash flow would be near $150 million U.S.

*And then? What would I do after that?*

In March 1987 Myron and I, in light of the future prospects we saw for the company, felt that we owed it to ourselves to increase our meagre 7-per-cent stake in Cineplex Odeon. We approached the board for additional options, or, alternatively, an interest-free loan to purchase a large block of shares in the corporation we were building. In both instances we were refused. Jimmy Raymond and Skip Paul, sitting on the compensation committee, were immovable. Finally, after several heated exchanges with Sid Sheinberg and Leo Kolber, Myron and I convinced the board to permit the sale to us of 1.5 million treasury shares at $19.00. We paid for the stock with a $26.25-million loan from First City Trust. This took our total combined holdings to about 3.5 million shares and represented our strong endorsement of the future prospects of the corporation, just as we were about to engage a new public offering to coincide with a listing on the New York Stock Exchange.

And then . . .

On October 18, 1987, Cineplex Odeon stock was trading around $19.00 a share.

The following day the stock market crashed.

*I was sitting in Myron's office, watching the Quotemaster, and when I saw Cineplex Odeon stock plummet $6.00 in a millisecond, I almost went into shock. We had each just lost $10 million apiece.*

But the crash had more serious implications for Cineplex Odeon than for us personally. The market subsequently rallied somewhat, but investor confidence had been fatally damaged. The market's perceived volatility drove out all the ordinary investors, leaving only the professional players – brokers, institutions like pension and mutual funds, and the arbitrageurs.

The sea had emptied of all the fish but the sharks.

And they were *hungry*.

The crash was a culmination of a change in the psychology of the market that had been evident for a number of years, and the change meant bad news for Cineplex Odeon. Historically, the major corporations had been built on the faith and financial support of a large number of diverse people and institutions, all of whom believed they were building something to last. In the get-rich-quick eighties, the typical investor strategy was in-out-thank-you-ma'am – get out fast, with as much money as you can, and to hell with the company, to hell with the other shareholders, to hell with the employees, to hell with the very idea of building something. I had incurred considerable corporate debt building Cineplex Odeon into arguably the most influential and powerful circuit in North America, and, in the new climate, too much debt made you vulnerable.

Myron and I both understood Cineplex Odeon stock might become prey for the shortsellers. In the postcrash market, the short-sellers would emerge as the arbiters of many a company's fate. A shortseller, remember, borrows stock, usually from his broker, and sells it, gambling on his judgement that the stock is shortly going to fall and that he'll then be able to buy the stock for less than he sold it. When shortsellers zero in on the stock, say, of a company with large debt or management problems, their activities start to influence the analysts and the business reporters, who then start predicting trouble. Unsurprisingly, predictions of trouble usually beget real trouble. The best, perhaps the only, response from a beleaguered company is to pare down debt as quickly as possible, or perhaps, if the value is evident, to enter the market to buy its own shares, thus keeping the price up.

With our stock at a postcrash low of $11.00, the board agreed to buy back two million shares.

After the market crashed, Myron and I began to kick around an idea. At these ridiculous prices, why not take Cineplex Odeon private? Our stock had crawled back from its lows to around $12.00. Why not raise the money to buy all the outstanding shares and take it off the market?

The only reason I could see for staying public was to raise more equity, but we were on the verge of completing our master plan for expansion anyway, and the cash flow would pare down or reduce the debt in proper time.

We took our privatization plan to Jimmy Raymond and Leo Kolber, and they were prepared to play along – Leo always preferred investing in private companies anyway, and so did the reclusive Charles Bronfman, who never wanted his investments to attract public attention.

We had been greeted with strong interest from the Bank of

Nova Scotia and Citibank, and we felt optimistic we could swing a $1.1-billion buyout at $14.00 a share.

*One billion dollars! In 1982 Cineplex Odeon had been down to its last $100,000. Now the company was worth a billion.*

Not unexpectedly, MCA was lukewarm.

"I don't think it works for us," Sid said. "And you'll never be able to finance it."

Forget it, in short.

We took it to one more stage, to a meeting over sushi at Sid's apartment in Manhattan's Trump Tower (co-tenant Steven Spielberg wasn't there). Lew showed up, and so did Skip Paul and Hal Haas.

What we proposed was that MCA would get back all the money it had invested – some $200 million – and retain a much smaller residual equity, a carried position, without any further investment or liability.

Lew didn't like it. He didn't want his $200 million back. He didn't want to be a minority shareholder.

"We bought into a public company," he said, "and we want it to remain a public company. You have a mandate to complete your three-year business plan to build the circuit, no matter how much you have to borrow. The bankers have plenty of money that they're dying to spend. Use leverage. Don't worry about equity."

He munched on his sushi and stared at me. I didn't say anything more.

Maybe I should have, but I didn't.

# CHAPTER

## EXPANDING HORIZONS

The logic of the business, the imperatives of the company I had built, and my own creative dilemma pushed me to expand our Canadian distribution business into the United States and, ultimately, throughout the world.

It's one thing, as I was discovering, to have hundreds of screens, it's another thing to keep them filled. A U.S. distribution arm would provide us the distinct advantage of having an inventory of several films readied for release and capable of filling two or three hundred of our screens if, for some reason, there was a lull in the majors' release schedules. We were always in need of that potential cushion.

To take us into distribution south of the border, I restructured our old distribution company, Pan-Canadian, renaming it Cineplex Odeon Films (COF). I appointed Joel Michaels, my former partner, who was based in Hollywood, president of the division. The idea was that COF would pick up not only North American but worldwide rights to independently produced films, often doing so by way of "negative pick-ups." That meant COF would set out the important criteria for a movie's production and obtain the right by contract to approve the screenplay, budget, principal cast, and director, without being exposed to any liability for budget overruns. We would pay the agreed amount only when the finished film was delivered. If we bought world rights, we would sell them off territory by territory even before we had to pay up, thus reducing our total commitment to the picture. Although our negative-pick-up guarantees ranged between $1 million U.S. and $5 million U.S., we, of course, still needed to be discerning. North American distribution costs, including prints and advertising, for even the smaller films were rising, sitting at anywhere from $2.5 million U.S. to $5 million U.S. a picture.

Sid Sheinberg raised no objection to COF's move into the United States; in fact, MCA backed the idea, mainly because of the home-video tie-up. We had folded the former Pan-Canadian's flourishing videocassette and pay-TV business into MCA's much-larger organization, and as a consequence, MCA agreed to advance COF 50 per cent of the costs of the negative pick-up of each COF release. It also agreed to provide up to a maximum of another $2.5 million U.S. a picture for release prints and advertising.

But the Bronfman contingent openly distrusted my intentions. Leo Kolber was the one who articulated the notion that I was just trying to become a movie producer again, using "his" money. Eventually Myron and I flew down to Claridge's offices in Montreal and confronted Leo and Jimmy Raymond on the issue. Jack Richer, the third Bronfman nominee on our board, was there too.

"Leo," I said, exasperated, "this is just a pragmatic business decision. I have no great desire to be in the trenches of film production again, fighting with IATSE and Teamster crews, psychoanalysing irrational actors and soothing a temperamental director. I haven't any time to handle the creative aspect of film production or to line-produce films – and I'm well aware of it."

In the end it was the incremental COF print business for Film House that finally won them over; they saw how that would minimize any exposure that distribution would bring in its train. That and my agreement to limit our capital contribution to the expanded division to $15 million.

Film House was part of the complex synergies of our company. It, too, had been acquired to diversify the company so as not to have to rely solely on exhibition for earnings. It worked this way: Say we acquired seven films a year, and let's assume those seven films needed three to four thousand release prints, a reasonable assumption. We would take those printing jobs to Film House; that would bring Film House an additional $8 million worth of business. At our margins, that would have meant something like $2.5 million of additional cash flow.

When we bought Film House for $15 million worth of Cineplex Odeon shares in July 1986, Doug MacDonald had already built it into Canada's largest motion-picture laboratory. In 1986 it grossed $15 million in annual revenues. The Canadian dollar was about 75 cents U.S., a clear incentive for the Hollywood majors to send their print business north of the border.

So I decided to spend $7 million more, broadening its earning capacity with the installation of one of the most advanced post-production sound facilities outside Hollywood and new and more efficient printing equipment.

But spending that kind of money would make even more sense if I got Sid Sheinberg's firm commitment that Film House would handle substantially all of MCA's North American release printing. This would mean twenty thousand prints a year and a boost to our annual cash flow of between $8 million U.S. and $10 million U.S.

After the customary internal political squabbles at MCA, Sid, with some degree of reticence, gave me the commitment.

Then, in my enthusiasm, I made a foolish mistake that dampened the otherwise overwhelming success of the Film House transaction. The producer, Jerry Weintraub, who had been head of MGM about twelve months earlier, had abruptly left to set up his own production entity and was being touted as a coming Hollywood power. I recommended to the board that Cineplex Odeon invest $7 million U.S., partly by way of a loan and partly by way of equity, in his newly financed, $230-million U.S. theatrical motion-picture business, in return for his agreeing to process his first forty releases at our lab. Alas, Jerry Weintraub went spectacularly bust after his first five pictures, and Cineplex Odeon had to write off most of the $7 million U.S.

Cineplex Odeon Films started off modestly. We bought the North American rights to Tony Bill's *Five Corners*, starring Jodie Foster (who went on to win Oscars for *The Accused* and *The Silence of the Lambs*), Tim Robbins (who became the hot young actor-director in 1992 for *The Player* and *Bob Roberts*), and John Turturro (the oddball star of *Barton Fink* and *Quiz Show*). Our second movie was Bruce Robinson's *Withnail and I.*

The first release, despite its superb cast, lost money, while the second was a marginal success. However, COF was now at least attracting a modicum of attention in Hollywood.

In April 1987 I got a call from Michael Ovitz, the president of Creative Artists Agency (CAA), the super-agent who was the Lew Wasserman of the eighties, a smooth-talking, button-down guy who had become the supreme dealmaker in Hollywood, with far and away the most prestigious list of clients. (Ironically, it would be Ovitz, the matchmaker of matchmakers, the dealmaker of deal-makers, who manipulated the sale of MCA to Matsushita for more than $6 billion U.S. in 1990, thereby ending Wasserman's long reign as Hollywood's uncrowned king.) Ovitz told me that one of his clients, Robert Redford, wanted to meet me. Redford had been impressed, Ovitz said, with my ideas about financing low-budget films, and he wanted to talk. "Can you call him?" Ovitz asked, "He's at his home in Sundance."

I called Redford that night, and he asked me to fly out and spend the day with him.

He had built his Sundance Institute to help train young filmmakers. It was located on a six-thousand-acre spread, six thousand feet above the North Fork of the Provo Canyon in Utah's Wasatch Mountains, a spectacular setting. He had fallen in love with the country when he was making *Jeremiah Johnson*, and he had acquired the property shortly afterward. I knew how overwhelming it was supposed to be, but I was still knocked out by the setting when I first saw it.

I arrived on a perfect spring morning and met him at the Tree-house Café, which was part of the Sundance Ski Resort.

"Hi, I'm Bob," said a familiar tousle-headed figure, taking off his sunglasses.

In his blue jeans and cowboy boots, Bob still looked boyish at fifty. He whirled me off in his Jeep on a tour of the property, talking all the while about movies, about what he wanted to accomplish, about people and politics and the environment – a non-stop stream of consciousness. I found myself in complete sympathy with his values. He insisted – and I believed him – that films over which he had some creative control had to in some way elevate the audience – they had to *mean* something.

*What a relief from Hollywood! What a relief from the body-obsessed airheads! What a relief from the cynical titans of Hollywood!*

Bob explained his reasons for bringing me to Sundance. "I want to refine the process of how smaller pictures get to the screen," he said, leaning forward earnestly. He meant simplify, rather than refine, it seemed – he wanted to get rid of the middlemen who cluttered up the process. With this in view, he was setting up his own independent production company, North Fork Productions, with the mandate to make quality, low-budget films. He had a certain contempt for the studios. He knew they would always finance a Robert Redford star vehicle, but they would show little interest in distributing low-profile films, made with care and integrity, that had something to say about the human condition. I knew from bitter experience how difficult it was to get an independent film enthusiastically distributed by one of the majors, to say nothing of trying to overcome their accounting practices.

We wound up the day at Bob's stunning French-style château, which he had built in the middle of a picturesque thousand-acre Utah field. As we drove up, the setting sun lit up the mountain tops, and I could see hundreds of deer gliding about in the dappled meadowland in front of the house. Pearl had spent the day horseback riding with Alicia.

*There were worse ways to live.*

Over a drink by the fireplace, Bob sold me a chalet – and I don't even ski! He also invited me to come on the board of the Sundance Institute, and, by the time I got back to Toronto, I thought of him as a friend. A few days later Michael Ovitz called back to confirm that Redford had felt pretty much the same. "He was impressed with you," he reported. "He liked your observations about the business. He wants to take this further."

As a result, in October 1987, Bob Redford and I announced a joint venture: North Fork would make a minimum of five movies over five years, all with budgets of less than $6 million U.S., and COF would distribute them worldwide. In direct contrast to the usual Hollywood fare, Redford was committed to making films about the cultures and minorities of North America. The first proposed film was *A River Runs Through It*, about a Scottish Presbyterian family that settled in Montana at the turn of the century, and Redford himself planned to direct it.

I was terrifically turned on by all this. Redford was exactly the kind of person I wanted to be associated with in the movie business, and in business terms, the agreement gave COF even greater credibility in the marketplace. But what I didn't appreciate at the time was that Bob moved at his own stately, deliberate rhythm. To my disappointment, he had yet to produce a single movie under our agreement by the time I left Cineplex Odeon more than two years later. For one thing, he became distracted by the problems of the $18 million U.S. *The Milagro Beanfield War*, which he was directing, and by the ongoing financial pressures and administrative hassles of Sundance. It wasn't until 1992 that *A River Runs Through It* was released, but then it lived up to all the expectations I had of our agreement, pleasing both the public and critics. Subsequently, Bob also directed *Quiz Show*, a movie that confirmed his growing directorial reputation as an artist who made thoughtful, intelligent, significant films.

The only other deal COF made that fall of 1987 was for *Madame Sousatzka*, John Schlesinger's $5.5-million U.S. film starring Shirley MacLaine. Shirley had literally begged for the role after Vanessa Redgrave had dropped out; she badgered and pestered Schlesinger, and unilaterally cut her usual fee to a negligible sum if only he would give her the role of the eccentric Russian piano teacher. I committed to cover the entire negative cost on the strength of a $3.5-million U.S. pre-sale of foreign rights and the MCA home-video advance of $2.5 million U.S. A no-brainer, I thought. But as it turned out, North American box office barely reached $5 million U.S., not nearly enough to cover our distribution costs. Bill Soady told me later that the movie flopped because nobody could pronounce its name.

Nevertheless, it was a winner for me in one respect, because I finally got to meet Shirley MacLaine. After falling in love with her all those years ago in *The Apartment*, I was thrilled to be seated beside her at the 1988 Venice Film Festival, where she won a Silver Bear for her performance. Later she also won a Golden Globe for best actress, and I believe if the movie had performed better, she would have won an Oscar.

*I left for Cannes the day after the wonderfully sentimental occasion of my daughter Alicia's bat mitzvah for what was to be one of the more magical moments of my tenure at Cineplex Odeon. When I had first gone to Cannes in 1973, I had been a law student moonlighting as a publisher; I was little more than a movie groupie, awestruck by the stars, seduced by the glamour, feeling like a hick in my Lou Myles tux. This time I was one of the honoured guests, strolling across the red carpet towards the steps of the Grand Palais. The paparazzi were out with their strobes, trumpets were blaring, the surging crowds pressed against the barricades and stretched out their hands.*

Okay, so it wasn't for me, exactly, that they were stretching out their hands. It was for Paul Newman and Joanne Woodward, who were in the back seat of a Mercedes limo. I was fascinated, and a little unnerved, at the intensity of emotion that the stars drew. I was there because Cineplex Odeon Films had underwritten $3.1 million U.S. for the worldwide distribution rights to Newman's provocative film adaptation of Tennessee Williams' *The Glass Menagerie*, which was in the main competition.

Still, I confess my cool somewhat deserted me as, flushed with pride, I entered the Grand Palais with Newman and co-stars

Woodward, John Malkovich, and Karen Allen. After the screening, the magic continued for me at a dinner at the Moulin des Mougins. I forget what I ate, but I remember the guests: Gore Vidal, Mel Gibson, Marthe Keller, Roger Moore, Christopher Walken, and film producer Jerry Weintraub. Still, the high point for me was when Yves Montand joined Norman Mailer and the Newmans at my table.

That same year I persuaded our board to help out Robert Lantos's film company, Alliance, which was in rocky shape financially and riven with internal dissent. I remember Robert calling me for advice and, ultimately, help. The advice was easy – because I had confidence in his judgement, I told him to buy out his partners and run the company himself, which he later did, with spectacular success. The help amounted to Cineplex taking an equity position for $1 million, with a further $2 million in loans.

Robert told me later that he thought it a courageous decision on my part, since Alliance's balance sheet hardly justified the investment commitment.

I remember phoning Robert only a few weeks later, after the stock market had plummeted.

"I just want you to know," I said, "that we won't try to renegotiate the terms of our agreement. I'll stick with my decision."

Years later Robert told me he knew the pressure I had been under and greatly appreciated my steadfastness.

In retrospect, this was a superb investment. The loans were retired within the first two years, and Cineplex Odeon has made well over $20 million since then.

COF was, I thought, making respectable progress up to this point. It hadn't yet achieved a major success, but I was optimistic.

*For once, my optimism was unjustified. COF would continue to be a relative bust, at least while I was still chairman of Cineplex Odeon.*

*On the other hand, our disappointments caused only a minor tick on the earnings and on our balance sheet – a far smaller effect than one would think from the angry attention the board paid to it.*

One of these busts was with Taylor Hackford, who had made his name as director of *An Officer and a Gentleman*; I had met him while working with Columbia Pictures on the marketing of another of his movies, *White Nights*. He was quite a character, tall and angular with chiselled looks and a bobbing ponytail. He looked like a hippie and talked as if he came from Harvard; he was widely touted as the "new" Hollywood. He caught my attention because he had always demonstrated real flair in his choice of music for his films. He had picked Phil Collins to write the songs for *Against All Odds* and *White Nights*, and when he screened *La Bamba* for me a few months before its summer release in 1987, I took notice. The soundtrack of late-fifties rock 'n' roll (*Aah! My music!*) was superb, and in anticipation of a potential breakthrough film, I immediately issued a directive to smother our screens with *La Bamba* trailers. The movie in fact did very solid business.

So when Taylor approached me about a joint venture, I was glad to listen. It involved his production company, New Visions, and his distribution company, New Century, where Norman Levy was ensconced as president and CEO, having left Fox after the arrival of Barry Diller. Taylor proposed to produce, and in certain circumstances direct, up to twenty-five films in five years, all with budgets under $8 million U.S. COF and New Century would divide the distribution rights. The joint venture was to be financed by a $50-million U.S. line of credit.

The investment seemed to me well justified. It would beef up our overseas distribution profile, and it would mean a further steady stream of films for our North American theatres. It would also give Film House an estimated $7 million U.S. a year in printing and post-production revenues.

Well, you can never tell when it comes to the movie business. Within weeks of signing the agreement, Taylor went right off the deep end. He rushed five films into production, the first three of which proved to be box-office poison. Then, within a year, the venture lost Norman Levy's involvement, because Taylor insisted on meddling with Levy's expertise and marketing approach to the first picture, with disastrous results. Norman abruptly bailed out.

Talk Radio, our next catastrophe, started as a great script. I hadn't seen Eric Bogosian's play at New York's Public Theatre in the spring of 1987, but I was both fascinated and appalled by the subject: the murder of Alan Berg, an outspoken Denver talk-show host, who was killed by anti-Jewish thugs. Obviously, it wasn't the kind of movie that studios run after, even though Oliver Stone was the director, so we were able to buy the worldwide rights for $10 million U.S. We immediately sold the foreign rights for $6.5 million U.S. That was a good start.

But then I ran into board politics. Our initial U.S. pay-TV and video agreement with MCA had expired. Fox then came to the table and offered us $8 million U.S. for the rights. And MCA? Although Sid Sheinberg had told the Cineplex Odeon board that Talk Radio was the best movie he had seen in the past ten years, MCA – my partners and shareholder! – offered us a paltry $4.5 million U.S.

If I acceded to the deal, I would be in trouble, so I called Sid.

His tone was far from friendly. In fact, it was downright menacing. "In light of our ongoing support of Film House and the losses MCA has suffered to date in its video deal with COF, I don't think it's advisable to accept the Fox offer," he said. Menace – and threat. He went on to suggest, in his Texas drawl, that Universal "might have trouble" continuing to send its film processing to Film House if I signed elsewhere. Here was my 50-per-cent partner playing the heavy with me! Cineplex Odeon would have to suffer a $3.5-million U.S. shortfall! Such was the price of keeping the relationship stable.

Lamentably, Talk Radio died at the box office, and after that the Bronfman and MCA contingents on the board turned against me on the issue of distribution. I felt obliged to remind them how Sid Sheinberg had waved his index finger at me while he was busy praising Talk Radio and costing Cineplex Odeon $3.5 million U.S.

But it didn't matter. Nobody listened. Board allegiances were already noticeably crumbling.

Around this time Norman Jewison and I had become close. Among other things, I was co-chairman of the Canadian Centre for Advanced Film Studies, which he founded. In his office one day, he had told me he was having trouble convincing Columbia and its chairman, my good friend David Puttnam, to greenlight his next project.

"I want to make *Moonstruck*," he said. "It'll only cost $10 million U.S., it has Cher, and a screenplay by John Patrick Shanley, but I can't seem to get a decision."

*I was taken aback. Only $10 million U.S., with a star like Cher and a screenplay by one of Hollywood's comers? I knew the writer's merit because* COF *had financed his* Five Corners. *It was hard to believe.*

At around that time Sid Sheinberg had fired Frank Price as head of Paramount and had installed Tom Pollock in his stead. I saw an opening.

"Hold on Norman," I said, "let me read the script and I'll get it to Sheinberg and Pollock. I'm sure they'll make your movie."

"You've got a week," Norman said.

I read the script overnight and then called Sid.

"I can't make a deal now," he said. "My son's getting married, I've got too much on, I can't do it right now."

"Sid," I said, "just say yes. Don't think, just do it. You can't lose."

But he wouldn't budge.

I called Pollock.

"I can't deal with it now," Pollock said. "I'll be on vacation in Hawaii. No, I can't do it."

In the end, *Moonstruck* cost $11 million U.S. for UA/MGM to make – and grossed $200 million U.S. worldwide!

A little later Richard and Lili Zanuck came to me with the script of *Driving Miss Daisy*, starring the late, great, gracious wonder, Jessica Tandy. Joel and I read the screenplay and just flipped; we were absolutely knocked out. I knew it would be a major artistic success. And it would only cost $8 million U.S. to make!

But I was still reeling from the trouble over *Talk Radio*, and constrained by the budgetary limits for our distribution company, so

I knew I would have no support at the board. Joel implored me to do it, but I had to say no.

Of course, the film grossed $125 million U.S. domestically; that film alone would have made our distribution company a gigantic success.

Board relations deteriorated even further in the contretemps over Martin Scorsese's *The Last Temptation of Christ.*

It started off blandly enough. In the spring of 1987 Tom Pollock had approached me about sharing the cost of the movie. I read the script with fascination over a much-needed weekend retreat at Los Brisas in Acapulco, and I agreed to put up half the $8-million U.S. budget for the film. Again, it seemed a no-brainer. Pollock's analysis showed little exposure for either party, because of MCA's lucrative network-TV deal, projected home-video revenues, and a substantial pay-TV deal that could be struck as part of the MCA package to HBO or Showtime.

Before I knew it, I was once again in the thick of controversy. The politics of the movie were positively Byzantine. Nikos Kazantzakis's novel, which had demystified Christ by portraying him as a human and sometimes sexual being, had evoked an hysterical reaction from Catholics and evangelicals alike. Scorsese, who had once studied to be a priest, had been longing to make a film from the book for years, but nobody would back him. A previous agreement with Paramount was abandoned when fundamentalists inundated the studio and its parent company, Gulf + Western, with protests. So why had Pollock picked up the idea? I later discovered he had agreed to take it on only to help lure Scorsese into the Universal stable. (*Cape Fear,* starring Robert De Niro and Nick Nolte, was the first spectacular success that came to MCA from this relationship.) Pollock needed my theatres. He feared, rightly, that the film might otherwise never see the light of day.

I had no idea what I was getting into. I didn't believe that religious bigotry could possibly be such a flaming issue in 1988. How wrong I was!

Protests began even before the film was finished. They were followed by death threats. Sally Van Slyke, the vice-president of

Universal's field operations, had to have security guards watching over her full-time for three months. Pollock and I were stunned by the intensity of the opposition and the enormous amount of publicity given the film, including a cover story in *Time*. It made me realize how thin is the veneer that masks the bigotry and the prejudice constantly smouldering beneath the surface of our society – and how little it takes for these hateful passions to pierce through and burst into public view. As predicted, every other exhibitor in America sent out signals that they would refuse to play the film.

Pollock decided to open the film a month early, in August 1988, to try to stem the pressure from the mounting protests. Cineplex Odeon was the only circuit to play the film; we opened in eight theatres and did record business, notably at New York's Ziegfeld Theatre, which grossed $200,000 U.S. the opening week.

But it's expensive being controversial. We had to keep extra prints on hand at each theatre where the movie played as insurance against vandalism; we hired bomb squads with sniffer dogs and security guards. I received mountains of hate mail, all anonymous. One envelope enclosed nails, with a note that said, "These are for your coffin." I was forced to hire twenty-four-hour security guards at my Toronto home for three weeks.

In the end there was only one truly effective protester: he found his way into the projection room at our Center Theatre in Salt Lake City, unspooled the film, and shoved it into the air-conditioning ducts.

But there was other damage. Lew Wasserman was outraged by the entire situation. There were vile anti-Semitic demonstrations outside the Black Tower and his home in Beverly Hills, where a group of fundamentalist Baptists staged an anti-Semitic tableau: a man dressed as Jesus was carrying a large cross and another man, supposedly a film producer, was stepping on his back. A plane flew overhead with a streamer saying, "Wasserman fans Jew hatred with Temptation." I never talked to Lew directly about it, but Sid acted as though it had been my idea to make the film – that *I'd* gone to Universal and asked them to participate, instead of the other way around. Wasserman couldn't wait for the movie to come off the screen, which it did pretty quickly.

Much later I learned indirectly just how sick Lew had been of the film. In December 1988, at the opening of the new Cineplex Odeon sixplex in Marina del Rey, Will Tusher of *Daily Variety* asked me whether *Temptation* would be released again.

"It's strictly up to Universal," I said. "I suppose the decision will be based partly on the attention it gets at the time of the Academy Award nominations. I believe the industry won't let it go unnoticed." (In fact, it received only a couple of nominations in minor categories, Hollywood once again showing its cravenness and unwillingness to recognize hotly contested material.)

The next day's *Variety* reversed my quote and had me saying that if the movie garnered significant Oscar nominations, I expected Universal to re-release the movie.

Wasserman became irrational. I didn't see it, but I could imagine it. There were always three stages to his tantrums. First he took off his big black-rimmed glasses. Then he banged a book on the table. Finally he took off the $30,000 Rolex. My misinterpreted remark about *Temptation* was definitely a Rolex blow-up.

He ranted, first at Tom Pollock, then at Sid Sheinberg and Skip Paul. "Who's in control of Cineplex Odeon? Don't we have any control over Drabinsky? Don't we own half the company?"

From all accounts, the subtext was pretty unsubtle. *"Who will rid me of this meddlesome priest?"* And I was cast as the archbishop – Garth Beckett Drabinsky.

The final irony about Cineplex Odeon's short but lively history as a distributor was that the last film commitments I made were the Martin Scorsese production of *The Grifters*, starring Annette Bening and Anjelica Huston, which was nominated for four Academy Awards, and the Merchant–Ivory production of *Mr. and Mrs. Bridge*, starring Paul Newman and Joanne Woodward, which also garnered an Oscar nomination. Both films made money.

We had become a magnet for great material, partly because the creative minds in Hollywood could see that Joel and I cared, that we weren't a threat to them but rather a supportive haven for projects they cared deeply about.

But Leo Kolber and Jimmy Raymond never stopped fussing on the subject of distribution; they couldn't see past the fact that we'd gone $15 million U.S. over our original estimate for the start-up costs of COF; they just refused to see that, after a mere thirty months, we had become seasoned players in U.S. distribution.

It was so frustrating! I had made mistakes, sure, but one *Moonstruck* or one *Driving Miss Daisy* would have wiped out the costs of all the mistakes put together. It showed, I believe, how naïve the non-MCA segment of the board really was. They just couldn't see that, in just a few short years, with a little more support and encouragement, we would have done magnificently well. Perhaps we had too much profile too soon, but it was still a bitter disappointment when I had to shut the division down in 1989, just as COF's momentum and profitability were finally going in the right direction.

Late in 1987 another incident brought further discontent from MCA and the Bronfmans. I abruptly stopped playing Columbia films over what I thought was its improper handling of Bernardo Bertolucci's *The Last Emperor.*

This classic film had been produced by Jeremy Thomas and picked up for distribution by David Puttnam during his short-lived tenure as Columbia's boss. I loved the movie and opened it solo in November at our Century City Theatre in L.A. to outstanding reviews (and, not surprisingly, to a first-week's gross of $100,000-plus U.S.). I convinced Columbia to add another run at Universal City for the always-lucrative Thanksgiving weekend. But a few weeks later I learned that Columbia's new boss, TriStar chairman and CEO Victor Kaufman, had illogically ordered Dawn Steele, then the head of Columbia's film division, to reduce the number of runs of *The Last Emperor* by two-thirds over the Christmas season. The order came down in the first week of December, when there was no longer any time to replace these bookings with other first-run Christmas product. Most of the runs had been booked into our finest screens all over the continent. What irked me even more was that this was the first potential breakthrough picture in more than two years from Columbia; I had loyally stood by during their successive management upheavals and had been rewarded with turkeys like *Ishtar*, the Elaine May comedy starring Dustin Hoffman and Warren Beatty, and *Punchline*, starring Tom Hanks and Sally Field. (I was involved only in a peripheral way in the *Ishtar* débâcle. I had hated the advertising material the studio had churned out for the film – camel dung would have been a polite term for it – and my view had become pretty well known. At the prodding of Mike Ovitz, Warren Beatty called to discuss the public response to the screenings; he already knew of my marketing orientation, and he knew the clout I wielded with the number of screens we owned. I spent something of a wild weekend with Elaine May, Dustin Hoffman, and Warren, partly in New Haven, Connecticut, partly in Toronto, and partly in the editing suite in New York. I haven't seen much of Warren lately – he's been too busy learning to be a father, I guess – but I've maintained a cordial relationship with Dustin.) Pulling *The Last Emperor* would make a big dent in our box office. The only picture in sight was from Columbia's sister company, TriStar's *Leonard Part VI*, starring Bill Cosby, and the word was that it was a turkey of pterodactylian proportions.

I smelled the stench of studio politics. *The Last Emperor* had been Puttnam's choice, and Puttnam had been forced out by Victor Kaufman; clearly, Kaufman didn't want to add to the profile of anything Puttnam had done. To hell with that. Why should I get hurt in their petty and spiteful quarrels? I got Kaufman on the phone and – let's be straight here – went a little crazy.

"I've waited patiently for a decent picture from Columbia," I yelled into the mouthpiece. "This is going to hurt me enormously. It's too late in the day for me to mitigate my losses."

There was silence.

I took a deep breath. "Either you reinstate all runs for *The Last Emperor* or I'll pull every date of the Cosby film."

He didn't blink. "Okay, we're out of business. Pull the dates."

I didn't blink either. I pulled all 153 *Leonard* dates that afternoon, including every date in Manhattan. I relished the thought of what Cosby (whose television show was also produced by Columbia) must be saying to Kaufman. Served the bastard right.

Kaufman retaliated by moving Columbia and TriStar in Canada to Famous Players. Sid was on my case at once.

But I stood my ground. "You would have done the same thing," I said, and he didn't deny it. But he made it clear he didn't much like it.

# CHAPTER

## THE DÉBÂCLE

I had welcomed MCA's equity interest in Cineplex Odeon in large measure because of the possibilities of mutual reinforcement that our partnership presented. The whole point of having an investor of MCA's wealth and stature was that it would be there to help Cineplex Odeon move in other fruitful directions.

One of those "fruitful directions" was Orlando.

It was Sid Sheinberg who suggested, soon after the MCA deal was completed in 1986, that I explore possible areas of co-operation with Jay Stein, the president of MCA Recreation Services. Stein had been recruited by Lew Wasserman some twenty-five years earlier to put together Universal Studios' Hollywood Tour at MCA's headquarters, on the 428-acre parcel of land known as Universal City.

The Universal Tour was a huge hit and rapidly became the fourth-most-popular theme park in the United States; by 1987 it would be drawing almost five million visitors a year.

The idea was to take tourists behind the scenes of the movie and TV business. In the early eighties, flashy additions kept the L.A. attraction competitive; one of these was the debut of a howling, growling, thirty-foot-high, thirteen-thousand-pound mechanical King Kong. (*And no, he said hastily, I will resist the temptation to use it as a metaphor for MCA.*) Then, in 1986, MCA announced a $142-million U.S. expansion featuring, among other attractions, the "Starship Enterprise," to which visitors were, of course, "beamed"; "Earthquake, the Big One," designed to offer a closer look at movie-making mechanical effects when visitors in a mock San Francisco tram get caught in an 8.8 tremor; and a *Back to the Future* attraction that would take tourists time-travelling.

I met Jay in the sixteenth-floor boardroom on top of the Black Tower. As we chatted, he mentioned his frustration over MCA's stalled plans to open a similar studio tour in Orlando. I sat up and started really listening. I knew theme parks, with their wholesome fantasy environments, represented one of the major entertainment trends of the eighties, tapping into as they did the seemingly insatiable family market – the largest and broadest of all markets. Orlando, moreover, was the capital of theme parks. Disney World, Epcot Center, Sea World, Busch Gardens, and Cypress Gardens were all easily accessible from Orlando's super-modern airport. These attractions were served by some seventy thousand hotel rooms, second in the United States only to New York City.

Jay showed me the numbers, and my enthusiasm mounted even further. A quarter of the thirty million visitors to Florida named Orlando as their primary destination, and Orlando tourism was growing by 15 per cent annually.

So what was holding Lew Wasserman back? The new tour had been announced as long ago as 1981, but Lew had been dragging his heels ever since, because, as he told Stein, he didn't want to proceed unless he had a partner to share the risk and keep the debt off MCA's balance sheet.

The reason for his caution was obvious: Disney. Just a few miles from MCA's Orlando spread, Disney was opening its own studio tour at Disney World, which itself drew twenty-one million visitors a year. Never before had a competitor opened an attraction of the same genre in Disney's backyard. It would be a ferocious competition – the ultimate battle between two revved-up marketing machines. I guessed that Wasserman had reservations about going head to head with Disney because he lacked the confidence that his own management could pull it off.

The situation was further complicated by Sid Sheinberg's ongoing feud with Michael Eisner, chairman of Disney, which I learned about from Jay. Originally the Orlando tour was to have been built jointly by Universal and Paramount, in the days when Eisner was president of Paramount. No sooner did he move to Disney, however, than he announced the Disney/MGM tour and all hell broke loose. Sid accused Eisner of stealing his idea. He called him an immoral man with a sense of failure in character. He even told a Florida newspaper that Disney's role in Florida was more reminiscent of a "ravenous rat" than Mickey Mouse.

Eisner, for his part, contemptuously dismissed the theft charge. He asserted that Disney had planned to add a studio and tour ever since the opening of the Magic Kingdom in 1971. In a return salvo, he accused MCA of trying to cream off the millions of tourists Disney World attracted to Orlando because of its international goodwill and inspired marketing efforts.

Later I would get a personal taste of the dislike the two men had for each other. I was visiting Sid at his Malibu beach house over the July 4 weekend in 1987, and as we strolled along the beach, our path crossed that of Eisner, who was a near neighbour. Neither man even nodded in recognition.

Still, the feud didn't dampen my enthusiasm for the studio tour. After carefully analysing the projections with Jay Stein, I felt confident about bringing a joint-venture proposal to the Cineplex Odeon board. Once again my imagination, sometimes more of a curse than a blessing, was fired up. I loved the idea. I saw the value of pooling the entertainment and exhibition skills of the two companies. Cineplex Odeon wasn't going to be the hind legs on this donkey. Our large architectural and engineering department could make a real contribution, and our theatres all over North America would be a terrific tool for promoting the tour. Each year I had a captive market of 125 million in my theatres. In addition, as a powerful exhibitor

I had some leverage with the film companies other than Universal, companies that wouldn't necessarily bend over backwards to advance the interests of Wasserman and Sheinberg. I was sure, for instance, that I could get the rights for attractions modelled on films like *Ghostbusters*, which were controlled by Columbia – *and I did.*

The opening was planned for June 1989. This gave us about three years to complete construction, on 130 acres, of a state-of-the-art film and TV studio, including two filming stages and one videotape stage, an office complex for entertainment companies, as well as fifty-one backlot locations, from Beverly Hills' glamorous Rodeo Drive to San Francisco's picturesque Fisherman's Wharf. Live shows, exhibits, and film demonstrations featuring a selection of filmdom's most celebrated movie sets and special effects would make the visitors actual participants in the movie experiences. Of course, all the mainstays of the Universal City Tour in L.A. were included too. Sheinberg had convinced his friend of twenty years, the exceptionally gifted Steven Spielberg, to serve as our exclusive creative consultant, and he had come up with a raft of attractions which he described as "fun-scary." A bike ride taking E. T. home was planned. So was a re-enactment of the *Psycho* shower scene in the Alfred Hitchcock Pavilion. Other features included a Hanna Barbera animation adventure; "Kongfrontation," which had an ominous King Kong manhandling a tourist tram from Roosevelt Island; and a *Jaws* adventure, with a twenty-four-foot great white shark menacing a pleasure cruise boat. (Even here, MCA couldn't get Eisner and Disney off its mind – the shark was designed to crunch up the boat, and among the debris that was supposed to float to the surface was a pair of Mickey Mouse ears.)

MCA's estimated total cost was $220 million U.S. Cineplex Odeon and MCA would each put up $65 million U.S., and together would take out a $90-million U.S. bank loan. Initial attendance was projected at between 4 million and 5 million visitors a year, with 5-percent annual growth. Revenue from tickets, parking, and concessions was estimated at $24 U.S. per visitor. Based on these projections, the bank debt would be retired within nine years.

The negotiations with MCA went on through the fall of 1986. All through our discussions, Lew Wasserman kept asking me, "Are you sure you want to proceed with this?" At the time I took it for a reflection of his natural caution about, and aversion to, Disney.

After the customary haggling over approval rights, management fees, the payment of dividends, and buy/sell provisions, we concluded our deal. MCA was going to be both operator and developer.

Sure, I had some nervousness. Our commitment of $65 million U.S. represented almost 40 per cent of Cineplex Odeon's total equity, which meant that a huge slug of capital would not be contributing to our earnings for two and a half years. It wasn't as onerous an investment for MCA, because it put up its share only partly in cash, the balance coming from the transfer of the Orlando site to the joint venture at fair-market value.

We were fifty-fifty partners, which meant that, should there be cost overruns, we would both have to come up with the additional funds required in equal shares.

Again, that meant little to MCA, which could handle any budget overage from its substantial cash flow and its limitless lines of credit. In our case any major deviation from the anticipated funding schedule would put pressure on our lines of credit. We were operating safely, but we couldn't afford any calamitous slip-ups by our partner, the project manager.

That's how I came to hire Jeff McNair as Cineplex Odeon's watchdog in Orlando. Jeff had been vice-president of operations for Expo 86 in Vancouver and, before that, the director of marketing for Canada's Wonderland, the entertainment park just north of Toronto. I met him just after he had turned down MCA's offer of the top marketing job at Orlando. He didn't want to be part of the MCA culture. Instead, he joined Cineplex Odeon as a senior vice-president for special projects, and he, Myron Gottlieb, and I, along with Wasserman, Sheinberg, and Stein, comprised the joint-venture's executive committee of six.

Jeff is a tall, laconic Ontarian, as phlegmatic as I am effusive, and he proved his worth almost immediately. At the very first meeting of the six, it was obvious that MCA's team were badly divided. Sid

Sheinberg couldn't stand Jay Stein and regularly tore strips out of him. Stein, whom I had liked at first, was by now revealed as a classic neurotic. He used to sit at the table and squeeze a ball in the palm of his hand in order to release his tension and frustration. Later I learned that Stein was completely frustrated by his life at MCA and couldn't stand the bureaucracy. He expressed his frustration in a purely Hollywood way, by driving around in a red Mercedes 450SL with his wife's name on the back licence plate, the kind of whimsy abhorred by button-down MCA.

We soon discovered that Stein's recreation services' staff was a collection of talented but unrealistic people. While its members came up with some exceptional ideas, they were entirely incapable of achieving complete design integrity without substantially upping the original budget estimates. The building-project managers were worse: they couldn't meet deadlines. As for the financial controls, the estimating, budgeting, and cost-tracking were a joke.

Lew Wasserman's legendary golden touch also took on a tarnish. To drum up commercial sponsorships, he recruited a company called IMG, run by Mark McCormack, the marketing-genius-turned-super-sports-agent for such luminaries as Arnold Palmer, Jack Nicklaus, and Björn Borg. McCormack had written a book called *What They Don't Teach You at Harvard Business School*, in which he saluted Wasserman as the most influential person in his life. McCormack projected tens of millions of sponsorship dollars for our theme park, but month after month would go by without achieving any targets.

And then there was Disney, the spoiler. During the summer of 1987 Disney launched a major offensive in MCA's own backyard in Burbank. It bought a forty-acre parcel of land from the City of Burbank, a mere five minutes away from Universal City, and announced it was going to use the site to build a themed environment to compete with Universal. MCA bounced into court, contending futilely that the City of Burbank had never invited MCA to bid on the land.

Before it had got to that point, Jay Stein had told me that a Disney executive had called him and suggested a deal: Disney would back off Burbank if MCA bowed out of Orlando. Since I didn't have the emotional antipathy to Disney, I saw a possible solution to our growing problems. Why couldn't MCA and Disney merge both projects and put to an end to what was turning into a potentially explosive battle?

Reluctantly, Sheinberg agreed to my suggestion that we meet Eisner and Frank Wells, Disney's president.

Sheinberg was on his best behaviour and didn't make a single mouse joke, but it was soon apparent that the companies were so set in their ways, their philosophy and approach so different, that nothing could persuade them to find any common ground. The meeting went nowhere.

Back at Orlando, costs continued to soar. By September 1987 Jeff was bringing me figures that showed that construction costs (attractions, street sites, and landscaping, in particular) were escalating by millions of dollars. Jeff kept showing us how inexperienced management was killing us. He warned of insufficient product and inadequate pre-opening marketing budgets. The more he screamed at me, the more I pummelled Sheinberg with questions and pressed him to replace Jay Stein. The fabric of our relationship was being shredded.

Then, in October, MCA officially revised its projections. Now the tour was going to cost $388 million U.S.

But Jeff, who had never believed any of MCA's figures, was projecting $468 million U.S., more than twice MCA's original budget. At this rate, even with a revised banking arrangement, Cineplex Odeon was going to have to advance at least $120 million U.S. of equity to the venture, rather than the original $65 million U.S. Disaster was imminent.

The next joint-venture committee meeting, in the executive dining room on the Universal lot, was the capper. I asked Sheinberg and Wasserman straight out whether they thought we were even now getting a full and true disclosure of the project's real costs. I believe to this day that they themselves were being kept in the dark by Stein, to whom they swiftly referred my question.

Stein was unequivocal in his reply. "There's no way this project is going to go over $400 million," he said. "It's going to be capped at $390 million."

This was too much for Jeff. He glared at Stein and said, "You're lying, Stein. You're lying. There's no way the total cost won't reach $450 million and more – probably $500 million. And that doesn't take into consideration capitalized interest – only the actual money going into the project."

Sid Sheinberg's face turned beet red and he lost all control. He turned to me and said, pointing at Jeff, "I want you to fire this man. He's incompetent. He does not belong on this team. He does not have any regard for what it takes to build one of these projects. I have no use for him. As far as I'm concerned, he's dead."

I kept my cool, but my mind was racing. What was going on? Up to now, Sheinberg had had no time for Stein. Now he was defending him. Why?

I was uncharacteristically soothing. I didn't appreciate, I said, either the lecture or the attack on Jeff.

I left the meeting deeply frustrated. Sheinberg either didn't understand or didn't care that, even if Stein's figures were correct, the costly miscalculations were already placing great financial pressure on Cineplex Odeon. The bank financing that Myron had so skilfully assembled without the assistance of costly investment bankers couldn't be raised beyond $275 million U.S. until the tour was up and running and the cash-flow projections were being met. And that seemed further away than ever.

This miserable situation dragged on into 1988, with Jeff reporting cost overruns to me daily. One day he just laid it on the line. "Garth, the whole thing is out of hand. Not only am I projecting costs of more than $500 million, but to compensate, Stein has slashed the marketing budget to a meager $30 million."

According to Stein, we didn't need a North American advertising campaign. "We'll just wait until they all come to Florida!" he said blandly.

I was aghast. Was the man mad? We were head to head with Disney, which now had its studio tour well under construction. Every day both MCA and Disney carried out helicopter surveillance of the other's project, and it was obvious that the well-schooled Disney management would open on schedule in June 1989, while the woefully inadequate MCA team would be at least a year late. When I raised this with Sheinberg, he just shrugged his shoulders and said, "What can I do?" I was desperate. I knew we had to get out, fast.

By the time I flew to L.A. for a Cineplex Odeon board meeting in the fall of 1988, I had already made my frustration and anxiety about Orlando's out-of-control costs clear to the non-MCA members of Cineplex Odeon's board. Our credit lines were in jeopardy, and soon the public would become aware of our constantly growing Orlando-related obligations. I found, to my astonishment and disappointment, that the Bronfman segment of the board was unwilling to assert itself against MCA. Kolber and Raymond, once my staunch supporters, were now cozying up to the other side.

The other shoe had really dropped just before our annual general meeting in June. The L.A. *Times'* Kathryn Harris did a hatchet job on us under the heading, "PUSHING IT TO THE LIMIT." Harris pointed out that, as of March 1988, our long-term debt was $537,411,000 U.S., which exceeded the debt-equity ratio allowed by one of our largest lenders. Harris had interviewed Myron, who acknowledged the violation, but made it clear that we had the lender's agreement to do so, pending a renegotiation of our loan agreement.

Harris didn't mention this. Nor did she mention that our debt problem was due to the pressure being placed on Cineplex Odeon by the cost overruns in Orlando. Instead, she wrote, "A perception persists in Hollywood that Drabinsky is flirting with disaster because he has predicated Cineplex Odeon's growth on the most optimistic view of exhibition."

I had a well-founded suspicion that this "perception" had been shaped by someone in MCA's Black Tower. Soon afterwards, financial analysts began to criticize the "liberal" depreciation policies of Cineplex Odeon, which set us up for a siege by the shortsellers, the hyenas of the stock market.

The *Toronto Star* would later compare my performance at the subsequent annual general meeting with the movie *Raging Bull.* I certainly put my reputation on the line. I pledged that our debt-equity ratio, then at about 1.7 to 1, would never exceed 2 to 1.

I survived the meeting, but the aftermath was dire. I had to make that pledge good by selling assets, and I had to prove to a now-sceptical investment community that those assets were valuable.

The first asset to go was Film House. By this time I had put my brother Cyril in charge of the facility. I was proud of the gains we had made in the printing division and the reputation enjoyed by our post-production sound labs as the finest in Canada. Film House's revenues had bounded upward from $15 million in 1986 to $46 million in 1988, even though Universal was still giving me unbelievable amounts of aggravation. Sheinberg wouldn't or couldn't ram it into the heads of certain Universal executives, namely Tom Pollock and Bill Soady, that by sending printing to us rather than to DeLuxe or Technicolor, they were dramatically improving Cineplex Odeon's bottom line and, by extension, MCA's.

Shortly after the annual meeting, Technicolor was sold to a British company, Carlton Communications, for a record price. It gave me my opening. I said to Skip Paul, Jimmy Raymond, and Myron at an executive committee meeting, "If Universal will play ball and maintain a long-term relationship with Film House, then, based on the Technicolor sale, I believe I can make a deal to sell the facility for around $100 million U.S. That's $75 million more than our total investment in it to date."

At about that time, Rank, a competitor of Technicolor and a mighty British conglomerate with broad interests in leisure and entertainment, had decided to expand its lab business in North America. For $100 million U.S., it had bought the Bell & Howell video-duplicating lab in Chicago. Universal was Bell & Howell's largest customer, and that's how James Daly, the managing director of Rank's film and TV division, came to meet Sid Sheinberg and ask whether Film House was for sale. Sid said, "You'd better talk to Garth Drabinsky."

Daly did so, and by December 1988 I had closed what I still consider a masterly deal. Rank would pay $73 million U.S. for 49 per cent of Film House, with an option to buy the remaining 51 per cent within the year for an additional $76.5 million U.S. Cineplex Odeon would continue to manage the lab and, as part of the deal, Universal agreed to continue its allegiance to the lab. In our two-and-a-half-year ownership of the lab, its value had appreciated sixfold.

That eased the pressure for a short while. Then, in January 1989, an idea was presented that would have helped even further. My real-estate guru Ira Mitchell and Larry Spungin, MCA's head of real estate, came up with the notion of getting the renowned architect/developer Chris Hemmeter to create an enormous destination resort hotel on the Orlando site. Hemmeter would pay the joint venture $25 million U.S. for thirty-seven acres, on which he would build a spectacular $300-million U.S. resort, in which the joint venture would retain a residual interest. Since Sid Sheinberg had called Hemmeter's Westin Kauai Hotel the "Spielberg of resorts" – visitors could swim with dolphins in man-made lagoons, take lunch in bamboo forests or Japanese sculptured gardens filled with Pacific art treasures – I thought he would jump at the suggestion. But he and Wasserman did one of their classic MCA negotiating put-downs (their familiar "you're shit, we're it" stance) and irritated the developer, thereby losing the chance to bring in a much-needed $25 million U.S., not to mention two hotels, a giant conference centre, and a health spa – all assets that would have competed with the best of the Disney resorts.

Meanwhile the Orlando cost estimates continued to zoom upward, soon reaching $510 million U.S. Our share of the obligation would have to grow to a staggering $117 million U.S. In order to justify this level of investment, the projection of first-year attendance was also revised upward, beyond five million. Jeff, however, kept looking at me and saying, "I have no confidence in MCA's numbers."

Reluctantly, I concluded we had to get out. It was time to sell. I instructed our friends at Gordon Securities to start looking for high-probability buyers, and, after a week or so of exploratory phone calls, Myron and I flew to London to meet Michael Gifford, Rank's chairman and CEO. During the Film House negotiations, we had found Gifford and Doug Yates, his mergers-and-acquisitions maven, to be straight-shooters.

Rank was of sufficient size to be able to hold its own with MCA, and it seemed intent on expanding its relationship with the Black

Tower. MCA was already looking at a site in Spain for a studio tour to compete with Euro Disney, which was scheduled to open in 1992 in Marne-La-Vallée, just outside Paris, and Britain was likely to be its second choice for a location. Rank owned the legendary Pinewood Studios (home of the James Bond pictures), so it was a good fit. Collaboration seemed possible.

Over dinner at Les Ambassadeurs, the plush West End dining club, I discovered to my fury that Skip Paul had already almost scuppered us. Gifford announced that Paul had told him that, in the circumstances, we would be pleased to sell our interest in Orlando at cost! I was seething. I found it difficult to contain the disgust and contempt that I felt toward Paul and Sheinberg – they had just taken away whatever leverage we had for negotiations. It also revealed how tattered our relationship was with MCA. Clearly Sheinberg was willing to sell out Cineplex Odeon for the long-term gain of a Rank relationship.

Back in my hotel, I called Sid. In the harshest words I had ever used with him, I warned him that Skip Paul had no jurisdiction in these negotiations. Henceforth, his status was only as an observer.

"Muzzle him," I said.

Fortunately for us, Gifford badly wanted this deal, and over the next two days Myron and I fought for the best one we could get.

Even as Skip Paul was telling Jimmy Raymond, who relayed the information to us, that we would be lucky to close a deal at $120 million U.S., I was able to push Rank to close at $150 million U.S. As Cineplex Odeon's total investment in Orlando thus far had been $92 million U.S., we ended up with a tidy profit of $58 million U.S. I also hung on to a significant ongoing residual interest, pegged to attendance, which would pay Cineplex Odeon up to $10 million U.S. a year, and a percentage of Rank's revenue of any commercial development of the Orlando site.

Without any resistance, Rank also gave us a first refusal on any theatre complex to be built on the site, but MCA, in a startling display of venom, vetoed it. Why? Why was it not prepared to grant a simple concession to the company that, in Sheinberg's own words, had provided "expertise and counsel during the project's early stages," the company in which MCA continued to hold a substantial interest – a simple concession that wouldn't cost MCA a cent?

It was perverse. But that's where our relationship had gone.

In its press announcement, Rank said it would be investing a further $50 million U.S. in Orlando. I didn't say a word. I didn't even roll my eyes. I just thought, "Little do you know. The end is nowhere in sight."

How right I was! The Universal Studio Tour would finally open in June 1990 – with only half of it functional. The first year's attendance was 3.5 million, substantially below projections. The final cost was more than $700 million U.S., excluding the capitalized interest on each of the partners' investment. It wasn't until 1993 that attendance figures surpassed 6.5 million. Nevertheless, it will be years before Rank sees any meaningful return.

Cineplex Odeon got out, thank God. If we had remained involved with the sorry mess, we would certainly have gone bankrupt.

*I emerged from Orlando feeling bruised and exhausted. What was I doing, dipping into my personal well of creativity to fight my own partners? What was I doing, so far from home, staring blankly at yet another hotel wall, fiddling with yet another TV remote, listening to yet another CNN program about some war in some far-off place? I could feel my life going by in an accelerating rush, and for what? To extricate myself from one more disaster caused by the ineptitude of my partners? To build yet another movie screen to show yet another movie?*

*I had lost my boyhood to the surgeons' knives. And here I was, in danger of losing more years, my life spinning out of control.*

*I was portrayed in the press as a bully, crass and pushy, a man who just wanted his life to be bigger than anyone else's. How could they know? I yearned, ached, for a more creative life.*

*But I had no time!*

Here's how it went, those years:

Remember, I was based in Toronto, dealing with L.A. on the one hand and England on the other (because Cineplex Odeon was expanding into England, too). I would start work at eight o'clock in the morning and not finish until seven or eight o'clock L.A. time, which meant nearly eleven o'clock for me. This was my life, five days a week. And then the weekends. . . . They were for catching up on business foregone.

I can't tell how many evenings I would get home at two or three o'clock in the morning. I would begin screening films at ten o'clock at night. I had a projectionist come in and set up the projection room next to my office. I remember making judgements in the small hours about which movies were going to be hits, and I made plans for those films in our theatres. I had to be able to extrapolate what was going to happen to those films, how many people would want to see them, how many more runs we would need. If I saw a film I thought would be a hit, the next morning I would scream at my bookers, demanding that they go out and get the film on forty more screens, because every run was going to be worth another $10,000 or $15,000 a week. The work had to be done, and I felt negligent if I didn't screen two hundred and fifty to three hundred movies a year. That's another six hundred hours, the equivalent of another fifteen "normal" work weeks. Then I had to read scripts and pore over plans. All of this on top of administering a sprawling public corporation.

We were also still building theatres all over North America. Ira Mitchell would put together a dozen opportunities for me in a particular city. They would all come together in a bundle. We would analyse them with our architectural people, who would be able to see, at least within a twenty-, thirty-, or forty-thousand-square-foot framework, what sort of theatre layout we could generate. Pro-formas were then drawn up, and, of course, we then went down to take a look at the locations. In order for me to even consider a deal, I had to have been there, had to have seen the site, talked to the people, thought about the implications.

Which meant the trip down, up in a helicopter, survey the entire city, see what the competition is doing and so forth, and back to Toronto.

On top of that, it was Orlando every month, to see what was being perpetrated there. And then I had to travel constantly to L.A. and New York, because that's where the base of our business was. I used to go down to L.A. to deal with our film department, to deal with the distribution division of the company, and to deal with the other companies we were doing business with. And of course to deal with MCA. To make those flights more efficient, I would take two or three of my executives with me every time I got into a plane, which would give us another four or five hours to sit and talk. I would leave L.A. at six or seven o'clock at night, after a full day there, and get back to Toronto at one or two o'clock in the morning, in time to be more or less intelligible the next day. As though that weren't enough, I had to finalize our U.K. deals, assemble an overseas organization and energize them, too, so I flew over there once every three or four weeks.

We had our own plane, because that schedule would have been literally impossible on commercial flights.

This didn't stop the press and others from criticizing my lifestyle. That, I expected. But so much of the criticism was so woefully ignorant! Critics somehow imagined I loved flying around in a corporate jet, living the high life. They pictured me living like a mogul, as though that utilitarian little plane was some kind of flying palace, some kind of Hefneresque sybaritic fantasy instead of what it was – a mobile office and me with a phone glued to my ear.

My life at that time was a triumph of superior metabolism. I never had time not to be well. In twenty years of business I haven't missed a day of work for illness, other than when I had to go into the hospital and have surgery for a severely broken humerus from a fall in Antigua on New Year's Eve 1987, and even then, I was out in forty-eight hours. I just never, ever, didn't go to work. I don't know what it is to call in and say, "Oh, by the way, I've got the flu, I'm going to be home today and tomorrow." I've never done it.

One alternative, of course, had always been to move our offices to L.A. But I never came close to doing that. Partly for business reasons, substantially for personal ones.

The business reasons were easy enough: it was more cost-effective to stay put. If we moved, we would have had to re-employ all our head-office staff in U.S. dollars, which would have cost us a bundle. For example, our architectural and engineering division, which had grown to almost a hundred people, was better employed in Canada. You can't budget the outside architectural and other professional costs associated with theatre construction, like interior design and engineering consultancy, for less than 5 per cent of the total cost of a new theatre, which was generally running somewhere between $4 million and $5 million. So these services, if purchased outside the corporation, would amount to at least $200,000 a project. Given the number of projects we were building, it would result in a total cost of about $5 million a year. Infinitely more expensive, of course, in U.S. dollars. We were spending on our inhouse organization less than one half that amount annually. On balance, I thought then, it was better for the finances of the company to stay in Toronto and for me to maintain my punishing travel schedule.

But the undeniable fact is that, if I'd been living in L.A., I would have had more one-on-one contact with the studios.

*That I didn't move to L.A., I believe, was the biggest reason it all went wrong for me, that I blew it. I was always considered the Canadian outsider. I should have been there, to further nurture my relationships with the film companies, to spend more time with Sid Sheinberg to allow him to understand my philosophy, to hold his hand.*

*But I also truthfully believe that if I had gone to L.A. for business reasons, I would have gone alone.*

*It's painful for me to contemplate, but I haven't been a good family man.*

*Cineplex Odeon stole my life for more years than I'm able to count.*

*I suppose the trade-off in any entrepreneur's life has always been family versus the obsession of the business.*

*From the time I first started making movies, I was always on location somewhere. I wasn't making those movies in my backyard: I had to be in whatever place the script called for. The same when I was building theatres or acquiring rights to films – my business was always taking me to* far-away places. The Cineplex Odeon story was a worldwide story, and it took me out into that world. There were long periods when I spent months of my life on the road.

Pearl would never have gone to L.A. She hated the place, she hated the business I was in, she hated the people in the business. The times we spent together in L.A. only contributed to her disenchantment. She found the people shallow, the place ugly – an ugly place with an ugly value system. Some of the extraordinary events we attended in Hollywood – such as Sid Sheinberg's son's wedding, an intimate little affair for eight hundred, complete with a manmade sunset and held under the clock where Back to the Future was shot – only reinforced her views.

She was, essentially, raising the kids by herself, which she has done unbelievably well, and she was determined to do that in Toronto.

I must say this: I've got two wonderful kids, a daughter who's in college, a young woman who's wildly talented in the arts; and a son, a handsome, attractive kid with his own style about him, an intelligent kid with tremendous integrity, a boy's boy much loved by his peers (and with a knowledge of sports to rival my own!). Both kids are incredibly warm and loving, both are balanced, bright kids who've never caused me a day of grief in my life, and that's a huge tribute to Pearl. It was hell being at home alone, her husband thousands of miles away, while a baby cried all night with an infection.

I've already recounted how Pearl got her Masters in French linguistics; she's a terrifically gifted lady, a perceptive and intuitive person who has never led me astray.

Ours has been a twenty-three-year marriage, but not without a great amount of strain.

Sure, there were times when we laughed together, for we have a kindred sense of humour, but in truth I don't recall having much of a family life for fifteen years now, since the Cineplex Odeon wheel started turning and my life started spinning with it.

I have always tried to get back to my family for the holidays, for important birthdays, for anniversaries. We have always tried to go away together over Christmas. But I was away a lot, too much.

*It has sometimes been achingly, unspeakably lonely, both for me and for Pearl.*

*Obviously, being married to me has been no picnic.*

*I console myself with the thought that she has had these wonderful, wonderful kids around her.*

*My life, as I've described, was a life on the run. I spent more time on the road than at home, feeling more and more cut off from my family and from the creative juices that have fuelled me.*

*I was in L.A., I was in New York, I was in Chicago, I was in Salt Lake City, Utah, I was in Montreal, I was in Orlando, I was everywhere but home. My children were growing up and my wife was a single mother, and I had a billion-dollar company to run that consumed every waking vital moment of my life. And again I ask – for what?*

*So often I looked down, through the porthole of some airplane, into the blackness of some anonymous patch of North America, and saw the lights of some town below, twinkling forlornly in the dark, and I felt a wave of loneliness wash over me.*

*I had started the wheel turning, but now the wheel was turning me; I felt I was losing control, not of this creature I had built, but of my life.*

*And I saw no way out.*

*Yes, of course there were satisfactions. First of all, I did some extraordinary restoration of theatres. The architectural awards, the recognition . . . all that was very important to me. Taking the most difficult spaces and building theatres where nobody thought they were possible – that I loved doing. Like the one in the air above Canada Square. Like building the largest theatre in the world at Universal Studios, after everyone had turned the project down, and notwithstanding the naysayers.*

*But it wasn't enough, that's the point. After a while it was only a question of looking at your grosses and determining how much you're making on the bottom line, and that's all it was. Building theatres and looking at grosses. Night after night after night. It was just a game of numbers. It wasn't a business that could satisfy me. Especially when I owned only 4 per cent of the company.*

*Something was going to have to change.*

*Whenever I looked out through the portholes of my plane into the black sky over America, I was also looking through a window into my heart, and looking curiously at the vacuum I found there. Where had my life gone? I could read my curriculum vitae like anyone else and plainly see the assets that I had created, but . . . where did my twenties go, my thirties? What had I really done? Where was the quality of life I so yearned for? I saw my whole nature change as well. Big character changes. Changes I didn't like. I became a much harder human being, less patient, less forgiving.*

*I loved life a lot more in my twenties, when I was practising law and when I was making motion pictures. And then, slowly, the joy of life was sucked out of me by the pressures of Cineplex Odeon Corporation.*

*I knew what was happening. I knew I had to get out of the movie-theatre business, or at least to irrevocably alter the structure of the company so as to change my destiny.*

*Why? Because I couldn't stand Leo Kolber's face any more, or Jimmy Raymond's face, or anybody at Claridge. I couldn't deal with Sid Sheinberg any more. I couldn't stand the people in the business, the Monday-morning fights, the constant disloyalty, the lack of inspiration, the waste of the business. . . .*

*A showdown was coming.*

# CHAPTER

## SHOWDOWN

*If Cineplex Odeon were a Shakespearean tragedy, Orlando would be the villain, the leering assassin who would knife the Prince and bring the Royal House crashing down.*

*I didn't feel much like a Prince. But I knew the crowd of spearcarriers (the Wassermans, the Sheinbergs, the Pauls, the Kolbers, and the Raymonds) was getting restless. And those spears were not turning out at a hostile world. They were pointed at me.*

The miserable Orlando episode crystallized my problems with the board, many members of which were now mired in some form of postcrash anxiety. Suddenly the company's rapid expansion and outstanding record of achievement were being used against me. There was a lot of agonizing reappraisal. What had seemed farsighted, bold, and imaginative only months before was now being questioned. What had seemed wise was now called foolish.

During the first two years of the MCA marriage, Leo Kolber and Jimmy Raymond had steadfastly supported us in our private sessions, when Myron and I, in a growing state of irritation, harshly criticized Orlando's out-of-control budget. But publicly they were never ready to risk a showdown during our acrimonious altercations with MCA, and through 1988 they began to distance themselves from us and draw closer to MCA.

They were aided and abetted in this, I'm sure, by Jack Richer, the Montreal accountant who was the third Bronfman nominee on the board.

I didn't know Jack before he came on the board, but I sensed right away that he disliked me. He was a staunch conservative, perfect for the shaky business climate that prevailed at the end of the eighties. As head of our audit committee, he took great pleasure in sniping at me during board meetings, attacking the level of debt I was incurring to renovate and build our circuit. He loved to deride the efforts of our distribution division. It wasn't hard to see what he was doing: he was showing off for MCA.

It worked, too. He eventually gained the confidence of the board, and MCA actually labelled him "astute." This despite Lew Wasserman's instruction to me not to worry about leverage; the bankers, he had said, "have plenty of money they're dying to lend."

Richer was joined in his negativity by the aggravating Skip Paul, who had by now been given more jurisdictional clout over Cineplex Odeon's affairs by Sid Sheinberg.

Although the corporation reported an overall profit in the third quarter of 1988, there were substantial losses from exhibition, which gave Skip further ammunition. It was luck of the worst kind. Exhibitors and distributors fight all the time, but we had fallen out with two, Columbia and now Disney. Disney, feeling very confident with its Christmas 1988 line-up, suddenly decided to reverse its policy of allocating its pictures in non-bid zones and instead put Disney films up for bids everywhere. My film buyers told me that, if we agreed to this move, it would cost us millions. I adhered to their advice. I refused to play. Disney refused to deal. We lost a couple of runaway hits, *Three Men and a Baby* and *Good Morning, Vietnam*. At a December 1988 executive committee meeting, I could tell from the glances exchanged between Skip and Jimmy Raymond that an alliance was being forged.

This became even clearer when, at the end of 1988, Jimmy, as head of the Cineplex Odeon compensation committee, refused to give Myron and me our year-end bonuses, the first time this had happened since the company started to make money. I challenged him about it. "I closed the Film House deal with Rank. In spite of the battles with our film suppliers, it's been a record year. Why no bonus?"

He said nothing.

I could see Richer's hand in all this. In the summer we had sold fifty-five Canadian theatres in non-strategic locations to a subsidiary of Edper's for $55 million U.S., and the sale boosted our bottom line by $3 million U.S. A little later we sold half of Film House to Rank. As a result of these two transactions, we showed a profit of $40 million U.S. at the end of 1988. But Richer persisted in pointing out, with gleeful satisfaction, that, without these sales, Cineplex Odeon would have reported a loss. That was inarguable. On the other hand, we used the transactions to write down the film costs in our distribution division. Since the accounting line for distribution was consolidated with theatre operations on paper, it could be said that our core business, "exhibition," was down. At all times, my responsibility was to generate earnings in spite of adverse conditions in one or other divisions of the corporation, and to date, this way of doing business had enormously enhanced the value of the Bronfman group's 7.2 million shares in Cineplex Odeon in a relatively short time.

By mid-February 1989, Skip's antagonistic rhetoric had escalated to such an extent that I had to confront Sid Sheinberg. I had breakfast with him at his well-guarded house in Bel Air and put it to him straight.

"Skip Paul has become abusive. He undercut me in my negotiations with Rank for the sale of Orlando. He's always going behind my back sowing seeds of disaffection with the Bronfman people, and he's certainly succeeded. As a result, Richer now seems to see himself as MCA's protector."

Sid said nothing. He just stared at me.

"Maybe this situation has gone beyond redemption," I said, "but

I'm still trying to find a way to work together. Sid, when you bought into Cineplex Odeon, you said you were investing in me. The company is much stronger today than it was when you came in. It's time to call off your dogs, otherwise there'll be serious implications."

Sid assured me he would comply. But in the end he did nothing.

So in late February, when I learned, with some astonishment, that David Fingold had quit the board, I knew another crisis loomed.

Before his resignation, the board numbered seventeen. MCA had five seats and the Bronfmans three. Management, including Myron and me, had four, and there were five independent directors who were friendly to management: Nat Taylor, Ted Pedas, Rudy Bratty and Jack Daniels, two of my most durable supporters, and David Fingold, who had helped us buy Canadian Odeon. In a crunch, therefore, we could fend off any hostile initiative by the MCA–Bronfman group.

But now the balance of power could shift. MCA couldn't nominate another board member to replace Fingold because of the standstill agreement, but the Bronfmans could. And if they did so with the backing of MCA, we would be in trouble. There would be nine MCA–Bronfman directors to eight of us.

As Myron saw the matter, our best stance was to leave the board at sixteen. "Why do we have to rush out and fill it? After all, the bylaws call for a board of variable size."

But within a few days of Fingold's resignation, Jimmy Raymond was on the phone to Myron. It was one of Jimmy's many early-morning calls, around half past seven, and he first talked, as he always did, about world politics, about business in a general way, and then he circulated slowly, amiably to the point. Claridge would like to fill the Fingold seat with Bob Rabinovitch, a former deputy minister of communications for the federal government who was now with Claridge.

Myron, equally affable, said, "No, Jimmy. No more Claridge directors. We'll only agree on another independent director."

Jimmy didn't back off, confirming our worst fears. He kept up the pressure. "There are too many members of management on the board!" he would charge. (That was nonsense. Compared to the top fifty Canadian companies, Cineplex Odeon had an average number of management board members.) "Besides," he said with a straight face, "we could back you and Garth better if we had a nominee."

"Bullshit," I said to Myron. "He's probably promising MCA the same thing."

I finally called Sheinberg. It was another tense conversation. I said, "Sid, if you back the Bronfmans in this, I'll consider it a declaration of war."

Sid was laconic. "I hear what you're saying," he said.

As February gave way to March, Myron and I finally confronted the truth: we were in the battle of our lives over who would control our company. The only option available to us seemed to be to buy out the Bronfmans. Huddling with Myron, I circled March 30, the next board meeting, as our deadline for doing so. In early March, Jimmy and Leo met Myron and me in my Toronto office.

I said, "We're frustrated; you're frustrated. If we can find the financing for your shares, would you agree to sell?" Jimmy and Leo gave us strong signals that they would be glad to walk away for the right price. Cineplex Odeon shares were selling that day for $16.25. They wanted $18.00 a share. At that price, Myron and I had to raise about $127 million.

For months MCA had been trying to push us off balance so they could take over the direction of Cineplex Odeon. We had to fight back. We had no option. The struggle was far from equal – we were small, MCA was a behemoth. Still, despite my growing feeling of disillusionment, Cineplex Odeon was my creation and my life. To MCA, Cineplex Odeon was just a minuscule part of a huge empire. I had to proceed.

The momentous decision made, the clock started ticking. The deal had to be made fast and secretly; I knew it would be fatal if MCA got as much as a whiff of our plans. Myron asked Richard Bain, an old friend of his and a corporate lawyer, to begin drawing up the papers for the purchase of the Bronfman's shares.

At the same time, Myron and I began to bat around the names of possible partners. On March 13 I called Rudy Bratty, who was vacationing at his Florida condo. I asked if he would come in on a proposition to buy out the Bronfmans. I said I needed at least $50 million from him. Rudy didn't back off. He was obviously interested and flush with cash. A couple of days later he called me back to say, "I'm in, but I've got a better idea. I'd like to take the deal to the new investment-banking arm that's just been set up as part of the Erin Mills group."

Erin Mills had been one of the great stories of the eighties boom. The Erin Mills group was formed in 1983 to buy the forty-seven-hundred-acre Erin Mills residential-development site in Mississauga, west of Toronto.

Everyone and his lawyer had been after the acreage when it was first put up for sale by Cadillac Fairview: Rudy, Jack, Marco Muzzo of Marel Corporation, Alfredo de Gasperis of Con-Drain, and Larry Robbins and Ellie and Norman Reisman of the Great Gulf group of companies were all manoeuvring to buy it. Finally, the Jews and Italians, as they called themselves, pooled resources and wound up paying cash of around $90 million in what was, to that date, the biggest residential real-estate transaction in Toronto's history.

Nobody had believed that these guys would be able to stand each other. But somehow the chemistry worked, and, by 1989, with a red-hot Toronto real-estate market, Erin Mills was worth a billion dollars and the group was looking for interesting investment opportunities. Rudy reported that, subject to gaining Jack Daniels' nod, Erin Mills had agreed unanimously to back us. The terms would be stiff, but we could have the money.

The only hitch was finding Jack, who was touring the South Pacific on a cruise ship. With the assistance of ship-to-shore radio and fax, Jack eventually okayed Erin Mills' participation; later, however, he said he wouldn't have done so if he had known MCA didn't know about the deal. To me, this doesn't make sense. He knew, we all knew, the world knew, that if I got control of the company, which is exactly what the deal was designed to do, MCA would be angry. Maybe the South Pacific air mushed his brain.

Myron lined up the other partners quickly: Ned Goodman of Dundee Capital and Jimmy Connacher, who had led the aggressive institutional and investment house of Gordon Capital from near extinction in 1983 to become Canada's phenomenal firm of the eighties. Connacher, in turn, brought in Andy Sarlos for a small piece. I might have winced a little when I saw Andy's name, remembering the events of 1982, but, since he was a major player in Toronto, it was inevitable I would do business with him again.

Later, after we had announced the members of the consortium, the press labelled them "savvy and sophisticated" and speculated that they were in for a quick kill. In fact, the group was in for the long haul. Under the terms of a trust document, Myron and I were given total voting control of all of the consortium's shares, which represented about 30 per cent of the company. This, together with our own shares, would give us effective control of Cineplex Odeon and *carte blanche* as to its direction.

We were now in the final stretch toward the March 30 board meeting. It seemed as if we had the basis of a secure deal, but we were wary. Myron and I decided we had to have it wrapped up before the meeting. We couldn't get rid of a lingering fear that the Bronfman group would weaken and give in to MCA when it came to the crunch.

On March 20 Skip called Myron, saying he had talked to Jimmy about the new Bronfman nominee and that MCA was still on the fence. Before hanging up, he said, "You know, you and Garth could be out of here any time."

Okay, so we knew.

The board meeting was to be held over the phone. We flew into Montreal that morning, and an hour before the call, we met Leo and Jimmy at one of the Execaire offices at Dorval airport. The negotiations were brief and to the point. We badly wanted their stock. They badly wanted out.

We shook hands on a price of $17.50 a share, and they agreed not to press for an extra board member. A $3.6-million deposit would be wired to Claridge's bank account to confirm the transaction. We reminded them that the sellers of a "control block" could not by law consist of a group of more than five shareholders without the permission of the Quebec Securities Commission (QSC). Jimmy and Leo assured us that the five largest shareholders owned about 80 per cent of the stock, and that they were content to sell only these shares for the time being. In our presence, Kolber then confirmed by phone to his counsel, Michael Vineberg, that they had made a deal with us to sell the shares of the five largest shareholders. The agreement would be documented by the end of the first week of April. It was essentially a simple deal.

Leo and Jimmy had done handsomely over the six years. Everyone was satisfied. And at noon we were all plugged in to the conference operator, Myron and me in Montreal, Leo and Jimmy, who by now had flown to Toronto, and Sid and Skip in L.A. As agreed, the Bronfman group withdrew their request for another nominee to the board.

Two problems nagged me as we flew back to Toronto later that day: Sid Sheinberg's reaction and Jimmy Raymond's mouth.

I decided to tell Sid about the deal in that narrow window of time between the moment when the deal actually closed and when it was to be made public.

I wasn't looking forward to it. My gut told me that, once he knew he had been outplayed, Sid would be unforgiving. It would be no holds barred. He would go, I knew, to any lengths to undermine me.

Jimmy Raymond's loose tongue was something we couldn't control. Sure enough, almost immediately rumours came bouncing back from Montreal that the Bronfmans had sold their shares. And we were at least a week from closing.

Then Michael Vineberg called Richard Bain and dropped his bomb. The Bronfman group had, without disclosing it to us, asked the QSC for an exemption, not for five but for all the shareholders in the Bronfman group.

"How many?" Richard asked.

Vineberg tiptoed round the subject. It turned out that the shares were held by a tangle of companies encompassing Bronfman family members and their associates. Phyllis Lambert, Charles Bronfman's sister, was in with her company Philotecton; the Bronfman children's trust, CRBT, was in; there were two companies owned by Jimmy Raymond's family, two Leo Kolber companies, and two companies belonging to Jack Richer. When the different shareholders were finally added up, the total number was seventeen!

Strategically, Vineberg explained, the Bronfman group felt they would have a better chance if the deal was presented to the QSC on an all-or-nothing basis.

Richard was taken aback. But Vineberg said, "Not to worry. It's a lead-pipe cinch."

When Richard relayed this conversation to me, I was livid. "The deal we made didn't involve anyone going near the QSC!" It was a flagrant breach of our agreement – an agreement concluded only days before.

I guess I only then realized the true arrogance of the Bronfman family. Charles Bronfman was either receiving hopelessly bad advice or else he really believed that, as one of Quebec's power barons, he could be denied nothing. What did it matter that the deal his representatives proposed broke the rules? The Bronfmans were above all that!

"It's a lead-pipe cinch!" I had to remember Vineberg's cockiness in the months ahead. Huh! He was the faulty O-ring seal in the negotiation, the guy who caused the deal to leak away.

I was almost out of time. If we believed that the oral agreement made with Leo and Jimmy on March 30 was binding, then we had to file a 13-D schedule describing our intentions to the Securities and Exchange Commission (SEC) within days. Immediately, MCA would learn of the transaction.

What a position I now found myself in! Suddenly, far from having a secure deal, we had only an arrangement that was subject to the uncertain outcome of an administrative hearing. And I knew that regulatory bodies are almost invariably intimidated by controversy.

On April 2, a Sunday afternoon, Richard, Myron, and I met at Myron's house. We sat in the sunroom, playing through all possible scenarios. We concluded that, if there were any danger that the QSC would hold up the deal, then we should drop the whole thing now, before MCA got a whiff of it.

The key was the trustworthiness of Leo Kolber. Could he sustain a blitzkrieg from MCA? Would he remain steadfast?

In the middle of all this we placed a conference call from Myron's house to Leo in Montreal. "Leo," I said, "we are all in this predicament because you guys went off after that bloody exemption without our approval. Damn it, you made a deal with us. You committed. And your smart-asses have screwed it up. The whole thing is cratering."

Leo was entirely reassuring. "I'm telling you, Garth, you have a deal. At the very least, we'll sell you the shares of the five largest shareholders, and these will be enough to give you control. I guarantee it. We want you to cooperate with us when we try to get the exemption, but if we're refused, I'm telling you, one way or another, the five largest shareholders will sell to you at the price set."

I was yelling at him, "The whole company may be riding on your word, Leo."

Leo answered, "You have my word."

I was satisfied. I had never wanted to believe that the Bronfmans would sell us out, whatever the provocation or however difficult it became.

It was now time to tell Sid Sheinberg.

On April 3 I started calling Sid. He didn't return my calls. Unusual. Perhaps, I thought, he was still annoyed over the business of the new board member. I knew that on April 7 he was going off to Spain for a meeting of the United International Pictures (UIP) board. Time was evaporating. We had to speak soon. That same day I heard that Jimmy Raymond had confirmed to *The Financial Post* that the Bronfman shares were as good as sold.

For four days I placed repeated calls to Sid and got no response. In one conversation with his secretary, I said I was prepared to fly to L.A. to meet with Sid whenever he was available, as long as it was prior to his departure for Spain. Sid left for Europe without speaking to me.

Now we had to file the 13-D schedule, as our purchasing group was formally in place. We would file on Monday morning, and MCA would know immediately what we had done.

On Friday night, April 7, Myron called Skip Paul in L.A. and left a message on his answering machine.

I don't think I slept much that night.

The next morning I read in *The Financial Post* that there was speculation I was buying the Bronfman shares. Soon afterwards, Skip was on the phone to Myron. Myron patched Skip into my car and then said, "Skip, we've negotiated a deal to buy the Bronfman stock."

For the first time ever, Skip was speechless. If I hadn't been so nervous, I would have laughed.

Then he said, "Well, I figured you might try to do this over the next month. I told Sid this. I wanted us to sit down and discuss it."

More chat, then Skip asked, "Why didn't you tell us?"

I pointed out that for the past five days I had tried to meet Sid to explain our actions but had been ignored. As for telling Skip, I didn't see any point in being diplomatic. "In any event," I said, "we could never trust you."

Skip was placating. "There was no reason not to."

Myron chipped in. "That's not true, Skip. You've been supporting the Bronfmans and threatening our position as management. All we want is for our relationship to be on a level playing field."

Skip ended the conversation, apparently reconciled to the reality of our imminent success. "Go ahead and close the deal," he said. "We're going to work together to make this happen. Congratulations."

So it was quite unexpected when, later in the day, Skip phoned Myron. "I phoned Sid in Spain and Lew in L.A.," he said. "They both hit the roof and instructed me to kill the deal at whatever cost." Talk about Dr. Jekyll and Mr. Hyde.

"Maybe we can find another buyer," Skip suggested.

Myron blew up. "You're crazy! We're buying the Bronfman stock."

"This is going to cause serious problems with MCA," Skip said brusquely. "You're going to hear more about this."

Jimmy Raymond called Myron that same evening. He was fretting. Skip had called him to ask, "Why didn't you tell us you wanted to sell your stock? We could have found a buyer at a higher level." This was a typical MCA "end around" and substantiated our charge to Skip that MCA could never be trusted. Smelling defeat, they were now going to be ruthless.

That same night, I faxed to Sid Sheinberg in Spain a copy of the press release going out on Monday. I added a personal message, "Sid, call me."

Sid got the fax Monday morning in his hotel room in Madrid. He later told a reporter, "Sure I was shocked. How would you like to be sitting in Madrid and learn your wife had run off with another man!"

He called me that day, and before I could say a word, he said in an icy voice, "I'm extending the courtesy to you that you have not extended to me. We have retained legal counsel and we intend to oppose you every way possible until we defeat you and this deal."

Sweat broke out on my forehead. I knew he meant it.

Rudy Bratty got a call that night from Skip. Rudy had just returned from his Florida vacation, and Skip asked him whether he and Erin Mills wanted to go through with the buyout. Rudy said he did, and then Skip made, as expected, a few derogatory comments about my management record. Rudy later told Myron that he decisively brushed Skip aside.

On Tuesday, April 11, MCA fired off the first of its missives: a letter from its Toronto lawyers to the QSC objecting to the transaction on the grounds that it was against the public interest.

We were now pressuring Leo and Jimmy to get a second agreement prepared, in case the first arrangement was turned down – which was now a distinct possibility. The second deal, which was announced on Friday, April 14, called for only the five largest shareholders to sell their shares in the first instance, with the other shareholders being guaranteed the same price if, within a reasonable period thereafter, they sold their shares for less than $17.50 on the open market.

On Monday, April 17, the QSC announced that, because of MCA's objections, a hearing would be held that Friday.

I fought panic. It was apparent now that Vineberg had been disastrously wrong. I still believed the Bronfmans would stick to the deal. I still believed that Leo Kolber wouldn't go back on his word. And yet – I couldn't ignore my instincts. I said to Myron, "We're in terrible trouble."

And that trouble was not long in arriving.

*In the middle of this nerve-racking week, Cineplex Odeon celebrated its tenth anniversary. On Wednesday, April 19, we threw a huge party at the Art Gallery of Ontario. Ontario Premier David Peterson made a congratulatory speech, and we distributed a book of the works of art that had been commissioned for Cineplex Odeon theatres. It should have been a champagne occasion for me. But instead of hearing talk of celebration and conquests as I shook the hands of friends and well-wishers, all I heard was speculation about the impending battle.*

The next day saw hostilities increase. A letter arrived by courier from Skip Paul. He accused me and all the members of the board, other than MCA's nominees, of having betrayed our "fiduciary duty" to the shareholders. Directors of a public company are in a position of trust and must act in the best interests of all shareholders, and if there is even a smidgen of evidence that they are not doing so, they're liable to be sued. MCA was accusing Myron and me, Jack Daniels, Rudy Bratty, and the Bronfman group of putting our own interests ahead of those of the company and its shareholders. They zeroed in on our 13-D filing, which outlined our plans, including the possibility of our consolidating our control by buying up more shares once we had closed with the Bronfmans. In addition, MCA said any change in the control of the company was a matter for the whole board to judge. Skip wanted the deal raised at the next day's board meeting. That didn't leave enough time for either side to prepare its arguments, so the meeting was rescheduled for April 27.

Later the same day there was even worse news. MCA had obtained an interim injunction to block the deal.

I called attorney Mark Hayes, and he went over to MCA's Toronto lawyers, Fraser & Beatty, to get a copy of the affidavit filed in support of the injunction. It was an eye-opener. MCA's claim that certain directors on the Cineplex Odeon board were "extremely critical" of the financial reporting practices and management procedures was routine stuff, but Skip Paul had sworn that the information had been collected by Jack Richer, head of the audit committee.

*Jack Richer! A member of the Bronfman selling group. He was one of those being sued! Or was he? I felt the prick of cold steel from a knife in the back.*

The tension eased a bit when Ron Rolls arrived from Montreal where he had been on a brief. He wasted no time telling us how we would attack the injunction. In the first place, an *ex parte* injunction – one given without notice to the opposing party – is only granted if the opposing party is unavailable when the application is heard by a judge. Clearly that had not been the case here. He was confident he could get the injunction quashed.

Early the next day, Friday, April 21, Mark Hayes was dispatched to get an appointment to see Chief Justice William Parker in his chambers as soon as possible. He came back with the news that a hearing was set for Monday morning.

In the meantime, the onslaught of bad news continued. Kellogg Associates, the publisher of a relatively new financial newsletter for money managers, came out with a special report on Cineplex Odeon. It directly attacked our reporting practices. The timing was too good not to be suspicious. Lorne Kellogg clung to his assertion that the timing was entirely fortuitous, but nobody believed it. Kellogg Associates had been in business just a year, and they were looking for a high-profile controversy to establish themselves as the security industry's Ralph Nader. We all believed that the information on Cineplex Odeon had been leaked to Kellogg by Hal Haas, MCA's treasurer, who was a member of our board. Indeed, our chief financial officer, Ellis Jacobs, said he had seen a copy of the report peeking out of Haas's briefcase before it was published. It had DRAFT stamped on it.

On Saturday I spent hours with Ron Rolls and Mark Hayes constructing and then destroying arguments to be made against the injunction. Rolls was confident that he had MCA dead to rights. As shareholders, Myron and I had a legal right to deal with shares as we wanted. MCA, however, didn't. In our shareholders' agreement with them, MCA management had agreed not to take any steps to affect the control of the corporation. But that was exactly what they had been trying to do by allying themselves with the Bronfmans, even before we took any steps to secure control of Cineplex Odeon.

And they were still trying. That very week Jack Daniels flew to L.A. on other business and Skip Paul asked him to lunch. Skip asked, "Is there any way you guys could buy the company with us and we can avoid all this hassle?" Skip was proposing that the Erin Mills group sell us out and go in with MCA, buy out the Bronfmans and all other shareholders, and become fifty-fifty partners in Cineplex Odeon. The first move, of course, would be to get rid of Myron and me.

On April 24 Ron Rolls went before the Chief Justice and, as he had promised, persuaded him to throw out the injunction. I heard the news in midmorning and felt the world had just been lifted off my shoulders. I shouted to Myron to come to my office, and when he came in, I hugged him. I was exhilarated. Victory had been won where it counted – in court.

*That was the last time I felt lighthearted until it was all over.*

MCA now attacked with the ferocity of a wounded lion. Its lawyers, Herb Wachtell and Martin Lipton, were experienced anti-takeover counsel, and they had spent years finding ways to stymie such deals. They operated with a single-mindedness found only in the United States, where litigation is akin to nuclear warfare. MCA also had pockets deep enough to bring out the best (or worst) in their lawyers.

So that same day, Monday, April 24, three class actions against the directors were launched in L.A. Eventually all the class-action suits were folded into the one filed by Three Bridges Investment of Philadelphia, a company widely known and ridiculed as a class-action junky. The principal complaint was Cineplex Odeon's accounting practices. The financial statements, it was claimed, had been misleading, so Cineplex Odeon's shares had been trading at artificially high prices.

This was so laughable it surely didn't merit a response. All our numbers were audited without qualification. Our policies were fully noted in the financials, and, most importantly, we had been rigorously scrutinized in the financial press for almost a year.

The curious aspect of the suits was that not one of them named any of the five-man MCA contingent on the board of directors as defendants. In fact, only two days previously Skip had spoken to Myron on the phone. If we didn't back off, he had told Myron, we would be faced with more lawsuits. Evidently, therefore, MCA was fully aware of the impending lawsuits and had known they weren't being named. It was, of course, just another attempt by MCA to coerce and intimidate the Bronfmans by making them notorious all over North America, especially in the eyes of the SEC.

Meanwhile back in Toronto, MCA appealed the Chief Justice's decision and announced that, until the appeal was decided, it was MCA's contention that the injunction stood. We had no sooner responded with our own announcement disputing MCA's position than, on Tuesday, April 25, the QSC announced its ruling.

It summarily rejected the first deal – and the second deal, too. We had been assured that the second deal fell squarely within QSC regulations, but the QSC agreed with MCA's objection to the indemnification provision as being unfair to the other shareholders.

The Bronfmans had overreached; they had torpedoed their own deal through greed. Unfortunately, we were headed for the abyss with them.

But there was no time to brood. Our backers stood firm, and so did the Bronfmans. A third deal was coopered together. This one, surely, had to be acceptable, because it was so thoroughly unobjectionable: only the five largest shareholders would sell their 5.8 million shares at $17.50, and there would be no top-up provision for the other twelve shareholders.

Meanwhile Myron was receiving his daily tongue-lashings from Skip Paul about our manoeuvres. After one particularly vituperative call, Skip suddenly asked, a little anxiously, "Are you taping this conversation?"

April 27 was the day of the crucial board meeting at Cineplex Odeon's head office. It was scheduled for 1 P.M., but the directors began drifting in earlier. To emphasize how seriously they were taking the legal onslaught from MCA, there was also a growing contingent of lawyers. Ted Pedas had flown in from Washington, D.C., with his lawyer, Mike Klein, and I had several detachments, Ron Rolls and Mark Hayes representing me personally and David Stone from Weill Gotschal & Menges acting as the buying group's New York lawyers.

The Bronfmans were represented by Michael "Not to Worry" Vineberg. And then, just before 1 P.M., there was a bustle in the reception area and the double oak doors to the executive wing were pushed open. There were the MCA directors, Sheinberg at their head, surrounded by a retinue of lawyers. It was the usual MCA grandstanding shtick. There were now about fifty people in the room, and at least thirty were lawyers. I figured about $10,000 in legal fees were being rung up every hour.

Skip Paul, in his capacity as Sid's gofer, handed around two letters in brown envelopes. The first was a notice that MCA had obtained leave from the Supreme Court of Ontario to sue all the directors (except, of course, themselves) and planned to do so as of May 10. The other was a flat-out assault on Myron and me, recommending that we be fired immediately.

What was noteworthy, however, was that MCA had opened a possible escape hatch. They would go along with our deal if the offer of $17.50 a share was made to all shareholders.

This was ridiculous. We had offered $17.50 as a premium for a pivotal group of shares. The market price that day was $14.00. MCA had now upped the stakes from $125 million U.S. to $1.3 billion U.S. (including the assumption of all corporate debt).

Until then I had been sure the deal would go through. Sure MCA was yelling and screaming, but that was to be expected. They had been beaten. The Bronfmans had given their word. Leo Kolber had given an oath to stay with the sale no matter what.

However, as I glanced around the boardroom, I began to have grave doubts. I saw board members, with the exception of Ted Pedas and Nat Taylor, buckling. When Pamela Seymon, the barracuda now turned pilot fish for Herb Wachtell, started to describe the way the SEC would consider dereliction of fiduciary duties, I looked over at the Bronfman group. They were white, obviously intimidated by the constant references to "fiduciary duty" and "SEC censure" because of Seagram's heavy involvement in the U.S. market.

The board meeting was never called to order. Instead we all broke up into groups and brainstormed. I went off to my corner office with my lawyers and backers.

I was thinking hard. I could of course obstinately say to hell with MCA, we'll fight 'em all the way, even with the knowledge that everyone was losing enthusiasm for the battle. But should I? We had just had a taste of MCA's methods. Dirty was a polite euphemism for the way they had played. My name, Charles Bronfman's name, Myron's name, and the names of all the directors were going to be smeared all over the continent. And an all-out war would no doubt damage the company, drive down the price of the shares, and benefit only the shortsellers. At the forefront of my mind was how Charles Bronfman, with his obsession for anonymity, would feel about this.

The other option was to augment the buying group to make substantially more capital available, so an offer could be extended to all shareholders. Of course, we'd have to negotiate a more realistic price than $17.50.

I didn't have to make the decision. The Bronfmans did it for me. Jimmy Raymond and Michael Vineberg appeared in my office and, after all the lawyers had shuffled out, made it clear that the Bronfmans were withdrawing their agreement to sell the shares.

Jimmy looked sad. "We can't do it, Garth. The publicity would kill us."

Jimmy and Leo just had no stomach for a fight. Just like some politicians, their actions were going to depend on expediency, not on principle.

I picked up the phone and called Richard Bain, who was still in Montreal negotiating with the QSC, "You might as well come back, Richard," I said. "The deal's off."

Three hours later, when Richard arrived, he bumped into Leo Kolber in the hall.

"Leo," Richard said, "you're not believing all that crap are you? There's no possible way MCA can win a suit. The QSC are bound to let a deal through."

Kolber's facial twitch had become more and more pronounced during the day. Suddenly he began to yell. "The deal's off!" he cried. "I can't allow Charles to be sued."

In my office, Myron and I huddled for a couple of hours with Bratty and Daniels, taking them carefully through all the ramifications of a purchase of all the shares. I really believed we could pull off the financing. I asked the two of them, "Are you with me?" They said they were prepared to stay the course.

I was metaphorically waving a white flag as I went along to the boardroom with a bottle of 222s for Sid Sheinberg, who had the flu. In the ensuing discussion, MCA agreed to drop all litigation. I declared Myron's and my intentions to explore the possibility of making a bid for all the shares. Plans were made to reschedule the board meeting for May 15, at which time a special committee would be formed to handle bids for the company.

I was so glad for the reprieve that I didn't see the downside at all. But I think Leo Kolber did. Richard Bain later told me that, after Sid had left for his hotel around eight o'clock, he and Leo Kolber were left alone together in the boardroom, when Leo let loose with a barrage of profanity about MCA. "Profanity such as I had never heard," marvelled Bain – and this from a considerable profaner himself.

Sure enough, there was no truce. *Variety* had for months been planning its April 26 issue as an effusive salute to Cineplex Odeon's tenth anniversary, but MCA sank to the depths of pettiness by withdrawing its congratulatory ad and influencing others to do the same. It did the same thing at a B'nai B'rith dinner in New York on May 7 at which I was the guest of honour. This was supposed to be an upbeat occasion for me. I had been fêted as the first Canadian to receive the B'nai B'rith Distinguished Achievement Award, an accolade given previously to, among others, such heads of state as Golda Meir and Dwight Eisenhower.

My award was given for the creation of the Drabinsky Lecture Series, for which (with the dedicated help of Lynda Friendly) we had raised more than a million dollars and through which we intended to create a forum for world-acclaimed individuals to lecture at prominent venues in major cities across North America; for me, the overwhelming theme of the series could be summed up in one word: tolerance. (As I told the assembled dignitaries that night, "I don't think that there is one single way in which the human condition could be improved so much as by raising the level of tolerance among nations and among individuals.") MCA, predictably, further demonstrated its class by releasing its two tables, influencing other Hollywood companies to follow suit.

The dinner took place at the Pierre Hotel, and I was in a daze. I had spent the day with bankers, and now here I was, filling four hours shaking hands with friends and dignitaries while klezmer music was being played behind me at a dizzying tempo. I had to pretend that all I had on my mind was my acceptance speech. There was a good turnout of Canadians, from Ken Thomson to Allan Gottlieb, who gave the main address of the evening, and the Canadian media were well represented. Unashamed, Jimmy Raymond and Leo Kolber were there, too. Hal Prince and Robert Redford sat at my table, and so did Shirley MacLaine, who actually presented my award. As she handed it to me, she quipped, "This is not me you're seeing. This is Sid Sheinberg." Sid, as co-chairman of the event with Charles Bronfman, was supposed to have been the MC, a role that Myron had to take over at the last minute after Sid had ungraciously begged off.

I had flown into New York just for the dinner. I flew out the same night.

On May 10 Sid Sheinberg went to the MCA annual meeting in Chicago on his way to the rescheduled Cineplex Odeon board meeting. "Garth tried to steal the company," he told a reporter. He later amended "steal" to "take." But he made it clear that there was no going back to the status quo.

May 15 was a shocker – and set the tone for everything that happened in the next six months. The day began at 7:30 A.M. when Myron got his customary call from Jimmy Raymond. "I'm in the next room to the Kolbers. There's going to be trouble. Sandra and Leo have been pressured enough. They're prepared to go along with MCA and dismiss you and Garth at the board meeting later this morning."

My feeling was one of disbelief. Why were we at war once again?

The audit committee had found what they claimed was a discrepancy in the way certain loans to Myron and me had been reported. These were really advances on the bonuses we were still waiting for, and they were made to cover income-tax payments. Through an oversight, for which I was ultimately responsible but of which I had no knowledge, the loans had not been referred to in the information circular attached to the 1988 annual report. "It's a red herring," I told Myron, "but it won't do us any good."

When I got to the office, I called Jerry Banks, among others, and told him of the MCA plan to dismiss me. Only once before, Jerry said afterwards, had he ever seen me in a similar state, and that was when I was banging my head on the wall the night I thought I couldn't get the $1 million U.S. to George C. Scott in New York in time to save *The Changeling*. He was right. I felt exhausted – and completely at the mercy of others.

The meeting had been scheduled for 11 A.M., but was later postponed to 1 P.M. Ted Pedas, up from Washington, had hardly taken off his coat before he was approached by Jack Daniels.

"We're going to fire Garth today," Jack said, his face sombre.

Ted was stunned. "How are you going to fire Garth? And why? He's your partner!"

Sid Sheinberg arrived, accompanied by Martin Lipton, bristling with hostility.

By now anger pervaded the room. I reckoned that, if the meeting was called to order and a vote taken right then, I would be on my way out. It didn't happen only because it was clear to even the most hostile that there was no agreement as to who would replace me. Jack Richer's name was proposed but quickly dropped. The only decision taken was to ask Joel Goldenberg, of Goodman and Carr, a lawyer who had not been directly involved in Cineplex Odeon's affairs, to look into the unreported loans that very day and report to the board. The meeting then broke up in caucuses after agreeing to reassemble at 3 P.M., later postponed to 4 P.M.

The board members continued to lobby. Ted Pedas behaved in a way I'll always remember; he went out and, in his soft-spoken manner, fought for me. At one point he walked into a meeting the Bronfman group was having with Rudy Bratty and Jack Daniels and heard them talking about how they were going to give Myron and me a six-month leave of absence and then get rid of both of us. Pedas simply exploded.

"Do you realize what will happen when people hear Garth and Myron are gone? Jack, Rudy, why did you invest in the company? Was it because you believed in Garth and Myron or not? What's going to be the perception on the street if you guys decide to fire them now? The magic of this company is Garth and Myron. Get rid of them and watch the shares drop through the bottom of the market."

MCA was not, however, so easily defeated. The day went on for fourteen hours. My lawyers spent the time working out the lawsuit I intended to file against MCA if I was fired. When the board meeting was finally called, the first order of business was Joel Goldenberg's report on the loans. It was quite clear that, hard as Jack Richer tried to make Goldenberg say the loans were an offence for which Myron and I could be dismissed, the issue was far too complicated to be dealt with in such a summary manner.

But none of that really mattered. Looking around the boardroom table, I could tell from the faces of my colleagues that I was once again on the precipice.

*I stayed through it all. I put up with Sid's disdainful attacks. (From his behaviour at the meeting, no one could have believed that he later told Ted Pedas, "I felt betrayed. I loved Garth.") I put up with everything. I fought back. I just couldn't bring myself to let Cineplex Odeon go without a tenacious fight.*

I couldn't afford to show my anger. We had to come away with something. And we did: we were given until September 30 to raise enough money to buy the company. There were restrictions: for the first time, Myron and I had employment contracts with the proviso that we could resign or be dismissed on fifteen days' notice after the expiration of the term. Should that happen, we would receive payments of $3.5 million for Myron and $4.5 million for me. To keep me under ostensible control, an "office of the chairman" was set up, consisting of Skip, Jimmy Raymond, and me. Every material decision I might make over the next few months would be subject to challenge.

What occurred that day was a victory for MCA. Pamela Seymon of Wachtell Lipton derisively called the grace period a figleaf, and she was right. And as the meeting broke up around one o'clock in the morning, someone said to Skip Paul, "Well, you had to back off," and Skip said, "No, we got exactly what we wanted."

Myron and I left the building together and I said, "I feel unclean."

# CHAPTER

FABULOUS PHANTOM

The fight with my Cineplex Odeon partners was exhausting, but not so exhausting that I couldn't find some energy (left over from running a complicated company under the sceptical scrutiny of an increasingly hostile board) for the more creative side of my life. And so my next project pushed itself into my consciousness.

It had been during the first renovation of the Pantages into a single-screen movie theatre, from late 1986 to December 1987, that the transatlantic drums began to beat louder and more insistently for a gargantuan new musical by Andrew Lloyd Webber, *The Phantom of the Opera*, directed by Hal Prince, which had opened in London at Her Majesty's Theatre in October 1986.

All early indications were that *Phantom* would confirm Andrew's reputation as the most dominant composing force in the world of musical theatre. When it opened in London, it was to merely mixed or negative reviews. But it instantaneously soared to meteoric success.

Andrew had first burst onto the theatrical scene in 1968, when his pop cantata *Joseph and the Amazing Technicolor Dreamcoat*, written with Tim Rice, had captured the attention of the London critics. He went on to compose a remarkable series of popular musical hits including *Jesus Christ Superstar*, *Evita*, the 1981 blow-out success *Cats*, and *Starlight Express*.

There are other men of compelling genius in the theatre – Stephen Sondheim immediately comes to mind – but for the past quarter-century Andrew has been simply the hottest composer working in musical theatre. There was *A Chorus Line*, of course, which was a smash hit, but Andrew has otherwise been staggeringly omnipresent. Despite often lukewarm critical response, including sporadic allegations of plagiarism and of deriving musical ideas from such composers as Puccini, he single-handedly rescued musical theatre from the commercial stagnation in which it was then languishing on Broadway and in London's West End.

When I began my attempt to secure the Canadian rights to *Phantom*, *Cats'* international box-office gross had exceeded $1 billion U.S., more than two and a half times the North American gross of the movie blockbuster *E. T.* It made the box-office take of an Arnold Schwarzenegger action movie look like petty cash. By the spring of 1994 *Cats* was in its twelfth year on Broadway and was the most financially successful theatrical production in history, with an estimated box-office gross of $2 billion U.S.

I wasn't able to fly over to London to see *Phantom* for myself until January 1988. I sat in the back of the cramped stalls in Her Majesty's Theatre, my view of the stage partially obstructed by the awkward dress-circle overhang that blocked the famous chandelier effect. No matter. I was mesmerized by the ephemeral dream, the great love of a hideously disfigured composer for a beautiful young soprano. It's a marvellous rendering of the age-old tale of Beauty and the Beast, staged with precision and spectacular special effects by the legendary Mr. Prince.

The experience dazzled my senses and set my imagination on fire. And, remember, I was no longer the callow youth whose heart had been captured so effortlessly by Shirley MacLaine in *The Apartment*; I was now an experienced, knowledgeable theatregoer, my judgement honed over my fifteen years of seeing every major musical stage production of Western theatre – to say nothing of screening hundreds of movies every year. I regarded myself as a more-than-competent judge of what added up to box-office success, either on the stage or screen, and I knew at once that *Phantom* was the most entertaining work I had ever seen, the music, the emotion, and the cinematic flow of the staging all working in perfect harmony. If I, who can be so sceptical, could be so moved, for the average theatre patron who goes maybe twice a year, it had to be almost overpowering. As the audience stood and roared its approval, I became consumed with a burning ambition to bring the musical to Toronto – to stage the world's most spectacular show in the world's number-one theatre. After all, as Robert Browning wrote, "Ah, but a man's reach should exceed his grasp, or what's a heaven for?"

Indeed, for me this was the *only* show to open the Pantages; only *Phantom* would be grand enough for the theatre. It was perfect. I knew the public's perception of a theatre is influenced for years after it opens by what it chooses to present as its first attraction. For example, Toronto's O'Keefe Centre, despite its acknowledged imperfections, has always done surprisingly well at the box office, and one reason is that, when it opened in 1960, it was with a pre-Broadway production of the Lerner and Loewe classic *Camelot*, starring Richard Burton, Julie Andrews, and Canada's own Robert Goulet.

There was a footnote: I noted that evening at *Phantom* that the role of Christine was played by the ravishing Rebecca Caine, a Toronto-born soprano with a soaring voice. Years later I would have to deal with her recalcitrance and her bewildering mood swings; then, I just filed her performance in the back of my brain.

Back in Toronto, I heard that Tina Van der Heyden, who had been a co-producer with Marlene Smith of the two-year Toronto hit run of *Cats* at the Elgin Theatre, was trying to secure the Canadian rights to *Phantom*. I needed all the goodwill I could get with Andrew's company, the Really Useful Group (RUG), and I didn't want to drive the licensing fee up through further bidding. Since I had no prior relationship with either them or her, I decided to meet her. I had something no one else in Toronto had – a theatre that could handle the physical demands of *Phantom* and generate a weekly box-office gross of over $1 million. As I mentioned earlier, the O'Keefe Centre was consistently promised to the National Ballet Company and the Canadian Opera Company. Ed Mirvish had recently committed to Cameron Mackintosh to co-produce *Les Misérables* at the Royal Alexandra, but even if the Royal Alex had been free, it was too small to house the scale of *Phantom*'s design.

I arranged a meeting with Tina and asked her if we could join forces. "Look, where are you going to put it?" I said. "It's absurd to go after the rights to the show if you don't have a theatre." We reached an agreement.

I had one more serious obstacle: Cameron Mackintosh, an eminent theatrical figure and a man of very considerable achievements. He had already co-produced with RUG a number of productions of *Phantom*, including those in London and New York, and wanted badly to control the Canadian deal and the Canadian production, but he didn't have the Canadian rights. I understand from my London sources that Cameron made every effort in his meetings with RUG to denigrate me, despite the fact we had never met.

So how to get *Phantom* to Toronto for my wonderful theatre-to-be? Simple, really. Just convince Andrew Lloyd Webber and his associates to do business with me. Of course, I also had to convince my own board, with whom I was already in fractious and fretful argument over my handling of Cineplex Odeon, to go along.

I knew it would be difficult to contact Andrew personally. It was even difficult getting through to his executives. With all the support I had, and after repeated telephone calls to RUG, it wasn't until February 1988 that a meeting was finally set up.

By then a second production of *Phantom* had opened on Broadway, to an enormous advance sale of $18 million U.S. and featuring the original London leads – Michael Crawford and Sarah Brightman. New York greeted its arrival with levels of excitement and public hysteria rarely seen, even in the long and illustrious history of Broadway.

Andrew had first seen Sarah Brightman in the London company

of *Cats* and had been instantly mesmerized. Their romance flour-
ished as he wrote *Phantom*, giving credence to my theory that composers do their best work when they're in love, and he later married
her. However, by the time the Broadway production of *Phantom*
opened, the marriage was severely strained, the pressure augmented
by the hostility of U.S. Actors Equity towards allowing her to perform
in New York.

Off I flew to London and to RUG's corporate head office. I found
my way to Greek Street in the centre of London's West End theatre
district, where cabs have to crawl up on the sidewalks of narrow
streets to get by and quaint restaurants make up every second store-
front. RUG's offices were then squirrelled away on 20 Greek Street in
Soho, just up the street from the Palace Theatre on Cambridge Circus at the corner of Shaftesbury Avenue and Charing Cross Road.
(The illustrious theatre, built by Sir Richard D'Oyly Carte for the
presentation of Gilbert and Sullivan operettas in 1891, had been
bought by Andrew in 1983 and became the home of *Les Miz* in
December 1985.)

In a meeting room in RUG's second-floor boardroom, I unfurled
my plans to restore the Pantages and began my pitch to the assembled
executives. Among them was Brian Brolly, RUG's managing director,
a former MCA executive who had helped Andrew with the *Jesus Christ
Superstar* concept album when Andrew and Tim Rice were still
unknowns. Brian is a quiet, unobtrusive man, loaded with talent.
Keith Turner, RUG's lawyer, was also there. I had known him from the
foreign-sales aspect of the movie business. Finally, there was Biddy
Hayward, a longtime Lloyd Webber loyalist. Biddy was tough, cold,
and cynical; she simply assumed I was just another sycophant trying
to suck the blood of her beloved Andrew.

They listened politely. Clearly, though, they had no appreciation
of Toronto's potential. They didn't consider it a real theatre town.
*Cats*, for them, had just been a flash in the pan – an exception to the
rule. Still, they were willing to keep talking.

In one way my timing was perfect. True, Cameron Mackintosh
had been bad-mouthing me, but that was discounted by RUG because

Cameron was already in something of a conflict of interest; his focus was on *Les Misérables* and his forthcoming production of *Miss Saigon*, a musical by *Les Miz* composers Alain Boublil and Claude-Michel Schönberg, produced without RUG's involvement. I think Andrew resented this wandering allegiance, since at the time RUG had as its main priority the establishment of new territorial relationships for its productions. So this was a propitious time for me to obtain the Canadian rights to *Phantom*.

I came to the RUG meeting with full developmental plans and told them I could be ready by the fall of 1989. I was prepared to put up a $1-million advance, despite their scepticism about the reach of the Toronto market. This source of new cash flow appealed to RUG, whose public stock was then in the doldrums.

I was confident that my plans for the Pantages would impress the RUG executives – and they did.

Another propitious moment: As we were poring over the plans, I heard a door open and Andrew wandered in. I looked up, but he said nothing.

This was the first time I had seen him in person, and I noticed at once that his photos don't do him justice. What you usually see in the pictures is a skinny, chinless guy with wispy hair and an almost ostentatious absence of personality. In person, though, he has a real presence, marked by a perpetual air of confidence. He moves with a catlike delicacy, an impression enhanced by his slanted, soft brown eyes. I knew enough about him not to underestimate his feelings, which he kept under tight control. Many people had done so, to their later chagrin. They also tended to underestimate his business acumen. I would do neither.

In this first meeting he was detached and cool. I could almost hear his brain ticking away as he sized me up, carefully and deliberately. However, I got a glimpse of the passion underlying the dispassion when I saw his eyes light up at the Pantages' plans. By the time I left the office, I felt optimistic. Even Biddy Hayward was softening towards me.

Yet, irony of ironies, I don't know whether I would have secured the rights to the show without Sid Sheinberg's intervention. Sid had known Andrew from the early seventies, when MCA had produced Norman Jewison's film adaptation of *Jesus Christ Superstar*. I had of course filled Sid in on my plans, and he later told Andrew, who was in Hollywood negotiating the sale of the rights to the film of *Evita*, "I've never known anybody as crazed about doing anything as Garth Drabinsky is about doing *The Phantom*. You've got to support him."

I also had lobbying help from Bill Freedman, a dear friend of mine, who had been born in Toronto but was now a respected London theatre producer and owner.

I went to see him. "Bill," I said, "please tell Andrew about our long friendship. Make it clear to him that I'm a hard-working, committed producer and that I won't ever compromise the integrity of the production. All I need is the chance."

For what seemed a very long and nerve-racking time, I was kept in suspense.

By the end of March 1988 I closed the Pantages deal with Famous Players, even though I had no agreement for the rights to *Phantom* and therefore nothing to fill it with.

This was, I acknowledge, a ballsy move. Some people, in fact, might even call it flagrantly negligent, and though the Cineplex Odeon board didn't go that far, it certainly expressed reservations about becoming involved in live theatre. But the Pantages deal was a nicely calculated risk because the potential was so great. It was my one chance to secure the asset and I had to take it. Don't forget it was also a way of ending the feud with Martin Davis.

Throughout April and May of 1988 Brolly and I discussed the parameters of the deal, but it wasn't until June that we began to flesh out the material terms. I flew to London with my associate, Dan Brambilla, a leading New York theatrical attorney. I left him there and implored him not to leave until the deal had been inked.

I flew on to Israel, where I was to lead a group of Toronto Jews from the entertainment industry, keeping a promise to the United Jewish Appeal. It was my first visit.

I arrived in Jerusalem at four o'clock in the morning. Back in

London drafting was still going on, but for a while my worry and concern were banished in an overwhelming wash of five thousand years of Jewish history. As we drove through the Jerusalem night, with the cool, dry air fresh on my face and the sweet fragrance of flowers, lush, verdant gardens, and palm trees in the air, a tear trickled down my cheek. It happens to every Jew, I am told, arriving in Israel for the first time.

My guide, Victor Yagoda, asked me, "Where do you want to go?"

I paused, watching the famous honey-coloured Jerusalem limestone as the car passed the venerable buildings of Old Jerusalem, imprinted with thousands of years of grief and triumph. I shivered, sensing the press of the centuries, the millennia.

"The Wall," I answered.

We travelled through the meandering streets of Jerusalem, past mosques and churches, to the old city and finally to the Wailing Wall, bathed at that dawn hour in a golden light. I was mesmerized, and deeply touched, to see Jews there at that hour of the morning, *davening* in dozens of dialects, in front of that centuries-old symbol of Judaism. All through the next week I felt pulled between the extremes of one of the deepest emotional experiences of my life and the negotiations for a show I wanted dearly.

Finally we had a deal. At the end of the day we would retain 71 per cent of the profits and a significant gross participation for the rent of the Pantages. The deal meant we could recoup our investment within the first year. Thereafter, the cash flow from the theatre (restored at a cost of about $20 million) and the production would net $17 million annually for the foreseeable future, including profit from the show, rent, net operating expenses of the theatre, and contributions from merchandising, concessions, and corporate sponsorships. Considering that the original Toronto production, now in its sixth year, and the Canadian touring company, in its fourth year, have sold over 6.25 million tickets, generating about $425 million in revenues or almost 20 per cent of the musical's worldwide gross to date, the deal was – why not state it clearly? – a masterly stroke.

Soon after I closed the deal I bought out Tina Van der Heyden's position. She did all right: in addition to a healthy payout, she accepted an ongoing production credit, but in fact would have no further involvement whatsoever in the production of the show.

We still had a heavy schedule of work to do. A condition of the contract, signed in June 1988, was that the show must open by September 1989. This meant finishing the most complex theatre construction-and-restoration job ever attempted in Canada by the private sector within a time frame that was excruciatingly short, a little more than twelve months. The last three months would be spent moving in the physical components of – excuse another superlative but it's true – the most complicated theatrical production ever mounted on a Canadian stage to that time.

I had decided long ago that the Pantages was not going to undergo a mere renovation, but that we would restore the theatre to its early twentieth-century opulence with relentless, unswerving attention to detail.

The theatre had started its life in 1920 as a thirty-six-hundred-seat vaudeville house, designed by Thomas Lamb, the same theatrical architect who had designed the Elgin & Winter Garden theatres. The audiences of the time who flocked to it were as awestruck by its grandeur as those who visit it today. However, the restoration posed some problems: much of what had been beautiful about it had been destroyed by the clumsy way Mandel Sprachman had converted it into a sixplex in 1972, paying more regard to economy than elegance. The result was that many of the beautiful visual elements had been removed, destroyed, or painted over in raucously loud colours.

Luckily we were able to obtain Lamb's original drawings and other archival documents from New York's Columbia University. They aided our interpretation of the research findings we had accumulated from the partial refurbishment in 1987. A team of expert craftspeople began to refinish all that still existed of the theatre's original carved and gilded plasterwork and to recreate, from the drawings and photographs, all that had been destroyed.

On the functional side, the space was almost completely reconfig-
ured. The area under the orchestra seating was excavated a further
sixteen feet to accommodate dressing rooms, sound equipment, elec-
trical rooms, and other service areas. A fourteen-foot-deep trap room
was built under the stage floor to accommodate the mechanisms that
make possible some of *Phantom*'s more magical special effects. The
stage itself would have 190 trapdoors, many of them quite small, to
accommodate the glowing candles for the famous "lair" scene. An
orchestra pit for forty musicians was provided with an hydraulic lift,
permitting the musicians to play at any level required by the production. The stage tower was raised ten feet.

The highly effective Cineplex Odeon architectural-engineering-
construction team supervised a crew of 150 and put them on a fast-
tracking schedule. For example, the finishing trades concerned with
painting, gold-leafing, and marbleizing walls and ceilings were working busily on the site at the same time that heavy construction trades
were excavating, underpinning the foundations, and pouring concrete. The original palette of colours was carefully analysed so they
could be reproduced. Artist Srebrenka Bogovic-Zeskowski restored
two original murals, while another artist, Tony Philip, painted a new
(and less bowdlerized) version of the mural over the grand staircase.
The project design coordinator, Julia Strutt, even discovered a missing stained-glass window that had originally been set into an elaborate painted and gilded frame in a wall next to the grand staircase.
By chance, she noticed the missing window on display in a second-
storey window of a private townhouse while driving down a Toronto
residential street. The owners willingly agreed to return the window
in exchange for opening-night tickets to *Phantom*. Restored to its
original location, the window now serves as a focal point of the grand
staircase.

The theatre restoration well in hand, I turned my attention to the creative constituency of *Phantom*. In September 1988 I flew to New York
to meet the director, the remarkable Harold Prince. When I walked
into his office at 10 Rockefeller Center in the heart of Manhattan, I

was immediately reminded of entering Nat Taylor's office for the first time. Hal's shelves and walls were lined with memorabilia from his career, just as Nat's had been with movie mementos. I was also struck by how funny it was that Hal's name was even engraved in gold letters on his door.

I've met plenty of icons before, but Hal is without question the most-pleasant, least-assuming icon I've ever met in show business. I walked in expecting a huge ego. After all, Hal Prince is the most important musical-theatre creator of our lifetime and had been a Broadway producer and director for more than forty years – producing such Broadway classics as *Fiddler on the Roof, A Funny Thing Happened on the Way to the Forum, West Side Story, Damn Yankees*, and *The Pajama Game*. His musical directing credits included *Cabaret, Company, Follies, Pacific Overtures, Evita, Sweeney Todd*, and *A Little Night Music*. In his time he has collaborated with some of the most gifted talents in musical-theatre history, such as Stephen Sondheim, Jerome Robbins, Bob Fosse, and Michael Bennett, not to mention such stars as Angela Lansbury, Chita Rivera, Elaine Stritch, Len Cariou, and Joel Grey.

He was the quintessential Broadway director, a consummate manipulator of images, forever brimming excitedly with new ideas. That day, I found him sitting at his desk, glasses propped on his tanned, bald head, smiling. Later I learned that this was how he always appeared – unshakeable and in full control.

Hal's office was like *Phantom* Central, controlling the many productions being mounted all over the world. I wasn't a moment too soon. Hal was booked up with projects for a year and more, and, as he smilingly said, he took a lot of vacations in Europe. The fact that he always took three months off every summer, and six to eight weeks every winter, complicated my production schedule. But he had already agreed to make himself available to me for his usual "top and tailing" procedure. He would be in Toronto for the final casting, leave, and then return for the first day of rehearsals to introduce to the cast his *raison d'être* for the production; then he would come again when the cast went onstage in costume, and he would stay through previews until opening night. The rest of the work would be carried out by his longtime associate, the ever-flamboyant Ruth Mitchell, and by the impeccable choreographer Gillian Lynne.

We talked generally about the production, and I arranged for him to pay a three-hour visit to the Pantages construction site. We were four months into the project then. As we walked through the site, which still looked more like a bomb crater than a theatre, I knew he was worried. Concrete was being poured. There were hard hats everywhere. He laughed nervously and said, "Garth, it's going to be wonderful, but you're never going to get it finished on time."

I replied, with my usual enthusiasm and optimism, "It will be ready in eight months. I never miss an opening."

Hal said, "If you say so."

Later, I remember Hal reminiscing about that afternoon, how he saw the theatre at a stage when it was little more than an empty shell, but how he realized even then its enormous potential. He has always loved great theatres – he's a sucker for a pretty space. He acknowledged that, in spite of its size, the Pantages had a feeling of intimacy rarely found in theatres of its genre. He had already directed *Phantom* in London's Her Majesty's Theatre, in New York's Majestic Theater, and in Los Angeles' Ahmanson Theatre, but he soon came to believe that the Pantages would best serve the production.

*Phantom* is a baroque variation on the "backstage musical," in which the show must always go on. Hal's production, which recreates the opulent world of the Paris Opera House (including parodies of period operas such as the 1770s *Il Muto*), is a romantic fantasy, rooted in Hal's determination to reveal the Phantom's humanity, his normal, romantic urges and sexual longings that had become distorted by his physical deformity. Maria Björnson's design evoked sensuality with her use of curtains and her black-and-gold proscenium arch design of erotically cavorting neo-baroque nymphs, satyrs, and seraphs.

Yet the heart of *Phantom*'s staging goes back to Moscow's Taganka

Theatre and theatrical techniques derived from the early twentieth-century Soviet director, Vsevolod Meyerhold. Hal had visited the theatre in 1965 and been inspired by a political revue based on John Reed's pro-Bolshevik tract *Ten Days That Shook the World*, which used imaginative tricks and devices to evoke and suggest settings and scenes rather than recreate them in realistic detail.

Using black velour to create a "black box," Hal believed he could simply put a vivid prop on one section of a stage, leave the rest of it black, and the audience would fill in the rest for themselves.

Hal's *Phantom* is one of the greatest mirages of theatre. In reality it's a contained show, but it gives the feeling of immensity; it is full of tricks and illusions, but as Hal often said to me, "It's when to use them, and how, that surprises and overwhelms."

In addition to Hal Prince, all the remaining original creative team, including designer Maria Björnson, sound designer Martin Levan, lighting designer Andrew Bridge, choreographer Gillian Lynne, and music supervisor David Caddick, had agreed to come on board.

But what about my star performers? When I had seen the show in London, as I mentioned, the female lead was played by Rebecca Caine who, *mirabile dictu*, was Toronto-born and -raised. Surely, I thought, she would welcome the chance to return home to Canada to critical acclaim? Her agent was so enthused by this prospect that he didn't even return my calls. As far as he was concerned, Rebecca was about to commit to starring in a West End revival of *Carousel*, and that was that. Nevertheless, I still wanted to cast her. I was, as usual, persistent.

In September I was on my way to the Venice Film Festival, where *Madame Sousatzka* was in competition. I decided to stop in London, and, from my room at the Inn on the Park, I called Rebecca at home, where she was bedridden with the flu.

"You don't know me," I said, "but I'm from Toronto and I'm going to produce *Phantom* there. I'm leaving for the Venice Film Festival in five hours, and if you don't get over here to meet with me, you're going to miss the opportunity of a lifetime."

After a lot of whining, she reluctantly got dressed and arrived, pouting, at my hotel. After listening to my pitch for an hour, she was still not quite persuaded. She said she needed the weekend to think about it. I said I would call her Sunday night. When I did, she said yes.

Following the Venice festival I flew directly to Dublin to meet with Colm Wilkinson, the honey-voiced Irish tenor with an extraordinary two-and-a-half-octave range who had starred as Jean Valjean in the original London Royal Shakespeare Company and New York productions of *Les Misérables*. I believe Colm to be musical theatre's greatest tenor, and I had already pre-cleared casting him with Andrew and Hal Prince. Colm had also been Andrew's first choice to portray the Phantom, but was unavailable at the time, having already signed to do *Les Miz*. Nevertheless, Andrew had invited Colm down to his annual summer festival at his estate at Sydmonton, in Hampshire, west of London, where the *Phantom* project was first unveiled.

Colm is renowned for his 100-per-cent commitment to his work and for his constant search for the essential truth of a character. Even in this one-hour, one-act workshop version at Andrew's theatre in an old church, complete with makeshift set and primitive chandelier, Colm was totally absorbed. He had been given a real axe with which to cut loose the chandelier, and he got totally carried away, chopping and hacking off bits from the historic church's wooden beams. Splinters, dust, bits of wood flew into the air and audience; a huge chunk of wood hit a man who stood up, screaming. Ironically, he was the show's prospective insurance agent. The Phantom had his first victim.

Andrew was so impressed by the verisimilitude of Colm's performance that, during the car ride back to London, he turned to him and said, "You must forget this French revolution nonsense and do my play!"

Strangely, however, Andrew had first recommended Sammy Davis, Jr., to me as the Phantom. Andrew had flown with Liza Minnelli to Monte Carlo and had seen Sammy sing "Music of the Night" there and had been knocked out by his performance. I wasn't swayed in the least. "Save him for the first U.S. national touring company," I retorted.

I met Colm at Dublin airport. Over smoked salmon, I dangled an irresistible (meaning $1 million-plus) offer in front of him. I told Colm he and his family would fall in love with Toronto and assured him that the Toronto production would be world class. When we parted company, I had the basis of an agreement with him. With a little more long-distance negotiating, he was signed. The West End and Broadway's loss was Toronto's gain.

For the third lead, the romantic leading man, I was delighted to sign Byron Nease, an American who had a strong voice and convincing acting skills.

But for the rest I was determined that the production would be all-Canadian. Auditions were held in Toronto, Montreal, Vancouver, Edmonton, and Calgary. To the surprise and delight of both the creative team and myself, we were overwhelmed with exceptional Canadian singers, dancers, and musicians. This and other recent casting experiences have made me proclaim to theatre professionals around the world, with confidence, that Canada has a talent pool that ranks favourably with any. True, it becomes diluted when many productions are competing for the same performers. Musical theatre is still relatively new in Canada. We can't always expect to hire a completely Canadian cast, because the truth is there aren't that many well-trained and experienced triple-threat performers: people who can act, sing, and dance at equal levels of greatness.

This is changing. Some of the Canadians who were originally cast in the chorus of *Phantom* have, over the past five years, as we've gained confidence in the breadth of their capacity, progressed through the company to take on leading roles. For example, opera singer Glenda Balkan, who was originally hired as a chorus member, came to perform the role of Christine in the Toronto and Canadian companies.

*Some things don't change, though. One of them is the constant, inflexible, and interminable capacity of the cultural nationalists (many*

*of them members of the press) and the collectivist mentality to criticize*
*my casting of non-Canadians – anywhere and in any role.*

*This drives me absolutely crazy.*

*Do they know how many Canadian actors I've employed? Do they*
*know, or care, how many other jobs I've brought to the Canadian thea-*
*tre, how many musicians, costumers, sound, set, and lighting designers,*
*how many stagehands, and on and on I have employed over the years?*
*Do they know how much money I've brought into Canadian theatre? Do*
*they care how many buildings I've built and restored? Do they care how*
*many bums I've put into seats?*

*Crazy. They drive me crazy. They are absolutely beneath contempt.*

I was now assured that I had assembled the elements of a production
that would do us all proud, and I could move on toward meeting my
next objective – selling *Phantom* to the public. You may have on your
hands the best theatrical product ever produced, but it'll be gone in
an instant if you can't find ways to let the public know it exists.

I've also learned that filling the seats for an open-ended run is
much different from filling them just for a limited two- to three-week
engagement. It calls for an unremitting effort, comparable to that
involved in selling a product like toothpaste or a soft drink, a product
that you hope will be around for years.

*Effective marketing, in my opinion, is skilfully implanting in the*
*public's mind a strong sense that an extraordinary event is taking*
*place in their midst, one that they simply must attend to fulfil their cul-*
*tural lives.*

From day one our marketing strategy involved intensive mul-
timedia advertising campaigns to capture and retain consumer
attention, building upon the success already achieved by Dewynters,
RUG's British advertising agency. Dewynters' challenge had been to
create a campaign that would appeal to the widest possible market
worldwide, unhampered by any cultural references or language bar-
riers. As well, the show's visual identity, or "geo-logo" as Dewynters
calls it, had to be simple, representative, and dramatic enough to be

marketable in various types of merchandise to the primary European and North American market and secondary markets around the world, a strategy known as integrated packaging. Their success was undeniable; the Phantom's mask is the most successful mark in musical-theatre history.

At the outset, Anthony Goldschmidt, one of the great advertising minds of Hollywood, created four movie trailers for *Phantom* to be screened a year in advance of our opening, at all our Cineplex Odeon theatres throughout Canada. To coincide with opening night, our inhouse audio/visual department produced, in partnership with the CBC, a one-hour TV documentary special about *Phantom*, entitled "Behind the Mask," which featured backstage interviews and highlights of the evolution of this thrilling production.

To create and maintain top-of-mind awareness, we varied our creative elements.

I kept cross-pollinating ideas from my movie experience, which made me somewhat different from anyone else working in theatre. I brought back ideas from the old roadshow movies. I even used mail-order advertising. In later years I used colour in our daily newspaper ads. I changed our ads weekly to keep them fresh and to focus on different market segments – by now we've produced more than four hundred newspaper ads, a dozen TV commercials, and more than a hundred radio spots for *Phantom*. Our radio advertising was especially effective, largely because of the resonant voice of actor Graeme Campbell as the Phantom. His stentorian tone pierced through the radio clutter to deliver our message. We recorded more than eighty radio commercials with him and continue to use them to this very day. Two years after his untimely death from cancer, his voice is still heard and will be as long as *Phantom* continues to play in Canada.

All marketing has to be in tune with the prevailing *zeitgeist*. In times of recession, when the public is fretful, and in times of political uncertainty (the unnerving constitutional debate in Canada, events like Desert Storm in the United States), advertising campaigns must stress the themes of romance, fantasy, and escape. On the other hand, in times of public exuberance and robust economic expansion, the advertiser can move back to the hard sell. All our advertising was sensitive to these shifts in public mood. For much of my advertising and design work I've used Lenny Gill's Echo Advertising and Scott Thornley, whose design sensibilities I've learned to trust over the years.

Other innovations were introduced as well. Pepsi billboards in downtown Toronto would have a plain white surface during the day with the Phantom's mask in the corner. At night the sign would transform itself to black with glowing shattered-glass typeface letters saying "The Phantom of the Opera." A multifaceted educational program was developed to introduce our future audiences, at an early age, to the unique experience of live theatre. A year after the opening, I produced a music video of the title song to support sales of the original Canadian cast recording. I used segments of the video in subsequent TV commercials.

*Phantom*'s promotional value was enhanced and its revenue stream extended by marketing a broad range of merchandise associated with the production, much broader than the norm for such shows. In addition to the customary T-shirts, souvenir programs, posters, and cast albums, *Phantom* also spawned paperweights, musical dolls, glow-in-the-dark underwear, a pop-up book with a microchip that plays the Phantom's theme, papier-mâché masks, beach towels, and winegum candy in the shape of a mask. A popular souvenir is The Phantom Magic Mug, a black ceramic mug on which the famous mask, painted in heat-sensitive ink, eerily appears when hot liquid is poured into it. There was Phantom-inspired perfume and jewellery, including an Angel of Music brooch, replicating the sculpture on the proscenium arch, and even chandelier earrings.

Because the Pantages was still under construction, and in keeping with the spirit of *Phantom*, we created Midnight Madness: at midnight one freezing January 1989 night we opened a temporary box office, decorated with seductive curtains and candelabras in keeping with the design of the show, and for the first time began selling single tickets. The concept captured the public's imagination, and *Phantom* went on to set, by opening night, a new worldwide record box-office advance of $23.8 million. To this date it has only been exceeded by the New York productions of *Sunset Boulevard* and *Miss Saigon.*

I knew demand in southern Ontario would be strong throughout year one. But I was determined to do everything I could to keep sales at capacity into the second year and well beyond. That's when I realized Toronto's enormous potential as a commercial theatre centre. Toronto is not what one might call an automatic destination for tourists, unlike New York and London, which benefit from an elaborate and aggressively promoted tourist infrastructure – thousands of hotel rooms, numerous theatres and night clubs, world-famous dining rooms and bars, giving them a multiplicity of attractions for tourists who flock to the city without a second thought. In many ways the Toronto experience is antithetical to the West End and Broadway, so we had to sell Toronto as a destination. Also, I had a much larger theatre to fill than those in New York or London. The Pantages is 50 per cent larger than the Majestic in New York and 80 per cent larger than Her Majesty's in London. We had all the disadvantages without the advantages. We had a particular marketing challenge.

So I decided to take advantage of the fact that, within a two-hundred-and-fifty-mile radius of Toronto – including American cities such as Detroit, Cleveland, Pittsburgh, Buffalo, Rochester, and Syracuse – lives a population of about twenty million people, many of whom are willing to travel to Toronto to see a first-run production of a major musical rather than wait many years for a hit Broadway production to come to their city. There have never been home-grown versions of these shows in their cities, and they were markets ripe for the picking. Today, half of *Phantom*'s audiences come from the border states of Ohio, Michigan, and New York.

Against formidable odds, the Pantages restoration was completed within the requisite twelve months. And on July 5, 1989, more than two months before opening night, we received our first rave review: the Architectural Conservancy of Toronto Region gave me its Award of Merit for the purchase and renewal of the Pantages Theatre and for restoring and returning to future generations a landmark that would not otherwise have been preserved. My dynamic team of theatre architect David Mesbur and project manager and engineer Peter Kofman were also, quite rightly, honoured for their work.

*The honour was a vindication in the same way the whole Pantages restoration experience was a lifesaver for me. It also took my mind off the dreadful, day-to-day misery of those last nine months of tension at Cineplex Odeon. I was in the crucible of a $1.3-billion U.S. buyback, harassed constantly by the board's special committee, facing the indignation and outright hostility of MCA, hounded by the press, and either harassed or ignored by the investment bankers.*

*Often, at three or four o'clock in the morning, I would put on a hard hat and wander through the work site, watching the gilders at work, or the plasterers shaping their creations, or the carpenters putting together the intricate and splendid detailing. I love good craftspeople; I was happy to be among competent people doing work they loved. Watching them work, I knew my vision was right.*

The three-week technical period of the show was fraught with trouble. I was shaking down not only an operating crew of forty but a huge front-of-house staff for the Pantages. To tackle my first big assignment as a theatrical producer with a large musical, an intricate musical, and to open a new theatre at the same time. . . . It's sort of like opening a hotel and inviting all the fancy people of the world to stay there on opening night and wondering whether the elevators are going to work.

*I remember, a few days before the opening, Hal coming to me, distraught.* Phantom *works everywhere in the world but in Toronto, he moaned. I'm finished! He threw his hands up in the air and went gloomily back to his hotel room.*

All the previews were rocky. For example, the first-act journey to the Phantom's lair across a subterranean lake, one of the most stunning, imaginative, and memorable scenes in musical-theatre history, has, as an essential part of it, a radio-controlled boat that transports the Phantom and Christine. A propertyman in the wings uses a hand-held control to guide the boat through the fog and candelabras.

However, during the rehearsals the boat used to run wild, crashing into candelabras or the front of the stage. The problem, we found, was not the ghost in the machine but radio interference from passing ambulances and police cars and other vehicles outside the Pantages on Victoria Street. To solve the problem, the crew sought a dedicated frequency and switched to a totally encoded/decoded system, so that the boat could not respond to anything except the signal coming from its controller. Soon, we were licensed for the required frequency.

*But of course, everything was as smooth as silk on opening night.*

*And the première of the Fabulous* Phantom, *on September 20, 1989, a gala benefit for Toronto's Mount Sinai Hospital, was a night Toronto would long remember.*

Crowds bursting with excitement lined up outside the Pantages Theatre to see the first-nighters. Victoria Street was closed to through traffic. Celebrities and dignitaries began arriving, among them Olympic-gold-medallist figure skater Katarina Witt and Grammy Award-winning record producer David Foster. Andrew Lloyd Webber flew to Toronto in his private jet, bringing with him Prince Edward, who was working as a production assistant at RUG. Pearl and I took our seats. So did my board. So did Hal. So did Andrew.

From the first crashing Grand Guignol chromatic chords of *Phantom*'s theme, the atmosphere inside the theatre was electric. I watched anxiously, but the radio-controlled boat worked perfectly. Even the chandelier crashed on the exact musical phrase. The performance was magnificent, and when the final curtain came down, the audience leapt to their feet in enthusiastic applause. But my proudest moment of all was when Andrew, Hal, and I were called onto the stage.

*At that moment I wanted to forget the ugliness I was going through with the Cineplex Odeon board. I wanted to bask in the crowd's thunderous ovation, for it was obvious I had been right – my risk had paid off. I had brought off a double triumph: a mighty artistic success and the establishment of a whole new area for our company, one of incredible commercial potential. Yet, as I saw the expressions on the faces of the members of my board in the audience, Skip, Jack, and the others, it was* clear to me they just didn't care. I knew they secretly hoped the reviews the next day would be terrible.

The louder the audience cheered, the greater the anger that welled up in each one of them as they hungered vainly for my failure.

Well, my career as chairman of Cineplex Odeon was almost at an end. But I had forged two entirely new partnerships, one with the musical works of Andrew Lloyd Webber and the other with the artistry of Hal Prince.

That was my future.

I looked down at the stamping, cheering, clapping crowds.

The goddamn board could wait until tomorrow. I was busy.

# CHAPTER

## Cineplex Adieu

I should have been gone from Cineplex Odeon on May 15. Why did I stay on?

*Phantom* had something to do with it. MCA and the Bronfmans needed me to finish the restoration of the theatre and launch *Phantom.* They knew no one else would be able to do the job; I was to be their pawn.

*And me? I, too, wanted to protect* Phantom *and the theatre – from them.*

I was also there because I never give up without a fight, and I still believed I could raise the money to buy the company. So did Myron. But he and I were going to have to raise between $1.3 billion and $1.4 billion U.S. in a deteriorating economy (the roaring eighties were over and the bottom had fallen out of the junk-bond market, which up to that point could have provided interim financing). If we had succeeded, we would have pulled off what would have been the biggest leveraged buyout in Canada's history.

MCA was totally in control of the process. It had insisted on setting up a special committee to evaluate bids for the company. Morgan Stanley & Co. and the Canadian investment banking firm, RBC Dominion Securities, were engaged as advisers to this committee. Both firms were highly regarded in the financial community, but the people they assigned to act as "experts" in this field were absolutely pathetic – callow, completely lacking in knowledge of the entertainment industry in general and the exhibition of motion pictures in particular. In the ensuing months, they would spend an inordinate amount of time and effort taking the company's money and persuading the committee of their own brilliance and effectiveness.

The special committee is an idea imported from the United States. It's meant to be a panel of disinterested directors of the company in play. Its job is to ensure that shareholders get the highest possible price for their shares; it's also a board's first line of defence against a class-action suit by shareholders.

Among Cineplex Odeon's directors, there was only one who could fairly be described as truly disinterested – Ted Pedas. So obviously fair was Ted that even MCA felt obliged to pick him. But then they packed the committee with three of their own directors, as well as the three Bronfman directors. So the six included, of course, the irritant, Skip Paul, and his counterpart, the unpleasant Jack Richer, my two most unyielding critics. No wonder we soon came to call it the "special special committee." We should have realized then that it was game over; instead, we only slowly, painfully discovered that MCA was not going to let us succeed, no matter how attractive our proposal would be.

Leveraged buyouts, or LBOs, came to have a bad name, but they began as a perfectly respectable way of restructuring companies to realize the maximum value of their assets. In a classic LBO, a shell company of investors would buy out the shares of the target company, using mainly borrowed money, restructure it, and, by selling assets, pay off as much debt as possible. Then, typically, the revitalized company would be taken public again with the contributed equity of the takeover group being marked up, based on a generous multiple of projected earnings.

The LBO resembled a totem pole of financing. The buyer put up 10 per cent of the capital required, raised 60 per cent from the banks, using the company's assets as collateral, and obtained the remaining and crucial 30 per cent in the form of a short-term high-interest bridge loan. In the early eighties the raising of that final 30 per cent was dicey. Cash-rich companies like insurance companies were the best places to apply for it, but they took their own good time assessing the risks, and timing played an important part in a successful take-over when a company was already known to be in play and open to the highest bid.

Not until 1985 was this timing problem that affected all LBOs really solved. That was the year Michael Milken, a New York bond trader with the firm of Drexel Burnham Lambert, created a bond that was the perfect tool for the leveraged buyout. The junk bond, as it was derisively called, was an instrument of awesome simplicity. An investment bank would come up with the mezzanine layer of financing and then turn around and sell subordinated bonds in the company at very high interest rates. The bank, moreover, collected a handsome fee for the effort. As the cost of LBOs soared, so did bankers' fees. For the $23.5-billion U.S. LBO of RJR Nabisco in late 1988, the bankers picked up overall compensation of more than $1 billion U.S.

Financing a bid is very expensive, and a client must pay at each stage of the process. A bank may say, "We believe we can provide you with $50 million U.S., but if you need a brief letter that says we're interested, in order to show evidence that your money is in order, you'll have to put up a holding fee today." Then the bank has to perform its own due diligence before deciding whether it will make a firm commitment. That costs more in fees. When the bank has finished its investigation and is ready to commit, that firm commitment costs still more money. When the bank finally advances its loan, it deducts a final whack of fees and expenses.

On May 15 Myron and I reached an agreement with the board that it would reimburse us for up to $5 million in financing expenses – but only if we made a cash offer to all shareholders of $17.50 a share. We already knew that the $17.50 we had been prepared to offer the Bronfmans was inappropriate; it was a premium offer for a pivotal control block and initially was for only 7.3 million shares, later reduced to 5.8 million, representing the five largest selling shareholders.

So now Myron and I, along with Robert Topol, our incisive and proficient numbers-analyst, really got down to the chore of tearing apart Cineplex Odeon's assets to determine what they really would be valued at for financing purposes.

There were about 50 million shares outstanding in Cineplex Odeon. Fifty times $17.50 came to $875 million, which converted at the time to $743 million U.S. When the company debt of $590 million U.S. was added, along with the bankers' and lawyers' fees, the total came very close to $1.4 billion U.S.

But the value of the assets fell short of that amount. By our reckoning, the U.S. circuit could be sold for $850 million U.S. It broke down this way: the New York and New Jersey theatres, the prime asset, were projected at $400 million U.S., Chicago and Minnesota at between $100 million U.S. to $125 million U.S., Los Angeles at $125 million U.S., the Seattle/Northwest theatres at $100 million U.S. to $110 million U.S., Washington, D.C., at between $50 million U.S. to $60 million U.S., and the southeastern theatres for around $65 million U.S.

The rest of the assets came to $400 million U.S.. They included $250 million U.S. for the live-entertainment division (including the Pantages) and the Canadian circuit, $20 million U.S. for the U.K. circuit, $80 million U.S. for the residual interest in Universal Studios, Orlando, and other miscellaneous real estate, and $50 million U.S. for the remaining 49 per cent of Film House.

Together, it all totalled $1.25 billion U.S.. That is, in a perfect world, with no margin for error.

We knew that the sale of the assets might take a year to eighteen months; in the meantime, interest on the primary debt would mount, not to mention the interest on the junk bonds that would be needed to top off the financing.

So once again we sought out the calming, rational advice of Roy Furman, who had so often advised us in circuit acquisitions. While Jack Richer, showing a complete lack of common sense, was boasting all over the street that he expected bids of $20.00 a share (Cineplex Odeon shares were then selling for only $16.00!), Roy urged us not to overreach and not to be misled by the bombastic emanations from any member of the committee. We established that a correct bid for all the shares should be $14.50 cash, plus a $2.00 note for each. The total cash cost to us, including the assumption of all Cineplex Odeon debt, would be about $1.2 billion U.S.

It was do-able, but tight. Or tight, but do-able.

To begin, we needed to solidify our first tranche of equity. Jack Daniels and Rudy Bratty may have wavered briefly at the May 15 meeting, but they seemed prepared to continue to support our efforts, so we went to them. Still, they cut themselves out of the detailed negotiations for conflict-of-interest reasons (they already each owned large Cineplex Odeon positions) and turned over the hashing out of the details to another Erin Mills partner, Larry Robbins. I hadn't met Larry before, but he turned out to be a really warm guy. We needed $200 million U.S. in equity and asked Erin Mills to put up two-thirds, with Myron and me filling in the remaining third.

"No," said Larry, "$180 million will do it. We'll put up two-thirds of a hundred eighty."

He loved that figure, one hundred and eighty. Larry is a religious Jew who observes the Sabbath faithfully; he also prefers, indeed often insists on, basing deals on the magic number eighteen and its multiples. (When written in Hebrew, eighteen means life.) He had parlayed this eccentricity into a deal-clincher in all sorts of situations. With great good humour, he insisted that, for its $120 million U.S. of equity, the group should be given 54 per cent of the new corporate entity to be formed (eighteen times three, naturally), which was later reduced to 51 per cent. We were going to put the final third, or $60 million U.S., in place through a combination of a rollover of our own Cineplex Odeon shares, merchant-banking sources like Ned Goodman's DCC equities, and $20 million U.S. from some of the constituents of the original buyout group, including Gordon Capital, Alfred Taubman, Nat Taylor, and financier Joe Rotman.

Erin Mills' terms were stiff. For their equity of $120 million U.S., they insisted on an onerous shareholders' agreement, giving them a majority of seats on the board, and they wrote in provisions that would put a lot of pressure on Myron and me to meet the expected financial tests. That meant they would always be in the driver's seat. But I was willing to go along because of their simple and decent approach to business: they operated on a verbal commitment and a handshake; we had known them almost ten years and they had never crossed us.

The bulk of the financing, $850 million U.S., would have to come from the banks. There were only two banks in Canada with any real experience in the entertainment business, the Toronto Dominion, which had actively financed the cable industry, most notably Rogers Communications, and the Bank of Nova Scotia. The latter had joined a consortium of Cineplex Odeon bankers in 1987. Obviously, in light of our history with the TD, we favoured the Bank of Nova Scotia. In protracted discussions with Bruce Birmingham, then head of corporate banking at Scotiabank, and Peter Godsoe, then vice-chairman (and now its CEO), we received a letter of intent for $370 million U.S.

Of the U.S. banks we considered, we finally settled on Bankers' Trust, which gave us its letter for $380 million U.S. in late June. The only problem was that Bankers' Trust's terms didn't mesh very well with Scotiabank's. Bankers' Trust viewed the deal as a one-year bridge, whereas Scotiabank saw it more as an ongoing relationship over a reasonable workout period. But we were sure we could reconcile these differences into an arrangement satisfactory to all parties.

When we added up the equity and bank financing, we were $250 million U.S. shy of financing our $14.50 cash plus $2.00 note offer. We were going to have to resort to junk bonds to resolve the shortfall.

But by June the fallout from the Wall Street scandals was already affecting the marketplace. The previous December Drexel Burnham Lambert, the junk-bond kings, had been charged with illegal trading, and in March Michael Milken had been charged as well. In Canada the foremost junk-bond banker was Vancouver's First City Trust, and in late May Myron flew out to talk to First City's Sam Belzberg, who was an old friend. Belzberg agreed to take up $125 million U.S., but only if Drexel or Bankers' Trust was the other participant and, on behalf of both parties, would handle the necessary due diligence.

But Drexel was dragging its feet. By June there was growing concern over Robert Campeau's inability to pay the enormous debts he incurred in his junk-bond-driven takeovers of Allied Stores in 1987 and Federated Stores in 1988. Drexel itself wouldn't provide the bridge until the junk was placed and would only give us a "highly confident letter." For this they wanted their customary fee upfront, and we, in turn, would have to rely on their best efforts.

All of our debt financing would be considered soft until each of these segments could be unequivocally locked in. The upfront fees required would be in the neighbourhood of $10 million U.S.

What a bind! Since it was a condition of our equity players that they would not bridge any financing fees until they were certain that $14.50 plus $2.00 would be accepted by the special committee, for the time being, at least, we would have to rely on our own resources.

Myron and I soldiered on. By now we had an army of advisers, lawyers, and investment bankers. As a matter of routine each Saturday morning, in the Cineplex Odeon boardroom, we conducted strategy sessions over hot Kiva's bagels and cream cheese. The talent included Roy Furman and his colleagues, Brian Freedman and David Harris, Jon Levin of Fasken Campbell Godfrey, and Gar Emerson, then of Davies Ward & Beck and now chairman of Rogers Communications and head of the Rothschild Bank of Canada. There were also three lawyers from Weill Gotschal & Menges, a leading New York law firm in mergers and acquisitions.

On June 16 the annual general meeting took place at our Varsity Theatre. Sid Sheinberg arrived with Skip Paul a step behind, whispering in his ear like a courtier.

The meeting was a fine example of the theatre of the absurd. The Varsity was packed, and while the shareholders were pretty quiet, the press was in full cry. Much was made of the fact that I was accompanied by security guards. The press said it was to defend myself from shareholders. In fact, the shareholders were quiet and attentive; the guards were to defend me from the press, which was now treating me like a mediagenic rock star. Any other time I could have dealt with the attention – but not this day.

By comparison, the proceedings were mundane. Jimmy Raymond gave an inconclusive-but-factual report on the activities of the special committee. Then Jack Richer and Sandra Kolber took the floor. Both were carried away by the unaccustomed media attention and pro-jected all kinds of exaggerated notions about their expectations for share prices; they raised the phantom of "unidentified bidders for Cineplex Odeon." Myron and I had difficulty keeping our mouths shut.

Our strategy was to wait until after the meeting and then promptly deliver a letter to the special committee, stating that we were prepared to buy all outstanding shares for $14.50 cash, plus a $2.00 promissory note, and stating further that, if this were accept-able, we would make the offer firm within ten days. We intended by this to squeeze the special committee to truly act "in the interests of all of the shareholders," to use the phrase MCA put to the Quebec Securities Commission.

*There's no doubt in my mind even now that we would have been able to close the deal on this basis sometime in July if the special committee had been, as it claimed, trying to get the best deal for the shareholders, instead of pursuing MCA's hidden agenda to thwart us.*

Instead of telling us to firm up our offer, the committee continued their little gavotte with the phantom buyers. "How can we be sure," it asked, "that there aren't a lot of other people out there waiting to make a bid? We have to give the same specific information you already have to all prospective buyers, so everyone is playing on a level field."

*More of the stall. More bullshit.*

The committee decided to put the company up for auction and take bids for it, either as a whole or for all its parts.

And then it twisted the knife a little more. "At less than a $17.50 all-cash bid," the committee told us, "we can't undertake to reimburse you for expenses, because we'd be favouring you over other bidders."

We were effectively stymied. The "process" had to run its course before we were given any money to allow us to make a bid! It should have known – it must have known, in spite of all its posturing and blustering – that we were the only real contenders. So there was no reason for this except to cut us off.

In the meantime, conditions in the money markets were conspicuously deteriorating with each passing day.

The auction was patently harmful to the company. The freedom-of-information policy so piously announced by the special committee meant that anyone off the street could be supplied with complete financial data on Cineplex Odeon, no matter how confidential it might be or how much it would hurt the company if it ended up in the hands of our competition.

The Mirvishes, our main Toronto competition in legitimate theatre, had no serious interest in buying any of Cineplex Odeon's divisions, but lost no time in applying for, and being given, complete information on all aspects of our live-entertainment division's production of *The Phantom of the Opera*, including artists' contracts, union agreements, running expenses, sponsorship agreements, suppliers' contracts, service contracts, and all sorts of information that companies don't voluntarily make available to their competition.

This wasn't the end of the special committee's destructive actions. It directed, for instance, that bonuses totalling $2 million Cdn be offered to a chosen list of employees for cooperation in the process, especially in assisting any prospective purchaser other than Myron and me. Of course, people like Dick Roberts, Lynda Friendly, and Robert Topol were considered corrupted by their attachment to me and were not approached, but Jerry Banks was. With his usual impeccable propriety, Jerry helped where he could, but refused the money.

This bribing of executive personnel caused a deep schism in the company. Employees naturally thought their future was threatened unless they chose the winning side. This was reprehensible. As summer wore on, it became more and more obvious that Allen Karp had become Skip Paul's messenger boy. He was leaking things I told him to Skip. I knew this because Skip would then pass the information back to me.

In August I finally called Allen, who was somewhere sailing on Lake Ontario, and suggested lunch. I reminded him somewhat pointedly that his position at the company, his place on the board, was due entirely to me.

I put it to him bluntly. "Where's your allegiance, Allen? Are you with me, or not?"

He kept his eyes downcast and didn't answer.

I suspected then that the idea of succeeding me as head of Cineplex Odeon had been dangled before him, and that visions of a glamorous Hollywood-style existence were dancing in his head. The temptation was clearly too much for whatever loyalty he might have felt toward me. Proof that he had already sold me out was not long in coming. Within days Skip Paul was accusing me of attempting to influence Allen's vote as a member of the Cineplex Odeon board.

After refusing to deal with our offer of June 26, the special committee first set July 15, then August 2, then August 15, and finally September 14 as the deadline by which all offers must be made.

*What offers?*

I wanted to scream. It had long ago become obvious, even to the committee, that we were the only bidders. During all those long, nerve-racking weeks, there was not one serious offer, not even a believable rumour of a serious offer.

Meanwhile Myron and I were scouring North America for money. The intent was to create a new financing model without using junk bonds. To reduce our reliance on substantial long-term primary bank lending, we would liquidate chunks of assets immediately after the purchase of the company. These asset sales would be firmly in place at the time of any offer we made to the shareholders.

Donald Trump, our landlord for Cinema III in New York's Plaza Hotel, was one possible buyer. The day we met him in his opulent-but-garish office high up in the Trump Tower in Manhattan, he hardly seemed to hear me as I pitched the sale of our New York circuit. He was completely distracted, and no wonder; his casino, his marriage, and his real-estate empire were only months from crumbling.

Another was Stanley Gold, a Hollywood entertainment lawyer whose partner in Shamrock Holdings was Roy Disney, Jr., Walt's nephew. Stanley had a big reputation as an honest broker. He had brought Michael Eisner and Frank Wells (who died in 1994 in a helicopter crash while skiing in Nevada) to the Disney studio, where their turnaround of that company's fortunes became a legend. We discussed the sale of the entire U.S. circuit to Shamrock, but we couldn't get together on the price. Stanley held the line at $700 million U.S., while we knew we couldn't accept less than $850 million U.S.

The high-flying (and later incarcerated) Italian, Giancarlo Paretti, finally took time out from his deluded pursuit of MGM to talk with us. A few weeks earlier Dino De Laurentiis had called me to make the introduction. Paretti had already bought Cannon Pictures from the Israeli-based team of Golan and Globus, which included the prestigious ABC–EMI theatre circuit in Britain. He was supposed to have access to limitless funds from undeclared sources.

Paretti was hard to pin down, but we finally caught up with him in Toronto's Sutton Place Hotel, where he offered to buy the whole company for a vast-but-as-yet-unspecified sum. I had to tell him that Investment Canada would never allow it! Then he said he would pay $900 million U.S. for the U.S. and U.K. circuits, if the New York brokerage house of Bear Stearns would support the purchase with the issue of an entirely unrealistic level of junk bonds. By then I knew he was operating in a fool's paradise; the more I pressed him for details, the less forthcoming he was, and his offers went up, down, and sideways. Later, when he actually succeeded in buying MGM, the studio's bankers, Credit Lyonnaise, found him to be such a flake that they forced him in short order to step down as CEO.

Frank Wells, the president and the paternal influence at Disney, was a bona fide MCA hater. Wells, I thought, would be likely to come up with an offer for the U.S. circuit if anyone did, just to get it out of the clutches of MCA. After a lot of discussion, however, the plan foundered on a conflict of interest. Disney's contract with its own Silver Screen film-financing vehicle restricted the studio's right to own an exhibition chain.

What about Coke and Pepsi? Could I possibly play these two giants off against each other? Coke dominated the continent's movie houses. Pepsi wanted to expand its share. I knew that whichever of them supplied Cineplex Odeon with the syrup, from which the drinks are made, would reap profits of $80 million U.S. over the course of the next ten years. Why not offer an exclusive ten-year contract to the one that would come up with a loan to us of $40 million U.S. (the present value of the ten-year stream of profits)? I flew to Atlanta to put the proposition to Coke's president, Donald Keough, and then to Purchase, New York, to pitch Roger Enrico, Pepsi's president. Pepsi gave me the green light. It was prepared to go the distance.

We also approached Mel Simon, Indianapolis's pre-eminent shopping-centre tycoon, about forming a partnership with Cineplex Odeon to own and operate its movie-houses in the Chicago area. It would have been a stretch for Mel – real-estate prices were beginning to slide. But Henry Plitt, from whom I had bought our first U.S. circuit only four years before, heard about my discussions with Simon and came looking for me. He was lost without his theatres and would have loved to get back in the business by buying the Cineplex Odeon screens not only in Chicago but in L.A. as well. But he wasn't offering nearly enough money.

In Canada our struggle would be a running front-page story for months. It was heartening for Myron and me to get supportive calls from the Toronto investment community. More surprisingly I got numerous calls of sympathy and support from Hollywood, which I had expected would line up beside MCA – one of its own, after all. In fact, I even got calls from some MCA executives who wanted to see the white flag raised and the relationship resumed between us.

Clearly that wasn't going to happen. MCA seemed consumed by malice toward us. It wasn't enough that the special committee was completely overpowered by MCA, but MCA was going behind even its own committee's back to further its own interests. Various industry players, such as Dick Smith of General Cinema and Sumner Redstone of National Amusements (he later parlayed his circuit into the acquisition of Viacom and Paramount Communications), were approached as possible partners for MCA in the purchase of the entire U.S. circuit or selected regions. So were our partners Erin Mills. At a luncheon in L.A. in August, Skip Paul once again made an overture to Jack Daniels. This time he suggested that Erin Mills join MCA in making a $1 billion U.S. bid for the U.S. circuit. None of MCA's overtures came to anything, but they showed in what contempt MCA held Cineplex Odeon's shareholders and, for that matter, its own creature, the special committee.

*All through this exhausting search for financing and the struggle for a resolution to the impasse in which we found ourselves, I was finishing the restoration of the Pantages Theatre, in pre-production of Phantom, and also running this billion-dollar company – fighting with distributors, worrying about earnings, doing everything that a conscientious CEO had to do. I ran the company as though it were my own, so that I would have something of value later, if I succeeded in buying it.*

On September 14, after being conned by the committee since June and after long months of eighteen-hour days and seven-day weeks, we were ready to make three separate proposals in writing. The first was an offer to pay $17.50 for all the shares, on the condition that the special committee find a buyer for the U.S. circuit at $1 billion U.S. The committee kept saying the U.S. circuit was worth at least $1 billion. We agreed – as long as they found the buyer. Our second bid was an offer to buy all the assets of the company, except the U.S. circuit, for $325 million U.S., based on our belief, when it came right down to it, that MCA would never relinquish the U.S. circuit. And third, we came back with our original offer of June 16. We would buy all the outstanding shares for $14.50 cash, plus a $2.00 note.

Because of the prodigious amount of work we had done since the middle of June, we felt confident we could put the financing in place for any of these transactions if they closed within a reasonable time, say 120 to 150 days.

Now that our proposals were on the table, the committee knew they would make a public spectacle of themselves if they didn't treat them seriously. But, unbelievably, they still kept making noises indicating they had better offers! No sooner had our three proposals been received than Jimmy Raymond was on the phone to Myron to say none of them was good enough. Who, then, were these phantom buyers? Jimmy was never a malevolent man, but he was a born promoter. "Mid-East investors have offered $900 million U.S. cash just for the U.S. circuit," he confided to Myron. Needless to say, these "Mid-East investors" never surfaced. It turned out to be more of the same hype that had characterized the process throughout.

MCA was still giving the impression that it would bless an all-cash deal for all of the shares. This was just a delaying tactic – they knew full well that no one wanted me out until *Phantom* opened and our employment contracts expired. Negotiations, therefore, continued at full throttle. The whipsawing continued. We would make progress with Jimmy and Leo one day, only to have it repudiated by Skip Paul on advice from MCA's lawyers the next. It was like the cartoon gag where a character nails down one side of a plank and then starts on the other, only to have the first side pop up and knock him out.

As the month wore on it became more and more apparent that MCA was determined to frustrate our deal. However, Jimmy and Leo told us that the Bronfmans were still willing sellers and were applying pressure on MCA to go along.

In the middle of all this Ted Pedas called me from Washington. Buy all the assets except the U.S. circuit, he said. "Take whatever you can and get out fast. These people are impossible."

But Ted didn't understand. We couldn't do it. We were caught in another catch-22. If we bought the non-U.S. assets, the Bronfmans would be left in a U.S.-asset-based company and couldn't avail themselves of the protection of Investment Canada. They would then be at the mercy of MCA, because the voting limit on MCA would no longer hold. To the Bronfmans, this would be a fate worse than death, and if we so much as suggested it, they would readily side with MCA to get rid of us. We were useful to the Bronfmans only as long as we were trying to put together an offer for all of the shares – and thus extricate them.

Finally, by October 25, we had hammered out a deal with the committee. It was an incredible reach for us, but our new offer was $16.40 for all 50 million shares. Even then, however, we couldn't get MCA and the Bronfmans to lock up their shares – they wanted to be free to sell to a higher bidder should one miraculously arrive, from where no one knew.

But we did wrench two concessions from the committee. If, by November 15, we were able to show we had the money to complete the deal and table a draft bid circular, and if, by November 23, we could mail our offer to all shareholders, then the special committee would reimburse us the $8.5 million U.S. we would spend financing our bid. And as part of the deal, MCA and the Bronfmans agreed to buy the eighteen-screen complex at Universal City for $57 million U.S. – not a bad price for a movie-house I agreed to build and delivered a couple of years earlier for only $18 million U.S. The sale of the Universal City theatre was also an important indication of the value of the circuit, which we were going to have to dismember to raise the cash for the buyout.

We had exactly three weeks to make good our offer.

Since no part of the purchase was to be funded by paper, and since the junk-bond market had now completely faded away, the interesting question was – where in hell was $1.325 billion U.S. in cash to be found?

In the four months from June, our equity financing had diminished from $180 million U.S. to $125 million U.S. Our principal partners, the Erin Mills group, became less enthusiastic about the deal – they themselves had taken a knock in the falling real-estate market. We were only able to keep them in by reducing their share of the equity from $120 million U.S. to $60 million U.S. In return, they agreed to stretch and give us a mortgage of $35 million U.S. on Cineplex Odeon's interest in a lucrative midtown Toronto property. Myron and I held to-gether our previously committed $60 million U.S. of contributed equi-ty and, in fact, raised another $5 million U.S. from the same sources.

We also made an unconventional but landmark deal with Al Taubman for the New York–New Jersey theatres, the crown jewels of the U.S. circuit. For $155 million U.S., Taubman would buy half the shares of all the Cineplex Odeon subsidiaries that owned and operated the New York and New Jersey theatres, leaving Cineplex Odeon the owner of the other half. Then the Chase Manhattan Bank, on whose board Taubman sat, would grant a stand-alone loan to those subsidiaries for an equal amount of $155 million U.S., which in turn would be passed upward as a loan to the parent Cineplex Odeon, making a total of $310 million U.S. in available cash – ten times the 1990 projected cash flow of the theatres. Taubman also got Chase to commit financing to the venture of $42 million U.S. to provide suffi-cient working capital to complete the scheduled construction of new theatres in the area to the end of 1992. Thus we retained management of the circuit and we guaranteed our fully financed expansion of the New York–New Jersey circuit over the course of the next three years.

We calculated that by 1992, after the circuit had been groomed, we should be able to sell the three hundred screens for perhaps as much as twelve to fourteen times their cash flow, and, under the formula we had worked out with Taubman, Cineplex Odeon would then be entitled to a residual of $105 million U.S. or more. This was a sweet deal for us, made possible by Taubman's knowledge of, and confi-dence in, our real-estate holdings and our strength in management.

The Taubman deal was the big one, but we had others in place as well, such as the sale of the Seattle–Portland circuit to Act III, Norman Lear's company, for $105 million U.S. (the committee's advisers had established a top value for that circuit of only $75 million).

Our primary banks were still supportive. The Bank of Nova Scotia was prepared to give us a mortgage of $225 million U.S. on the com-pany's Canadian holdings. With Bankers' Trust, we negotiated a mortgage of $200 million U.S. on the remaining U.S. circuit (after the sale of the Universal City theatre complex) – the southeast region of the U.S., Chicago, Minneapolis, Washington, D.C., and California.

Then we reached an agreement with Rank for the sale of our remaining half-interest in Film House for $40 million U.S. (After we left the company, Cineplex Odeon's new management, desperate for cash, would in less than six months let this half-interest go for $27.5 million U.S.) At the same time we arranged with Rank for a mortgage of $60 million U.S. on Cineplex Odeon's residual interest in Universal Studios, Orlando, the U.K. theatres, and certain pieces of other non-theatrical real estate in Canada and the United States.

This brought our total to $1.1 billion U.S, leaving us with a shortfall of $200 million U.S. This was pretty remarkable, considering we had been severely restrained by the special committee for the better part of four months. We needed only an extension to year end and a piece of mezzanine financing to bridge the deal, and we would be there. (Ironically, one half of that shortfall would have been satisfied by the $2.00 note component that we created as part of our original offer. I remembered what Herb Wachtell had told Myron and me on May 16, when we were lunching with him and Sid Sheinberg. Herb advised us – with Sid listening intently – that the deal would have to be structured cleverly and would almost inevitably require some paper if our buyout was to succeed. How right he was!)

MCA, of course, refused to extend and refused to accommodate us with respect to the notes. The shareholders would have taken home $16.50 Cdn. But victory at almost any cost was the only thing that MCA wanted.

*I say it again: MCA never wanted the deal to happen – despite the damage their intransigence was inflicting on Cineplex Odeon's shareholders.*

On November 15 the special committee issued a press release, stating baldly that Drabinsky and Gottlieb had failed to come up with the cash. We immediately countered with a press release of our own, pointing out that all we needed was a little more time and a little accommodation by way of the note component of the deal.

The Bronfmans offered us our only chance to survive. In the next forty-eight hours Jimmy, Leo, and Sandra, along with their adviser Bob Rabinovitch, were flying out on the company plane to meet Sheinberg and Wasserman at the Black Tower. Myron and I had been pointedly not invited, but we went along on the plane, hoping to persuade the Bronfmans to support our request for an extension or to work with us to find another solution.

I decided to try a change in tactics. During our sequestered five hours to L.A. I worked hard to convince the Bronfman contingent that a return to the status quo might be in everybody's interest.

"Let's holster our guns," I suggested. "Myron and I will give up trying to buy the company and return to running it profitably."

I pointed out that in the seven months we had spent trying to raise the purchase money, our entrepreneurial talent had discovered limitless opportunities. The future would find us all in fat city, stronger than ever. Take the Taubman deal – Jimmy and Leo had really liked that. I reminded them that it wouldn't go through unless Myron and I were still in charge of Cineplex Odeon. Taubman had no confidence in any managers who might succeed us. Carefully, slowly, point by point, I took Jimmy and Leo through an examination of the company that would remain if we sold off New York and New Jersey, Seattle, the half-interest in Film House, and some secondary regions in the Southeast. I showed them a company with a yearly cash flow before interest and G&A of $80 million U.S. to $90 million U.S. and only $125 million U.S. of interest-bearing debt.

Finally, I emphasized the horrendous consequences to our shareholders if we failed to come to an accommodation.

Jimmy and Leo told us it didn't really matter what they thought. MCA would consider such a standoff a victory for Myron and me, and they wouldn't hold still for it.

Like a trainer prepping a battered fighter between rounds, I kept drumming it into Leo that MCA was powerless if the Bronfmans threw their support behind us.

The four of them went off together, apparently poised and prepared for the coming altercation.

Two hours later they were back. I could tell at once, by the looks on their faces, that our worst fears were about to be realized. Sid and Lew had made mincemeat out of them.

"You're out," said Leo, almost as soon as he walked into the room of the Registry Hotel next door to Universal City. "Leave quietly and we'll sell you a couple of assets."

*A bone for a good doggie! I was too stunned even to be angry, even to feel the contempt that would wash over me later. The loss of Cineplex Odeon was staring me in the face.*

In one last-ditch stand to show how real our $1.1 billion U.S. was and to convince Leo to hold MCA at bay until we worked out the last $200 million U.S., I got Al Taubman to invite Leo and Sandra to dinner with Myron and me at his West Bloomfield, Michigan, estate. Al's son Bobby and Bernard Winograd, president of Taubman Investment Company, were there too.

At dinner Al confirmed the deal negotiated for the New York–New Jersey theatres. But Leo, displaying a complete lack of couth and manners, spent the evening trying to keep the agreement in place – even if Myron and I were let go. He knew well enough not only that the deal had been cleverly conceived but that it was critical for the company, for in one pass it would reduce the company's debt by half.

But Al was adamant. Myron and I must remain. If we did, he would complete the deal, and to show his commitment to the new partnership and to the current management, he volunteered to buy a substantial number of treasury shares in Cineplex Odeon.

However, when he asked the Bronfman group whether they would do the same – that is, stay in for the long haul and not dump their shares – Leo, embarrassingly, refused to commit.

Desperate by now to achieve peace with both MCA and the Bronfmans, I asked Al as I was leaving his home to soften his demand that Myron and I remain at the head of the company and to instruct his advisers to provide me with a fully negotiated agreement, ready for signature, that I could produce at our forthcoming board meeting.

Al, bless him, agreed to everything. *There's just no substitute for class.*

＊   ＊   ＊

The sand in the hourglass continued to trickle out.

Jimmy Raymond, the nearest thing we had to an ally on the board from the Bronfman group, had seemed unusually depressed in the past few months, his usual buoyancy absent. I had put it down to stress, but it turned out to be worse. He wouldn't be able to attend the crucial November 27 board meeting; instead he would be in Toronto General Hospital for cancer surgery. I went to visit him there. Standing by his bedside staring down at his unshaven face, I wondered what I would do without his stabilizing presence to influence Leo. He himself was demoralized. He talked about the grave differences developing between him and Leo. He even talked about the possibility of leaving the Bronfmans.

In the end he said, "I'm sick Garth. I can't help you."

"You're sick, Jimmy," I muttered, "but I'm near death."

Between the November 16 press release and the scheduled board meeting of November 27, Skip Paul pushed the idea I had long suspected MCA of harbouring: MCA would support our purchase of all assets other than the U.S. circuit. This would have been acceptable to me. I would be able to start again, with a new base; the whole exercise wouldn't have been wasted. We began to talk about this. MCA's initial asking price was $400 million U.S. against our offer of $332 million, but eventually we closed the gap to acceptable levels. Then we asked the Bronfmans for their concurrence. They reacted exactly as I had told Ted Pedas they would: frantic with fear that they would be "stuckholders" under the domination of MCA.

No deal.

*So I had to face the future without Cineplex Odeon. What would I do? Could I – would I have to – leave the entertainment business? I wouldn't go back to law, I knew that. For a moment I was lost. I saw only a terrifying absence; I saw myself slipping below the grey and shimmering surface of the featureless future, bereft and alone.*

*I broke down only once during those emotionally draining and tormenting seven months. It was Friday, November 24, and I could no longer internalize the pain. I sat alone in my office after everyone had left the building and came face to face with the harsh reality that Cineplex Odeon was no longer to be mine. I couldn't help it. I cried.*

November 27 was the blackest of many black days. Sid marched into the meeting followed by his usual entourage and handed out another letter to everyone, signed by Skip Paul. In the letter Skip accused Myron and me of everything short of sexual relations with small animals.

Myron and I had one last card to play. In an attempt to stave off execution, we had plotted a careful strategy for the meeting. Cineplex Odeon shares were selling that day at $10.50. We recommended to the board that Cineplex Odeon complete the Taubman transaction, the Rank transactions, the sale of the Seattle theatres, and use part of the resulting proceeds of over $500 million U.S. to repurchase approximately 40 per cent, or ten million, of its outstanding common shares (excluding MCA's) for a premium price of $15.00. This would boost the morale of the shareholders and utterly destroy the short-sellers, who now had built up a huge, and utterly exposed, position. In addition, it would significantly reduce the float of shares, thus helping to maintain the price of the stock considerably above the current market. Even if this was done, I said, the total debt at year's end would be about $250 million U.S., less than half of the company's current debt. It was focused, responsible, in the best interests of all shareholders. It was perfect!

But nobody wanted to listen. It all fell on the deaf ears of a jaded, exhausted, and, finally, confused board.

Nat Taylor rose to the occasion and made one last pitch in support of us, just as he had done back in 1982 in similar circumstances.

"Without Garth's management, the company has no future," he insisted.

Sid's face never changed expression. A one-hour adjournment

was called. Myron and I left the boardroom. Sid followed me out and confronted me in the hallway. "Did you read the letter?" he asked.

They were the first words to me that had passed Sid's lips since our May 16 lunch with Herb Wachtell. I turned away in disgust without responding.

Sid and Leo met in my office during the adjournment, and in that brief meeting the details of an MCA/Bronfman treaty were concluded. MCA would let the Bronfmans nominate another two board members, making them equal with MCA at five apiece. Leo would become chairman. Together they would take the company to glory.

We were called back into the boardroom, and in a voice empty of emotion, showing no awareness of responsibility for his part in the events that had just occurred, Leo told us how things were going to be. Our resignations were to be handed in by December 1. We would have until then to make a deal to buy any of the assets on a list they gave us. The assets comprised the live-entertainment division, the midtown Toronto property, the U.K. circuit, and the distribution division.

*I said nothing more. There was nothing to be said. Finally, in the end, they had taken my company away from me.*

There was one final indignity – the board had nominated the execrable Jack Richer to negotiate with us.

After the meeting ended, Jack wasted no time bouncing into my office, gloating and vindictive.

"You were the cause of all Cineplex Odeon's problems," he said, gracious to the end. "And now you're out of here. Claridge and MCA are running things now. The market is at $10.50 today, and Claridge is going to buy a lot of stock."

So they did, adding more than 1 million shares to the 7.3 million they already held. They paid about $8.50 a share.

In his mean-spirited manner, he asked us what assets we were interested in buying. I told him only the live-entertainment division and the midtown Toronto property.

"So make an offer," he said.

"I already have an understanding with Kolber and Raymond," I pointed out. "I established a price on our return flight from L.A. a few weeks ago."

But when Jack heard the details, he shouted, "No way! We'll never sell for those prices!"

He ended that first session by telling us to deal only with him. Any attempt to discuss matters with any board member would kill any chance for a deal.

*Oh, he was a sweetheart.*

I later learned that Jack Richer had been promised a bonus for whatever he could gouge out of us. And gouging it was: the prices he put on the Pantages, plus the *Phantom* rights and the midtown property, were so outlandish that I immediately said we were no longer interested in the real estate.

"Okay," he exclaimed, irritated. "But you'll now pay a lot more."

And did we ever!

Throughout the negotiations, his style was venomous; he managed to be both coercive and evasive at the same time. Frequently we came to what we assumed was a full agreement; then Jack would disappear and come back, hours later, with new terms and a "take the deal, or you leave with nothing" attitude.

Here's a small sample: At one point in the discussions I called Lawrence Chernin, a Goodman and Carr lawyer with whom I had worked for four years and who was now acting for Cineplex Odeon, to inquire about something technical but trivial. It was the form of consent that would permit the transfer to us, on closing, of the two lucrative *Phantom* sponsorship deals with Pepsi and John Labatt Corporation. But Jack Richer went berserk when he heard about the call. As a punishment, he said, the deal was off – unless we let Cineplex Odeon hold on to the $2.1 million of Pepsi sponsorship money.

This was bargaining in good faith? Because of one innocent phone call, he extracted another $2.1 million from us.

The Labatt deal, however, was different from the Pepsi one. Because its agreement extended corporate-wide and not just to

*Phantom*, it was not severable in the same way, and in the end Labatt refused to consent to the transfer. Instead, it took the opportunity to void the whole arrangement. Like Al Taubman, they had no confidence in Cineplex Odeon management without Myron and me. This cost us $2.7 million U.S. and cost Cineplex Odeon an additional $4.5 million U.S. in lost revenues over the next couple of years.

Shortly afterwards Richer came into my office, again wearing his obnoxious smile. I remember asking him, with as much disgust as I could project, "What's it like to negotiate with someone whose pants are down, both his legs and hands are bound tightly, while you're holding a gun pointed at the victim's head?"

*We paid too much, far too much, for what we took away from Cineplex Odeon. Any intelligent person would have walked away from the deal. In the end, though, I had to agree to whatever he asked. I had no choice. I needed the glorious Pantages and* Phantom *to build a new future. They were my lifeline, and I was drowning. Without them I know I would have spiralled downward into despair, because at that exhausted moment I had nowhere else to turn. So he stuck us – there's no dignified expression for it – for a total of $75 million U.S. ($88 million). This was about $28 million more than the agreement I had negotiated with Leo on what was supposed to be a fair and equitable basis. Our original separation agreements, which guaranteed me a parachute of $4.5 million and Myron $3.5 million, were essentially torn up. The severance payments were now to be folded into our purchase of* Phantom *and the Pantages. Cineplex Odeon on closing would book a profit of $21 million for a division that had been operating fully for only two and a half months.*

A few days before we moved out, Richer had the unmitigated gall to ask me if Cineplex Odeon could rent my art collection, which hung on the walls throughout head office.

"No, Jack," I said. "The art goes with me. For Cineplex Odeon, culture stops on Friday, December 14."

I left my office that Friday night and went home. As I said at the start of this book, I told my family what I could.

"Don't be sad," I said to them. "I'm not. There's plenty of opportunity and challenge in what I'm going to do next. Things aren't going to get boring."

Afterwards, I went down to the Pantages in a state of shock. I sat in the orchestra and stared blindly up at the stage, fighting back misery. After the show was finished, I went up on the stage behind the closed curtain and spoke to the cast, musicians, and crew. They were quiet, some of them with tears in their eyes.

I was choked with emotion. "You are now officially my new family," I said, meaning every word. "My corporate family. I love this theatre. I love all of you. With good fortune, *The Phantom* will play for many years."

I never take tranquilizers, nor do I ever take a drink, so I had no way to come down off the terrible humiliation of losing my company. I do remember calling some of my friends, among them Jerry Banks. I remember telling him of the glorious future of The Live Entertainment Corporation of Canada, which was to be the name of our new $88-million venture. It would be as great – no, greater – than Cineplex Odeon, I insisted.

That was when Jerry said something like, "You know, Garth, it's only been a couple of hours. You have a right to feel sad."

Well, it passes. The next morning at eight o'clock, the phone rang. It was Prime Minister Brian Mulroney and his wife, Mila. "I just read about your resignation," the prime minister said in his chocolate-rich baritone. "I regret the outcome of your struggle. You may be down for a short while, but you're never to be counted out." I was very touched. The following week, the *Globe and Mail* editorialized, "Garth Drabinsky is the latest in a long line of entrepreneurs who have burned their way through the pages of Canadian history like supernovas." In New York the *Village Voice* said that I ought to be remembered as "nothing less than one of the most influential operators in motion-picture history." And the *Montreal Gazette*, looking back at what it called the Drabinsky decade, said, "In Canada, a country whose chilly conservatism is a smug façade for collective cowardice, Drabinsky proved that Canadians can make a foray into the world and grab a piece of the action." Dozens of comforting letters followed, some from people I knew well, some from strangers.

I felt a surge of hope. I had *Phantom* and the Pantages and, as I kept telling myself, live theatre, not the movies, had been my first love.

*I had come down from the heights before, I had crashed before, landed before in a fog of despair and anger. But in the end I had always managed to shake off the chill, to imagine the sun's rays warming my back. All I had to do was climb again, back to the warmth, up into the heights, a little closer to the sun.*

# PART

III

LIVE ON STAGE

# CHAPTER

## RESURRECTION

I woke up on December 16 a full-time theatrical impresario.

Within a few days I had designed the logo for our new company, The Live Entertainment Corporation of Canada, which I was already calling Livent. I took the ornament of the gryphon from the ceiling above the orchestra pit of the Pantages – next to the Phantom's chandelier – and stamped it in gold on a deep blue ground. The image made me feel better right away. I thought of it as a phoenix rising from the ashes.

*We had paid too much as a partnership for what we'd got, but we had also paid too much personally. I myself was in debt up to $8 million or so. Eight million dollars!*

*Afterwards, I went to see a psychiatrist for a while. I had never done this in my life – I had never sought help from anyone. I had always been completely self-confident, self-contained, and self-sufficient, but now, for the first time, I needed to talk, to reflect, to assess my life, my career direction.*

*Did it help? I think so. I needed someone to talk to. But in the end, I think, what ultimately pulled me through was my own life and the way I had lived it.*

*I had been there, you see. I had stared the dogs of adversity in the muzzle before. They held no terrors for me. I could reach back to other problems more terrible than they and see how I had emerged from them, unbeaten, unbowed, once again ready for a challenge. Why not again?*

*I turned my attention to the future.*

*In Greek mythology, Icarus plunged into the sea when he flew too close to the sun. It's supposed to be a lesson in the sin of hubris.*

*I think the bastard just gave up too soon.*

*He should have gotten himself another set of wings and taken off again!*

*So, I thought to myself, I know the downside – the immense risks, the depression at losing something I had built, the shameful betrayal by people I had considered friends and whom I had helped make large sums of money. Yes, the downside was easy. But there was an upside too – the upside was I felt as if a huge load had been lifted off my shoulders. I was back in the business I had wanted to be in all along – the theatre. I was finally living my dreams, dreams that went back to the first time I walked into a darkened auditorium to come upon a high-school play in rehearsal, dreams that I had been trying to fulfil in various ways through all the years in between.*

In our attempt to buy back Cineplex Odeon, Myron and I had formed a fifty-fifty partnership called the MyGar Partnership ("At least it sounds better," Myron said, "than GarMy"), and it was MyGar that two months later acquired the Pantages Theatre in Toronto, the Canadian stage rights to *Phantom*, and a few other theatrical rights of no particular consequence. We promptly folded MyGar into our newly incorporated company (whose name we later changed to its present one, Live Entertainment of Canada, Inc.).

Later, *Variety* wrote, "Garth Drabinsky walked away with the only part of Cineplex Odeon that is profitable." If only it had been that easy! When Myron and I bought the Pantages–*Phantom* package of assets for $88 million and established Livent, that package was the only string to our bow – $88 million, essentially for one theatre and one musical production! Myron and I contributed $8 million of the $88 million by selling off all of our holdings in Cineplex Odeon at an average price of $9 a share. We also got a much-needed loan from the ever-supportive Joe Rotman, who held out a hand when we needed it. (I'll never forget my conversation with him; he was less interested in the payback terms than in offering support. All he said was, "I hope you'll do the same for me when I need it.") The deal closed on the strength of a $60-million line of credit with the Royal Bank, a substantial portion of which was personally guaranteed by the two of us. During our buyback efforts, I discovered that the bank was prepared to lend us money against the theatre's cash flow, but it was still an astonishing display of confidence in our entrepreneurial talent, even by the standards of the late eighties. I suspect that if it had happened a year later, we would never have had the bank's support – the economy was slipping so rapidly into recession. (I want to pay tribute here to Allan Taylor, the bank's chairman – Saskatchewan-born, you see – Prairie people stick together! And also to point out that five years later, in 1994, the company has relatively little bank debt and the Royal Bank has been completely paid out.)

At the start, Cineplex Odeon retained $20 million from the record-breaking $23.8-million advance ticket sales for *Phantom*, severely impairing our cash flow for the first nine months. Life was excruciating.

We were obligated to put on the performances, but we retained little revenue from the sold-out audiences that saw them. Of course, we sold future tickets to later performances, but we were barely matching expenses. Oh, we were having a lot of fun!

There were even more difficulties. The recession was upon us. Interest rates were rising from 10 per cent to 14.5 per cent – another blow to our cash flow. As the Canadian dollar strengthened to nearly ninety cents by the summer of 1990, tourist traffic began to spiral downward. The convention business simply disappeared, and hotel vacancies rose to an alarming 45 per cent. We couldn't have faced more formidable economic conditions in starting a new company – especially a fully leveraged undertaking in the unpredictable business of theatre.

Still, not all was gloom and uncertainty. There were lighter moments. I remember particularly the afternoon that Shirley MacLaine, in town for her one-woman show *Out There Tonight*, came to our home. Pearl had called her earlier to let her know that her friend Gwen Whittal (an ardent fan of Shirley and a student of metaphysics) had suggested Shirley might like to meet Rick Thurston, a well-known Canadian deep-trance medium. Would she! It took Shirley less than a second to say yes, cancelling all her scheduled interviews for the day.

As Pearl tells it, Shirley arrived late, dressed à la *Steel Magnolias*, right down to the white pumps. She looked slightly frazzled. She'd been driven to a house with an almost identical address to ours, an unexpectedly modest bungalow. Undaunted, Shirley told her limo driver to wait and rang the doorbell. The scene that ensued didn't reassure her that she had come to the right place.

"Is this the Drabinsky residence?" she demanded of the woman who stood stricken in the doorway.

"Oh my God! You're Shirley MacLaine!" the woman blurted, her eyes blinking rapidly and her mouth agape.

Shirley assured her that she wasn't and made her escape.

At our house, once introductions were properly made, Shirley set-tled in to interrogate Rick while she tucked into the pastries and tarts, a large bowl of cherries wedged securely between her knees. Pearl says it resembled the cherry-eating scene from *The Witches of Eastwick*.

Afterwards, they moved into the study for a little serious channel-ling. Rick would go into a deep trance, allowing the "transcendors," a group of never less than forty-three thousand spiritual entities who speak with one voice, to respond to a myriad of questions. Among them, Pearl was amused to hear, was advice to Shirley to curb her enthusiasm for sweets if she wanted to maintain her shape and health.

At 6 P.M. Shirley departed for a rehearsal and then her show. But she came back after for more channelling. So it was that, when I came home at 1.30 A.M., I was more than a little surprised to find everyone still in feverish discussion around our kitchen table. Gwen had just suggested to Shirley that she do a TV show to interview top

(Top) With Pierre Trudeau

(Centre) With Brian and Mila Mulroney at one of the opening galas of *The Phantom of the Opera* at the Pantages Theatre in Toronto in 1989

(Bottom) Receiving the 1994 Tourism Canada Person of the Year Award from Prime Minister Jean Chrétien and Carole-Ann Hayes of WHERE Magazines International, sponsor of the award, in Vancouver

Bayne Stanley

(Top) Nobel Peace Prize Winner Shimon Peres of Israel with me on Broadway at a preview of *Show Boat* at the Gershwin Theatre in September 1994

(Centre) With Teddy Kollek, the former mayor of Jerusalem, in front of the King David Hotel

(Below) With architect Moshe Safdie in 1994, on the roof of Safdie's Mamilla Development in Jerusalem

With my executives on the day Livent was listed on the Toronto Stock Exchange, May 7, 1993. Left to right: Senior Executive Vice-President Robert Topol; Executive Vice-President Dan Brambilla; Executive Vice-President Lynda Friendly; me, TSE Director of Original Listings Rob Cook; President and Chief Operating Officer Myron Gottlieb; TSE Manager of Original Listings Jerry Vickers; and Scott Paterson, Senior Vice-President and Director of Corporate Finance for Midland Walwyn

With Andrew Lloyd Webber

At a *Phantom* news conference in Singapore in 1994

(Below) With Hal Prince during *Show Boat* rehearsals in the summer of 1993 in the Main Stage Theatre of the then North York Performing Arts Centre

With Donny Osmond, his wife, Debbie, and their sons at the party at Toronto's Royal York Hotel in June 1992 following the North American première of *Joseph and the Amazing Technicolor Dreamcoat*

At the Toronto première of *Joseph*. With me, from the left, Andrew Lloyd Webber, the composer and producer of *Joseph*, and two of the stars of the original company of *Kiss of the Spider Woman*, Brent Carver and Anthony Crivello

Daily Telegraph (London)

Outside the Shaftesbury Theatre, in London's West End, home of the London production of *Kiss*, in September 1992

With Liza Minnelli at a news conference, announcing her recording of "The Day After That," the anthem from *Kiss of the Spider Woman,* as an AIDS fund-raiser

Tom Sandler

With Hal Prince and the ineffable Chita Rivera at the party at Toronto's Four Seasons Hotel following the world première of *Kiss* in June 1992

Onstage at the Gershwin Theatre with some of the stars of *Show Boat* on opening night on Broadway. Left to right: Lonette McKee as Julie, Joel Blum as Frank, Rebecca Luker as Magnolia, Mark Jacoby as Ravenal, John McMartin as Cap'n Andy, and choreographer Susan Stroman

With Lonette McKee and Lena Horne immediately following the final curtain of *Show Boat's* opening night on Broadway, October 2, 1994. Horne was considered for the role of Julie in the 1951 MGM film adaptation, but rejected in favour of Ava Gardner because of Hollywood's racist casting policies. McKee became the first black actress to play the role in the 1984 Houston Grand Opera revival of *Show Boat*, and went on to universal critical acclaim as Julie in our new production in Toronto and on Broadway.

A euphoric moment as Myron and I pick up the 1993 Tony for Best
Musical for *Kiss of the Spider Woman*

A portrait of me by Ludmilla Temertey, which she titled
"I Live My Dreams"

metaphysicians. Why didn't I produce her? Shirley asked. After all, we had already been linked in many different incarnations.

I finally gave up and went to bed at 3 A.M. I knew if I didn't leave soon, I would be heading for an out-of-body experience myself.

As a student of the entertainment business, I knew how powerful the Hollywood studios had been in their heyday, when the industry was still vertically integrated, before it was broken up by the anti-trust legislation. I had seen how they were edging back into another version of vertical integration in the Reagan era. At Cineplex Odeon I had learned the complicated synergies of the movie business, and though my partners never understood what I was doing, I had integrated that business as well as I was allowed to, considering the constraints of my board.

In my live-theatre experience I had seen how opportunities had been lost for lack of a proper venue for a show. I had seen how important it was to control as many aspects of the business as possible, not just production but exhibition as well, to be in control of your own destiny, to give you the maximum entrepreneurial freedom of action. It was this philosophy that I wanted to adhere to as my career in live theatre unfolded.

Myron and I assembled a stellar management infrastructure for Livent, covering all of the necessary disciplines of legitimate theatre, to facilitate our future growth. Once again, as at Cineplex Odeon, the team included Lynda Friendly and Robert Topol, people who shared my passion and interests and who hadn't been moulded by the archaic traditions of the legitimate theatre industry and so were able to implement the plan I envisaged.

At first our theatrical bow had only one string, as I've said. But what a string! As it turned out, *Phantom* came to be pure, unalloyed, high-assay gold. Within the first year I reseated the Pantages and increased its capacity by one hundred seats to twenty-two hundred seats. Based on the first of what would be a continuous series of research studies by Goldfarb Consultants, I rescaled the house, increasing the top ticket price from $75 to $85 and thereby increasing our weekly box-office capacity to nearly $1.3 million. Indeed, the Pantages became the highest-grossing theatre in the world for a continuous run. Eventually, it grossed yearly about 90 per cent of what Toronto's Blue Jays bring in from the SkyDome, a fifty-thousand-seat facility, and every other source of revenue!

Earlier, at the 1988 press conference where I announced *Phantom*, I was asked how long I expected it to run. I was being extravagant, I thought, when I said, "Three years." By now I knew that *Phantom* would play in Toronto at least five years. Nationally there was a pent-up demand. How could I service the rest of the country? I needed more cash flow. So, twenty months after the opening, in April 1991, we mounted a second, $10-million production of *Phantom* to tour Canada. That production starred the first Canadian Phantom, Jeff Hyslop, while Christine was portrayed by Patti Cohenour, Sarah Brightman's original alternate on Broadway. It was a bold move to have two *Phantom*s in one small country, but I strongly believed we could amortize the goodwill *Phantom* had generated and the payback would be substantial. I was right.

The Canadian tour's ongoing success enabled Livent to acquire from RUG the rights to present *Phantom* at the two-thousand-seat Blaisdell Theatre in Honolulu, beginning in October 1993. Box-office receipts for the ten-week run were $11.3 million U.S., a record for Hawaii. We had also acquired the licence to present the tour in Anchorage, Alaska, in 1994 and the rights to co-present the production in the Far East, opening in Singapore in February 1995, followed by a sixteen-week run in Hong Kong.

Other than RUG and the operations of Cameron Mackintosh, we were virtually alone in this – the taking of major theatrical productions into cultures very different from those for which they were originally written. It's an incredibly complicated and subtle undertaking to find a massive audience through marketing in cultures where even the media habits differ substantially from ours. It takes a very special expertise to bring it off. Livent has developed that expertise, and we're applying it to the world.

Because of *Phantom*'s longevity, we needed to find new ways of
marketing it to keep the Toronto production running at near-
capacity levels. In January 1993 we launched "The Phantom Express,"
a free one-day return-bus-trip package between Toronto and various
U.S. and Ontario border cities, including Buffalo, Rochester, and
London. With the purchase of a ticket to a Wednesday or Thursday
performance of *Phantom*, patrons would receive same-day return
bus transportation aboard a luxury coach. En route, the passengers
would view the video, "Behind the Mask." This was a substantial
value-added benefit to the ticket buyer. The economics were surprising. A full bus could be leased for $500 U.S., or less than $12 U.S. per
passenger. The profit off merchandising (typically, most passengers
would buy souvenirs) and the addition of a small administrative fee
per ticket almost covered the costs of the bus ride. The success of this
enterprise has surpassed our highest expectations, having sold tens
of thousands of tickets.

Another breakthrough was our Canadian cast recording of the
show.

In hindsight it may have seemed that producing a Canadian
album should have been an obvious decision, one that was enthusiastically embraced by everyone involved. This was not the case. Despite
constant demands from the theatregoing public for a Canadian cast
recording, it took me more than a year of persistent negotiations to
convince Andrew and Polydor to grant me the rights. They just didn't
believe that Canada could or would support another *Phantom* album.
In the end I convinced Andrew it would be a tragedy, in the case of
Colm Wilkinson, not to preserve for posterity his historic performance. Andrew and the record company finally acquiesced, and
Andrew has since told me in a private moment that Colm's performance of "The Music of the Night" on the recording is definitive.

The Canadian cast recording of *Phantom* was the only other
English-language recording besides the original London cast album,
which starred Michael Crawford. (Other recordings had been made
in Japanese, Swedish, and German.) In just four years since its release
on Polydor/Polygram in December 1990, the recording has sold, in

Canada only, almost 700,000 units, seven times platinum. Shortly after its release, the Canadian highlights album was outselling in Canada the original London album by ten to one. These sales have helped our promotional efforts enormously, catapulting awareness of our production of *Phantom* into the stratosphere. But the synergies go both ways – the album sells the show and the show sells the albums.

In my view, cast recordings are a tremendously helpful tool to the producer and cast. If it were possible, I would prefer to produce them even before the show begins, they're that important. What they do is allow the performers to understand the subtleties of the music better. Also, of course, the cast album has helped me produce dozens of sound bites for our radio and TV ads. The separate recording of the music track permits me to study the music's phrasing in order to extract many diverse musical moments around which thematic advertising campaigns are designed.

In the summer of 1989, about two months before the opening of *Phantom*, Hal asked me to participate in an audacious and ambitious new musical he was directing, called *Kiss of the Spider Woman*.

I was intrigued at the idea of *Kiss* as a musical, because some time previously one of my former executive vice-presidents, Cary Brokaw, who had left Cineplex Odeon to form Island Pictures with Chris Blackwell, approached me to become involved with their first production, the movie adaptation of *Kiss of the Spider Woman*, directed by Hector Babenco. Cineplex Odeon put up part of the financing and distributed the film in Canada. The movie gained a large following, and William Hurt won an Oscar for his portrayal of Molina, the gay window-dresser.

Hal told me that, beginning in May 1990, he was going to stage *Kiss* as a work-in-progress on the campus of the State University of New York College at Purchase for a very limited eight-week run as part of New Musicals, an ambitious enterprise headed by Marty Bell. Marty's concept was to develop new American musicals away from the economic and critical pressures of Broadway. The plan was to finish the workshop production, spend a year or so rewriting, and then mount a full production.

Hal loved the idea. Increasingly, he felt stifled and frustrated by the escalating costs of mounting an original Broadway production and by the power of the critics to close a show. Hal knew from painful experience, as I did, about the influence of the critics and the effect of word of mouth in Manhattan's theatre community and the gleeful *schadenfreude* of that crowd. Before *Phantom*, he had had a string of failures, including Stephen Sondheim's *Merrily We Roll Along* (1981), *A Doll's Life* (1982), and *Grind* (1985).

*Kiss* was based on the postmodern classic novel by the Argentine novelist Manuel Puig, whose books had been banned in Argentina for nearly a decade. The show had music and lyrics by John Kander and Fred Ebb (who had written such shows as *Cabaret* and *Chicago* and such hit tunes as "New York, New York") and a book by Terrence McNally, celebrated author of the Broadway hit *The Ritz*, among others, and playwright of *Frankie and Johnny*.

Puig's hero in *Kiss of the Spider Woman* is Molina, who is incarcerated in a Latin American prison on a morals charge. Molina, a social misfit with no political conscience, who allows himself to be eternally humiliated, is a romantic who uses the cinema as his waking dreamscape. He is obsessed with his dream creation, a movie goddess named Aurora/Spider Woman. Like a modern-day Scheherazade, Molina tells his cellmate, a Marxist revolutionary named Valentín, the movies he remembers from his childhood. He distracts Valentín, who is in danger of weakening from the terrible prison conditions and giving information to the authorities under the pressure of the horrific torture he endures. Through Molina's compelling, imaginative powers, both men are able to escape into a fantasy world to survive. By the end of the story, in a brave and selfless act, Molina finds the courage to act on behalf of another human being. Likewise, Valentín learns about humanity and compassion. As Canadian author and critic Alberto Manguel once put it, "For Puig, it was important to depict a different kind of hero, someone who doesn't sacrifice himself for a cause he has embraced, but for a cause someone else has embraced. In Puig's eyes, only then does a revolutionary act achieve true nobility."

Hal told the New York Times that Kiss, although it is full of Broadway values, is "about two men . . . and the women they think of. One thinks of a lover, one a mother. It's about a life one of them creates for the other in the imagination. It's about what you do when you're sequestered, and it's about whether it's moral or not moral, cowardly or not cowardly, to retreat into fantasy."

Fred Ebb came up with the inspiration for a theatrical adaptation in 1986 and took it to John and then to Hal. Hal was interested in the dramatic contrasts – the dark, grim, shadowy world of the two men in a cell and Molina's fantasy life, which was light, happy, bright, and Technicolor, almost Betty Grableish. Hal knew if he could mix the two themes successfully, it would be a fresh musical, a musical about compassion.

Kiss's structure was reminiscent of that of Kander and Ebb's Cabaret, in which the Kit-Kat nightclub provided a fantasy, showbiz escape, with production numbers that commented, often ironically, on the narrative taking place in the real world outside the bar – the savage world of Nazi Germany and the Holocaust. In Kiss, the prison cell is the focus of the harsh, totalitarian reality, while Molina's dreams are the showbiz escape. One of the challenges was to make the prison scenes as dramatically compelling as Molina's fantasies were entertaining.

The major problem structurally with the early version of the musical I saw at Purchase was that Molina had only one fantasy movie with one continuous plot. As the action shifted between the movie in Molina's mind and the prison cell, audiences became confused in their attempt to track both stories. There were two linear plots instead of one, and many who saw it couldn't remember the last sequence of the dream they saw. Each movie sequence needed to be unique unto itself. That would take a great burden off the audience.

Also of great importance was that the creative team had to find a way of writing more moments in which the Spider Woman could

weave through the musical's action. She had to be a mysterious, ominous, omnipresent figure.

Moreover, the scenes in the cell were simply not harrowing
enough. The writers of the show seemed frightened of their own
material – the dark themes of totalitarianism, torture, homosexuality
– and pulled back, which meant the script was fatally compromised
from the start. In a way they had created the movie portions as an
escape for the audience from the unrelenting gravity of the theme;
what they finally admitted to themselves at Purchase was that the
audience became involved with the two guys in the cell and didn't
seem to need all that much relief.

Though I loved the notion of working with Hal again – clearly, he
and I were forging the early stages of a collaborative relationship – at
that juncture it was impossible for me to participate. I was still trying
to buy back Cineplex Odeon and preoccupied with the opening of the
Pantages and *Phantom*. I just didn't have the time, or the mental
energy, and declined.

Unfortunately, *Kiss of the Spider Woman*, New Musicals' first and only
presentation, was sandbagged by the critics. They had had – or
thought they had – an agreement with the New York media that no
critics would make the hour-long trek to Purchase to review the show.
After all, this was just a workshop. But the creative team was unable to
enforce a critics' embargo.

Frank Rich of the *New York Times*, despite the producers' requests
for restraint, came anyway. The *Times* considered *Kiss* to be a full-
dress commercial production rather than a workshop. As well, since
this was Hal's first musical since his mega-hit achievement with
*Phantom*, he was, in the *Times*' opinion, newsworthy. By extension,
the show merited public criticism, workshop or not.

If one rereads Rich's review, he was quite fair and balanced, offering constructive criticism. Calling *Kiss* "the first large-scale American
musical told from an unapologetic and unsentimental gay point of
view," Rich called for more intimacy and a "dazzling musical-comedy
presence of the Chita Rivera sort." He did point out the show's flaws,

but all the flaws he found I had easily spotted and the creative team had already identified.

Still, his review, balanced as it was, was enough to scare off producers and destroy any chance the project had of an immediate transfer to Broadway. Hal, Marty, John, Fred, Terrence, and everyone else involved in *Kiss* felt betrayed and considered that their dream had been sabotaged. Everyone retreated to heal their wounds, and it wasn't until the spring of 1991 that I joined them to pick up the pieces.

In December 1989, just a week after moving into my new Livent office, I opened the Toronto *Globe and Mail* and read that a new three-theatre performing-arts centre was being built in North York. To my astonishment, the article reported that the leading candidate to program and operate the centre was – me! I was, to say the least, taken aback. After a bruising, and horribly public, nine-month squabble over Cineplex Odeon, some politicians somewhere still felt that I wasn't damaged goods? This was reassuring!

In any case, I thought it was worth investigating what it was I was supposed to be the leading candidate for. I put in a call to Glenn Garwood, executive manager of The North York Performing Arts Centre Corporation, and asked him what was going on. He explained that the corporation had put out a call for tenders internationally in London, New York, and Toronto. In response, the media had called repeatedly asking Glenn if I had put in a bid yet.

"I told them, no, he hasn't bid yet. But I'm sure he'd be interested," Glenn told me. Apologetically, he said the press had taken his response and misquoted him, assuming that he had said I was already interested.

Then he added, "Now that I have you on the phone, may I send you this information package?"

"Sure," I said, "send it down."

Why was I interested? I expected *Phantom* to have an extended run at the Pantages, and we weren't in a position to grow beyond it. If Canadian rights to another mega-hit could be acquired, I would have to pass, because we didn't have another suitable theatre in Toronto. We were stifled.

The new theatre was to be located at the geo-centre of Metropolitan Toronto, a short drive from a major east-west expressway interchange. After Toronto, North York is the richest city in Metro. It had a gleaming new city hall and civic-centre complex adjacent to the site of the proposed arts centre. More importantly, it also had a mayor with vision, drive, and *cojones* in Mel Lastman, so I knew the project had a strong likelihood of actually coming to fruition. It wouldn't get bogged down in interminable political debate – Mel would push it through. Although the proposed arts centre was seven miles north of the Pantages Theatre up Yonge Street, it took only about fifteen minutes to make the trip on the subway.

*In any event, Nat Taylor's advice to me was always, "Shows make theatres; theatres don't make shows." In other words, it doesn't matter where a hit show is presented. Audiences will seek it out.*

I soon learned that Ed and David Mirvish and Concert Productions International (CPI) had each submitted bids for the management rights to the centre. However, I was not so quick to respond. When I looked over architect Eberhard Zeidler's plans, I was disappointed. I admired Zeidler and still do. His successful projects in Canada include Toronto's Eaton Centre and Vancouver's Canada Place. But in this case, I felt he had been given wrong advice. The recital hall, for example, was planned to have only seven hundred seats, but it needed to be expanded to at least a thousand seats to attract and economically support a varied schedule of leading classical artists, while still retaining its intimacy and acoustical integrity. The main theatre's design had two balconies, but a seating capacity of only fifteen hundred, with a backstage depth of only forty feet. In order to make it practical and financially viable, the main theatre needed eighteen hundred seats, with a backstage facility large and flexible enough to handle big-scale musicals as well as international ballet and opera productions. I also thought it needed an orchestra pit large enough to handle up to eighty musicians, the size of a Verdi opera.

To effect economies in the design, I convinced Zeidler to rethink the public spaces and to compress his oversized lobby areas. In return, those savings could support the auditorium and backstage enhancements that were required.

When I met with officials of the City of North York, it was clear that Livent was their first choice. Within two months of our first meeting, we signed an agreement to become the exclusive manager of the three-thousand-seat facility. Livent was engaged for an initial term of ten years from the opening, with option rights exercisable in our favour to extend our tenure to up to forty years.

Now all I needed to do was find a production to open the theatre.

A production that would rival *Phantom* in prestige, scope, theatricality, style, verve, and sheer bloody wonder.

*One cool September evening in Toronto, near the first anniversary of my Phantom, I was on Yorkville Avenue, on the sidewalk outside a restaurant, when I glanced across the road and realized I was standing just outside the place where I was born. The Yorkville district is now to Toronto what Georgetown is to Washington – lined with boutiques and European-style cafés, where Torontonians make the most of a short summer. But No. 88 Yorkville was an anomaly, a derelict, two-storey building with peeling paint, waiting forlornly for the wrecker's ball. I felt a sudden twinge of nostalgia. Forty-one years earlier this building had been Mount Sinai Hospital, but more like a boarding house than a true hospital, in a modest neighbourhood going to seed. By the sixties, when Yorkville transformed itself into Toronto's version of Haight-Ashbury, the hospital had long gone, the building an empty shell, peopled only by ghosts.*

# CHAPTER

## LIVENT

In 1990 I took the Concord over to London for a meeting with RUG about the possibility of acquiring additional territorial rights to *Phantom*. On my way into town from Heathrow, I browsed through *The Times* and noticed that a revival of the Jerome Kern/Oscar Hammerstein II classic 1927 musical, *Show Boat*, was playing at the London Palladium. It was a production of Opera North, in cooperation with the Royal Shakespeare Company. Curiously, in all my years of going to the theatre, I had never seen a production of what has been called the first modern musical.

So that night, my curiosity piqued, I showed up at the box office and bought what ticket I could. Unfortunately, the production wasn't very memorable. Like most other productions since 1946, the physical show didn't reflect the immensity of Ziegfeld's epic. Other than in its initial Broadway and London premières, and perhaps the subsequent restagings in the thirties, *Show Boat* had never been graced with a lavish production with a budget that would enable a producer to fully realize the majesty of its score, its sweeping, multigenerational story, and its Mississippi River setting. Nevertheless, I was impressed by the emotional impact it had on me. After all these years the incredible score and story still retained their power.

The London critics had loved the show. Richard Morrison of *The Times* wrote, "If Tolstoy had written a musical, he might have produced something like *Show Boat*. . . . Here is a chronicle not simply of individual destinies, but of a nation. . . . With just one song, 'Ol' Man River,' Kern and Hammerstein created something so truthful that the time and place of the original context is transcended. It speaks as directly to today's audiences as to 1927 Americans." *

After the show I went off for a ruminative supper. I went to Zen Central on Queen Street off Curzon (the street where it all began for me in London, so many years ago). During a substantial meal of deep-fried shredded beef, sautéed chicken, and lobster in black bean sauce, I mulled over the musical I had just seen.

As we enter the new millennium, I reflected, audiences will want to continue to revisit what was great in popular culture and entertainment in this century. I believed that the appetite for nostalgia would continue unabated. And *Show Boat*, after all, is one of musical theatre's greatest legacies. It's considered by theatre historians to be a landmark work, an American musical masterpiece.

Sitting there alone over dinner, I decided, if I could assemble a dynamic, creative team of the world's finest talents and acquire the world licence I would need to justify the costs, this would be the ideal musical to open the Main Stage Theatre at the North York Performing Arts Centre (now called the Ford Centre for the Performing Arts).

The missing link was a director who could bring to the story and its sublime characters a certain boldness and renewed vitality. Naturally, for me there was only one man for the job, and his name was Harold Prince. By this time, I regarded *The Phantom of the Opera* as the most satisfying creative association of my career. How wonderful it would be to act as a catalyst, allowing Hal Prince to touch his golden hand on the early as well as the latter end of the modern musical spectrum.

It took me six months of hard-fought negotiations with the estates of Edna Ferber, the author of the 1926 novel upon which the musical was based, Jerome Kern, and Oscar Hammerstein II for the worldwide rights, but I finally got them. At one point I remember urging

Ted Chapin, president of the Rodgers and Hammerstein Organization, "You've got to finish the deal quickly because Harriet Pilpell [who represented the Edna Ferber estate] may die." Sure enough, soon after the deal was signed, she did, in fact, die.

One reason I needed Hal was for his dramaturgical skills. There was still no definitive script for *Show Boat*. It existed in many forms and there were many options for the director. Fortunately, a plethora of songs, lyrics, and dialogue existed from which to choose.

The next thing to do, of course, was to sign up Hal. I was in New York when I finally culminated the rights negotiations. It was the end of October 1990, a beautiful fall day, and I've always loved New York best when it moves close to the festive season. I called Hal for a meeting at his office at 10 Rockefeller Center. I was cautiously optimistic. I really believed he would agree to do the show. How could he resist? In many ways, Kern's *Show Boat* was his contribution to American opera, and I knew Hal loved the art form, with its larger-than-life scope. He had directed opera all over the world, including New York's Metropolitan Opera.

I knew Hal didn't, as a rule, direct revivals, but that wasn't going to stop me. I sat him down and said excitedly, "I want you to direct a show for me. It's a revival."

Hal replied, "If you're going to ask me to do *Carousel*, I pass."

I was momentarily distracted. "Why?"

"Because I could never figure out the problems of Act Two," he confessed.

I said, "Well, you're off the hook. It's not *Carousel*. It's *Show Boat*."

Hal did a double take, then he grinned. "Isn't that the funniest thing! I've been thinking about *Show Boat* for the past couple of years." He went on to say he had never seen a production of *Show Boat* that he liked, that he felt did justice to the musical. For one thing, the book needed substantial revision, especially the second act.

We talked about it at length. Hal said he considers *Show Boat* to be the first great contemporary modern musical – the first to merge the traditional, happy-go-lucky naïveté of Broadway musical comedy with serious themes. It also was the first marriage of what was the popular, conventional American musical-comedy form and operettas defined in Vienna in the golden days. He called it "Jerome Kern's *Porgy and Bess*," and the score was "the best ever written for a musical." Ironically, Florenz Ziegfeld, the colourful impresario renowned for his *Ziegfeld Follies* shows and who produced the original *Show Boat*, considered the musical to be an inspired aberration.

Hal and I were in sync from the outset. Our goal was to create a production with a realistic, "gritty" documentary feel, not one full of the usual make-believe Hollywood nonsense, a pretty, pastel, empty thing. I wanted it to reflect the real attitudes of the time, not some sanitized version of them.

Hal agreed. He said he had never seen a *Show Boat* that established the musical tale's historical context and properly depicted the passage of time. The story spans a forty-year period, moving from the post-Reconstruction Deep South in the 1880s to industrialized Chicago, all the way through the jazz age and the Roaring Twenties. This was a turbulent time in American history, as democracy was reconstructed following the Civil War and the country plunged into the First World War. Against this panorama unfolds the story of the Hawks family, of a show-boat captain, his daughter, and her bittersweet romance with a river gambler, of the tragically fated singer, Julie, and the people who lived and worked along the banks of the Mississippi River.

In creating his artistic statement, the stagecraft would incorporate the latest developments in automation, computerization, and lighting. Earlier *Show Boats* had been hampered by the limitations of the technology of the day.

Hal said he considered the 1927 version of the play to be more "modern" than the 1946 revival, which, while slick in 1946 terms, lacked the sweep and historical punch of the original. Also, he wanted to restore some songs that had been cut from the 1927 opening, especially Queenie's beautiful spiritual lament "Mis'ry's Comin' Aroun'," which was omitted by Ziegfeld because he deemed it too serious for its time. (Kern and Hammerstein got around this setback by incorporating the song into the overture.)

Later, in rewriting the book, Hal, in consultation with me and other members of the creative team as well as Bill Hammerstein (son of Oscar Hammerstein and a director/producer in his own right), showed great sensitivity in the elimination of any inadvertent stereotyping in the original material that, although it might have escaped comment in the past, could have caused offence to some segments of society today. In light of the events that followed, this became even more important.

We talked about the creative team we would need. Multi-Tony-Award-winner Florence Klotz, who has designed dozens of superb shows, would design the more than five hundred costumes needed. Eugene Lee would create the sets – he had already won two Tonys with Hal (for Bernstein's *Candide* and Sondheim's *Sweeney Todd*) – why not another? Richard Pilbrow would do the lighting. He had many Broadway credits to his name; he is also the author of the standard text on stage lighting and in 1982 was given an award by the U.S. Institute of Theatre Technology for his contributions. The choreography would have to be by the brilliant (and adorable) Susan Stroman. Susan, too, has innumerable illustrious credits to her name (she swept the 1992 theatre awards, winning the Tony, Drama Desk, and Outer Critics' Circle awards for her work on the smash-hit Gershwin musical *Crazy for You*). She had already worked with Hal on *Don Giovanni* for the New York City Opera.

The score with which Hal had to work was a treasure trove of such timeless melodies and classic theatre songs as "Ol' Man River," "Can't Help Lovin' Dat Man," "Bill" (with lyrics by P. G. Wodehouse), "Make Believe," and "You Are Love." The imaginative orchestrations and arrangements would trace the development of musical styles from Victorian ballads and spirituals to early Mississippi Delta blues, Dixieland, ragtime, and jazz.

The next step, we decided, was for Hal to prepare the reworked material for a reading in New York so we could see what we had. I left, confident that the premier attraction for the gala opening of the North York Performing Arts Centre was set: a full recreation, not a revival, of *Show Boat*.

The year 1990 was full of activity. While I was busy negotiating the rights to *Show Boat*, the Canadian touring production of *Phantom* was being prepared.

Wherever it has played, *The Phantom of the Opera* has literally transformed theatres which have housed it. In the case of New York's Majestic Theatre and Toronto's Pantages Theatre, renovations were necessary to adapt the stage and auditorium to Maria Björnson's opulent production designs.

With the ingenious and elaborate engineering necessary for "permanent" productions, the challenge of creating a national Canadian touring production that would recreate the marvellous spectacle on the road without losing any of its wallop was a substantial one. How do you transform theatres, from Vancouver to Montreal, into the Paris Opera House? How do you accommodate the candles' mechanisms when most theatres on the road don't have adequate trap rooms? How do you safely install in each new venue a chandelier, which has to crash nightly without injuring anybody?

Our production team, under the capable stewardship of Peter Lamb, began preparing the touring production with the same effort they brought to the original, only now they also had to consider flexibility and economy. The essential difference was refining the set so it could be installed in a theatre relatively quickly and taken out just as fast, so that we could maximize the amount of performance time we had in each city.

The technical demands of *Phantom* – the special-effect tricks and illusions, the light cues and scenery movements – present many unique challenges and make it almost impossible to have an absolutely perfect show. (Three out of the many times I've seen the show, the damned chandelier refused to move: each time it was excruciatingly embarrassing.) In fact, as my production stage manager, Pat Thomas, said to me, "Most shows can't be perfect unless you have only one set, three light cues, and two actors." *Phantom* has more than nine hundred light cues – two hundred and ten of which are called – and about a hundred and fifty scenery moves, not to mention all the prop setups and costumes.

To take *Phantom* on the road, the Canadian touring company would use nineteen tractor-trailer trucks, the same number used to transport the Rolling Stones' 1990 Steel Wheels tour. Installing and dismantling such a large show called for meticulous scheduling to make sure that each truck arrived in order and at the time it was needed. Indeed, the tour was an international effort. Whereas the Toronto production was very much Toronto-based, the touring production had automation devices from New York, scenery built in Calgary, lights and sound produced in Winnipeg, costumes built in Toronto and New York, and sculptures and drapery from London.

It was while we were working in Vancouver in May 1991 on the setup for *Phantom* that I got *Kiss*ed again.

During a break I invited Hal and Ruth Mitchell to take a trip over the mountains with me in a de Havilland Sea Otter to Whistler, B.C. Somewhere in the air high over the Rockies, Hal told me that, over the past ten months, he and his colleagues had found the way to "unlock" the problems with *Kiss*. When we got back to the Pan-Pacific Hotel, he handed me the revised script and I read it quickly. I saw at once that they had solved the difficulties that had surfaced in Purchase and had met the challenges head on. As I read I felt flushed with possibilities. I believed the musical had the potential of being an artistic breakthrough, one that could push the theatrical envelope to a new dimension. I believed it could become the quintessential Hal Prince show. We went out for Chinese food to celebrate, and over the stir-fried chicken I agreed to produce *Kiss*. The one thing I remember we all agreed on was that we bring in Chita Rivera to play the title role.

At the same time I was also involved in producing Andrew Lloyd Webber's first musical after *Phantom*, *Aspects of Love*. Why would I do so, you might reasonably ask, since the show had lost its entire $8-million U.S. nut on Broadway? Well, I thought I knew what had gone wrong. *Aspects* is a show of intimate chamber music, whimsical and poetic, and it had been overwhelmed by its staging – by gargantuan production values and lavish-but-oppressive sets. Although it was set in a villa in the sunny south of France, Trevor Nunn and Maria Björnson chose to depict the piece in sombre shades of grey and brown. (Trevor was later gracious about my organization, despite my opinion of his *Aspects*. He wrote me a letter after he had visited Toronto in 1994 saying, "I came to Canada expecting I know not what, and with a vague and uncomfortable sense that you hadn't liked my version of *Aspects of Love*. I left with a feeling of great stimulus and zest because of the sheer energy, professionalism and vision that I encountered, and I even allowed myself to believe that my work was not without its admirers on your formidable team. . . ." I am thrilled that Trevor and I will be collaborating, in the fall of 1995, on Andrew Lloyd Webber's latest sensation, *Sunset Boulevard*.)

Set in France between 1947 and 1964, and based on Bloomsbury author David Garnett's 1955 novella, *Aspects* is a story of love and jealousy spanning three generations. The story begins with Alex, a British seventeen-year-old who is smitten by an older woman, a French actress named Rose Vibert. Alex invites her to spend a surreptitious fortnight in his uncle's villa in the south of France. She, in turn, falls in love with Alex's sybaritic and bohemian uncle, George Dillingham, an art forger, who shows up unexpectedly. George is also having an affair with an Italian sculptress, Giulietta Trapani. The story also suggests a liaison between Rose and Giulietta.

The simple fact is that Andrew's *Aspects of Love* was an intimate, transitional piece. And although the score had some of his most beautiful, enlightened, Mozartean writing, it never captured the public's imagination.

Nevertheless, I decided that when you have a relationship with a composer and his company, you don't cherry-pick. Loyalty is important. You're in for everything. It's part of the quid pro quo. Livent had had great success with Andrew's work. In addition to two productions of *Phantom*, we had mounted a concert presentation of songs and music composed by Andrew titled *The Music of Andrew Lloyd Webber* that was based on a similar limited-run presentation in England in 1988. We gave the show its North American première in Vancouver and followed this engagement with a staging at the

O'Keefe Centre in Toronto in July 1989, two months before *Phantom* opened. Starring Andrew's then-wife, Sarah Brightman, both engagements were completely sold out. Our production toured North America from the fall of 1989 until the fall of 1992, featuring, from time to time, Miss Brightman and Michael Crawford.

*Aspects* was a show very close to Andrew's heart, and I agreed to produce it largely because of that, but only if I was allowed to supervise the reworking of it as a chamber piece.

I decided to produce an entirely new staging conceived by Robin Phillips, who had become director-general of Edmonton's Citadel Theatre. Phillips's restaging acknowledged that *Aspects* is essentially a memory play. Phillip Silver's sets used white, diaphanous curtains and scrims, through which characters materialized and vanished. Ann Curtis's costumes created a beautiful look that transcended the time period. It was reminiscent of many of the Stratford Festival's stylish shows during Robin Phillips's tenure in the seventies and eighties.

The exceptional cast was headed by Australian actor Keith Michell, known to television audiences for his performance in the title role of the BBC series "The Six Wives of Henry VIII." We opened on September 1, 1991, at the Citadel Theatre and were very well received. Andrew attended the gala première. Throughout the performance he displayed his customary fits of anxiety, but in the end thought it a great improvement over what had gone before.

After a six-week run, the musical moved to Toronto's Elgin Theatre, where it opened on December 3, 1991. The space didn't quite suit the show's intimacy, once again revealing the problem of the paucity of Toronto's available commercial theatre spaces.

Undaunted, we mounted a touring production that began in Chicago in April 1992 and played throughout the United States to mixed reviews. But, in the end, *Aspects* was never going to find its audience, and the tour ended in June 1993. We wrote off a portion of our investment and moved on.

In June 1991 the next Andrew Lloyd Webber project was already in the works.

Under the invigorating direction of Stephen Pimlott, Andrew had remounted a colourful production of his very first show, the one he had written with Tim Rice, called *Joseph and the Amazing Technicolor Dreamcoat*. This time it starred Australian TV heartthrob Jason Donovan, and premièred at London's Palladium to overwhelming critical acclaim.

A few weeks earlier I had had one of those special moments in my theatrical life. Andrew had called me into his private study at his Sydmonton estate and played for me the mega-mix of *Joseph*, a roof-raising recital of all the show's tunes. And from the first moment I saw Andrew's new version at the Palladium, I had said, "We're doing this show." Pimlott, better known in England as a director of operas and Shakespearean theatre, had staged a marvellous, playful, campy, and witty, tongue-in-cheek production that made the most of Andrew's musical-pastiche score and Tim Rice's irreverent lyrics.

The story, of course, was from Genesis, and tells the tale of Joseph being cast out by his eleven brothers, his subsequent sale into slavery, and how he eventually acquires power in Pharaoh's court through his interpretation of dreams. Its climax has Joseph flown high above the orchestra's first few rows, trailing his long coat of many colours. Anthony Van Laast's choreography was a panoply of funfilled gyrations, twirls, and kicks. More than a musical, this was like a party that rocked the theatre. Mark Thompson's designs were bright and geometric, playfully evoking the musical's Egyptian setting.

One of the most charming elements, one that showed Andrew's theatrical genius at its most subtle, was the participation of a children's choir, which gave the show a sweetness and a gaiety impossible to find any other way.

I was at the première and the black-tie reception that followed at the British Museum of Natural History. There, dining among the dinosaurs, I began to press Patrick McKenna, managing director of RUG, for the rights. I continued to pursue the licence with my usual prodigious effort, and thirty days later we had it. We would give the show its North American première at Toronto's Elgin Theatre in June 1992.

* * *

In October 1991 we moved ahead with the musical reading of *Kiss of the Spider Woman*. To see how far we had come and what more was needed, we gathered in a rehearsal studio in Michael Bennett's former building at 890 Broadway. Richard Thomas, well-known to television viewers for his role as John-Boy on "The Waltons," portrayed Molina with great vulnerability, while Anthony Crivello performed the part of Valentín. The always sprightly Chita Rivera, looking years younger than her birth certificate indicated, read and sang the pivotal role of Aurora/Spider Woman.

We were all thrilled by what we heard. Something genuinely new and daring was evolving. And yet there was still some residual uneasiness in my mind. The earlier version had failed at Purchase. And the work dealt with exceptionally difficult subject matter.

I wasn't used to being uneasy or uncertain. So one day, sometime after the New York reading, I called Jay Scott and asked him over to my office. Jay, who died of AIDS-related causes in 1993, was Canada's most erudite, intelligent, and witty movie critic, and I had always had a profound respect for his writing. Jay had also been a strong believer in the original concept of Cineplex and of smaller screens devoted to the art of specialty programming, the kind of films he loved to review.

I sat him down and told him about my plans for *Kiss*.

"Look," I said, "I'm still not sure whether I really want to do this or not. I'm just not sure, Jay. This is really a tough call for me. I think I love it and I think it's right. But, given its subject matter, homosexuality, incarceration, some pretty tough areas. . . . I want you to listen to this."

I put a tape of the New York reading on the DAT machine. I even allowed him to smoke – and I allow *no one* to smoke in my office – but Jay couldn't handle an hour and a half without tobacco.

"I'm going to put this on and I'm going to go do some other work in the boardroom. I'll leave you alone. We'll talk afterward."

Jay was absorbed, enthralled. Later we went to dinner at Sisi Trattoria across from my office, and, over his second glass of cabernet, he leaned forward and said, "Garth, do it. I think it will be an incredibly important piece of work, a watershed." His encouragement gave me the added confidence to proceed.

I scheduled *Kiss* to open in Toronto in the summer of 1992 at the St. Lawrence Centre. If it worked, I planned to take it to London's West End that October. After the devastation of the Purchase experience, I felt we needed the critical imprimatur from another respected world theatre centre before we dared bring *Kiss* to Broadway. It was the only way we had a chance of getting a fair shot, of avoiding critical prejudgement against the project. I believed that London, regardless of the New York critics, would welcome *Kiss* and view it on its own merits. Hal agreed with me on this, though we both understood it would add considerably to our costs. At least this stepped process could be halted if it became necessary; if we absolutely had to, we could terminate it in the West End. With luck, the wave of enthusiasm and praise generated there would carry the show to Broadway. Toronto, for all its strengths, just didn't carry the heft that London did. I pencilled in the spring of 1993 as a possible Broadway date.

We had already engaged a creative team we were certain could further elevate the project. Our new choreographer was Vincent Paterson, acclaimed for Madonna's Blonde Ambition tour and her movie *Truth or Dare*. He had also created the choreography for Michael Jackson's controversial music video "Black or White," as well as Steven Spielberg's motion picture *Hook*.

Hal first became aware of Vincent's work when he reluctantly saw *Truth or Dare*. He's a self-confessed Puritan and went to the theatre thinking, "Why is Judy [his wife] dragging me to this?" Yet he loved the movie and called it "a fascinating study of her brain." More importantly, he thought the dance numbers were stunning. When he got home, he called Vince immediately. But when he identified himself, Vince hung up, thinking it was a prank. Hal called back, then called me and Chita. We all agreed to hire Vince.

Hal also concluded that *Kiss* needed a realistic-yet-overpowering prison setting that could instantaneously metamorphose into any scene from one of Molina's intriguing and often elaborate movies. Hal wanted to collaborate with Jerome Sirlin, whose stunning scenic designs and projections had thrilled audiences in the Philip Glass/David Henry Hwang performance piece *1,000 Airplanes on the Roof.*

I also had a hunch about the role of Molina. I loved Thomas's readings for the role, but I was a touch nervous about the strength of his singing voice; this would, after all, be his first musical. Brent Carver, a Canadian actor who for twenty years has earned the love and respect of audiences for his many memorable performances in regional theatres and the Stratford Festival, auditioned for us at the St. Lawrence Centre, where he was starring in Molière's *Tartuffe.* His reading, before all of the authors and Hal and me, was so compelling that I convinced Hal that we should hire him as Thomas's alternate. Richard would play the role of Molina six times a week and Brent would perform it twice a week, just as actresses who shared the role of Christine do in *Phantom.*

*God, I love that feeling, that feeling that only theatre can give, when actors, alone on an undressed stage, insert themselves so completely into a role that they capture the auditorium and everyone in it, holding them spellbound. It is absolutely breathtaking. And then, in a performance, when each actor is charging his or her lines with meaning, feeding off the others and the audience, creating something greater – it's an overwhelming feeling when theatre is really cooking. There's nothing in movies like it, nothing.*

My instinct about Brent was eerily good. Fortune must have been smiling at me, because before our rehearsals even began, Richard Thomas called me in Anguilla where I was sailing and told me he had to withdraw because he was going through a messy divorce. Brent stepped effortlessly into the part and won the instant admiration of his colleagues.

I consider myself to be a creative producer in the old-fashioned theatrical tradition. Hal, bless him, confided to a radio reporter once that I am "defining producing again, as a creative process. There are very few creative producers, and they are very much needed." Perhaps Hal's greatest compliment to me was his attestation to my marketing savvy. One day he turned to me and said, "If you were producing *Fiddler on the Roof*, it would still be running today."

In a return to standards Hal was brought up on, he keeps saying, in his graceful way, "I work for him." That means a great deal to me, since Hal's teacher was the great dramatist, director, and actor George Abbott. For my part, I still keep saying, simply out of respect for our collaborative relationship, "No way. I work alongside him."

Hal taught me what true artistic risk is and how important such risks are. The shows that have boosted his reputation – *Follies, Pacific Overtures, Sweeney Todd* – never recouped their Broadway production costs, but they rewarded him profoundly in other ways, in his creative heart.

I learned a lot from him, but I hope I have given him something back too. On Broadway today there's hardly ever an effective and protective interface between the artist and the business elements of theatre, between artists and the collaborative struggle.

I was initially in awe of Hal during the early days of *Phantom*. But I came to know him well and to learn something about his inner nervousness and his need for assurance. Over the years, despite minor differences of opinion, Hal and I have never had a huge argument. Our partnership is a creative journey. Seldom, for instance, have we ever disagreed on casting. I've come to understand his temperament and have learned when I can approach him firmly and when I should leave him alone, when to nudge, when not to push. Working with Hal, I learned how to nurture artists, how to sustain them and keep them going. I know how to stop them cannibalizing themselves.

Hal demands closed rehearsals, but every few days he invites me to come and see the progress of the piece. He works very fast. In the first week he will put the first act on its feet and in the second week, the second act. Thereafter, rehearsals will be run-throughs of each act. By that time I'm already weighing the piece, assessing what problems I see. If I say something like, "There's still a lack of coherence here," he's likely to respond, "Hold on! I'm not finished yet!" But I believe that he does now respect my initial reactions and visual sense.

*Kiss* got closer to launch date. Jay Scott, to my delight, did a major advance piece, a full-page feature in the *Globe and Mail* in which he predicted the "darkly stirring" work "had the potential of becoming a classic musical."

The excitement continued to build during previews. Hal said he hadn't felt this good about a show since *West Side Story* opened in 1956. Chita said much the same thing.

However, by the time we opened in Toronto, we knew we hadn't solved all the problems. Surprisingly, Vince Paterson's choreography was disappointing; it didn't take full advantage of Chita's talents or show her to her best advantage. The Kander and Ebb score sagged in the middle scenes. One song in particular, "Don't Even Think About It," although entertaining, just didn't work in the context of the story. We needed a showstopping song that better clarified and defined the relationship between Molina and Aurora, the fantasy movie queen of his dreams. Terrence McNally also needed to make substantial changes to the book to clarify characterization, motivation, and plot. In particular, at the top of Act II, we needed to have staged one of Molina's imaginary movies so the audience themselves could understand their attraction to Valentín.

Still, I was ecstatic when *Kiss* premièred, and the opening-night audience rose to its feet, shouts of *bravo!* echoing through the theatre. Maybe, I thought, Toronto was at last mature enough to embrace a musical of this nature. At the post-opening reception at the Four Seasons Hotel in Yorkville, one of the highest accolades came from Carlos Puig, who was the executor of his late brother's estate. He spoke little English, but he had no difficulty communicating: he hugged Brent Carver when they met and wept tears of joy. After all, Molina was one of the most heroic and beloved characters in all of Manuel Puig's fiction, and Brent's heartbreaking performance would live long in memory.

The next day's notices were mainly upbeat, even enthusiastic, except for an inexplicably pathetically written piece in the *Globe* by the then-theatre critic Liam Lacey (who neglected even to mention that Hal Prince had directed the production!). Many of the critics shared the opinion that Brent's performance as Molina outshone William Hurt's Oscar-winning performance in the movie.

Perhaps the most insightful review was written by Robert Cushman and published in the *Globe* nine days after Lacey's drivel. He had been "thrilled, gripped and moved," he said, and called *Kiss* "a rare serious musical, the best prison musical since *Fidelio*." On the face of it, it was an eccentric comparison, juxtaposing as it did a Broadway musical with Beethoven's opera, but I could see his point. *Fidelio* is part of the "rescue opera" genre, in which an innocent hero of noble character faces death, only to be ultimately saved by a force higher than himself. I knew Hal would consider the comparison arch and pretentious, but I understood – at least Robert was moved enough by our work to draw the connection.

In a subsequent article, written for London's *The Independent*, Robert added, "I've been saying for years that there are only three American musicals of tragic dimensions: *Porgy and Bess, Camelot* and *Sweeney Todd*. Now make that four."

Despite these reviews, despite the fact that we had a cast and creative team comprised of some of the finest talents in the theatre, despite the fact that the musical was adapted from a best-selling novel that had inspired an Academy Award-winning movie, I just couldn't excite a Canadian audience to come and see it, just couldn't pierce that national reticence.

I concluded that Canadians still needed to read the critical endorsement of the foreign press before they would turn out. It's so frustrating! I would like to see Canadians willing to experience and support new material, to make up their own minds, and to trust their own judgement.

After opening night, Hal, who was exhausted, left for his inevitable three-month summer sojourn. It was torture for me; he waited just twenty-four hours after the show opened and then jetted off. I wanted to dig in right away and implement the revisions I knew we had to make. We had so much work to do but, alas, the changes would have to wait until the end of our three-month Toronto engagement. To complicate matters further, Fred Ebb, who had been suffering

angina pains throughout our Toronto rehearsals, underwent quad-
ruple open-heart bypass surgery within days of the opening, and his
health was very fragile. I was afraid we would lose him altogether.

Over those twelve weeks the fax machines hummed and grew hot
with missives from Hal deep in darkest Europe, urging, cajoling,
demanding of John and Fred repeatedly, "Write a new song to replace
'Don't Even Think About It.'" They thought about it and eventually
responded with their own fax saying, "We're tired of your faxes."
Then they sat down and wrote the new song in less than an hour. It
was titled "Where You Are," a brassy, syncopated blockbuster in the
great Broadway tradition. When they later played the song for Hal
and me for the first time in a little room next to the main rehearsal
hall at the Elgin Theatre, I knew at once that they had succeeded, that
this was going to be a major showstopper.

During July 1992 I accumulated all the authors' notes and then off
I went to Positano to meet Hal.

It was a typically bizarre day in my life. I was in London. I got up at
the crack of dawn, took a private plane to Naples and then a limo
skirting the crowded beach to Positano. I spent four hours with Hal,
getting his blessing on the changes, and then a helicopter arrived to
take me back to the airport to pick up my plane to get to the Concorde
in London to fly back to New York to get to Toronto so I could have
the changes orchestrated and rehearsed prior to Hal's return.

Hal returned to Toronto during the final week of August, the last
week of Kiss's Canadian engagement, to put in some of the changes
we had agreed on. At that point we replaced Vince Paterson with a
new choreographer, Rob Marshall. We added the new Act I showstopper, "Where You Are." We also introduced a new number at the
top of Act II, "Russian Movie/Good Times," a depiction of one of
Molina's over-the-top movies, with Chita as a doomed cabaret star.
And the finale's choreography and staging were changed so that now
the Spider Woman and Molina would dance an increasingly tense
tango of death which culminates in Molina bravely embracing her
and seizing her kiss – literally and triumphantly embracing death –
to the cheers and bravos of the people in his life, members of an

audience viewing this ultimate movie fantasy of his in the moment before his death.

Just ten days after we opened *Kiss*, on June 24, Livent's production of Andrew Lloyd Webber's *Joseph and the Amazing Technicolor Dreamcoat*, starring pop singing sensation Donny Osmond, received its North American première for a limited eleven-week engagement.

Casting Donny Osmond was a real coup. After his astonishing success as a child pop star and his hit TV variety series during his teen years with his sister, Marie, Donny had vanished from public sight. In his thirties he attempted a comeback with a new rock-and-roll image, but his success was only moderate. He had been thinking of turning to acting, and *Joseph* gave him his chance. And he took it – did he ever take it! His performance was magnificent. The onetime *Teen Beat* heartthrob, the object of fans' adoration, was once again a knockout. Women who had loved him when they were teenagers brought their children to see him, and the *kids* smothered him with affection.

I can take only part of the credit for casting Donny. I got a call one day from Arnold Mungioli, a young New York University theatre graduate. He was then freelancing with our New York casting agents Johnson Liff, though he's now in my casting department. He phoned me cold and said, "Donny Osmond. What do you think?"

I hadn't followed Donny's career recently. I didn't know whether this was a brilliant or an off-the-wall notion.

But hey, I'm receptive to any intriguing idea. I called my receptionist and switchboard operator, a young woman in her early twenties, and I said, "Donny Osmond. What do you think?"

"Are you kidding?" she said. "I wouldn't wash my hand again if he came in here and he shook it. That's how mad I am about him."

So on the strength of that astute piece of marketing analysis, I called Arnold back. "Let's pay for a first-class ticket and bring him in to New York for an audition," I said. I had already auditioned everyone I could think of, even Olympic diving champions. I needed a gorgeous body with a gorgeous voice, an icon. For our promotional focus, he had to be ideal in nature and in form.

Donny flew overnight from L.A. and came off the plane unshaven (with perfect stubble), in skintight jeans and a black leather jacket. He looked great. First thing he said was, "I really haven't had a lot of time to learn the music, but before I sing a song from the show, I'd like to perform a piece of my music."

And I'll be goddamned if he didn't ask the piano accompanist to get off his seat. He sat down and started to play and sing. He was terrific. Then he got up, walked to the corner of stage right, squatted down, and started to sing "Close Every Door." It was mesmeric. The empty house, with its lights up, immediately became a darkened sanctuary; everything centred on him; with no props, no lighting, no theatrics, he could hypnotize an audience as sceptical as a casting committee. I knew at once I had my star.

Another stroke of luck: we signed up Johnny Seaton, one of North America's best Elvis impersonators, to amuse and enthrall crowds with his campy, swivel-hipped performance as the Pharaoh, blue suede shoes and all.

*Kiss* opened in London's West End, at the thirteen-hundred-seat Shaftesbury Theatre on October 20, 1992. This was a special experience for me. I had never before produced a show in the West End, where theatre is in everyone's blood – even the cab drivers knew about *Kiss*. During the two weeks of teching the show, I spent almost every night going to the theatre, especially to see the other two musicals opening the same time as ours – the Norwegian entry, *Which Witch?*, and *Radio Times*. I wasn't impressed, and though I couldn't guess the British critics' reaction to *Kiss*, from everything I saw and heard, especially opinions from audiences at our previews, I was convinced we had a winner.

*We were rehearsing in the midst of Yom Kippur and Rosh Hashanah, and for the first time I was away from my family during those holy days. I ended up going to synagogue alone in London, because I just couldn't afford to be away from London at so critical a juncture. The pressure was so acute. We had actually lost money during the run in Toronto, but I somehow had found the confidence to go the next step and take it to*

*London. I couldn't stop now. It was too good. It was too important. But there in London by myself during the holy days, for a brief period I wavered. And I was desperately lonely.*

There was one completely unexpected, and potentially devastating, hitch to our London prospects – an IRA bombing campaign. Just a couple of weeks before *Kiss* opened, a bomb exploded in a nearby pub, killing one man; another went off no more than a hundred yards from where I was holding casting sessions with our resident director, Annie Allen, our vice-president for casting, Beth Russell, and our resident music supervisor, Jeff Huard. While Londoners tend to take terrorism in stride, I still had a horrid feeling that our part of the West End might be avoided by theatre patrons for a few weeks. On the other hand, previews continued to sell well and the buzz on the show was hot. Nightly, such celebrities as Robert Downey, Jr., Robert Wagner, and Eartha Kitt came to catch the musical.

On opening night security precautions were paramount. Tracker dogs sniffed the theatre and it was pronounced safe before the glamorous audience began arriving. Stockard Channing, Ben Kingsley, Joan Collins, Twiggy, Sir Ian McKellen, Gillian Lynne, Cleo Laine, John Dankworth, Dame Judi Dench, Peter Hall, Conrad Black, and Barbara Amiel were among those who showed up for the gala. Pearl was there with me, and afterwards we went to dinner at Orso's with Andrew Lloyd Webber, his wife, Madeleine, and the ever-luminous Plácido Domingo.

London is an unusual city for theatre people; there are so many daily and weekly newspapers that it can take three or four days for all the reviews to come in. But the next day, and in the days to follow, the reviews were extremely favourable. In fact, Hal received his best British notices. The *Daily Telegraph* said, "This is a musical that combines emotional generosity with an often dazzling theatricality. It deserves to thrive." Benedict Nightingale in *The Times* said, "This is a show that sacrifices neither a serious subject to entertainment nor entertainment to a serious subject: a feat to respect and enjoy." Michael Coveney in *The Observer* called *Kiss* "a triumph . . . deeply moving."

Kenneth Hurren in *The Mail on Sunday* proclaimed, "the best musical for a decade!"

Shortly after it opened, *Kiss* won the 1992 Evening Standard Award for Best Musical.

I had been waiting to make my final preparations for Broadway until I saw the London reviews – bad reviews would have given me serious second thoughts. But now my strategy of taking the show to London seemed to have paid off. With these strong notices in hand, and the award, I could use London's reaction to overcome any residual American uncertainty from the show's initial mounting in Purchase. Almost immediately I put on hold New York's Broadhurst Theatre, on 44th Street next to the Majestic, which housed *Phantom*, and planned to begin previews within six months, in April 1993. The Broadhurst could bring us good luck, I hoped – that was where Hal had teamed up with John Kander and Fred Ebb to stage *Cabaret* in 1966.

The next step was to record the original cast album, which we did at London's Olympic Studios. It was released in England on First Night Records in February 1993 and in May in North America on RCA Victor.

Hal and I decided to open *Kiss* on Broadway on May 3, just before the deadline for the 1993 Tony Awards. *Kiss* had proved itself in London and I believed it would stand out against the other contenders for the Best Musical Award. To be sure, I had flown to La Jolla to see an earlier incarnation of The Who's *Tommy* and to Chicago on New Year's Eve 1992 to see a preview of the musical adaptation of Neil Simon's *The Goodbye Girl*, starring Martin Short and Bernadette Peters, which was getting mixed reviews. I concluded that our Tony chances were strong.

One of the unusual aspects of our London *Kiss* was our taking the original Canadian cast to the West End; the same cast then departed for Broadway, and we recast the show with Bebe Neuwirth, well-known to TV audiences for her role as Lilith in "Cheers," as Aurora/Spider Woman, Canadian Jeff Hyslop as Molina, and Charles

Pistone as Valentín. By July, despite five Olivier Award nominations – *Kiss* won for Howell Binkley's lighting – we had to close the show in London because we couldn't adequately replace the principal cast from the U.K. As well, the box office had begun to suffer – the unusually hot summer was murder.

*Kiss*'s New York debut was an unforgettable moment for me. Here I was, back on Broadway, memories of my awful experience with *A Broadway Musical* nagging at the back of my mind. But this time it was entirely different. I got a sneak preview of New York's reaction during our invited dress preview. With many of New York's theatre and social élite in the audience, including actress Elaine Stritch and George Furth, author of such Sondheim/Prince musicals as *Company* and *Merrily We Roll Along*, the atmosphere was electric. At the finale the audience rose in unison to its feet, stamping and roaring its approval. One New York society doyenne who sat next to our director of communications, Dennis Kucherawy, said to him, "My, that was wonderful! I'm going to tell my family to come and see this." When Dennis thanked her, she replied, "Please allow me to introduce myself. I'm Patricia Kennedy Lawford." As Dennis said to me later, "Some family!"

Opening night attracted another star-laden crowd, including Gregory Hines, Lena Horne, Liza Minnelli, Michael York, Tony Randall, Jack Klugman, Betty Comden and Adolph Green, Beverly Sills, Lynn Redgrave, Lucie Arnaz, Joan Rivers, and Fay Wray. Harry Belafonte sat beside Pearl and me; when I glanced over at him during the poignant moments of Act II, I noticed tears streaming down his face. At the curtain the standing ovation seemed to go on forever. Harry turned to me and gave me an enormous hug, congratulating me for having the courage to stay the course.

After the première, I didn't go to the celebratory party. I walked with Pearl over to the offices of LeDonne, Wilner and Weiner, our New York advertising agency. There, I unbuttoned my shirt and settled in eagerly to monitor the entertainment beats on TV and await print reviews.

This certainly was not *A Broadway Musical*. The reviews were overwhelming. *Time* and *Newsweek* both loved the show. Howard Kissel of the *Daily News* wrote that the musical "manages to be beautiful, funny and moving." Michael Kuchwara, drama critic for Associated Press, called it "a thrilling evening of theatre . . . outdazzles every other song-and-dance extravaganza on Broadway."

Of course, the crucial review, to see if we had overcome the Purchase experience, was that of Frank Rich in the *New York Times*. Rich wrote, "For those who dote on Broadway musicals, Mr. Prince's new work would be worth seeing just for the Fellini-esque finale, a flashback to an old movie palace that is a variation on the famous Loveland sequence in his 1971 *Follies*. When he finally brings Mr. Carver into Ms. Rivera's arms to seal his fate with her long-awaited kiss, you cannot help feeling a shiver of pure theatre. Not because the kiss realizes this musical's lofty intentions, but because it consummates the showmanship of a director who wrote the book on how to spread a web of white heat through a Broadway house."

After reading the *Times* review, I felt an enormous sense of relief. Pearl and I rode over to Hal's exquisite Upper East Side two-storey apartment, where he and Judy fêted the cast in grand style. Hal and I went to a quiet corner and together relished the knowledge that the rest of the world had vindicated the judgements we had made through our four-year journey, and that *Kiss* was, at last, a sweet victory.

We didn't have an excessive box-office advance, but it built substantially following the first day's notices. Then came the Tony Awards. I had never been to a Tony ceremony before. And it was a real nailbiter for us. We had almost a dozen nominations, but so did our main competition, *Tommy*.

We started off the evening winning three or four awards very quickly. And then we stopped, and the momentum of the evening went to *Tommy*. They picked up some technical awards and the choreography award. I was beginning to get worried. What was upsetting me was that for the past week I had been hearing rumours that the industry was not prepared to give the Best Director Award to Hal Prince. The reason? Hal had already received nineteen Tonys – and there's a weird sense of balance that's injected into any voting procedure for awards. You can see it at the Academy Awards every year. But I just couldn't conceive how Hal, who had brilliantly reworked the piece over the year between Purchase and Toronto, and who had directed three nominated performances (Chita Rivera, Brent Carver, Anthony Crivello) – how could he not get Best Director?

Of course, Hal saw it differently. "The most important thing," he kept saying to me before the evening, "is that we must win Best Musical." In one way he was right. Had Hal received the Best Director Award, to which he was justly entitled, while we were overlooked for Best Musical, then commercially the show's future would have been in doubt.

And Hal genuinely did want the award for me. He wanted me to get Best Musical. He and Judy were sitting in front of Pearl and me, in the first row. And across the aisle was Manny Azenberg, one of the great producers on Broadway, who has been in Neil Simon's corner for at least twenty-five years. Manny kept looking across the aisle at me and mouthing the words, "Relax! You're going to win!" I've been through a lot of motion-picture award ceremonies, and I've won and lost my share, and I know how these things go. Still, I was tightly wound and pretty nervous by the time *Tommy* won three in a row. And then when Hal lost to Canadian Des McAnuff, director of *Tommy*, I became really upset, because now the fiscal health of the show was all, essentially, down to one award.

The weekend before the awards, Dick Roberts, who was quite literally days away from dying of ravaging cancer, stumbled up from his apartment and came into my office, lying down wearily on the couch. You could see he wanted to live long enough to see me win the award. It was important to him in some fundamental but obscure way.

"Dick," I said, "I gotta figure out what to say if I'm going to win this thing. I don't have more than about twenty seconds to do it. What do I say?"

I wanted to get across two things: to pay tribute to Hal Prince in a way that all of America, Canada, and the industry would hear. I don't think this had been done nearly enough throughout Hal's illustrious career. Our industry, as in all segments of the entertainment industry, has a shadow of envy and jealousy that creeps into everything. And here was Hal, a man who had done more than anyone else, who reshaped musical theatre as we know it, and I wanted to remind people of this.

The second thing I worried about was Canada. It was important to me to get across that the show had been rescued and revived in Toronto. If there was a theatregoing public watching the awards in Toronto, at least on that night I wanted them to realize once and for all that we're capable of creating outstanding work.

So I had it all worked out.

The final award, the big one, was to be presented by Michael Crawford. "How wonderful," I thought, "if I win this." Michael had starred in our production of *The Music of Andrew Lloyd Webber*, and he was the original Phantom, and *Phantom* had been so crucial to my theatrical life, giving me the economic strength to go on, and Hal Prince had directed *Phantom*. . . .

When the announcement came and I had won, I had a great, instantaneous sense of exhilaration, the kind of feeling that comes only rarely in one's life. So much effort had poured into that one moment, so much toil. I remembered how Marty Bell and the others had been sandbagged by the critics up at Purchase. I remembered the little plane trip Hal and I had taken over Whistler, when he'd told me how he'd reworked the script, and how I'd read it later and had known at once that it was a triumph, and here I was, scooping up the most-coveted theatrical award in the premier theatrical city of the world. The award was for me, for Hal, for all of us – for Fred Ebb, who ten months before had open-heart surgery; for Terrence McNally, who so desperately wanted it; for Myron, who had shared the risks with me and was now sharing the rewards; for all the hopes and aspirations of all the people who had helped make it work; for all the performers and crew; for the spirit and the morale of our own company;

for my family; for Pearl and the kids (I thought of their worried faces the night I had gone home, after my ousting from Cineplex Odeon). The euphoria I felt was for all of us.

Nothing else I've won has come close to this. For the rest of my life I can always be introduced as the Tony Award-winning producer. Well, that's a nice title to have.

As I went up to the stage to get my award and make my little tribute, I thought *I hope the camera doesn't follow me up. I don't want twenty-five million people to watch me lurch up to the stage. It never leaves me, I guess.* And they were sensitive to it – I watched the videos later and they never showed me limping at all.

At Livent's party afterwards at Manhattan's Symphony Café, Hal told those present, "The only regret I have about not winning Best Director is that I was unable to say publicly, to all those millions watching, that Garth was the only producer anywhere who had the vision and the courage to produce *Kiss*."

And so, within a month after its Broadway opening, Livent's production of *Kiss of the Spider Woman*, which had already won big in London, made theatre history when it became the first musical to go from a Toronto stage to international success, winning not just Best Musical but six other Tony Awards. (Our other Tonys included Best Actress: Chita Rivera; Best Actor: Brent Carver; Best Featured Actor: Anthony Crivello; Best Musical Score: John Kander and Fred Ebb; Best Book: Terrence McNally; and Best Costumes: Florence Klotz.) *Kiss* also was given five 1992-93 New York Drama Desk Awards, including Outstanding Musical, and the 1993 New York Drama Critics' Circle Award for Best Musical. (It's significant to note that this prize wasn't awarded in 1994.) In Toronto the show won seven Dora Mavor Moore Awards, again including Best Musical. *Kiss* also received the 1994 New York Outer Critics' Circle Award for Outstanding Musical, and Chita won the prize for Best Actress. In fact, *Kiss* became the first musical since *Les Misérables* to sweep every Best Musical award on Broadway. In November 1994 our production of *Kiss* began a two-year North American tour, again starring Chita.

Meanwhile, I had hired the pop diva Vanessa Williams as Chita's replacement on Broadway, the first black female star on Broadway for a long while, possibly since Pearl Bailey. She has had fabulous critical response since she appeared, but it does illustrate an interesting point – simply appointing her didn't sell advance tickets in any numbers. Theatre audiences are reluctant to accept cross-overs from pop music to musical theatre. It was only after her stunning reviews that we started to sell tickets in substantial quantities.

And in all this, not once did the story make it to the front pages of the Canadian newspapers. It was the first time a Canadian had won the Tony for Best Musical, for a show that had started its run for glory in Toronto. I had spent four years of my life on a project that had won me international acclaim – and not once did I bump from the front pages the election of another municipal politician or the arrival in town of another raccoon or whatever else Canadian editors judged to be the news of the day. I've been cynical about the press for some time, but even I found that hard to take.

*Well,* Kiss *was a vindication of my artistic judgement and an affirmation of the multiple talents I had assembled around me. But it was even more than that. It had been vital for me and for the company I was nurturing to follow a licensed production like* Phantom *– no matter how successful, how well executed, how artistically sound – with a show of our own, one that we had created and developed, that belonged to us alone. It was equally relevant to demonstrate that we had the verve and the nerve to tackle difficult subjects in a theatrically exceptional way. Doing the show at all immediately garnered me recognition as a producer of significant work and enhanced my stature in the industry almost overnight, in a way that I could never have done by reproducing the proven works of Andrew Lloyd Webber, no matter how successfully. That was worth everything. I knew now where our company was going.*

# CHAPTER

## COMING HOME

With *Kiss* successfully launched on Broadway, it was time to devote greater attention to *Show Boat*, the rehearsals for which were beginning in only three months.

*Kiss* had drained me of so much of my emotional, creative juice, and I was exhausted. Yet again I was confronted with a mere sliver of time to resuscitate before pre-production began on a musical of epic proportions. What made it even more difficult was the decision, taken by both Myron and me, to issue shares of our company to the public, in what would be the first listing on a North American stock exchange of a company devoted entirely to live theatrical production.

Why go public? I knew only too well the administrative and accounting hassles it would bring in its train, but it was the only viable way of raising much-needed equity and strengthening our balance sheet for future growth. We wanted to grow the company with minimum reliance on traditional bank financing and at the same time to see our ownership position appreciate through market recognition. The only way to do this was through public financing. So once again we embarked on a week-long series of public roadshows across the country, endless speeches, endless meetings with the retail and institutional components of the marketplace.

But in the end, it was done. The shares were well received by the public and we could look with increasing confidence to the future.

We had staged a reading of Hal's new scripted version in October 1991. As I listened to the drama of the story and the lush score, I wept. I knew our completely rethought production of *Show Boat* would captivate audiences not only in Toronto but throughout North America, even the world.

In revising Hammerstein's book, Hal gathered material from the first 1927 production, the London script, the 1936 film, and the 1946 Broadway revival. He consulted John McGlinn's 1988 EMI–Angel recording of the complete *Show Boat*, consisting of the 1927 production and all the musical material written for it over the years, as well as Miles Kreuger's superb historical chronicle, *Show Boat: The Story of a Classic American Musical.*

Hal decided, among other changes, to replace what he called the "conventional" and "irrelevant" second-act opener at the Chicago World's Fair and to return instead to the principal story with the birth of Magnolia and Ravenal's daughter, Kim, in a thunderstorm. This was a departure because, from 1927 until well into the fifties, the musical tradition was to wake up the audience at the start of Act II with high-energy entertainment, devoid of strong story content.

But as I've said, Hal and I were determined to mount a gritty, documentary-style portrayal of the period. That's one of the reasons why we brought in Eugene Lee, who, with his love of natural materials, would be adept at recreating the look of Natchez, Mississippi, *circa* 1887.

I've always been attracted to historical themes and I feel comfortable in historical research. With this in mind, in the fall of 1992 I flew down to Natchez on the Mississippi. I had never spent any time in a southern plantation town and I thought it important to do so, both from the point of view of truly understanding the script and because I thought such an understanding would help my marketing efforts. In the debilitating heat and insufferable humidity I toured a riverboat and visited a cotton plantation across the river in Louisiana. I picked a pod of cotton, that potent symbol of enslavement and oppression, and broke it open, smoothing the silky fibres inside. As I did so, I felt an almost atavistic jolt of understanding of the contradictions inherent in the Deep South. I returned to Toronto loaded down with books and cassettes to use in our research.

To be the voice of *Show Boat* on all our radio and TV commercials I engaged the eminent actor James Earl Jones, who is perhaps best known as the voice of Darth Vader in the *Star Wars* movies. He has one of the most distinctive voices in show business, a majestic basso profundo that I knew would penetrate the radio clutter and deliver *Show Boat*'s message effectively. Throughout his career James has been an outspoken supporter of black causes. In the late seventies he played Paul Robeson on the stage, the actor who gained fame for his portrayal of Joe in *Show Boat* and for his magnificent performance of "Ol' Man River." I was fascinated by James's professionalism and the efforts he had to make to overcome his speech difficulties.

It's always tough, of course, to advertise a show that hasn't been produced yet. You can't use video clips and you can't use audio recordings of the performers. In Canada it was doubly difficult, because *Show Boat* reflected an American, not a Canadian, heritage. But James's voice did exactly what I had predicted – it gave our promotional efforts a coherence and a focus and effortlessly pierced the "noise" of radio.

Public acceptance of *Show Boat* seemed certain. Goldfarb Research tested our radio commercials and the results went off the scale. Not only did those polled say they wanted to see the show – reassuring in itself – but they also identified *Show Boat* from the ads as relevant and historic.

Meanwhile, we were scouring North America to assemble a fascinating, diverse, integrated cast, including two-time Tony Award-winner Robert Morse as Cap'n Andy, one of the musical theatre's most celebrated and coveted roles, and Emmy Award-winner Elaine Stritch as his domineering wife, Parthy. It was a broad sweep – we looked at many hundreds of actors in those months – because we needed to assemble the cast equivalent of two full *Phantoms* and three of most Broadway shows. We needed no fewer than nine principal leads. Our performers came from opera, pop music, Broadway veterans, and Broadway newcomers. We scooped up in total seventy-three performers, the largest cast on a Broadway stage since 1927. The reason? We judged Kern's music would never be given its proper due without it – we owed it to the music and to ourselves to do it right.

Two years earlier, in the spring of 1991, when I announced at a widely reported press conference that *Show Boat* would open the new North York Performing Arts Centre in the fall of 1993, among those attending were Hal Prince and Bill Hammerstein. Hammerstein told the press how he had grown up with *Show Boat*. He was nine years old when the original Ziegfeld production had its debut in 1927, and he reminisced about how he used to stand onstage and watch the show from the wings. In 1946 he acted as stage manager of the last revival before Jerome Kern died. He spoke eloquently about how the original production had transformed audiences' perceptions about musical theatre.

"The first thing that happens as the curtain goes up," he said, "is there's a group of black workers on stage. And they turn to each other and they sing 'Niggers all work on de Mississippi, niggers all work while de white folks play.' Can you imagine how that went across with the audience of 1927? When they'd come to the Ziegfeld Theatre to see a Ziegfeld show, and that was the first thing that struck them? It was a shocker. In those days there was no consciousness, as there is today, about the plight of being black in our society. But it worked; it made people think. And the rest of the play is about a riverboat gambler and the naïve daughter of the owner of a Mississippi show boat, who meet and obviously long for each other. The audience knows it, the mother knows it – but resents it. They get married and have a pretty miserable life until the end of the show. But you believe in their love for each other. You know that they're inherently wrong for each other, you know that they're going to make each other unhappy. Nevertheless, you care about them so that, in the end, you want to see them come together.

"When Garth came to us and told us what he planned to do, I was thrilled. And I was triply thrilled when he got Hal to direct it. Nobody could bring more of a new life to this show than Hal because of his talent, his sense of convention and imagination, and certainly his ability and past experience."

Since the plight of the newly emancipated American blacks is a central element of the story, I was mindful, throughout Hal's development of the script, of the language we would use in the show, especially the use of the word "nigger." I wanted to ensure that our production would be a meaningful experience for the black community in Toronto, so many of whom came from the Caribbean and are not necessarily aware of American history. Long before the opening I wanted to learn what the local sensitivities were. Interestingly, *Show Boat* had been rewritten by Oscar Hammerstein through the years to reflect changing social attitudes. "Niggers all work on de Mississippi" became "Colored folk work on de Mississippi." I needed to determine whether to use the original or revised lyric. In the two years that followed I consulted widely inside Canada and out with such people as entertainer Harry Belafonte and Washington lawyer and civil-rights advocate Vernon Jordan, whom I had met at one of Prime Minister Mulroney's dinners at 24 Sussex in Ottawa and who later led Bill Clinton's transition team when he assumed office. Both men encouraged me to use the original lyrics, because it reflected the history and social condition of post-Reconstruction America.

Of my own volition, I held a consultation meeting with members of Toronto's black community on October 5, 1992. The list of invitees came from Lincoln Alexander, the former lieutenant-governor of Ontario. The meeting generated quite a bit of discussion about the intended tone of the production and a warning that radical younger members of the black community would likely not understand the historical accuracy or importance of the piece. While they wouldn't constitute its natural audience either, they posed some hazard of "discomfort" because of the lack of understanding.

At the meeting, suggestions were made that we use *Show Boat* in some way to raise funds that would benefit the Toronto or North York black community. At Lynda Friendly's suggestion, we agreed to reserve the night following opening night as a benefit evening for charities related to black causes, like sickle-cell anemia, and resolved to invite black groups to organize fund-raising events around it.

For a while that seemed to be that. There were no rumblings of protest from the black community, although the show was still receiving wide publicity and coverage. And then, on February 15, it all hit the fan, when Stephnie Payne, an elected North York board of education trustee, introduced a notice of motion alleging that *Show Boat* was "hate literature in the form of entertainment" and demanding that the board condemn the show and, in effect, boycott it if it went ahead.

Even in this early broadside, there were hints of the extravagant rhetoric that would later characterize the affair. Although Payne had, of course, neither seen the show nor read its script, her motion referred back to the Edna Ferber novel on which it was based, saying it "contributed to the negative images and stereotypes used to denigrate people of African ancestry, portraying them as subhuman savages, dimwitted, childlike, lazy, drunk, irresponsible and devoid of any redeeming human characteristics. . . ."

I knew that whatever my thoughts were about this motion – and they were, I assure you, pretty bleak – I would have to confront the issue. I had seen what had happened three years earlier at the Royal Ontario Museum, where a protest by the black community against an exhibition called *Into the Heart of Africa*, an exploration of the impact of missionaries on the continent, had escalated past all reason and had ended with the curator harassed and threatened, eventually banished, and museums all over the continent cravenly caving in to the worst forms of politically correct excess. I also knew that this was not something a corporate leader could delegate. This was something I should take charge of myself, be front and centre in.

I urgently needed to meet with Payne herself to learn firsthand what the problems were. So I called a private meeting with her at my office for the next day. Without consulting with me, she showed up with a cross-section of the black community; also present were some watchful members of B'nai B'rith.

I spent some time explaining the background to the piece, why it had been a seminal work, how it depicted the realities of its time, how it had played without incident for sixty-six years in many cities with black majorities. I spoke eloquently, I think, but to no avail. The meeting was rancorous and there were threats of escalating conflict. At one point Payne stood up and shouted, "I can't stand this! I'm going to strangle you!"

One of our initiatives had been to create an educational program, at a cost to us of $250,000. Part of our intention was to produce a forty-five-minute video and student/teacher resource kits that would have sections devoted to discussing the show's social background, the history of blacks in the South, issues of racism, and so on. But the mere mention of the money seemed to inflame paranoia, as though we were trying to buy consensus. "Who in North York authorized this?" Payne demanded. "Why wasn't the board of education consulted?" I explained patiently that it was a private initiative and we were using our own money, and that we'd be happy to have input from black educators. This seemed to mollify everyone.

The discussion ranged back and forth inconclusively. I took what I thought was the extraordinary step of volunteering Hal Prince's presence to meet privately with the group and answer their questions; this was after I had refused to yield up the script for their scrutiny.

On this I was adamant. "I will not get involved in a censorship situation," I said. "We will not have our integrity impeached. What does this request say about the democratic process? Do you think Spike Lee would have shown the script for his movie of Malcolm X to the Nation of Islam leaders? No, he would have gotten up from the table and walked away!"

At the end, it was agreed (sort of) that "progress had been made." We agreed to deal freely and frankly with everyone and to keep the discussions open. Payne even agreed to discuss delaying her motion, though it was clear her mind was already made up.

A week later, on February 24, the North York board of education voted, at a raucous, rancorous, and highly charged meeting, to "defer" debating or voting on Payne's motion, "pending further discussions between the producers of the show and members of the black community." For my part, I was prepared to meet as often as they liked. But I was not prepared for them to rewrite our script or to tell us what we'd be allowed to produce, and I told them so.

A day later, in any case, Payne almost self-destructed when she recklessly allowed herself to be picked up by a CTV cameraman saying that white men, especially the Jews, were always the ones responsible for "racist" plays that denigrate black people. The reference to Jews, and to the tender sensibilities between the Jewish and black communities, changed the nature of the debate immediately from our putative "racism" to Payne's newly revealed anti-Semitism.

Three days after her inflammatory televised remarks, the North York board convened again. The meeting was even more raucous. There were demands for Payne's resignation. She refused.

And so it went. There were forums and symposiums and press conferences and meetings. The United Way, which had reserved an early Show Boat performance for a fund-raiser in collaboration with the Canadian National Institute for the Blind, was pressured to withdraw; it refused, and reaffirmed its commitment to the production, causing considerable internal dissent. The Coalition to Stop Show Boat asked the Toronto Police Services Board and Ontario Human Rights Commission to intervene. (The commission, to my delight, later issued a report giving no credence to the notion that Show Boat was racist, but nonetheless raised the ominous view that "such things must not be allowed to happen again.")

I went ahead with the meeting I had offered to hold with Hal and me. More than sixty people showed up in the fourth-floor audition room of my head office, some in support of Show Boat, some vehemently opposed, others with no opinion. The meeting was chaired by Toronto's former mayor, David Crombie, and there was a full airing of views. And such views! The meeting was characterized by irrational statement, sneering, insult, hyperbole, and disrespect. It seemed to have little to do with *Show Boat* and more to do with airing of frustrations; it was politics as therapy. There was no recognition, apparently, that they were confronting one of the most politically sensitive directors of all time, who dealt with Nazism in *Cabaret*, totalitarian oppression and homophobia in *Kiss*, and racism in *West Side Story*. Hal and I stood firm; we refused to cave in to the strident tone and relentless pressure of the meeting and pledged to present *Show Boat* "in a manner that sustains the highest standards of integrity and decency," which was easy enough for us to promise since we had intended to do so from the beginning. Hal himself explained how he had only committed to do the show in the first place after everyone had agreed to re-examine any potential stereotyping.

Throughout the meeting, the United Way delegation looked on warily, trying to ensure that its support for *Show Boat* not be eroded through bullying and harassment.

Ralph Agard, a member of a black group called Harambe and also a United Way board member, demanded to see the script.

I remained defiant.

"I will not," I said. "It's censorship. It's repugnant."

As the weeks dragged on, the vile rhetoric spread rampantly. One flyer called *Show Boat* "an economic and cultural holocaust which transforms any performing arts centre into a gas chamber functioning at full strength at each production, in order to annihilate in the thoughts of the black child any hope of equal opportunities. . . ." For thirty continuous weeks I was subjected to scurrilous, hysterical, anti-Semitic commentary in *Share*, a weekly tabloid aimed at Toronto's black communities.

As for Stephnie Payne, she was caught trespassing in the *Show Boat* box office during one of the regular Saturday protests. There she threatened a black employee of mine. "I can't believe you need the money that bad," she snapped. She later denied having been there, but a videotape clearly showed she was. And on May 19 her motion finally came to a vote at a heated North York board of education meeting and was soundly defeated.

But I wasn't going to let it rest there. I was determined to do everything possible to confront and meet every opposition point of view. Why not? I had confidence in my production; I knew none of the protesters had seen the show or knew in any way what they were talking about. I persuaded Harvard professor Henry Louis Gates, Jr., the distinguished American black historian and civil libertarian, to read the script and give his honest, critical opinion. In October, as part of the Drabinsky Lecture Series, he delivered a major address at the North York Centre's Recital Hall. He called our production of *Show Boat* "a victory for tolerance and sensitivity." The problem with the protesters, as he pointed out, was that they made no distinction between a work of art that depicted racism and a work of art that was racist. And he denounced, in a ringing phrase, all efforts to suppress art. "Censorship for any reason," he said, "is to art what lynching is to justice, and we ought to fight the former as ardently as we fought the latter."

I don't want to give the impression that my life in this time was dominated only by the shock troops of political correctness. I was watching our production of *Show Boat* take shape under Hal's masterly direction; and at the same time I was watching the North York theatre complex take shape.

I was so proud of that building! For months, whenever I had any spare time, I would call up small groups of friends, or one or two journalists at a time, and I would walk them through the building. I would swing them through the raw concrete of the building site. Here, I would say, are where the public areas will go. Here, the bars will be set up, here, the concession stands – we'll sell the cast album of the show and related merchandise here. I pointed out the exceptional sightlines, the great size of the stage, the substantial dressing rooms. I showed them where the boxes were situated. I pointed out the airflow system under the seats, similar in design to those of early Thomas Lamb theatres. I could picture it all: the twinkling lights, the gorgeous colours, the richness of the detailing, the tumultuous applause, the crashing chords, the entrancement of the theatre.

The journalists would look at each other in that cynical way they have and grin. But I didn't mind. I was no longer Darth Grabinsky in the press. They had begun to see how much I loved theatre – and some of that would surely rub off!

And it all came to pass. The theatre complex opened on time and on budget, to rave reviews.

And then, the opening night of *Show Boat* approached.

Hal had asked me what to do about the critics.

"Well, I'll tell you," I said. "It's easy. This is the first time anyone has ever seen the Hal Prince version of *Show Boat*, and we're also opening a brand-new theatre complex to the world. It's also our first show together since winning the Tony for *Kiss*. So there's no doubt in my mind that sometime over the next few weeks, all the New York press contingent will want to come up and see the show anyway. I want them to see it and be swept up with the excitement of an opening gala. I don't want them trickling in during previews. I want to roll the dice. Let them be here with their Canadian counterparts. Let's make it a memorable event."

So I brought them all up, gave them a lunch at the Pantages (another chance to show them what I could do), and talked with them about my feelings and the project. I wanted to get to know them; they were, after all, going to be an essential influence on me for a long time.

Another reason I wanted the New York press contingent there was I had learned from *Kiss* that Canadians often need the imprimatur of foreign critics to endorse the production before they'll turn out to see it. As I told Hal, "They're going to want American critics telling them the show is wonderful. So I need those reviews to support my marketing strategy. I need a positive *New York Times* review in my first ad."

They all came, too – including of course the *Times'* Frank Rich. A fantastic turnout. There must have been two hundred and fifty press in the theatre that night, a who's who of theatre criticism.

For the first time in modern-day theatre, I believe – certainly for the first time since *Camelot* in 1960 – virtually every important North

American theatre critic had gathered under one roof at the same time to see a performance of a musical.

Was I nervous? Of course. And for another reason too: the press is not a demonstrative audience, obviously. And two hundred and fifty of them in one auditorium can end up dampening the enthusiasm of a whole crowd. It surely was a risk. On the other hand, the show wasn't playing in their cities, so at least they didn't have to run out afterwards to make a deadline, writing a hasty review. They could think about it a bit.

Talk about tension, though! I went backstage prior to the show, and though it was only six or seven minutes to curtain, Bobby Morse was still prowling the halls with his bathrobe on, as nervous and skittish as a pregnant doe. Not a good sign, not a reassuring sign at all.

Even on normal occasions the adrenaline levels are cranked up to Everest heights on opening nights. You just can't control it. For *Show Boat*, the preview audiences were filled with enthusiasm, and the research indicated an unequivocal smash. I knew what I had up there, but I wanted everyone else to love it too, all at the same time – I positively *willed* them to love it, to have as great a passion for the work as I did.

It's never been a business for the weak at heart. I can't sit through an opening performance without feeling that I'm going to die fourteen times during every mistake, mistakes that only I can see, that are invisible to the audience. It just destroys me inside. *Oh my God, where's that lighting cue? What happened to that sound effect, where is it? What happened to the timing of that transition scene? And why aren't you. . .?*

The first act played, on the whole, very well. But Bobby was clearly off. He was under the weather, his voice was hoarse and raspy from the rehearsal period and the exhaustion of the previews and because he smokes. He was nervous and it showed. At intermission, Hal was almost beside himself, convinced we had blown the whole thing because of Bobby's performance. I spent the entire intermission calming him down.

Everyone else was performing superbly. Act II went off without a hitch. Bobby was much more in control.

The pathetic protesters were huddled outside, as irrelevant as a wisp of fog left over in the dawn from a forgotten night of dreams. Inside the theatre, I sat with Pearl and the kids, my two brothers, and both sets of parents, Pearl's and mine, all there for the first time. I carefully observed the rapt crowd, mesmerized as the intricate production unfolded before their eyes, smoothly, silkily, as effortlessly as honey flowing off a spoon. And when Michel Bell, who was playing Joe, moved to centre stage and, in his powerful voice, began to sing the wrenching, heartrending, melancholy lyrics of "Ol' Man River," my heart almost seized up from pain and joy and that thrilling kind of triumph that only the electricity of live theatre can bring you, and I remember thinking to myself, "Yes, this is it, this is what it was all for, all those years of toil and preparation, all those defeats and victories, this is where they were meant to bring me. They brought me into the theatre, where I'm at home."

By the end of the evening I knew that we had done it; the response of the audience told me it was an overwhelming success. Hal was not so sure. "Hal," I said, "relax, it's going to be gigantic." This was pretty hilarious. He's been through these scenes ten times more than I have, and I'm sitting there telling him to relax? But I was reading the situation a little more accurately than he was.

In a curious kind of way, the history of controversy and protest helped us. It made the occasion more significant than it otherwise might have been. It put pressure on the critics. It wasn't just another review they would be writing. They were discussing a major turning point in cultural politics in Canada. It also helped that, as far as all the American press in attendance were concerned, the protesters had been criticizing a beloved American work.

At the festivities following the curtain, the feeling was undeniably positive. You could sense the excitement. The press were turned on. *I hated the party, as usual – although this one was a memorable, even magnificent, event, I always hate opening-night parties. There's always too much to worry about. You worry about the reviews, you worry about the word of mouth, what people are saying in the corners and in the washrooms. I always want to be everywhere, just to hear those first mumblings of "Well, do you love it, or not?" People always lie to me on opening nights. You have to ferret out the truth. It's never easy.*

I stayed up all night, as I usually do, waiting for the papers. They bring them to me at two o'clock, four o'clock, five o'clock. And of course the next morning is spent in the office dissecting all the reviews, including the electronic ones, and trying to figure out how to position the show.

I felt a great sense of relief. And not just because the reviews were ecstatic, though they were. (And some of them dealt directly with the highly charged political issues that had been raised by the now-dispirited protesters. *New Yorker* critic John Lahr, who had actually stolen into the show four days before the opening, wrote that "the black experience, in both its triumph and its tragedy, is at the heart of the show's perception of America.... History is ambiguous, and so is the idealism of love and hate. *Show Boat* puts that paradox centre stage.... Anyone with a demitasse for a hat can see the intention. Not, however, the Coalition, a politically correct sign of our winded times, which wants freedom for everything but thought ... *Show Boat* still speaks to the informed heart of democracy...."

In the end the sad consequence of the protests was only to diminish the credibility of the accusers and to embarrass the overwhelming majority of the Toronto black community who were prepared, as all reasonable people are, to judge for themselves after the show opened whether there was any offensive subject matter. It had another negative consequence, however: because part of the strategy was to use the show to vilify Jews, in the way made familiar by the atrocious Louis Farrakhan in the United States, the black community found reduced support among those on whom they had always relied for alliances in their campaigns against racism; it set back the relations between Jews and blacks in Toronto, I hope not severely.

Later, after the show opened and the protests died away, buried under the weight of their own creaking rhetoric, I put down some of my thoughts in a talk to Toronto's Empire Club on the whole idea of artistic freedom. The speech clearly touched a nerve in the community. It was rebroadcast over and over; it got more currency than anything I had ever done. I talked about how freedom of artistic expression can be compromised, even lost, in a vain effort to placate specific groups whose goal was to limit rational discourse and stifle thought through the politics of anger, ignorance, and obfuscation. Adopting the parallelism of Professor Gates, I reminded my audience that censorship is to art as arbitrary authority is to freedom. I had refused to bow to that small group of demagogues among the black community, so ardently represented by Trustee Payne. We had faced them down and we had prevailed in the end. But at what cost?

What really happens when *ad hoc* groups with hidden agendas demand the curtailing of other people's freedoms while asserting their own democratic rights to argue their case of alleged intolerance, racism, prejudice, and inequality?

I took my audience first through the story I recounted in an earlier chapter, the story of the attempted suppression of Martin Scorsese's *The Last Temptation of Christ*. I sketched in what everyone knew – the lamentable rise of political correctness, the cult of the victim, and the emergence of self-appointed arbiters of legitimate discourse. I discussed the allegations against *Show Boat* and pointed out that they were, and remain, false, nefarious misconceptions based on a simple lack of knowledge and a cynical disregard for the truth (actually proving once again the proverb that "art has no enemy but ignorance").

I then became more pointed. What disturbed me most about the whole affair was the public silence of our political leaders. To a person, they ducked the issue. Despite being invited, not one of them attended the show's opening night.

*No one came, not one federal or provincial government or opposition leader, not one provincial cabinet minister, not even the city of Toronto's mayor.*

*Not even one.*

*They all turned out to be cowards, governed by fear instead of principle, more concerned with not giving offence than with leadership.*

*All of them.*

∗   ∗   ∗

Well, the show has been open for months and has been seen by hundreds of thousands of people. The protests died away within days, leaving only astonishment and regret that they ever happened. But there are still reverberations.

An example: as part of our responsibility to the theatre, and for our own good long-term self-interest in inculcating among the coming generations (our future audiences) a love for great theatre, we have made available, through student councils, discounted tickets for university students. Student councils readily took us up on these offers for selected performances of *Phantom*.

But in the case of *Show Boat*?

Not one student council permitted our offer to even be distributed!

Not one risked giving their own student body the choice to see our show.

Not one wanted their members to think for themselves.

Not one small voice was mustered against this disgraceful bowing to the worst excesses of political correctness.

Not one independent voice was raised – in the very citadels of academe, in the very places where free expression was born and is supposed to be nurtured.

Like the politicians – not even one.

There was only silence.

Remember, I told the Empire Club in my speech, remember Paul Simon's lyric, "Silence like a cancer grows."

After an opening, there is always a draining away of tension. I may work seven weeks non-stop during the rehearsal period of a show, just as, when I was making movies, I would be up all night, all day, for days on end, going, going, going. Then, after the opening, your body just collapses.

But after this one, I didn't have time. I had to run back into the editing room and finish off the *Show Boat* documentary with the wildly talented Colin Smith, head of our audio/visual department, for the CBC one-hour prime-time special. There were just so many things to do: I had to run to Vienna for the opening of *Kiss* there; Myron and I were in the middle of closing a special warrant financing, amounting to $20 million of fresh equity; there was a trip to the Far East to finalize the marketing strategy for *Phantom*; there was a *Phantom* opening on the tranquil island of Oahu; there was the completion of the development permit for the Safdie-designed theatre in Vancouver (I was excited by this project. It's the first time Safdie has been commissioned by anyone in the private sector in Canada to do a building, and I've always admired his work. His buildings are accessible creations, never forbidding monuments to government or corporate authority. They encourage life, activity, and social interaction. They are buildings people want to live in, work in, visit. If architecture is, indeed, "frozen music," then Safdie is a virtuoso); I was immersed in the world of classical music (North York's Recital Hall had a full program of international stars); and I found time, when I could, to look at my beloved paintings in my office, my home, wherever they were.

In October 1994, of course, *Show Boat* opened on Broadway to what started in the early hours of the morning as a trickle, then became a torrent, then a flood, then a veritable tsunami of overwhelmingly laudatory press coverage. The Americans, who knew the context as the Canadian didn't or couldn't, understood what we had done and effortlessly rose above the Toronto protesters' pettifoggery and miserable carping to just accept the glorious music, Hal's wonderful stagecraft, and the riveting performances of the cast. All the majors loved the show – the *Times*, *Newsweek*, *Time*, the *Post*, the L.A. *Times*, the *Daily News*, *Newsday*, *Variety* – but more than that: New York's ever-vigilant black media loved it too. The *Amsterdam News*, for example, called it "magnificent, fabulous . . . new and innovative . . . Prince highlights the role of the African-American . . . gives them important roles . . . an extraordinary production that must be seen. . . ." The *New York Beacon* observed that "the *Show Boat* cast shows the harmony of African Americans, Whites, Hispanics and several ethnic backgrounds working together for one common cause, and in this production the cause is to entertain you. At a time when we all could use a bit of positive race relations, here it is happening right on the Great White Way. And at the helm of all this is Hal Prince and his outstanding assortment of ethnic personalities. And they are working hard in a production that is dealing openly with a story subject that is centered around Black and white conflicts. So while *Show Boat* is what this review is supposed to be about, it's so much more important to 'show', or should I say witness, people who have thrown race aside to allow purpose and understanding to forge ahead." Not a hint of the ghastly rhetoric we had suffered in Toronto. Only joy, delight, wonder, admiration, and celebration.

I sat in my hotel room that morning surrounded by clippings, the congratulations pouring in, a warm glow of satisfaction permeating my being.

For six of its first seven weeks, the show broke its own weekly box-office gross records. Hal and I were the toast of Broadway, again.

Time to move on, again.

I had things to do, again and again and again.

It never stops, I just never, ever stop.

# Epilogue

Even now, more than five years after the opening night, there are times when I'll slip into the Pantages to see *Phantom*. I'll stand at the back of the auditorium or sit on the staircase (I very seldom take a seat; I have my own step in the balcony where I sit down quietly, unannounced, so my actors can't discern I'm there), and I *know* when the performance is cooking, I can see the audience completely absorbed, and in the end they're usually on their feet. And, yes, I take an immense pride looking around and saying to myself, "I did this; I made this theatre come to life again, I was responsible for putting these performers here, I brought this diverse audience here to be entranced." And then sometimes, in the evenings, I'll go up to *Show Boat* and I'll sit in the back by the sound desk watching with Annie Allen, and I'll whisper to her about what I like, what I don't like, whatever interests me; and sometimes the beauty of it just overwhelms me, that marvellous physical setting and *Show Boat*, with all its history, and it makes me feel very satisfied, because I know that it's the end result of a lifetime of creative effort, of a relentless pushing, pushing, pushing to get things done *right*.

*I lost so many periods of my life. From 1981 to the middle of 1983, I went into a terrible tailspin, having constantly to struggle to take hold of a company in extremis and save it and turn it around. Two and a half*

489

*years of my life just taken away from me. Then again in 1988-89 and the first year of Livent* . . . *more periods of emptiness, years of my life spent clawing my way through the quagmire of business, merely to survive. It depleted me of so much, of what I really loved to do.*

But now. . . . All my many encounters with live theatre in all its aspects, all my successes, all my disappointments, all my efforts, all my grit and grind, they were all part of the necessary education that brought me here, to this time and this place. All my long years at Cineplex Odeon, all that time sweating out the difficulties of creating and marketing a new sort of space for viewing motion pictures, all that effort to construct and refurbish theatres, all that time learning the craft, working with the overweening egos and maniacs of Holly-wood, all that time with the baying hounds of MCA at my heels, it was all equally necessary as background experience. I've learned to accept with equanimity the stark truth behind Murphy's seemingly absurd paradox, "Doing things the hard way is always easier."

Five years have passed since I left Cineplex Odeon and, with Myron, founded what is now Livent. With Myron's considerable administrative help, I now run what is demonstrably Canada's largest live-theatre enterprise, a company that, in 1994, grossed almost $250 million. Myron and I have created what is in essence a new kind of artistic enterprise, having brought sophisticated management and creative techniques to an industry dominated by archaic rules and moribund traditions.

And I'm still surrounded by the paintings I love. My home and my office are filled with striking works; at the office they spill out of the personal offices and boardrooms into the corridors and reception area, giving our corporate space a kind of glorious glow. I've also been able, once more, to express my love of art in a direct and public way. Back in 1987 I started talking with David and Marilyn Burnett about our opening a commercial gallery together. I knew this was some-thing I couldn't realize immediately because of my commitments to Cineplex, but it was an idea I liked to keep in the back of my mind, liked to think about in those rare, quiet moments.

The day after my Black Friday, I stood in the lobby of the Cineplex offices with the Burnetts, who were supervising the removal of my art collection. Depressing as it was to watch this, the art helped me look beyond the darkness of the moment. I put my arms around their shoulders. "Well," I said, "now we can get moving on our gallery."

In September 1990 I opened The Drabinsky Gallery with the Burnetts in Toronto's Yorkville. We opened with a retrospective of Harold Town and attendance measured in the thousands. Our aim from the start was to represent people whose work we believed in, not just because they were anointed with the diluted oil of art-world fashion. And this we've accomplished.

In its scope and quality, the programming of North York's Recital Hall, which my company manages, now ranks alongside those of Carnegie Hall and Lincoln Center in New York as the foremost in North America.

In a situation that is unique in the world of classical music, we use our rental earnings from commercial live-theatre productions at the eighteen-hundred-seat main stage to help underwrite the cost of operating the recital hall, and thus reduce the break-even threshold of bringing the very finest classical artists – Perlman, Stern, Pollini, Kiri Te Kanawa among them – to enrich the cultural life of Toronto. I have shown that cultural entrepreneurs can use profits generated in a market economy to finance cultural activity that, by its very nature and rarefied appeal, needs subsidy of some kind.

*I can barely remember the terrible days after I lost Cineplex Odeon, when I was afraid to go into a movie theatre for fear the anger and frustration would overcome me; those days seem impossibly far away, the nightmare of another life. I read in the* New York Times *that the MCA–Matsushita merger is "dysfunctional"; I read how Wasserman and Sheinberg visited their parent company's head office in Tokyo to pitch an idea, only to find it dismissed before they got there and to be insulted further by Matsushita's president showing up casually two hours late for the meeting; I read how they felt "treated like children" and "want more autonomy." The irony is simply delicious.*

I've now got the perfect circumstances to use my talent, taste, and judgement to bring to fruition projects with which I choose to become involved and to coax, cajole, and inspire the most out of a great many gifted people with whom I have had the good fortune to work in a variety of endeavours. The late, great Joe Papp once said, in the *New York Times* (September 22, 1991), that the role of the producer was "to make it possible for artists to do their best work and to find an audience. To accomplish this he has to possess the cunning of a master politician, the wiliness of a snake-oil salesman, the fanatical drive of a megalomaniac and, given the eternal precariousness of the theatre, nerves of steel. It doesn't hurt, either, to have some taste and a consuming passion for the stage."

Maybe he could have been describing me.

Hal Prince, when he was talking to a colleague about me in the embryonic stages of our relationship, said, "I give Garth boundless credit for the guts it took to produce *Kiss*. He's the only producer who would have taken it on. But more important than that, Garth instinctively knows the difference between hype and art; he would have done *Kiss* even if he'd never made a nickel from it. He always wanted to be a creative producer, and he is. *Kiss* was fundamental for him, in that it was his, he created that production, it wasn't a revival, or something done under licence, but a new and original work. And because he did that, he can go on, now, to do anything he wants."

*Anything he wants!*

And what will that be? Where do I go from here?

When you enter a theatre, in Hal's view, you must cast off all doubts, all armour, and just let it happen, be hypnotized, let yourself be taken on an apprehensive, maybe frightening, maybe fascinating journey. *Kiss*, *Phantom*, *Show Boat* all share one thing – they are all humanistic, all about intense human relations, about people reaching out to people, taking them at face value, not judging them on the colour of their skin, on some disfigurement, on their sexual orientation. When audiences see *Kiss of the Spider Woman*, they may perhaps sit down with a certain narrowminded belligerence, but at the end of the journey they have been obliged to see things more fairly than they've ever done. *Show Boat* is about love of theatre and love of family; it honours the continuity of generations. People are moved to tears and to exhilaration. *Phantom* is a romantic, erotic musical, and that's its pull. It, too, takes people on a journey from the dark headlines of the real world. *Phantom* is a condemnation of superficial responses to someone born disfigured but with the soul of a poet. The mask the Phantom wears is a half-mask, so the audience can look into his eyes, see the pain, be taken into his emotions – they want to respond to the poetry, not to the external disfigurement. Instead of seeing something ugly and recoiling, they are engaged.

In this way, what I've done is a clue to what I will do. Something that will engage the passions of people – their passions, emotions, and intellect. Something with substance. Something magical. Something *worthwhile.*

I have productions of *Phantom, Kiss, Joseph, Show Boat.* I have touring productions scurrying about the world. I'm going to continue to exploit all our current assets, whether it's *Phantom* in the Far East or *Joseph* still going strong in North America. I have E. L. Doctorow's *Ragtime* (a sensational book bristling with ideas and rich with history) under development, brought to me by Marty Bell – it had been on Marty's menu of projects when he came here to head up our creative-affairs department; in many ways this is my personal sequel to *Show Boat.* Terrence McNally is writing the libretto, unlocking it theatrically, and it'll be wonderful. Barbra Streisand, in her magnificent return to live performance, did a tribute to my *Show Boat* at the opening of her concert and followed with a rendition of "Can't Help Lovin' Dat Man" that gave everyone who heard it goosebumps – without question, it was the most memorable concert of my life. I have a theatre under construction in Vancouver, the first new live-theatre project that I am overseeing from the conception stage to fruition. I have a company the bank debt of which has been reduced to vanishing point. I have the capital to work with.

*I can, within the bounds of corporate and fiscal responsibility, do most anything I want.*

In this business I have always to be thinking three years ahead, because the gestation period of a new show is at least that long. I have to worry about the availability of people, of the kind of talent necessary for a great production. So I'll bring *Sunset Boulevard* to Toronto when *Show Boat* opens in Vancouver. And what then? When will *Phantom* run out of steam? In a year? Two years? Five? I have under development a musical based upon Ernest Lehman's brilliant film *Sweet Smell of Success*, which David Brown has brought under the umbrella of Livent because he and his flamboyant wife, Helen Gurley Brown, loved *Show Boat* and respected its meticulous production standards (he'd written Hal a personal letter telling him so). With an eye to the future, I launched in the summer of 1994 a seven-week festival of workshopping new productions, giving younger authors, especially, a chance to hone their talents and get their work performed by superb acting and singing talent. I hope the festival, which I plan as an annual event, will make a meaningful contribution to musical theatre. After all, as I said in my statement of purpose for the festival, "It's an art form that is all of our livelihood and all of our passion." So for me, 1996 and 1997 are going to be full of new, superb, original creations, pushing the envelope even further.

I'm at a time and a place in my career when I've built up a lot of goodwill and momentum. People are calling me because they understand by now that if they do business with my company, the work will be done well, we'll do it right, do it full justice, with taste and sophistication. They call me because they know who I am and what I've done, and they want to work with me.

Not just for my business sense. They know I've developed an ability to handle the creative constituents of any project I'm involved with, to interface with talent. It takes a strong person to be able to get everything you want and at the same time keep people from destroying each other. But I've got to the point where I can walk into the dressing rooms of major stars, listen to them rant and rave, and say, "Believe me, I'll look after it. Go back to work and consider it done." And to have them trust me to do just that, to know that it'll be handled properly. I've had so many of these relationships and associations, I've held the hands of theatrical personalities so many times that they're now absolutely confident I'll protect them. For example, Vanessa Williams agrees to do the Spider Woman on Broadway – and she's never done a musical before. So she's putting her trust in me in an important way. But she met me, felt confident in me, felt strength in me, and said, "I want to align myself with him."

Well, here's the hard part: how much time do I have to spend at all this and still leave myself any time for a life?

How big do I grow the company?

How much pressure do I want to impose upon myself? How do I see the last half of my life?

I've proved, even to myself, my own toughest critic, that if I focus on something, whether it be in charitable work, in business, in the arts, I will do it well. I never back down on a commitment, I always do what I say I'll do.

*But – yes, it's true, I admit it – I've been running pretty hard all my life.*

I'm successful because I am who I am. I trust my own judgement and the people I need around me trust my judgement too. But I also know that the bigger you grow a company, the further removed you are from the source. And one thing I've never been able to do is delegate taste.

I've been so fortunate in life. I was Dick Roberts's protégé. I was Nat Taylor's protégé. It isn't exactly right to call myself Hal Prince's protégé, but he taught me so much I might as well have been.

And now I'm cultivating my own protégés, people I can properly nurture in the artistic/business process.

*Who am I? I'm a man who makes up his mind, who knows what he wants. I don't run and hide. I'm quick to deal with an issue. To postpone is foolish. If there's a cancer in my life, I don't wait for the surgeons – I cut it out. I deal with things now, not tomorrow or the next day. I refuse to let things build up. I'm the same with all my associates. I'm quick to know when someone around me has a problem; I'll call them in at once and we'll have that tough conversation we need, so they don't spend all their private moments with the problem festering beneath the surface.*

*People say I'm driven. I don't understand the phrase. I don't know what it means. I think driven is a comfort word for the lazy, for people who don't know what to think. I'll never let an enticing opportunity go by without trying to take advantage of it. Is that driven? I don't know how to do anything unless it's to the best of my ability. Is that driven? I can't compromise. If that means that I'm driven, I'm driven. I'm committed to do the absolute best I can do every time out.*

*Was I driven to leave the practice of law, to build Cineplex Odeon, to create Livent from the ashes and fashion it into a force in the theatrical world? No, it was done from anxiety and fear and opportunity and desire; it was done because there was a window open and I had to slip through it before it closed, because the Magic Garden was on the other side and the sun was shining there, and I had to reach for the sun; it was done because the drops from the sprinklers on the lawn have always glittered like diamonds.*

# Note on Sources

The following titles were drawn on for material on the early years of movie exhibition:

Neal Gabler. *An Empire of Their Own: How Zukor, Laemmle, Fox, Mayer, Cohn and the Warner Brothers Invented Hollywood.* Crown, 1988.

Thomas Schatz. *The Genius of the System: Hollywood Filmmaking in the Studio Era.* Pantheon, 1988.

David Naylor. *Great American Movie Theaters.* Preservation Press, 1987.

———— (introduction). *Picture Palaces: Views from America's Past.* Preservation Press, 1988.

# Index

Squibb, Wayne, 46, 84
Stallone, Sylvester, 165, 170
Stanley, Jonathan, 125
Steele, Dawn, 333
Stein, Jay, 336-38, 340-43
Stein, Jules, 248-49
Steinberg, David, 87
Sterling Recreation Organization, 305
Stewart, James, 314
Stone, David, 371
Stone, Oliver, 282, 307, 328
Stoppard, Tom, 125, 286
Strauss, Robert, 249
Streisand, Barbra, 493
Stritch, Elaine, 388, 464, 472
Stroman, Susan, 447
Strouse, Charles, 127-34
Strutt, Julia, 387
Sunset Boulevard, 450, 494
Susskind, David, 88
Sutherland, Donald, 14, 89, 93, 95, 97, 110
Sutton Theatre, Manhattan, 303
Sweet Smell of Success, 494

Tacoma, Washington, 305
Taganka Theatre, Moscow, 389-90
Talk Radio, 328, 329
Tamara, 293-94
Tandy, Jessica, 329
Tanenbaum, Anne, 120
Tanenbaum, Howard, 197
Tanenbaum, Larry, 197
Tanenbaum, Max, 112, 118, 120-21, 156, 166, 181, 201
Tarragon Theatre, Toronto, 292
Taubman, Alfred: Beverly Center, 184-87, 192; buys New York–New Jersey theatres, 415, 417-18, 420;

Cineplex investor, 201-3, 205-6, 209, 404
Taubman, Bobby, 202, 418
Taubman Construction, 187, 202
Taylor, Allan, 315, 431
Taylor, Nat: background, 66-70; Canadian Film Digest, 58-59; Cineplex birth and delivery, 141-50, 152-53, 206; Cineplex debt, 187, 196-97, 198; Cineplex growth, 155-57, 173, 175, 177, 181-82, 184, 191; Cineplex investor, 201, 225, 358, 372, 404; GHD's mentor, 59-62, 64, 71-75, 77, 80-81, 83, 85-86, 302, 441, 495; MCA takeover, 2, 420; meets GHD, 55, 56-57; movie investor, 19, 98, 118-19; theatrical investor, 130, 134, 138
Taylor, Yvonne, 69
Teatro Stabile dell'Aquila, Italy, 294
Technicolor, 345
Telefilm, 76
Terms of Endearment, 166
Theatre in the Dell, Toronto, 123, 127
Theatre Passe Muraille, Toronto, 292
Thistletown Hospital, Toronto, 15
Thomas, Jeremy, 333
Thomas, Pat, 448
Thomas, Richard, 453, 455
Thompson, Mark, 452
Thompson, Paul, 292
Thomson, Dick, 152, 181, 187, 196
Thomson, Ken, 151, 374
Thomson, Rogers, 80-81, 84-85, 90, 96
Thornley, Scott, 395

Three Bridges Investment,
    Philadelphia, 370
*Three Men and a Baby*, 357
Thurston, Rick, 432
Tiberius Productions, 107, 118, 158,
    164, 166, 177
*Tie Me Up! Tie Me Down!*, 167
*Time*, 465, 486
*Times, The* (London), 462
*Times* (Los Angeles), 344, 486
*Tommy*, 151, 153, 463, 465-66
Tony Awards, *Kiss of the Spider
    Woman*, 30, 83, 463, 465-68
Topol, Robert, 253, 259, 403, 408, 433
Toronto: *The Amateur* site, 168-69;
    *The Changeling* site potential,
    110; Cineplex Odeon centre, 256,
    348-52; cultural life, 35, 491;
    Festival of Festivals, 148; film
    market, 51, 63-64, 92, 147, 153-55,
    176, 219-23; *Show Boat*
    sensitivities, 474-75, 477-78,
    483-84; *The Silent Partner* site,
    98, 102, 143-44; theatrical market,
    124, 127, 286, 289, 291-95, 297,
    396, 467; *Tribute*, 163, 165; why
    GHD stayed, 168
Toronto Free Theatre, 292
Toronto International Studios,
    Kleinburg, Ontario, 56, 85
Toronto International Theatre
    Festival, 291-95
*Toronto Star*, 135, 312, 344
Toronto Theatre Awards, *By
    Strouse*, 128
Toronto Truck Theatre, 289
Town, Harold, 250, 491
Towne Cinema, Toronto, 73
Transcanada Theatres, 65
Traverse City, Michigan, 276

*Travesties*, 125, 286
*Tree of the Wooden Clogs, The*, 148,
    151
*Tribute*, 119, 158-66
TriStar, 209, 306, 334-35
Trudeau, Pierre, 5, 165, 296, 315
Trump, Donald, 202, 409-10
Turman, Larry, 158-60
Turnbull, Douglas, 239
Turner, John, 85
Turner, Keith, 382
Turturro, John, 322
Tusher, Will, 332
Twentieth Century-Fox. *See also*
    Fox: distribution deal, 163-65;
    history, 67, 237; loan to Cineplex,
    187-90; Pantages Theatre, 280
Twentieth Century Theatres, 67, 72,
    143
Twickenham Studios, England, 95
Twiggy, 462

United Artists. *See also* MGM/UA:
    film distribution, 211; history, 68,
    70; merger with MGM, 237;
    Taubman's interests, 203
United Jewish Appeal, 384
Universal: *The Deer Hunter*, 155;
    film distribution, 209, 301, 304-5;
    Film House business, 328,
    345-46; history, 68, 154, 224; *The
    Last Temptation of Christ*, 330-32;
    theme parks, 244, 336-39, 341-42,
    347-48, 403, 416
Universal City Cinema, Hollywood,
    247, 250-51, 268, 313-14, 333, 414
University of Toronto, 38, 46, 47-48,
    49
University of Western Ontario,
    London, Ontario, 46-47

Williams, Tennessee, 325
Williams, Trevor, 102, 109-10
Williams, Vanessa, 469, 494-95
Wilson, Nancy, 35
Winger, Debra, 166
Winnipeg, 155, 157
Winograd, Bernard, 418
Winter Garden Theatre, Toronto,
    61, 286-91
Wise, Robert, 314
*Withnail and I*, 322
Witt, Katarina, 398
*Wizard of Oz, The*, 314
Wolinsky, David, 37-38
Wolinsky, Leonard, 37
Wolinsky, Sylvia, 37
Woodward, Joanne, 308, 325-26,
    332
Wray, Fay, 464
Wright, Bob, 28
Wysocky, Chuck, 173

Yagoda, Victor, 385
Yankovitch, Bob, 54
Yates, Doug, 346
Yonge Street Theatre, Toronto,
    287-88

York, Michael, 464
York, Susannah, 100, 103
Yorkdale Shopping Centre,
    Toronto, 70
Young, Ken, 53
Young Presidents' Organization,
    Toronto, 130
Young, Stephen, 98, 102

Zahorchak, Bob, 182, 224-26, 228
Zahorchak, Mary, 226-27, 228-29,
    233
Zahorchak, Michael: buys Odeon,
    72, 255; death, 224; distribution
    wars, 154-56, 175; scorns
    Cineplex, 182, 225; trailblazer, 229
Zanuck, Lili, 329
Zanuck, Richard, 329
Zeidler, Eberhard, 441
Ziegfeld, Florenz, 446
Ziegfeld Theatre, Manhattan, 306,
    331
Zimbert, Dick, 104
Zipprodt, Patricia, 296
Znaimer, Moses, 124-25, 286-87, 294
Zukerman, Barry, 179, 197-98, 208
Zukor, Adolph, 61, 62-67, 236